THE INTERNATIONAL
ORGANIZATION OF HUNGER

A PUBLICATION OF THE GRADUATE INSTITUTE OF INTERNATIONAL STUDIES, GENEVA

Also published in this series:

The United States and the Politicization of the World Bank
Bartram S. Brown

Trade Negotiations in the OECD
David J. Blair

World Financial Markets after 1992
Hans Genberg and Alexander K. Swoboda

Succession Between International Organisations
Patrick R. Myers

Ten Years of Turbulence: The Chinese Cultural Revolution
Barbara Barnouin and Wu Changgen

The Islamic Movement in Egypt: Perceptions of International Relations 1967–81
Walid Mahmoud Abdelnasser

Namibia and Southern Africa: Regional Dynamics of Decolonization 1945–90
Ronald Dreyer

THE INTERNATIONAL ORGANIZATION OF HUNGER

Peter Uvin

KEGAN PAUL INTERNATIONAL
London and New York

First published in 1994 by
Kegan Paul International Ltd
PO Box 256, London WC1B 3SW, England

Distributed by
John Wiley & Sons Ltd
Southern Cross Trading Estate
1 Oldlands Way, Bognor Regis
West Sussex, PO 22 9SA, England

Routledge, Chapman & Hall Inc
29 West 35th Street
New York, NY 10001–2291, U.S.A.

© The Graduate Institute of International Studies 1994

Set in Palatino
by Intype, London

Printed in Great Britain by JT Press Ltd

ISBN 0 7103 0466 8

British Library Cataloguing in Publication Data
Uvin, Peter
International Organization of Hunger.—
Publications of the Graduate Institute
of International Studies, Geneva)
I. Title II. Series
363.8
ISBN 0–7103–0466–8

US Library of Congress Cataloging in Publication Data
Uvin, Peter
The International organisation of hunger / Peter Uvin.
334p. 21cm.—(A Publication of the Graduate Institute of
International Studies, Geneva)
Includes bibliographical references and index.
ISBN 0–7103–0466–8
1. Food supply—Government policy. 2. Food relief—
International cooperation. 3. International relations. I. Title. II.
Series: Publications de l'Institute universitaire de hautes átudes
internationales, Genève,
HD9000.6.U98   1993
363.8'83—dc20   93–24952
                                                                CIP

Dedicated to Geert Roose,
an angel who brought me love and compassion

There is another defect which the Law of Natural Selection has yet to remedy: when people of today have full bellies, they are exactly like their ancestors a million years ago: very slow to acknowledge any trouble they may be in . . . This [is] a particularly tragic flaw . . . since the people who [are] best informed about the state of the planet, and rich enough and powerful enough to slow down all the waste and destruction going on, [are] by definition well fed.

Kurt Vonnegut, Galapagos, 1985

CONTENTS

CONTENTS

CONTENTS

FOREWORD

All who write on world politics hope to reduce the intractability of their complex subject matter. Some proceed by a massive simplification and soaring abstraction. Others sketch patterns of details in the hope of uncovering a guiding system. Still others concentrate on one or another element of the policies and political life of a state or two, usually choosing the strongest in military and economic terms or those about which it is easiest to learn.

All too rarely, it grieves me to note, do scholars of international politics attempt to understand cooperative behavior in the light of the theories developed by the observers of both conflict and of cooperation. Peter Uvin has written a book which expands the short list of such works and does so with insight, a wide range of scholarship and a willingness to test particular cases against existing theory. The result is not only the hoped-for expansion of knowledge but also a thoughtful improvement of existing theoretical approaches.

Uvin's universe of enquiry excludes military power and its application. It concentrates on the long-term, complex organization of cooperative transnational behavior and its rationale. Its focusses on functional issues involving world hunger, a haunting background and result, and perhaps even one cause, of the dreadful violence that characterizes our world even as the threat of catastrophic nuclear warfare has declined. But Uvin avoids thinking of world hunger as either a narrow or a technical issue. Rather it is part of a world that embraces economic and social theory and practice, state policy, and patterns of relationships among authorities. It also admits the complexity to international relations of participants other than governments, such as non-governmental charitable organizations, interest groups and private corporations.

The result of Uvin's analysis is a new clarity for one of the standard but deficient approaches to explaining international cooperation, regimes theory, and its union with considerations of power. To achieve this result Uvin uses the tools of the logician, the economist, the sociologist and the political scientist. It produces a new understanding of both world hunger and theories of international relations.

As Uvin freely employs sociological concepts, I yield to the temptation to point up a social aspect of his book that supports its cosmopolitan perspective. It is a product of a genuinely transnational intellectual effort. Uvin is a Belgian national whose daily work in Geneva, where he drafted this work, was largely in French. Most of the intellectual groundwork for his exploration was written in English and most of that by scholars based in the American environment where he also worked. His colleagues, whose help he acknowledges at chapter headings, came from several countries, many of them to study at the Graduate Institute of International Studies. Moreover, he benefitted from direct observation and participation in development projects in areas where hunger is a daily manifestation.

Leon Gordenker
Professor Emeritus
Princeton University

ACKNOWLEDGEMENTS

Before all, my gratitude goes to Professor Leon Gordenker, who not only encouraged me all along these years of writing, but also instilled in me his love for the study of the field of international organization.

I also thank Professors Thomas Weiss, from the Thomas Watson Jr. Institute of International Studies, and Robert Kates, from the Alan Shawn Feinstein World Hunger Program, both at Brown University: they, and their excellent staff, offered me a great occasion to finish up the writing of this book.

The Graduate School of Development Studies, where I have been teaching for some years, has offered me a stimulating environment in which to research; its director, Jacques Forster and my colleagues, especially the assistants, have been of great help.

Finally, without the friendship and love of Mary-Josée Burnier, Daniel Fino and Marc Hufty, this book would not have been written.

PERMISSIONS

The author and publishers express their grateful thanks to the following institutions for permission to reproduce illustrative material:

The World Bank: Grilli, E. R. and Yang, M. C., 'Primary Commodity Prices, Manufactured Goods Process, and the Terms of Trade of Developing Countries: What the Long Run Shows', *World Bank Economic Review*, vol. 2, no. 1, 1988, p. 21; Figure 4.4. *World Development Report 1986*, Washington D.C., 1986 (a), p. 117; Table 4.8.

Johns Hopkins University Press: Murdoch, W. W., *The Poverty of Nations*, Baltimore, 1980, p. 71; Figure 3.3.

ABBREVIATIONS

DAC	Development Assistance Committee, of the OECD
EEC	European Economic Community
FAO	Food and Agriculture Organisation
GATT	General Agreement on Trade and Tariffs
IDA	International Development Association
OECD	Organisation for Economic Cooperation and Development
UN	United Nations
US	United States
USAID	United States Agency for International Development
USSR	Soviet Russia

in chapter 5

WFP	World Food Programme
CFA	Committee on Food Aid Policies and Programmes
IEFR	International Emergency Food Reserve
FAC	Food Aid Convention
LIFDC	Low Income Food Deficit Countries

in chapter 6

UNFPA	United Nations Fund for Population Activities, recently rebaptized United Nations Population Fund
UNICEF	United Nations International Children Emergency Fund
WHO	World Health Organization
IPPF	International Planned Parenthood Federation

in chapter 7

BWI	Bretton Woods Institutions
IMF	International Monetary Fund

xv

ABBREVIATIONS

HIC	High Income Country
LA	Latin America
MIC	Middle Income Country
SA	Structural Adjustment
SSA	sub-Saharan Africa

INTRODUCTION

This book analyzes the international organization of hunger as well as its effects on the incidence of hunger. It is an international political economy study, situating itself in the theoretical debates of the discipline. Yet, to analyze its subject matter, it touches a variety of other disciplines or fields of study, such as trade and development economics, demography, international finance, rural development, etc. For each of these fields analyzed, the basic data related to our interest will be presented and critically interpreted.

More specifically, this book has four aims, two of which are theoretical and two empirical. The first theoretical aim is to test, or more modestly, to apply the theoretical framework of complex interdependence as developed by Keohane and Nye, two of the leading scholars in the field of study of international relations. This well-known theory predicts specific outcomes of international politics if conditions of so-called complex interdependence prevail. If their theoretical framework applies, this implies a quite fundamental change in the way most scholars of international politics and international political economy approach their subject matter. This debate is known since quite some time now; yet, due to weaknesses in the definition of some central concepts involved, it has not really progressed. The second theoretical aim of this book, then, is to define, and apply, some important concepts – most notably interest, preference and regime – in a different and clearer way than is usually done in the discipline of international relations. The way these concepts will be defined is perfectly compatible with Keohane and Nye's framework: they should be the basic building blocks for the construction of a sociological approach to international politics, drawing from

1

their innovations, and adding to it some insights of other schools of thought and disciplines.

This book does not search to present any grand new argument on Third World development, nor a prescription for solving the problem of hunger. It studies the functioning of the international organization of food and hunger. This divides in two distinct, but related, empirical questions. First: what are the international outcomes in the food/hunger issue area? And second: what is the impact of these international outcomes on the incidence of hunger? Answering these two questions constitutes the two empirical aims of the analysis.

Most of the issue areas analyzed here, with the exception of international finance, are little studied by international relations scholars: this kind of development-related, non-strategic, usually 'low politics' issues, in which international organizations play an important role, is not very popular in the branch. Yet, tens of thousands of people continuously deal on the international level with these issues, and billions of dollars are yearly spent on them; they take up a large share of Third World's policy makers' time and energy. This book intends to remedy the neglect of these issues.

The case studies are important for our theoretical aims. They not only allow us to innovate using relatively neglected issue areas; they also act as tests of the explanatory force of the theoretical framework presented in chapter one. They help to answer such important questions as: do regimes matter? Does our distinction between interest and preference and the relation posited between them enlighten our understanding of the issues studied? Do international organizations matter as much as Keohane and Nye's theory would have it? The originality of this approach consists in the use of what can be called the 'development literature' – Third World politics, development economics, rural development studies, and the other disciplines refered to above – to test theories of international relations.

Just as the case studies are central to the theoretical preoccupations of this book, its theoretical developments are crucial to its empirical aims. Indeed, our theoretical framework draws attention to different elements and brings us to ask different questions than what would have happened had we employed another theoretical approach. In other words, we will analyze the issue areas studied in this book quite differently from what is usually done. This is especially evident as far as the relation between international and domestic politics goes. On that fundamental question, there basically exist two positions within the development community as well as within the international relations branch; they have a high ideological content. The radical one holds that the international system, and the place of Third World countries in it, is responsible for underdevelopment and hunger, while the dominant, liberal one absolves the international system for what happens within countries – for hunger for example. The latter is a matter of good policy (usually meaning minimal government intervention) and technical progress. There exists little or no middle ground between these two incommensurable approaches to North-South relations, to development or to any other subject matter. We have a political aim here: we deliberately try to look for a middle ground, as rigorously critical as possible of the usual approaches and their preconceptions. With middle ground we do not mean equidistance from both approaches nor some impossible synthesis of them, but rather an attempt to avoid the usual clichés of both sides.

In the two chapters that make up part I of this book, we will present our theoretical framework and supply some important background information on domestic food production policies in the world. Both are necessary for understanding the rest of the analysis.

Part I

INTERNATIONAL POLITICS AND FOOD: THE FRAMEWORK

ONE

COMBINING SOCIAL SCIENCES: THE SOCIOLOGY OF INTERNATIONAL POLITICS*

The field of enquiry of international relations has been dominated for 40 years by the so-called Realist school of thought. Following Osgood, we can define Realists, with capital 'R', as those who 'believe that nations, as a matter of fact, are moved by self-interest' and Realism as 'the approach to international relations which is inter alia based upon this assumption.'[1] Realism has recently come under considerable attack from different sides, questioning even its most fundamental assumptions, and presenting different paradigms[2] This study, while keeping Realism's basic assumptions on the nature of international politics intact, wants to add to it some insights of other social sciences, in particular sociology. Such a venture situates itself in the global context of the present search by various scholars for a synthesis approach, drawing from both Realist and Liberal insights about international relations.[3]

The most innovative and coherent contribution to this venture up to our days remains Keohane and Nye's *Power and Interdependence*. Sadly enough, notwithstanding much lip-service, its research agenda has been largely ignored. The issues brought up in this path-breaking work have neither been falsified nor verified, but rather forgotten, buried under the rapidly changing fads of the discipline: regimes, declining hegemony, game theory.

Complex interdependence has been defined by Keohane and Nye as having three characteristics: multiple channels connect societies (transnational, transgovernmental, and interstate); the

* This chapter profited from discussions with Jan-Peter Heyer, Thomas Oatley, Daniel Warner and, especially, Prof. Leon Gordenker and Marc Hufty.

absence of hierarchy among issues ('meaning ... that military security does not consistently dominate the agenda') and the minor role of military force.[4] This gives rise to four distinctive political processes. First, linkages between issues become less effective, and, as a result, the outcomes of political bargaining increasingly vary by issue area. Second, the international political agenda is increasingly affected by international and domestic problems created by economic growth and increased sensitivity interdependence. Third, national interests are defined differently on different issues, at different times, and by different governmental units. Fourth, international organizations play a bigger role, putting items on the international agenda, and acting as catalysts for coalition formation and as arenas for political initiatives and linkage by weak states.[5] Finally, they present an 'international organization model' that is 'likely to apply under complex interdependence conditions' to explain international outcomes. The model expects 'international organizational norms and procedures and their associated political processes to affect patterns of regime change,' with the term international organization referring to 'multilevel linkages, norms and institutions.'[6]

The food issue area is usually considered a typical case of complex interdependence. Keohane and Nye themselves repeatedly refer to it to illustrate their theory, while the OECD, WFC, UNCTAD, FAO and other international fora often talk about food interdependence; so do many authors.[7] In this book, we will analyze whether the characteristics and the consequences of complex interdependence which Keohane and Nye described indeed exist in the international food issue area, and, if that is the case, if the 'international organization' model they developed to explain such situations holds.

The concepts of interest, preference and regime are very important to the international organization model or any similar attempt to enrich Realism with the insights of other schools of thought or disciplines. Yet, they have not always been used with much clarity or unanimity about their meaning. Hence, we consider it necessary to define and delimit these concepts clearly, as well as the relations among them.[8] This is what we now set out to do.

1 Regimes

Since the mid–1970s, Realists have been talking about a new and increasingly popular concept: regimes. In the early 1980s, they were defined with remarkable unity as 'principles, norms, rules and procedures around which actors expectations converge.'[9] This was a useful attempt to deal with a major lacuna of the Realist study of international relations: its theoretical and practical incapacity to deal coherently with anything that cannot be subsumed under the basic categories of self-interest or power. Yet, despite their popularity, regimes cannot easily be handled within Realist assumptions about international relations. Thus, their definition has become too restrictive, which has undermined their far-reaching interest. We set out to redefine regimes in a coherent way, and to assign them a central role in a modified, dynamic, but still essentially Realist framework.

A The trouble with regimes

In this section, we will argue that the consensual nature that is usually attributed to regimes is overly limiting and that the concrete relation between regimes, interests and outcomes is still unclear.[10] As a result, regimes have not lived up to the hopes placed in them by their defenders in the first half of the 1980s.

The fact that 'actors' expectations converge' around the regime content is usually taken to mean that if some party disagrees, there is no regime whatsoever, or at least not for that party. Thus Haggard and Simmons, for example, find the concept of implicit regimes misleading, because explicit commitment is required before there is a regime.[11] This implies the un-Realistic assumption that regimes are based upon the explicit consensus of all.[12] It is doubtful that any one case exists where all actors engaged in an issue area have consented consciously and explicitly to the norms and principles that apply to it – except for ratified treaties. This way Keohane and Nye, trying to avoid 'the charge of operational obscurity sometimes raised against the concept' warn against extending regimes 'beyond the institutionalized results of formal interstate agreements.'[13] If regimes have to be defined this way to escape the charge of obscurity, the cost is too high. Their study becomes hardly more than the study of international law[14] – and even there the notion of 'custom,' *i.e.* implicit, non-formal norms, is basic!

This evolution of the definition of regimes reflects a long-standing habit of mainstream American social science to treat norms as consensual, cooperative, and beneficial.[15] This produces disastrous results in international relations, as the consensual nature of norms in social sciences is incompatible with the basic assumptions of Realism. For Realists, states act only according to their self-interest in an anarchic world. Thus, they can hardly agree to be bound by norms that limit their freedom of behavior; where norms exist, they have to be, like cooperation, unstable and constantly violated following the changing interests of states. If Realists try to account for norms and principles (treated as consensual), they will tend to restrict their presence and role as much as possible. One way of doing so is by reducing them to international treaties. Hence the fact that norms and principles are defined in terms of consensuality – a definition reflecting mainstream social science habits – in combination with basic Realist assumptions of power and interest restricts the usability of regimes to the equivalent of treaties.[16]

Moreover, it remains most unclear what the position of regimes is in relation to outcomes. This refers to the important question: do regimes matter? – in other words, are they independent variables in the analysis of international outcomes? Theorists disagree on the question. For classical Realists, regimes can at best be intervening variables, reflecting the distribution of power, but not changing it.[17] In the concluding article of the International Regimes volume, Krasner hints at the possibility that regimes could be something more, rightly pointing out that in such a case the whole fabric of Realism is under question.[18] For authors such as Oran Young, it is possible, under Realist assumptions, to treat regimes as independent variables.[19] This has been attempted among others by Krasner in his *Structural Conflict* or by Keohane in *After Hegemony*.[20] To do so, however, Keohane ended up assuming an exogenously given demand for cooperation, which amounts to the 'Liberal' assumption of common interests.[21]

Hence the far-reaching possibilities of the concept have been largely lost. At present, either regimes end up being defined as explicit treaties, in which case they are allowed to play a small ad-hoc role within a Realist approach which places its emphasis solely on power and interest, or they are defined in a less restrictive way, but linked to notions of common interest and an exogenously given demand for cooperation, in which case they fall squarely within the Liberal tradition. We set out to avoid both these outcomes.

B The sociology of regimes

In this section, we will develop a definition of regimes that does not display the above mentioned deficiencies and yet remains compatible to Realism's basic assumptions. To do so, we will draw from the social science that is specialized in the study of norms and social action: sociology.

As sociologists and anthropologists have explained time and again, human behavior is influenced by norms and principles, *i.e.* people's actions are guided by certain cognitions and norms that explain the environment upon which they act and the way they ought to do so. That does not mean that these are always perfectly known or strictly adhered to: they can be regularly violated. Such norms and principles can be of an ad-hoc nature, or they can constitute a large and homogenous body, like an ideology or a religion. They become interesting to the political scientist from the moment they are shared by many actors over a certain period of time, *i.e.* when they become institutions.[22]

What, then, are the norms of a group? As said earlier, most people spontaneously limit norms to consensual constructs. They usually defend this definition by pointing out that 'consensual' does not mean 'unanimous,' and that a 'normal' amount of violation does not impinge upon the consensual nature of a norm. Any other, larger, definition of norms, defenders of a definition in terms of consensuality argue, mistakes norms for power or habit.

Strangely enough, those authors very often end up doing the opposite, exaggerating the amount of consensuality in the world and with it the presence of common interests. For, in practice, this reasoning often concludes that, whenever there is a norm, it must be a consensual construct. Even if this error is avoided, the problem of vagueness remains: when does something become a norm, defined as a consensual construct? When 5% of group violates a candidate norm, it probably remains a consensual construct, and thus a norm. But when 15% does so, or 25%? Where is the boundary? In international relations, is there a difference between the violators of a would-be norm all being OECD countries, or them being African countries? Norms do not even have to be violated to be non-consensual. Imagine 5% of a group does not agree with a norm (when questioned individually, they deny its validity), but refrains from violating it (for example, because they perceive a penalty upon doing so). Is it still a norm, defined in consensual terms? How about when 15% does so, or 25%? Is liberalism the basic consensual norm – and comparative advantage the principle – of the post-war trading system, even though it originated only among a few rich countries, most developing countries do not share it, and many developed ones consistently violate it[23]? Thus the problems with the spontaneous definition are both that it is blurry and that it overestimates the presence of consensus and common interests.

It seems better to define norms and principles without including consensuality or individual opinions. The way to do so, in line with the expectations of political science, is to look at what is **dominant** – not what is generally accepted. We propose the following definition: norms are the dominant standards of behavior (defined in terms of rights and obligations) that apply to a particular issue area. Similarly, principles are the dominant beliefs of fact and causation regarding a specific issue area.[24] Principles concern what is defined as a 'problem' and what is not, as well as how such problems are related to other issues. Norms define the 'right' behavior to solve, or avoid, problems. To ask for the regime for a particular issue area is to ask for the dominant beliefs and standards of behavior that apply to that issue area. That does not mean that all actors spontaneously share these norms and principles, nor that they always abide by them. To answer our earlier question: yes, liberalism is the regime of the post-war trading system, not because it is consensual, but because it is dominant.

There are different ways in which social phenomena, including norms and principles, can be dominant.[25] The usual way, as political scientists (should) know, is through power. Hence the conflict-sociologist Ralph Dahrendorf writes, for example: 'norms are established and maintained only by power, and their substance may well be explained in terms of the interests of the powerful.'[26] If an actor (or a coalition of actors) within a group has the power to do so, he can sanction or induce the others into accepting the norms and principles he prefers. This is, in a nutshell, the origin of the above mentioned liberal post-war trading regime. International norms are, then, the norms of those states which possess the power necessary to sanction them. This notion of regime is akin to the approach that pervades the work of the founding fathers of Realism: see for example Edmund H. Carr, when he writes:

> The contents of . . . a treaty reflect . . . the relative strength of the contending parties (. . .) Theories of social morality are always the product of a social group which identifies itself with the community as a whole, and which possesses facilities denied to subordinate groups or individuals for imposing its view of life on the community. Theories of international morality are, for the same reason and in virtue if the same process, the product of dominant nations or groups of nations.[27]

A second, but less common, way in which norms and principles can be dominant is through common agreement. One would expect this to be more frequent in groups where the composing elements have a roughly equal power than in groups where this is not so. In such case, regimes are likely to be of a compromise nature. A third, interesting, case of consensual dominance is where norms and principles which were originally imposed become internalized over time: in this book, we will find such cases with the family planning issue area and, to a lesser extent, structural adjustment. This phenomenon is one of the causes of the inertia of social institutions.

We argue that all issue areas, at all levels, are characterized by a dominant set of norms and principles that apply to the activities undertaken by the actors within them. The nature or content of this set is linked to the power of the different actors within the group. All issue areas thus 'have' a regime – not because there always is cooperation or consensus, but because there are always patterns of norms and principles for all issue areas in which individuals engage.[28]

Regimes can be classified according to the criteria of nature and institutionalization. The *nature* of a regime refers to its content, to 'the objects promoted' by it.[29] We will argue, for example, that the nature of the food aid regime is increasingly developmental. That means that the object promoted by food aid is the furthering of economic growth and the relief of hunger. Second, the *insti-*

tutionalization of a regime refers to the extent to which it has been formalized and to which organizations exist to monitor, coordinate or execute its provisions. It should be seen as a continuum, rather than an absolute, 'either-or' situation, allowing regimes to vary from simple, uncodified, quite unconscious ones to elaborate, highly organized ones, with formally written down rules and procedures.[30] This holds for both imposed regimes and consensual ones.

This definition of regimes differs from the one which is dominant in the discipline by the fact that it is larger in scope and more sociological in nature. It draws heavily from the so-called conflict model in sociology, which starts from the assumption that the most important element of social order is the dominance of certain groups over others and the resulting conflict.[31] The prime example of a conflict model of society is Marxism, but also liberalism, in the European meaning of the term, is a conflict-theory. To quote Ralph Dahrendorf again:

> From the point of view of this model, society and social organizations are held together not by consensus but by constraint, not by universal agreement but by the coercion of some by others. It may be useful for some purposes to speak of the 'value system' of a society, but in the conflict model such values are ruling rather than common, enforced rather than accepted.[32]

The conflict model in sociology as well as Marxism share with the Realist approach to international relations their focus on power, interest and conflict, and are specialized in dealing with the concepts of institution, organization and social action[33] As such, they provide an approach to norms and principles which is compatible with Realism's basic assumptions, while not suffering from the theoretical and operational flaws of its usual definition.

C Some methodological problems

Yet, important problems remain. For one, this definition of regimes is not particularly easy to operationalize with any scientifically desirable exactitude. Another, but no less grave, problem is circularity, whereby norms and principles are derived from behavior, and then used to 'explain' behavior – an often made error in international relations.[34] Both these difficulties are

14

inherent to the nature of the concepts of norms and principles, and, more generally, to the field of social sciences. Yet, evidently that does not signify these concepts have to be abandoned.

Faced with these problems, many scholars in practice take the road of what Galtung once called 'enlightened essayism.' The analysis of principles and norms then takes the form of an exercise in knowledgeable speculation by the researcher. This is considered undesirable by the dominant positivist-behavioral methodology in the field – another reason for the limited role attached to regimes in international relations. But, if done carefully and honestly, and enriched by a profound knowledge of the history of the issues under study, this might well be the best we can do at the present state of the social sciences.[35] And, as said, the methods and conceptual tools of sociology can be of great use.

Concretely, it is relatively easy to analyze norms when they are put down as such, for example in treaties.[36] Things become much more difficult when such purposefully explicit normative documents do not exist. One solution is to engage in an analysis of the discourse of actors. This is not new. In discussions on international morality – one of the origins of the discipline of international relations – authors have taken the position that the existence of international morality can be deduced from the rhetoric of statesmen.[37] In the same vein, Hedley Bull reasons that the fact that states feel compelled to justify their actions by reference to some standard – even when the action in question is exactly a violation of the standard invoked – is proof of the existence of international morality.[38] We would agree that this points to the existence of certain norms – whether or not international morality exists is not what interests us here. Thus, if we operationalize the search for the dominant norms of a group to the authoritative discourse by actors within that group (and certainly the powerful actors within it), we can try to avoid the dangers of vagueness and circularity.[39] In all this, we shall keep in mind the level-of-analysis problem. The discourse can be different on different levels. They should not be confused.[40]

2 Issue area, outcome and process

An issue area is defined as any 'subject matter concerning which actors can desire a diversity of possible outcomes'.[41] The element of choice and conflict in this definition makes it appropriate for use in the study of politics. Issue areas can be defined by the participants in them, or they can be constructed on logical grounds by researchers for the purposes of their study. Issue areas can exist at different levels of analysis: there exists both an international and an US hunger issue area.

Every issue area has an outcome, a term signifying nothing more than the general notion of the situation, the reality we study – what does the issue-area look like? What is going on in it? Outcomes are the usual object of study in international political economy. They are composed of two interacting but analytically different components: process and regime. The concept of process refers to the standard range of action going on in the issue area: it is the behavioral part of outcomes. Regime refers to the set of norms and principles that apply to the issue area: it is the normative element of outcomes. The two – process and regime – interact with each other and are under continuous pressure for change.

3 Interests and preferences

The basic assumption of Realism is that states act in their self-interest, while interest is an objective concept, derived from structural characteristics of position and 'defined in terms of power.'[42] This is without doubt the most fundamental insight of Realism, differentiating it from previous paradigms of international relations, most notably Idealism or Liberalism. Yet, fundamental problems exist in the application of this insight, with both central concepts – interest and power – being subject to considerable ambiguity in their definition. Concerning interest, there are basically two different strands of application. Most international relations authors treat interest as 'everything any group or person claims as an interest'[43] – or usually what the scholar thinks is an interest – thus turning interest into a subjective concept and reducing it to the notion of motive.[44] Others, assuming perfect rationality and knowledge, implicitly treat states' actions as always being in their interests.[45]

Interest is thus either reduced to motive, or interest and motive by definition coincide. Both these twists are undesirable and have been warned against by the founding fathers of Realism.[46] Yet, we believe it is crucial to have a clear distinction between the notion of interest and motive or preference, as well as a model about the relation between them. We propose one here.

Preferences (motives, intentions) are anything actors desire to achieve. They are subjective, *i.e.* depend on perception and the intention of the actors concerned. The process through which they are defined can and should be studied in a pluridisciplinary fashion: it is of central importance for our sociological approach to international politics.[47] *Interests* are everything that preserves or enhances the (relative or absolute) position of an actor in an issue area. Interests are relative to position,[48] but objective to person, meaning that they are independent of the conscious goals, objectives, motives or intentions of the actor in question. Indeed, it is possible that an actor is not aware of his interest, or even that he thinks the exact opposite about it (in which cases his preference goes against his interest).[49] Interests are a structural concept, based on the 'guiding principle' of the issue area under consideration.[50] In international relations, the interests of different actors usually conflict, for the gains of any actor are either absolutely (zero-sum games) or relatively (the distribution of gains) a source of losses for another actor.[51] Having made a clear distinction between both these concepts, we can now tentatively develop some theoretical hypotheses of the possible relations between them; together, these should provide us with a more dynamic approach to international relations. They will be tested throughout this book.

To begin, we assume with Realists that people's preferences are usually of a self-interested nature, *i.e.* people usually prefer what they think to be in their interest; they look for advancement and gain. Yet that does not mean that their preferences and the actions based on these preferences always are in their interest. Analytically, we can distinguish three basic categories of factors which can cause preferences to differ from interests. In the first, most common, category, people want to enhance their interests but fail to adopt the right preferences to do so. In other terms: actor's preferences are of a self-interested nature, but barriers residing in the complexity of the world and their limited knowledge of it or in their irrationality render their preferences contrary to their self-interest. In the second case, actors can have contradictory interests in different issue areas at the same time: any gain in one issue area then threatens to be against the self-interest of the same actor in another one. Finally, we allow for the fact that actors' preferences can be consciously different from their self-interest: charitable impulses for example.[52]

The first reason why actors' preferences might be against their interest resides in the ignorance and irrationality of human beings. People are very often blind, stupid, stubborn, shortsighted, manipulable, lazy, ignorant and almost always badly informed. Thus they act emotionally, follow prejudice, tradition and habit rather than objectively analyzing their situation, necessary in an extremely complex world.[53] Following Rosenau, individuals may be conceived of as habit-driven actors, whose 'actions are stemming from a combination of past experiences, cultural norms, memories, beliefs, personality, role expectations, and cognitive styles to which they have long been accustomed. That is not to say that habit-driven actors do not seek to act rationally.'[54] They merely do not manage to do so!

Second, actors' self-interests in different issue areas can be conflicting: a preference which is to one's interest in one issue area can at the same time be to one's detriment in another issue area. The existence of this problem is basic to Gilpin's hegemonic cycles model.[55] It is also close to the notion of 'externalities,' which has been used in international relations *inter alia* by Aggarwal. In other terms, the problem is caused by the existence of linkages between different issues. The latter can have two major origins: either the participating actors in different issue areas are the same, or there is some technical link between them.[56] In both cases, outcomes can be non-intentionally against one's interests.

The existence of both these phenomena implies that international outcomes are often largely unintentional – something which is not easy to take into account for Realists, one of whose working assumptions is the perfect rationality of actors.[57] We would expect this to be more the case under conditions of complex interdependence which are highly difficult for actors to grasp and master.[58]

The last possibility, that actors prefer not to act in their self-interests, happens quite often at the level of individuals: human beings are at times sharing, altruistic, considerate etc. Even at the level of large groups, such as states, it is possible for preferences of a non-self-interested nature to be dominant. A good example of this is provided by the reaction of all states in the case of famine

4 Towards a sociological pre-theory

We can now turn to making explicit the relations between the previously defined concepts. First, and most important, the degree to which outcomes satisfy the preferences of the actors involved in the issue area reflects the distribution of power between these actors. This derives from Realism, with this central difference that outcomes do not necessarily reflect interests. It is only to the degree that preferences of the powerful coincide with their interests that outcomes satisfy their interests. As we have seen, there can be different reasons why this is not the case.

Second, regimes play a central role in this dynamic process. From the outset, at least two relations can be distinguished. Primo, regimes influence the definition and redefinition of preferences for any given issue area.[59] Even if one held that states always act in their self-interest, then this self-interest has still to be defined: it is not given by God. The dominant set of principles and norms that apply to an issue area strongly influence this definition of self-interest in that issue area. The same holds for non-self-interested preferences. Secundo, the way outcomes are perceived is influenced by the existing regime for that issue area – which might explain the persistence of 'dysfunctional' outcomes. Where liberal principles and norms are dominant, actors will less easily detect that a particular liberal preference is dysfunctional to their self-interest; when they do so, it will be harder to redefine a preference which is very un-liberal.

Third, this difference between interests and preferences creates a strong dynamic of social change. For if outcomes do not reflect the interests of the powerful (although they did reflect their preferences), then two changes can occur. First, the latter, perceiving the dysfunctionality of outcomes to their interests, change their preferences.[60] As a result, to the extent that they possess the relative power to do so, the nature of outcomes will change. Second, the powerful do not perceive the dysfunctionality of outcomes to their interests and as a result the relative distribution of power within the issue area alters. This will lead to changes in outcomes (for other actors manage to realize their preferences to a larger extent). Hence, in both cases – actors redefining their preferences and/or actors losing relative power – outcomes are bound to change.

In this chapter, we have outlined a dynamic pre-theory of a

'sociological' type, i.e. 'which stresses the role of ... the impact of cultural practice, norms and values that are not derived from calculations of interest.'[61] It draws together strands from sociology, from 'classical' Realism, from Marxism and from interdependence theory. We believe this pre-theory to be entirely compatible with Keohane and Nye's theory of complex interdependence, and indeed to constitute a further development of some points of it. The main features of this tool box are a rigorous operational distinction between the concepts of interest and preference, commonly and interchangeably used by most Realists, and the redefinition of the concept of regime in a more sociological way, allowing it to have some more operational relevance than it usually has.

We believe the advantages of this pre-theory to be the following: it starts from a realistic assessment of human nature, in which greed, ignorance, habit and charity coexist; it can integrate domestic and international political processes; it assigns a fundamental, and not an ad-hoc, role to the factors of perception and knowledge, and finally, it is open to process and change, avoiding the determinism which so often characterizes bad social science[62] Throughout the rest of this book, we will be able to verify if our theoretical framework is indeed superior to Realism. We will do so in the usual Popperian way of testing if our pre-theory manages to explain at least as much as the usual Realist approach in a more coherent way. We will come back to this in the conclusion.

Notes

1 Osgood, 1953: 8.
2 See *inter alia* Holsti, 1985: *passim.*
3 The Liberal paradigm stresses the importance of domestic politics, learning, common interests and interdependence and cooperation. Among the works which most influenced us, we can mention Keohane & Nye, 1977 and their self-critique ten years later: Keohane & Nye, 1987; Keohane, 1984 & 1988; Young, 1980; Puchala & Hopkins, 1982 ; Krasner, 1982(a) & 1982(b); Nye, 1988: 238–9.
4 1977: 24–5.
5 Quotes resp. Keohane & Nye, 1977: 31, 32 & 35.
6 They go on to add: 'in our international organization model, these networks, norms and institutions are important independent factors for explaining regime change. One may even have international organization in this sense without any specific formal institutions.' Keohane & Nye, 1977: 54–7.

7 Keohane & Nye, 1977: 12, 15, 16, 20, 32, 35. OECD, 1984 (a): 15; OECD, 1984(b): 8, 100; see too Millman e.a., 1990: 308–9 or the title of the proceedings of the 20th international conference of agricultural economists: Maunder & Valdes, 1990.

8 Our pretentions in this are akin to Rosenau's, 1970, notion of pre-theory: we do not aim to account for iron laws nor to predict outcomes, but only to specify concepts and the dynamic relations between them in a coherent framework, which clarify and operationalize Keohane and Nye's international organization model.

9 See the special issue of *International Organization*, 36, 2, (Spring 1982) on international regimes. This issue was subsequently reprinted in book form: Krasner, 1984. Further references will be to the I.O. volume.

10 Other criticisms can be, and have been, voiced against the concept of regimes. The most notable among them probably still remains Strange, 1982: *passim*.

11 Haggard & Simmons, 1986: 493 & 494.

12 This interpretation of regimes is most 'liberal' or functionalist. Keman & Braun, 1987: 551–2 and Baehr, 1985: 502–4.

13 Keohane & Nye, 1987: 741.

14 For Keohane and Nye, 1977, chapter 5, for example, the collapse of the Bretton Woods arrangement in 1971–73 signifies that there is no regime anymore.

15 Keeley, 1990: 83–4; 86; 90; Young, 1986: 111.

16 This has been well explained by O'Meara, 1984: 245.

17 All the articles in Krasner's volume follow this line, except the concluding one by Krasner, 1982(b). See also Aggarwal's 1986 treatment of regime change of the Multifiber Agreement, or Haggard & Simmons, 1986: 492; Keohane & Nye, 1987. The same holds for the declining hegemony model.

18 Krasner, 1982(b). The same has been hinted at by Keohane & Nye, 1977 and by Keohane, 1982.

19 Young, 1986: 115 a.f.

20 Krasner, 1985, Keohane, 1984. See also Axelrod & Keohane, 1985.

21 O'Meara, 1984: 255. Having changed one of the basic postulates of Realism – that states have conflicting interests – into one that states have common interests, it is hardly surprising that he manages to 'explain' cooperation, even while keeping some other Realist postulates intact.

22 'Institutions involve the regulation of behavior of individuals in society according to some definite, continuous and organized patterns . . . These patterns involve a definite normative ordering and regulation'. Eisenstadt, 1968. For similar definitions in international relations, see Keohane, 1988: 383 and Young, 1986: 108.

23 See for example Ruggie, 1982; Bhagwati & Ruggie, 1984 and Krasner, 1985.

24 So as to minimize confusion, we choose to use Krasner's (1982(a): 186) standard definition of norms and principles.

25 The following discussion is indebted (although not identical) to Oran

Young's, 1986, discussion of imposed, negotiated and spontaneous regimes.

26 Dahrendorf, 1968: 140. This is also central to the theory of society of one of the foremost social scientists in history, Karl Marx. It is also a basic tenet of the (declining) hegemony approach.

27 Carr, 1939: 243 and 101.

28 This is similar to the approach to regimes offered by Puchala & Hopkins, 1982: 246, according to which 'for every political system (...) there is a corresponding regime'. It is what is implied by Krasner 1982(b) in labelling this definition 'Grotian'. For a good analysis of the Grotian perspective in international relations, see Bull, 1966 and Bull, 1977: 26 a.f.

29 Aggarwal, 1985: 20.

30 Concerning regimes, this point has been observed among others by Keohane & Nye, 1977: 20 and Young, 1982: 93. In sociology, among many, see Merton, 1968: 373 and Davis, 1949: chapter 3.

31 For a fundamental article, explaining the difference between the consensus model and the conflict model in sociology, see Coser, 1976.

32 Dahrendorf, 1968(b): 127. So as to avoid misrepresenting the thought of Dahrendorf, it should be noted that he also allows for the existence of cooperation and consensus; society is presented by him as a Janus-head – one side cooperation, one side conflict. See for that Dahrendorf, 1959.

33 This link between Marxism and Realism has also been observed by Keohane, 1986(c): 181.

34 For example: 'the real norms and procedures of a regime arise from the practice of its participants:' Donnelly, 1986; and 'whether a given rule exists is an empirical question, and the test is behavior:' Scott, 1982: 71.

35 One of the biggest problems with the contemporary study of international relations is precisely its a-historical nature. The present popularity of game theoretic and economistic explanations of cooperation is particularly open to this charge.

36 The methods of other social sciences, such as political science, historical critique and communication science, are most useful here.

37 Carr, 1939: 180 a.f.

38 Bull, 1977: 40 a.f. Among similar lines, see Frankel, 1979: 175.

39 The study of UN resolutions, the documents of different international organizations, the speeches of policy-makers at international fora, and the legislation of states, constitutes the basis for the search of the regime for a given issue-area. This is what specialists in international organization scholars used to do, and what European international relations scholars largely continue to do.

40 An example to clarify this: when the US Secretary of State speaks at the UN General Assembly about food aid to the Third World, he will stress the humanitarian and development objectives of aid. The same man, or his collegue from USDA, speaking before Congress in order to get the food aid bill passed, or before the Chamber of Commerce of an agricultural region, will refer to the foreign policy

and/or market creating role of food aid. This indicates that the norms applying to food aid are different on the international level than on the national US level.

41 Lampert, Falkowski & Mansbach, 1978: 151.

42 Morgenthau, 1949: 5.

43 Quote from Eastby, 1985: 60.

44 In Marxism, similarly to Realism, some scholars also ended up defining interest as a subjective concept; they have also been attacked by other authors. A very interesting debate on this took place in the 1970s between two modern Marxist authors: Poulantzas, 1977 and Milliband, 1977.

45 This, together with what Scott calls the intentional fallacy, constitutes the basic working assumptions of conspiracy theories. The intentional fallacy tells us that 'if something happened, or is happening, there must be a controlling pupose behind the event.... Actor purposes were the 'causes' that produced the 'effects' seen on every hand ... The fact of occurence, by itself, is conclusive evidence of intent.' Scott, 1982: 37 ff.

46 'The attempt to analyze the motivations of power politics purely in terms of interest would be to fall victim of excessive rationalism and a monist interpretation of motives. As in other fields, international action is normally prompted by a variety of motives, rational and emotional:' Schwarzenberger, 1964: 147–8. 'A Realist theory of international politics (...) will guard against two fallacies: the concern with motives and the concern with ideological preferences:' Morgenthau, 1959: 5–6.

47 Rosenau, 1986. This brings us to the study of domestic politics.

48 An essential element of Realism: Grieco, 1988: 487.

49 Thus whatever preferences guide the entrepreneur (impress his peers, improve the world, become rich fast ...), if he makes no profit (i.e. his interest), he will not survive long. Similarly, whatever preference drives a politician (improve the world, become rich fast, ...) without power (his interest) he will not be able to realize anything. This concept of interest is a typical Marxist one: see for example the distinction between 'Klasse an Sich' and 'Klasse für Sich'.

50 This definition of interest is related to Waltz, 1979: 73–4.

51 For the latter, see Grieco, 1988.

52 In simple words, we can synthesize the above as follows: actors' preferences can be against their interests because:
– actors were looking for their self-interest, but did not find it;
– they found it, but it was conflicting with their self-interest in another issue area;
– actors were not looking for their self-interest anyhow.

53 For what is often called a seminal statement on this matter, see Jervis, 1976.

54 Rosenau, 1986: 861–2.

55 Gilpin, 1981. See too Scott, 1982.

56 Lampert, Falkowski & Mansbach, 1983: 153.

57 As for social scientists in general. See Hirschman, 1971: 35: 'the idea that change, particularly major social change, is something to be wrought by the undeviatingly purposeful actions of some change agents is certainly far more widespread than the view that change can also occur because of originally unintended side effects of human actions which might even have been expressly directed toward system maintenance.'

58 Scott, 1982: chapter 2; also Sterling, 1974: 4.

59 This is a reformulation of basic sociological wisdom.

60 Assuming their original preference was self-interested.

61 Keohane, 1988: 381

62 It is clear that our pre-theory is closely influenced by, but not identical to, the so-called 'cognitivist' approach to international relations (as defined by Haggard & Simmons, 1986: 499), which stresses the intersubjective nature of regimes. This has been advocated *inter alia* by Haas, 1981: *passim*; Puchala & Hopkins, 1982: 247; Smith, 1989: 228; Young, 1986: *passim* and Kratochwil and Ruggie, 1986: *passim*. The link between regimes and cognition is also recognized by Krasner, 1982: 368, whose last line of his final article of the regimes volume reads: 'if regimes matter, than cognitive understanding can matter as well.' We agree.

TWO

FOOD PRODUCTION: THE POLITICAL ECONOMY OF INEFFICIENCY

Every cow in the US attracted $ 1.400 in subsidies in 1986, according to a celebrated calculation by the International Monetary Fund. At the time, this was more than the annual per capita income of half the world's population

Financial Times, July 14/15, 1990.

The food production policies of countries vary greatly: we could hardly analyze them in detail here. We will limit ourselves to a brief overview of the agricultural and food production outcomes of three groups of countries: the highly-industrialized, market-based OECD countries; the industrialized, centrally-planned Eastern European countries; and the low income, lowly industrialized, ones. We are aware of that food production policies within these groups are not identical, especially in groups one and three. Yet, to a large extent, basic patterns and fundamental constraints are similar within each group; where they are not, this will be mentioned. Hence, we set out to present the characteristics and origins of the food production policies in these three groups of countries, and their impact on food production, income distribution and economic growth.

The aim of this chapter is not to add to the existing body of knowledge on agricultural policy, nor to present a complete analysis of the determinants of food production, but rather better to understand the origins of the preferences of actors on the international level. Indeed, as we explained in the previous chapter, under conditions of complex interdependence, international policies cannot be separated from domestic policies and preferences. In chapter 7, where we discuss structural adjustment policy reform in agriculture, we will do exactly the opposite, and analyze the international origins of domestic policy outcomes.

1 The First World

A On the measurement of protection

Levels of protection in agriculture are not easy to compare between countries, even if, as for OECD countries, data abound. First, there are different ways of expressing protection, giving very different results. The classical representation, the 'nominal protection coefficient' (the ratio of domestic prices over border, or international, prices) only catches those policies that affect the price of agricultural products. Most of the EEC's or Japan's policies work through prices: they thus score high on this scale. Not surprisingly, this is the way favored by the US for calculating protection. Another way of measuring the extent of protection is by calculating total government expenditure on programs that benefit farmers. In this version, the US scores around as high as the EEC, as the latter loves to point out. Second, fluctuating exchange rates render any meaningful international comparison of protection very hard. Without any internal change in protectionism, nominal protection coefficients can vary dramatically, only because the exchange rate of the dollar, in which most international food trade is done, fluctuates. This happened with the EEC during the middle of the 1980s.[1] Third, as table 2.1 shows, there are different ways of disaggregating results. As Butler points out:

> while the EEC prefers to talk in terms of support per farmer, since that is the measure which favors its conclusion that European support levels are reasonable and fair, the USA with larger farms quotes figures on support for each unit of output.[2]

After a conflictual GATT meeting in 1982, the members of the OECD gave the latter's secretariat a mandate to research and measure the extent of protection of agriculture in their countries. For this, a new way of calculating the support afforded to commodities has been used, called the Producer Subsidy Equivalent (PSE): it measures all policies that affect farm prices. Originally developed by agricultural economist Tim Josling for the FAO,[3] these new measurements have been the subject of prolonged debate within the OECD. Eventually, a definition was agreed upon:[4] in 1987 the OECD started the publication of agricultural monitoring reports, complete with comparative tables of protection levels, measured in PSE, for each country and product.[5] Other official organisms, such as the US Department of Agriculture and the Australian Bureau of Agricultural Economics, have adopted the same measurements, although with slight differences. Hence, there has come into being a certain political consensus about the 'objectivity' of these measurements – a big step forward from the earlier situation when different actors did not even use the same measure for the same thing, and a testimony to the central role international organizations can play in the development of so-called 'consensual knowledge.'[6] Yet, this does not imply that states agree any more on the objectives they pursue, as the latest round of GATT negotiations shows.

Table 2.1 Measures of protection[7]

	Cost of the agric. policy	NPC	PSE	PSE, all products	PSE per farmer	PSE per ha.
	1980	1980	1980	1988	1988	1988
	billion ECU	%	%	%	US$	US$
EEC	56.5	35.7	36.4	43	9,000	590
Japan	23.8	83.5	54.3	75	16,000	9,640
USA	26.2	−0.1	14.5	35	24,000	114

B OECD countries' production policies: an overview

All OECD countries protect their agriculture. This holds for staples (in particular wheat and rice) as well as for other food crops (sugar and soybeans for example), agricultural commodities such as cotton and tobacco and the meat and dairy sectors. The extent of protection afforded to OECD farmers is high: farming is the most protected sector in the OECD (on the average around 50% at present) and the level has increased rather than decreased in the 1980s.[8]

These policies are old. Japan's protection of rice and other products began at the end of the last century;[10] the US Agricul-

Table 2.2 PSE's for wheat, rice and milk, in %[9]

	Wheat			Rice			Milk		
	79–81	84–85	88–89	79–81	84–85	88–89	79–81	84–85	88–89
Australia	7	12	11	16	25	26	33	52	27
Canada	15	41	36	–	–	–	74	97	70
EEC	28	36	27	15	68	51	67	56	56
Japan	96	98	94	71	86	88	79	82	67
New Zealand	00	13	11	–	–	–	20	14	3
USA	14	44	32	7	61	45	55	66	54

tural Adjustment Act was enacted in 1933; the Common Agricultural Policy of the EEC dates from the Treaty of Rome and functioned from 1967 onwards, but most members had prior protectionist legislation,[11] and the same holds for most other European countries.

The foremost objective of these policies is the maintenance of farmers' income, at least in 'parity' with industrial wages. The second one is to increase food production.[12] The latter plays a role in countries such as Switzerland, Sweden and Japan;[13] the former is central to the policies of all OECD countries. Finally, tertiary objectives include the preservation of the countryside as a way-of-living and as an ecosystem, and the stabilization of the supply of high quality foodstuffs. Hence, food related preferences play a varying and important, although usually not the most important, role in establishing OECD food policies: food production policies serve above all to maintain farm income. Considerations of (Third) world hunger are fully absent.

OECD countries have developed a complex variety of sector specific instruments to realize these aims.[14] Generally speaking, farmers' income can be supported either directly through income support measures, or indirectly through price support mechanisms; the latter also increase production. Governments can resort to import taxes and quotas, subsidies on inputs (seed, water, etc.) or outputs (production), direct public intervention (stockholding, marketing boards and deficiency payments), and export promotion measures. Most OECD countries, depending on their objectives, endowments and histories, use more or less of each. Yet, those measures that raise the price of agricultural products are the most common ones, accounting for around 70% of all PSEs in the OECD in the period 1979–81.[15] The US has been the most flexible in the pursuit of its objective to increase farm income, using both protectionist and free market measures as instruments. The EEC has developed an innovative and successful system of variable levies,[16] largely insulating its domestic production from world conditions. Most other countries present more 'ordinary' tariff-based, but not less heavy, forms of protectionism.

C Origins of these policies

Protectionism in the rich countries is usually explained by referring to the power of farm interest groups, and to the weight of elected representatives favoring farm interests.[17] This begs the question: if agricultural policies are protectionist in OECD countries, this evidently signifies that a majority of the members of its legislative bodies vote for such policies. Stating that farm interests are powerful or that they are strongly represented in Parliament is not an explanation, but a description. The puzzle remains: how can a group that commands only a small proportion of the votes secure such disproportional and almost unchallengeable benefits if other, often larger, also well-organized groups (miners, steel workers, teachers, medical professionals, public employees, to mention but some) do not manage? This needs more explanation than the usual reference to interest group strength.

The application of neoclassical public choice theory to agriculture provides such an explanation. Anderson & Hayami synthesize it nicely:

> First, the decreasing importance of food prices in household budgets as incomes grow ensures that political pressure from consumers and industrialists for low food prices diminishes with economic growth. Second, the relative declining importance of agricultural production and employment as the economy's industrial and service sectors expand makes it less and less costly politically for the government to succumb to farmers' demands for assistance measures designed to reduce the pressure for structural adjustment; moreover, the demands from farmers for such policies increases markedly once an economy has reached the point where the incentives for intersectoral adjustment are such that absolute numbers of farmers begin to fall. And third, there is tend-

ency for growing economies – especially densely populated ones – to lose their comparative advantage in agriculture and eventually become net food importers; this provides increasing scope for assisting farmers through covert policy instruments, such as import controls, that do not require budgetary outlays, and for justifying rural assistance on the grounds of food security.[18]

This approach presents some insights, which, though not new, remain valid. Food indeed constitutes a small share of household expenditure in rich countries at present; as such, any increase in its price passes by rather unnoticed. While budgetary costs are low, agricultural protection is thus not perceived as costly by most people.[19] This cannot but favor the continuation of these policies; yet, it hardly explains their origins.

The real weaknesses of this kind of explanation are its a-political and a-historical nature. It is a-historical because it reduces the past to a series of economic data. It is a-political for it treats politics in the same mechanistic, abstract supply-and-demand fashion as it treats the market for computer chips. It does not ask nor answer the important questions of who gains and who loses; who has what kind of power and who does not.[20] It reflects a typical confusion between 'political economy' and 'the application to political phenomena of modes of reasoning and analytical tools originally developed within economics' against which Alfred Hirshman warned two decades ago,[21] but which has become so popular now.

To put together the puzzle, we must consider the interplay between social, political and economic factors. Two points are worth stressing here. One is the longstanding existence in many countries of values favorable to farming and the countryside.[22] Their roots are linked to such fuzzy but strong emotions as tradition, preserving a way of living, and security of supply, with the precise mixture differing by country.[23] These values are often legally made explicit and well organized, as well on the farmers' side as on the government side, where large bureaucracies are engaged in mastering the processes set in motion earlier.[24] They constitute a strong brake on any change in policies.

But most important is that these policies are of prime importance to rural elites – large farmers, rural industries and commerce, political parties strongly represented on the countryside

(Christian parties in central Europe, for example) – and guarantee their support for and alliance with the modern state and economy. In all OECD countries, three quarters of the population live in cities and work in the secondary or tertiary sector; at the same time, at least three quarters of the territory is rural. Agriculture, although only occupying 3% of the population, is the heart of the functioning of this countryside. In tens of thousands of small villages and communes in the Western world, rural elites depend for their political, if not personal, survival largely on the fate of agriculture. Cutting the protection of agriculture would endanger the social and economic fabric of the countryside and the well-being of its local elites. It would undermine the alliance of the latter to those in power in the capital and endanger the stability of the territory. Agricultural protection thus benefits more than the 3% of the population directly engaged in agriculture: it is the price to pay to guarantee social peace between the rural and urban sides of modern states.

D The effects

OECD protectionist policies have several intended or unintended effects, five of which we will discuss in this section. They 1) increase OECD food security, 2) result in large internal food surpluses, 3) have regressive effects on income distribution within OECD countries, 4) are costly to government budgets, and 5) slow down economic growth.

By far the most important effect of these policies is to increase food production beyond what would have happened in their absence: in other words, OECD food security improved.[25] This comes about in two ways: directly, as less efficient farms keep producing; indirectly, as a result of the technological innovation induced by enhanced agricultural profitability. Hence, notwithstanding constantly declining farming populations, total food output increased continuously in all OECD countries. In the EEC, the growth rate of agricultural production has been around 2.1% to 2.4% during the period 1974–1983. As a result, against historic trends, the EEC is now more than self-sufficient in all major staples.[26]

Yet, while this growth in agricultural output took place, demand in the same countries was nearly stagnant: low population growth and full bellies account for this.[27] Hence, the second

31

effect of the OECD agricultural production outcome is the existence of large surpluses – the largest food problem of the rich countries.[28] Not only are these costly to store, but their existence and disposal also has international consequences that we will encounter in our chapter on food trade and aid.

Third, present agricultural policies have a regressive impact on income distribution. They are of disproportional benefit to rich and large farmers, and not to the small, poorer ones, in whose names they exist.[30] According to the OECD, 'over 75% of agricultural assistance . . . [in the EEC and the US] is received by less than 25% of all farmers.'[31] According to data by Paarlberg, the 2.1% of US farms that have gross sales of more than $ 500,000 a year take in on the average $ 105,000 in government subsidies, while the 78% of the small farms that have yearly sales below $ 100,000, receive only between 4,000 and 15,000 on the average.[32] Hence, the bigger farmers get bigger, while the small ones go bankrupt: in the US, since 1985, 400.000 farmers lost their lands.[33] The situation is similar in the EEC, notwithstanding attempts to the contrary.[34] Moreover, as a result of the dominance of price support as the main policy instrument, most policies end up increasing the cost of food to consumers. Because poor consumers spend a higher proportion of their incomes on food, this effect is socially regressive, especially in the EEC and Japan, where the largest share of farm protection is done through prices.[35] This effectively implies that the poorer consumers transfer income to the richer farmers and goes against the crux of post-war social policy in most OECD countries. This side effect holds less for those policies which are paid by taxpayers (i.e. payments by the state), for taxes are progressive.

The fourth effect is on government budgets. For surplus countries, (i.e. where domestic production is bigger than domestic demand), the costs of subsidizing inputs, buying food at guaranteed prices, storing it in warehouses and selling it on the international market through export subsidies, can be extremely high.[36] The policies of Japan and non-EEC European countries are less costly to their budgets, for they are net importers and their protectionism is thus mainly financed by consumers.[37] But the story is different for the EEC and the US. During the 1970s, when the EEC approached self-sufficiency in major cereals, the CAP budget cost increased fourfold; it doubled again from 1982 to 1986,[38] and has continued to skyrocket until the end of the

Table 2.3 EEC food self-sufficiency, in %[29]

	before 1945 EEC–6	1954–59 EEC–6	1960–64 EEC–6	1965–69 EEC–6	1970–74 EEE–10	1975–79 EEC–10	1970 EEC–12	1975 EEC–12	1980 EEC–12	1985 EEC–12	1987–88 EEC–12
Cereals	81	85	84	88	90	91	80	86	102	111	111
Wheat	n.a.	n.a.	94	107	97	106	87	101	123	120	119
Butter	104	100	100	109	101	110	81	80.8	117	123	127
Sugar	75	101	99	100	91	108	89	100	102	107	106
Beef	n.a.	n.a.	97	90	92	98					

1980s. Costs of the US program were low and stable during the 1970s, but exploded in the 1980s, when stagnating international demand dramatically increased stocks and export subsidies.[39] In total, the OECD estimates the cost of farm support to government budgets to be around $ 150 bn for the years 1985, 1986 and 1987.[40] Although no direct link can be made between expenditures for agricultural policies and budget deficits, the former are certainly of no use in solving the latter.

Table 2.4 Estimates of the cost of agricultural policy, in billion ECU[41]

Country	Cost to the taxpayer		Cost to consumers	
	79–81	84–86	79–81	84–86
Australia	0.5	0.7	0.2	0.8
Canada	1.6	3.7	1.5	3.2
EEC–10	21.1	30.4	36.7	49.8
Japan	10.2	13.7	17.3	41.3
USA	19.4	59.4	9.6	20.3

The final effect is on general resource allocation and, hence, on economic growth in the protecting countries. It is now commonly accepted that economic growth is slowed as a result of not only the budgetary weight of these policies but also the macroeconomic misallocation of resources that follows from the artificially high profitability of agriculture. Estimates of the efficiency losses differ very much, varying from $ 1.9 to $ 24.1 bn for the EEC; and from $ 0.3 to 5.5 bn for the US.[42] In Japan, overall economic growth, as well as consumer welfare, is supposed to dramatically improve in the absence of its agricultural protection.[43] The last OECD study on the subject concludes that protecting agriculture causes an annual income loss in the main industrial countries of $ 72 bn,[44] 'equal to the combined GNP of Ireland and New Zealand.'[45] Still, by itself, the fact that agricultural protection slows economic growth does not automatically justify its suppression: societies can chose to favor food security, environmental protection, urban-rural equilibrium, or guaranteed farm income to be more of a social priority than increasing the rate of economic growth.

2 The 'Second World'

A The outcome

The main characteristic of agriculture in the USSR and the other Eastern European countries (and communist LDCs such as Ethiopia, Cuba and China) until the late 1980s was its socialized, *i.e.*, public nature. There were few private farmers: instead, peasants worked on large state farms or cooperatives, which produce the bulk of agricultural output. These farms were governed in the same planned and centralized way as other sectors of economic activity. This collectivization of agriculture dates from the end of the 1920s in Russia, from the 1950s in the other Eastern European countries. Poland, where 76% of the land was tilled by smallholders constitutes an exception – but agricultural inputs and outputs were still supplied by government monopolies.[46]

In most Eastern European countries, agriculture has received a high share of government expenditure, especially in the last decades. In the USSR, for example, agriculture accounted for 20 to 30% of total investments under the 7th to 11th Plans (1960–1985).[47] As inefficiencies increased, government expenditures for agriculture soared.[48]

Most Eastern European countries, with the exception of Romania, subsidized food consumption. In the USSR, until the 1990s, the prices of food staples had not increased since 1962.[49] As a result, the demand for food largely outstripped supply, necessitating fast growing food imports.[50] Moreover, as the cost of producing food has increased over the years, government outlays for subsidies have augmented dramatically. D. Gale Johnson estimates that in Russia in 1983 the food subsidy on meat, milk, bread and potatoes accounted for 51 billion roubles, exceeding the value of total retail sales and amounting to an enormous 8–9% of GNP.[51] In the 1990s, all these subsidies are being abolished, bringing about hardship to food consumers.

B The effects

This situation had some important consequences. First, agricultural production growth was relatively high until the middle of the 1970s. For example, Soviet agriculture performed well between 1950 and 1970, the annual growth rate of output being

3,9%. In Poland, agricultural production grew at 2,2% per year in the first half of the 1970s, and in Hungary at 3%. Yet, this growth has been obtained at a high cost. According to Johnson, 'resources devoted to agriculture in the Soviet Union produce approximately half as much as the same bundle of resources would produce in climatically similar areas in the United States.'[52]

More recently, moreover, agricultural growth slowed down in all countries of Eastern Europe. In the USSR, for example, it was a miserable 1.2% a year during the 1970s[53] – below population growth. The reason for this is generally held to be not climatic problems (although they do exist) nor outdated mechanization (although that is often the case), but the socialized nature of the production system, which, combined with the unattractive way of living on the countryside,[54] takes away the incentive for farmers to produce more. The case of China, where the remarkable 1980s progress in agriculture is largely attributed to the privatization of land control, is a striking example.[55]

The second impact of the agricultural outcome has been a proliferation of inefficiencies. The case of the Soviet Union is most striking. Agricultural investment, which has been around a third of all national investment, was not only ineffective, but also took away resources from other sectors of the economy. The enormous fiscal drain caused by the food subsidies had heavy spill-overs on the rest of the economy.[56] According to the 1989 Pravda, out of 14 million people registered as working in the agricultural sector, 4 million were bureaucrats; and 'once the chairman of Gosagroprom has signed a piece of paper it passes through 32 stages before it actually reaches the farm.'[57] Moreover, according to some sources, up to one third of all crops harvested in the Soviet Union is lost as a result of negligence and bad transport and storage facilities.[58] Finally, the food imports necessary to bring domestic availability closer to demand were costly in foreign exchange. All Eastern European countries except Russia had to cut back their cereals imports in the 1980s; this was not the result of any decrease in need, but of lack of money. For many observers, this is not without importance for explaining the 1989 upheavals in these countries.

Indeed, a third important effect of this agricultural production outcome has been the declining legitimacy of the communist systems of these countries. Long food queues, and the lack of certain products, such as meat and sugar, especially in small towns, are factors which can not but undermine the workers' confidence in the socialist paradise and the powers-that-be. The USSR have known serious riots, with tens of deaths, in 1962, after retail prices for meat and butter had been increased; the 1970 Polish riots, which brought down Gomulka, were protests against the price of food.[59] And at the end of the 1980s, one of the crucial condition for Gorbachev's perestroika to succeed was generally thought to be the extent to which he managed to increase food availability for his population. He failed, and lost all popularity.

The failure of Eastern European agriculture has been recognized and policy reform has taken place all over Eastern Europe, starting even before the 1989 revolutions. Since the middle of the 1980s, Hungary, Chechoslovakia and Bulgaria decentralized their agriculture and/or increased farm gate prices. But it is the case of the USSR that is the most interesting. Since 1988, Gorbachev successively allowed farmers to lease land from the state farms for up to 50 years, which farmers could freely cultivate; started a 70 billion rouble investment program, so as to upgrade food processing and storage; liberalized most agricultural trade; and, in a final *coup de theatre*, offered farmers the possibility to be paid in hard currency for any grain and oilseed production above recent average production levels.[60]

By the beginning of the 1990s, the effect of these policy reforms was not impressive: the general state of chaos of most economies, and the weight of old habits among farmers and bureaucrats cannot be erased fast. But it is sure that Eastern Europe is at the beginning of a new era in its agricultural production outcome: the restoration of private agriculture proceeds at different paces, but the tendency is all over the same. Soon, for most of them the 'second world' production outcome will be the same as the one of the 'first world.' International food aid as well as aid to agriculture will reinforce the tendency towards the generalization of the West European mode of agricultural production.

3 The Third World

In sections a) and b), I will describe the usual diagnosis and explanation of Third World food policies. Sections c) and d) will present some observations that contradict this common wisdom, and present the basis of a more nuanced alternative explanation. Finally, section e) will briefly discuss some of the main effects of these policies, in the same way as above.

A Common wisdom: discrimination against agriculture

The study of LDC agricultural policies has become one of the 'boom' areas of development economics in the 1980s, equalled only by the analysis of financial markets. In both, the World Bank has provided a prominent forum for brilliant, liberal economists to advance their ideas and careers, according to the econometric and ideological exigencies of the discipline. The 1986 World Development Report – the yearly attempt by the World Bank at vulgarizing, agenda-setting and lobbying the rest of the development community – has been devoted to the subject.[61]

The 'common diagnosis'[62] of the development community concerning LDC agricultural and food production policies starts by the obvious observation that 'the prices of many agricultural commodities and inputs are influenced in a variety of ways by governments of developing countries. Government intervention can and does take place at the stages of production, marketing, consumption and trade.'[63] It then goes on to assert that, since independence, this intervention discriminates against agriculture, or against the countryside. Proof of this is found in the fact that farm-gate prices for agricultural products – food as well as non-food – in most Third World countries are below world prices,[64] meaning that the effect of government policies is that farmers' output is paid less than what it would have earned in the absence of these policies, i.e. free trade:[65] 'the profitability of farming is artificially depressed because of either macroeconomic or sectorial policies.'[66] This creates strong disincentives against agriculture, considered the major cause of low food production in the developing countries.[67]

We will not dwell here on the agriculture-specific or general macroeconomic policies which are taken to create this state of affairs: the subsidization of imported products, which compete with domestic production; the existence of monopsony state marketing boards, which set inferior prices for agricultural products; the taxation of export or import-competing crops; the existence of overvalued exchange rates, discouraging food exports and encouraging imports; the neglect of agriculture in government budgets, and so on. There exists a voluminous literature on these subjects, to which we can only refer in passing.[68]

At the same time they discourage domestic agriculture, governments subsidize food consumption: directly, through the use of food subsidies,[69] and indirectly, by some of the just mentioned policies (low exchange rates, for example). The official reason for this is to combat hunger, but it is widely believed that it is not only or even mainly the hungry who benefit, and that this is no accident.[70] As a result of these policies, demand for food, particularly imported, is higher than in their absence.[71]

B The usual explanations

The common explanation for both these policies – the squeezing of food production and the subsidization of food consumption – goes along pluralist lines. Its most popular version has been developed by Michael Lipton in 1977, when he introduced the concept of urban bias. Its political science tenet can be synthesized in his statement that 'the state is not neutral, but influenced by the powerful, the organized, the wealthy, and – under urban bias – the near.'[72] Indeed, according to this explanation, urban groups – poor and/or middle class – tend to be organized and prone to sudden revolt. Being food consumers, they have a strong interest in low food prices. The illiterate, dispersed and unorganized rural poor, on the contrary, pose no threat to the survival of most Third World governments.[73] Hence the existence of inefficient policies that keep food prices down at the cost of peasants and thus eventually cause hunger.

This notion of 'urban bias' is comprehensive and easy to grasp and thus popular in the international development community, especially with economists, who dominate the field:[74] no analysis or policy statement on agriculture fails to refer to it.[75] As we shall see in chapter 7 of this thesis, 'correcting urban/rural bias' is one of the basic axes of structural adjustment in the 1980s.[76]

Yet this explanation has some serious limitations. First, it tends to neglect international factors and explain the problems of developing countries solely by their own behavior. This is undoubtedly politically popular in OECD countries but it is also simplistic: if even in industrialized countries economic and social crises are at least partly explained by international factors, how much more does this hold for many poor countries, dependent on one export crop and with no reserves to cushion themselves against external shocks. Second, it neglects rural stratification (ranging from landless peasants to big estate owners), which is a variable of utmost important in Third World agricultural policy outcomes.[77] Third, it has little predictive power: why does sub-Saharan Africa, according to the literature, suffer most from urban bias-type of policies, while it is the least urbanized and least industrialized of all regions? The notion of urban bias should probably be viewed as a tendency among many, a similarity of outcomes, caused by different factors, rather than a theory, to be applied generally.

A different strand of explanation for Third World agricultural policies is represented by the 'radical' school. Some authors explain the incapacity of the poor to produce sufficient food by the privileged position of export crops and the development of large-scale commercial farming: 'they [export crops] withdraw from food production the most fertile lands, the strongest arms.'[78] De Janvry uses the notion of 'disarticulation' to explain the outcome against small-scale agriculture and food production in Latin-America: in economies based on low-cost production for foreign markets, food prices have to be kept down.[79] This brings us to what are properly called conspiracy theories, arguing that 'bad' Third World food policies are designed to suit the interests of foreign capital and its national allies.[80] Depressed living conditions in the countryside create a reserve pool of cheap labor, while low food prices guarantee a low reproduction cost of labor. Hence, agricultural policies (as well as the strategies of the aid agencies) are designed to benefit Northern elites, transnational companies and their allies in the South, all of whom have vested interests in their continuation.[81]

Several critiques can be raised against these radical explanations. The most important is their downplaying of the autonomous role of Third World governments, in favor of an 'international conspiracy' approach, usually with multinational companies and the US as the main culprits. More specifically, the oft mentioned conflict between export crops and food crops, with the former being imposed by foreign interests at the expense of the latter, thus causing hunger, does not hold. There surely are cases in which export crops are produced in regions where hunger, and even starvation, occurs, but this does not imply that foreign interests in export crops are responsible for such hunger

40

or starvation, nor that chasing such foreign interests would solve the problem. For one, it is untrue that export crops are only planted because they benefit foreign interests, against the will of peasants; they are very often rational and efficient actions for farmers, even small ones, who freely choose to plant them in the hope of making some money with them, so as to be able to buy other goods or services (health, schooling, beer, ...). Moreover, growth rates of both food crops and export crops tend to vary together, *i.e.* countries doing well in the one also do well in producing the other; both can expand together, and usually do so.[82] The conflict might hold for some individual cases, when land is very scarce or unfertile, but it should not be generalized.[83]

The critiques we made against both explanations are by no means specific to the issue area studied, but apply quite generally to both these approaches in development studies. But there is another, fundamental problem: the diagnosis on which they are based is incomplete if not counterfactual. That is what we now turn to.

C Some nuancing observations ...

A closer look at the data discloses some facts that put into question both the liberal and radical interpretations. First, and contrary to radical expectation, the discrimination observed tends to be stronger for non-food than for food products, and strongest for export crops.[84] This can be explained by the facts that export crops are administratively the easiest for governments to tax[85] and that many countries do have policies intended to favor food production. A second observation, which undermines the liberal diagnosis, reinforces the latter explanation: all evidence shows that the discrimination of food production results mainly from the side-effects of general economy-wide interventions, and not from specific food production policies, which are usually protectionist in nature.[86] According to Byerlee 'there is little evidence for the conventional wisdom that governments have maintained low producer prices in order to favor urban consumer-interest groups.'[87] Recent comparative research concludes that 'contrary to expectations, (...) direct policies have *provided protection* to the production of food in about 70% of the countries studied.'[88] Governments, or more precisely, branches of governments,[89] often subsidize inputs (seeds, fertilizer, rural credit) and/or outputs (marketing, storage), in an attempt to stimulate their food production. This has particularly been the case since the 'world food crisis' of 1972–74.[90] According to the FAO, for example, at least 70 LDCs have established guaranteed producer prices for their main cereals (maize, rice and wheat) since the middle of the 1970s.[91] World Bank figures show that 12 out of 13 African governments studied seriously increased producer cereal prices by the 1980s; an ILO study comes to the same conclusion.[92] Research on Latin America shows that government expenditure on agriculture underwent strong increases from the middle of the 1970s onwards in all countries under consideration, up to levels close to the one of the US.[93]

Hence, the picture that emerges is much more subtle than both the classical and the radical diagnoses have it. Most governments, especially in Asia, but, since the world food crisis, also in Africa and Latin America, have policies intended to favor food production; they have reoriented their spending towards the agricultural sector – most of all so for those products they are importers of, and for those produced by large farmers. Yet, as a result of administrative inefficiency,[94] the necessity to increase government revenue through taxation of exports and the side-effects of other policies,[95] disincentives against food production often continue to exist. World Bank figures show that for 6 out of the 12 countries that increased cereal prices, other policies outweighed the positive effects of these increases.[96] And the above mentioned Krueger e.a. study documents that of the 12 (out of 17) countries which have positive direct policies, 5 have indirect policies which outweigh the direct ones.[97] Not many countries escaped this outcome. Among those who did, and who consequently dramatically expanded food production, we find China,[98] India, Pakistan and Indonesia (all very large and populous) as well as Saudi-Arabia, Libya and the Asian NICs, countries whose food policy is better described by the 'first world' model than the third world one.

A critical look at the available data on actual food production reinforces our doubts about the classical diagnosis. The growth rate for food production (not only cereals, but also roots, tubers, etc.) in the Third World has been estimated by authoritative sources at 2.89% annually for the last 30 years;[99] 2.95% for the period 1961–1985;[100] and 3.1% annually for the last two decades.[101] Whatever the precise figure, this compares very nicely with a rate of 2.1% for the heavily protected, technologically intensive and expensive OECD agricultural sector during the same 1951–1981 period. Even if China is excluded, the annual food production growth rate in the Third World, according to the same sources, is still around 2.6% between 1961 and 1980. This also compares favorable with the growth rates of food production before independence: according to Etemad, all continents, Africa included, accelerated their food production growth rates after independence.[102]

Table 2.5 Food production growth rates, in %[103]

	Cereals		Major food crops	
	1911–50	1950–80	1961–80	1980–85
Africa	2.3	2.4	2.1	2.0
Asia	1.1	3.2	3.4	3.7
Latin America	2.0	3.9	2.8	2.2
Third World	1.4	3.2	3.1	2.9
China	0.2	3.0	4.1	5.5

Table 2.6 Per capita food production % growth rate, 1961–85[104]

	1961–70	1970–75	1975–80	1980–85
First World	1.0	1.3	1.2	0.7
Second World	2.1	1.5	0.1	1.3
Third World	0.3	0.1	0.3	0.6
Latin America	0.8	0.3	1.0	0.0
Asia	0.2	0.4	0.5	1.5
socialist Asia	2.1	1.1	2.4	4.1
Africa	0.0	–1.0	–1.0	–1.0
Maghreb	0.6	0.2	–1.3	–0.1

Admittedly, these figures become less good looking when they are disaggregated on a per capita basis, for the average Third World population growth rate during the same period was 2.5%, implying that the Third World as a whole has hardly increased its food production per person over the last decades. Indeed, according to FAO, the total increase in per capita food supply for the period 1961–1976 was only 3% in the Third World, with 7% for the middle-income countries and 0% for the poorest ones.[105] Yet, this constitutes no proof of the disincentive nature of the policies followed, but rather of the fact that population growth rates are high[106] (for further discussion, see chapter 5 of this book).

Moreover, these figures certainly underestimate food production, especially in Africa, the continent with the highest population growth rate and which is generally considered the best example of urban bias and disincentive policies. Gilles Mettetal, comparing the major sources on food trade and aid data for the Sahel, finds that differences between different sources for any given period that high that one can only conclude that there exists no certainty whatsoever about basic data.[107] Philip Raikes, after a detailed discussion of the FAO Production Yearbook figures for Africa (the most used data), describes their 'low level and downward trend in accuracy' and believes 'there is every reason to expect a significant downward bias in the reporting, and one increasing over time, for a variety of reasons.'[108] Among those reasons, we can cite the following. First, the fact that farmers switch to subsistence farming implies by definition that their production does not reach the market: it is accordingly impossible to measure it with any certainty. As it is food they produce and auto-consume, it is the figures for food production which suffer most.[109] Second, inasfar as farmers trade, they very often do so on parallel markets, beyond government's, and hence statisticians', reach. Recent studies of this phenomenon in the Sahel conclude that a very large part of food trade is done on these parallel markets.[110] Third, if the data for cereals such as wheat and rice are unreliable, that holds even more so for many staples, such as cassava and manioc, whose production has never been of much interest to those gathering the statistics, but which are important staples in large parts of the Third world – and in particular among the rural poor. This implies another bias to underestimate total food production. Finally, the common wisdom that Africa's food situation dramatically worsened since independence is also to a large extent based on the fact that its food imports increased strongly during the same period. But, as Sayre Schatz and Philip Raikes have argued, increased imports do not prove declining food production in Africa: they result from other, mainly urban, imperatives.[111]

To conclude: the neglect by Third World governments of their food sector is less general than is usually thought: in many countries, food production is promoted if not effectively protected. Insofar as discrimination exists, it is often partially unintentional, *i.e.* the side-effect of policies designed for other purposes. Finally, with 2.9 % to 3.2% annually, even the existing, certainly underestimated, figures on food production growth rates are not that bad: they are considerably higher than what has been managed by the developed countries in their own histories. Hence, we seriously question the uniform application of the usual liberal interpretation of Third World food policies, in which negative agricultural policies, implemented by selfish elites for the sole purpose of their staying in power, are solely responsible for low food availability, and, ultimately, of hunger in the Third World[112] – and whose subsequent solution is a good dose of state disengagement and free trade (see chapter 7).

D Towards an interdisciplinary approach to LDC food production

In order to understand the food and agricultural production policies in Third World countries, an ecclectic blending of disciplines is appropriate. Such approach should combine at least the following disciplines. First, economics is needed in order to grasp the complexities of relative prices and intersectoral linkages, the functioning of subsistence farming, the potential of surplus extraction inside and outside of agriculture, the effects of macroeconomic policies, the productivity of different farming methods and the like.

Second, we need to look at history, which gives us information about peasant modes of production as well as their gradual but usually incomplete insertion in the world market under colonial rule. Colonial governments usually vigorously promoted export agriculture, neglecting food crops.[113] Thus, a dualistic agriculture came into being, with modern, large-scale, and often foreign-owned producers coexisting with small-scale, largely traditional, state-neglected agriculture. Hence, already before independence, in many countries – most of sub-Saharan Africa for example – the growth rates of food production lagged behind demand, and these countries had become net importers of food.[114] The newly independent governments inherited this legacy and often added to it their priority for western-style industrialization, with the active backing of the international aid community.[115] While most of them also designed policies intended to boost agricultural production and promote rural development, these policies did not fundamentally alter the long-term evolution. The changes needed were much more dramatic and difficult to implement; administrative failure, powerful interests (usually mainly urban and industrial indeed) and the other aims of governments often worked against it.

Finally, the old rules of politics apply. In each country, the better organized an interest group, the more policies reflect its preferences. This holds between the rural and the urban sector – usually in favor of the latter[116] – as well as in the countryside. In the latter case, large farmers usually are the better organized.[117] In those cases where they produce food crops, these are more likely to be protected and, hence, aggregate food production to increase. Small farmers can benefit from this if they produce the same food crops, and depending on their access to inputs (seeds, fertilizer, credit). In Africa, the case of Zimbabwe is the outstanding example; in Asia, India.[118] If this constellation is not present, and given that small farmers and landless laborers are usually badly organized, have little access to inputs and often live on the brink of survival, special conditions are needed for really beneficial policies to exist for food production. These conditions are rarely present; they seem to have existed in socialist countries such as China and Cuba and in the Asian NICs.

To all this have to be added an understanding of the many technical problems of Third World agriculture: the lack of rural infrastructure and transportation; the poor quality of agricultural research and vulgarization; the absence of credit, seeds and fertilizers; political instability and warfare; the unadapted nature of the Green Revolution to local conditions; the bad quality of the land and its degradation, etc.

Explanations along the lines described above shun monocausality and generality and favor pluridisciplinarity and case studies. They will not be pursued in detail here: different authors have done so with interesting results.[119] The important point is to be aware of the complex nature of Third World agricultural policies and their origins.

E The effects

In order of importance, common wisdom has it that Third World agricultural production outcomes a) hold down agricultural and food production; b) increase income and asset inequality; and c) slow down general economic growth. The first effect decreases the supply of food available; the other two the entitlements of the poor to food.

The most important effect of the agricultural production outcome prevailing in most Third World countries is considered to be a lowering of agricultural production growth rates, for peasants switch to subsistence farming, lowering marketed domestic agricultural production. Bates sums it up nicely: 'the government's use of market controls to levy resources from agriculture lowers the returns farmers can expect from production for the market, both in absolute and relative terms. In and of itself, this fact would account for the peasant's turning away from cash crop production.'[120] This chain of effects is usually held to be a major cause of low local food availability, and, ultimately, of hunger in the Third World. Yet, as we saw above, agricultural growth rates have been high by historical standards in the Third World; much of their present decline, especially in Africa, might be due to biases in the data more than to real declining availability. There exists a generalization of the dramatic situation of some cases – Ethiopia, the Sahel – in order to explain all hunger in the Third World.

A second effect of these agricultural production policies is that they have been beneficial to the preferences of the rich. This impact may have been designed by powerholders to suit the preferences of important groups, or it may have been unintentional.[121] Different mechanisms are at work. First, the protection accorded to the agricultural sector has been monopolized by the larger and wealthier farmers[122] – in contemporary parlance, 'rents' have been created; rent-seeking behavior occurs, which is usually to the interest of the wealthy and the powerful.[123] The case *par excellence* is rural credit: the well-off, through their better capacity to deal with credit institutions (they possess collateral; they can read) and their closeness with powerholders, have benefited disproportionately from subsidized rural credit – amounting to 'redistribution in reverse,' according to Gonzalez-Vega.[124] Second, large farmers can switch easily to activities which are, for one reason or another, advantaged – in Latin America, mostly export crops; in Mediterranean countries high-value luxury crops; in Asia staples – thus monopolizing the rural surplus; having more land, they also simply earn more as a result of profitable new technologies.[125] In the context of the Green Revolution,[126] this has been called the 'talents effect,' implying that greater inequality often results from (certain kinds of) agricultural growth; it has been a hotly debated subject.[127] The extent to which this process takes place depends *i.a.* on the degree to which small farmers manage to switch to the more profitable crops. The latter is a function of the cost of entry into the new crop and the distribution of assets – both eminent subjects of rural political economy. What is important is that this implies that whatever increase in food production there has been – leaving aside the problem of its size – does not necessarily benefit the poor nor decrease the incidence of hunger.[128] Detailed case studies are needed to provide further verification.

The third effect has been the slowdown of economic growth. By distorting the relative prices of products and factors – cash and food crops, labor and capital – resources are wrongly allocated, away from agriculture and labor, and in favor of industry and capital.[129] In countries where agriculture is central to employment and gross domestic product, this leads to very suboptimal production outcomes.[130] Moreover, the high budgetary cost of these policies has to be financed by government in some way, thus decreasing the resources available for other uses. These effects by themselves are defendable: societies might seek objectives other than economic growth, and they may be willing to pay the price. Yet, in the light of the other effects, it seems that the welfare losses incurred as a result of these policies are unacceptable, particularly as it is probably the poor that are most hurt by slow economic growth. Contemporary structural adjustment policy reform professes to address exactly this problem.

4 Conclusion

This chapter examined the food production policies of various groups of countries. We saw that these policies are, in the words of the OECD, 'primarily and predominantly designed within the national context to achieve national objectives.'[131] Strictly speaking, they thus do not belong to the subject of this study, the international politics of hunger. Yet, although making abstraction of domestic politics can be, and is, theoretically defended by international relations scholars, it is practically meaningless to neglect the domestic politics of food production in the study of the international outcomes of food and hunger. This is because a) the objectives states pursue in the international issue areas we will study are intimately linked to their domestic policies in the food issue area and b) the impact of international outcomes on hunger is mitigated by these domestic processes. The validity of these claims will become clear throughout the rest of this analysis.

Generally speaking, we can conclude that agriculture-specific policies intend to favor food production almost everywhere. This testifies to the central importance of food in any country: almost nowhere is food production simply left to the market. Food consumption is also often subsidized, implying that many governments do attempt to guarantee basic food intakes, and hence avoid hunger, at least for parts of their populations. These subsidies can be extremely expensive, taking more than 25% of all government spending in countries as diverse as the USSR, Egypt and Sri Lanka until the 1980s; moreover, they are usually not very efficient, to the extent that their benefits do not only (or not even mainly) go to the poorest and neediest, but to different, usually urban, groups.

General macroeconomic policies, some of them very fundamental and longstanding, on the other hand, are often to the disadvantage of peasants and the poor in the Third World, cancelling the benefits of the direct policies. These policies result from severe political imperatives in favor of industrialization, state intervention, low urban food prices, and the like. The end-result – the combined effect of agriculture-specific and macroeconomic policies – is most positive for agriculture in the OECD, ambiguous in East bloc countries, and often to the disadvantage of small-scale agriculture in the Third World.

As a result of these policies, countries in the North produce more food than they would have produced in their absence, while many countries in the South produce less food than they would have done in the absence of their general macroeconomic policies.[132] This lies at the heart of a world characterized by unmanageable surpluses in the North and chronic hunger in the South.

Notes

1 OECD, 1988(b): 36, 77; FAO/CFS, 1987/3: 10; EEC, 1989(b):32; Madaule, 1990: 130, with interesting table.
2 Butler, 1986: 122. Also *International Herald Tribune*, June 27, 1988.
3 FAO, 1975.
4 See OECD, 1984(a).
5 The first report calculated figures for the period 1979–81; the second, published in December 1988, updated them to 1986; a more recent, 1990, one does the same up till 1988.
6 This does not mean such figures are not contested: *The Economist*, March 31, 1990, relates how Canada obstructed for months the publication of the 1990 OECD study, because it showed Canada to be as protectionist as the EEC – contrary to Canada's self-proclaimed position as a 'fair trader' and its membership of the Group of Cairns.
7 OECD, 1987(d): 134 for columns 1 to 3; columns 4 to 6, OECD, 1990(c): table IV.1, IV.4, and IV.5. The differences between column 2 and 3 show that U.S. protection does not work through the market price of food: as a result, domestic prices equal border prices. Yet, protection there is, as the PSE data testify, but it is in the form of subsidies, deficiency payments, and the like. The differences between columns 3, 4 and 5 have to do with the fact that there are less farmers in the U.S. than in the E.E.C. and Japan and that the average farm size in the U.S. is much larger than in both other countries.
8 Nogues, 1985: 119. Until 1987, PSEs increased in almost all countries; since then, they declined, but they are still above 1979–1981 levels: OECD, 1990(c): 97.
9 OECD, 1988(b): 28–9 & 105 ff.; OECD, 1990(c): Statistical Appendix.
10 Anderson, Hayami & Honma, 1986: 18.
11 Philippe, 1986: 50 a.f.
12 Ramses, 148: OECD, 1987(c): 42; FAO/CFS, 1987/3: 3.
13 Honma & Hayami, 1986: 120; George & Saxon, 1986: 98 a.f. According to Hathaway, 1987: 29–30: 'rice policy in Japan is probably the strongest case of food security driven policy that can be found in the world today.' I would argue that that distinction goes to Saudi Arabia, where wheat is subsidized at about 10 times the world price for food security reasons.
14 FAO/CFS, 1987/3: 3–5.
15 OECD, 1987(c): 14.
16 *i.e.* variable import taxes, set each week, making up the difference between the world price and the politically set (higher) internal price.
17 For a very good version, see Lindert, 1991: *passim*; see too Hathaway, 1987: 80 on Japan; Paarlberg, 1985: chapter 4 about the US; Nogues, 1985: 119.
18 Anderson & Hayami, 1986: 3; see too Honma & Hayami, 1986. The most famous theorist of this approach is Olson, 1982.
19 See too Paarlberg, 1983: 217.

20 'Power and domination are exluded definitionally.... It misses the institutional richness of political life:' Staniland, 1985: 40.

21 Hirschman, 1971: 3. Lipton, 1989: 1570, talks about 'political economy without politics;' For Staniland, 1985: 41, 'rather than applying a new synthesis, ... it simply applies the language of economics to institutions and behavior usually called political. This is a solution by relabeling, not a solution derived from fresh analysis. It makes politics into a colony of economics.'

22 These norms and principles remain generally shared up to our days. No major political party in the EEC, the US or Japan wishes to abolish farm protection, nor do, as far as I know, consumers' movements have it as a priority. Moreover, as we will see in the chapter on food trade, this regime is sanctioned on the international level.

23 Hathaway, 1987: 7.

24 Messerlin, 1983: *passim*; Destler, 1978: 75; Doyle, 1987: 307–8.

25 FAO/CFA, 1987/3: 6.

26 Tims, 1988: 150–1.

27 In the EEC, demand for agricultural products rose at a rate of around 0.9% a year during the period 1974–83.

28 OECD, 1987(d): 55–6; OECD, 1988(b): 90.

29 Columns 1 to 5: Rosenblatt e.a., 1988: 5 & 28–30; columns 6–10: OECD, 1988(b): 132–4; column 11: EEC Commission, 1990: table 3.7.3

30 Hadwiger & Talbot, 1979: 23, speak about 'a structure of elites that provided national leaders who helped secure federal policies amenable to large-farm agriculture notwithstanding the national-legal symbolisms favoring small-farm holdings.'

31 OECD, 1987(d): 59.

32 Paarlberg, 1988. 36.

33 *Financial Times*, July 28, 1989.

34 Well explained by the *Financial Times*, July 14/15, 1990.

35 According to the Australian BEA, 1988: S10, in Japan '1987 agricultural policies have effectively placed surcharges on income of about 8% for the 20% of households with the lowest incomes and about 5% for households with the highest incomes.' Moreover, 'the high price of land, together with the high price of food, has meant that purchasing power of Japanese consumers has been about 30% less than the purchasing power of US consumers.'

36 Tables OECD, 1987(d): 52 & 128–9. In the EEC; Ramses, 1986: 161.

37 Hathaway, 1987: 80; BAE, 1987: S8.

38 Hathaway, 1987: 75–7. Note that milk products are most costly to the budget, followed by cereals, oils and fats, and meat. For estimates of 1967/8, see Paarlberg, 1979: 84.

39 Hathaway, 1987: 84–7.

40 OECD, 1989.

41 One ECU = around 1 $. OECD, 1988(b): 39; see also World Bank, 1986: 112; OECD, 1987(d): 132; for Japan, for the period 1982–1986, see BAE, 1987.

42 World Bank, 1986: 121. The differences in figures are caused by

differences in the time periods, in the commodities included, and in the set-up of the model.

43 Already well described by Griffin, 1974: 164.

44 OECD,1990(b).

45 *Financial Times*, March 30, 1990.

46 The figures are 2.8% for Czechoslovakia, 5% for the GDR, 12% for Hungary and Bulgaria and 15% for Romania: Fottorino, 1989. For the case of Poland, see Tomczak, 1991: *passim* and *The Economist*, 21/10/89.

47 Ulyukayev, 1991: 277; Johnson with McConnell Brooks, 1983: 13–14.

48 All articles in the *Food Policy* issue of August 1991.

49 Wdekin, 1991: 183.

50 Sizov, 1991: *passim*.

51 Johnson with McConnell Brooks, 1983: 93 & 199.

52 Johnson with McConnell Brooks, 1983: 196; Demyanenko, 1991: *passim*.

53 Johnson with McConnell Brooks, 1983: 12; Paulino, 1988: 14.

54 Paarlberg, 1978: 93–4; Fottorino, 1989: 41, describes how this leads to rural exodus, leaving women and the old on the farms.

55 *International Herald Tribune*, 12/9/88.

56 Johnson, 1983: 201–2.

57 *Financial Times*, 7/3/89. Gosagroprom is an agricultural 'superministry' created by Gorbachev at the start of his agricultural reforms. It was abolished in 1989. See too Ulyukayev, 1991: 277 ff.

58 *Reuter cable*, 14/988; *Le Monde*, 7/7/89 and 12/8/89.

59 Malish, 1986: 77; Charvet, 1987: 25.

60 OECD, 1988(b): 157 ff.; *Financial Times*, 28/9/88; M.I.Goldman in the *International Herald Tribune*, 10–11/9/88; *Financial Times*, 11/8/89; *Le Monde*, 12/8/89. Bulgaria did the same for milk and milk products: *Le Monde*, 20/9/89. Not much progress has been made with this, though, due as well to administrative slowness as to the risk aversion by USSR farmers.

61 I will regularly refer to this Report: written by top economists at the most important development institution in the world, thoroughly researched, this represents contemporary consensual knowledge within the 'international development community.' See also the Asian Development Bank's 1989 brochure *Agriculture in Asia*.

62 Williams, 1981: 20; Leys, 1987: 45.

63 Tolley, Thomas & Wong, 1982: 1.

64 World Bank, 1986: 68; see too KIT, 1984: 33, for Zambia, Mali, Kenya and Rwanda.

65 Already in 1975, Saleh, 1975, concluded that 35 out of 40 countries studied undervalued agricultural commodities, thus creating serious disincentives to production.

66 World Bank, 1986: 150.

67 Based on this diagnosis, the remedy for the food problems of the LICs is to end government intervention and increase producer prices. As we will see in chapter 7, this is what structural adjustment in agriculture is all about.

68 A concise selection would include the following: World Bank, 1986, *passim* and its synthesis in Ray, 1896; on the effects of general macro-economic policies: Shuh, 1983, for some theory; Chhibber & Wilson, 1986 and Krueger, Schiff & Valdes, 1988 for empirical analysis.

69 USDA, 1987.

70 Structural adjustment also includes reform of these food subsidies: see chapter 7.

71 Byerlee, 1987.

72 Lipton, 1977: 323.

73 The urban bias thesis has much similarity with the works of collective action theorists on the same matter. Robert Bates, the most famous author along the latter lines, on peasants: 'they are small. They are numerous' (1980: 170) and on urban consumers: they 'are potent because they are geographically concentrated and strategically located. . . . They are therefore influential. Urban unrest forms a significant prelude to changes of governments in Africa, and the cost and availability of food supplies is a significant factor promoting urban unrest.' (1983: 170) In Africa, the literature recognizes one exception to this rule: Zimbabwe, where farmers' interests are well organized and policies thus more favorable to food production: Bratton, 1987: *passim* and Harvey, 1989. For North Africa and the Middle East, see Richards, 1983: 294 ff.

74 The inventor, Micheal Lipton, is himself an economist. For a critical discussion of his interpretation of political economy: Stanisland, 1985: 30–1.

75 As Braverman & Kanbur, 1987: 1180, note: 'there exists a consensus among economists on urban bias.' Some examples: OECD, 1984(b): 64; World Bank, 1981: 57; Nafziger, 1988: chapter 11; Bienen, 1990: 713 a.f.

76 World Bank, 1986: 92. During much of the 1980s, Michael Lipton worked for the Bank. He is now at the International Food Policy Research Institute, another of the great institutions of liberal research in the international development community.

77 On the latter, see RAO, 1978, and Elliott, 1975: fully.

78 Dumont, 1973: 40 (translated by us). See too, among non-radical american authors, Bradley & Carter, 1989: 117–20.

79 De Janvry, 1981 also contains an excellent theoretical introduction to radical approaches to agriculture. The author later applies the same concept to countries on different continents: De Janvry, 1983.

80 A famous version is Stavenhagen, 1975.

81 For a well-argued case, see Williams, 1981.

82 Mellor, 1987: 54; Giri, 1985: 107 ff.; Sender & Smith, 1987: *passim*; an interesting case study in Africa, see Christensen, Lofchie & Witucki, 1987.

83 World Bank, 1986: 77–8; KIT, 1983: 30; Sender & Smith, 1986.

84 See *i.a.* World Bank, 1986: 64–8.

85 Lindert, 1991: 74; Valdes, 1991: 111.

86 Cleaver, 1985; for Brazil, Calegar & Shuh, 1988: 43; for Egypt, Commander, 1987: 31.

87 Byerlee, 1987: 315; Prasada Rao *e.a.*, 1990: 215, 219 & 222 hold that 'conventional opinion as to the existence of significantly lower agricultural output prices in most developing countries is not supported by this study.'

88 Krueger, Schiff & Valdes, 1988: 266 (italics are mine); also Valdes, 1991: 94 ff.

89 If it is now commonly accepted that rich country governments should not be treated as unitary, rational actors, this should also be applied to Third World govenments. The fact that governments are composed of different branches, which have different preferences, might explain at least partially why direct policies are often positive, and indirect ones negative for food production. See Lipton, 1989: *passim* for an interesting discussion. An explanation of Third World food policy outcomes along these lines – with the preferences and the policies of different departments, regions, and parastatals going in different if not contradictory directions – seems to be at least as plausible as the usual approach; yet, it is almost never done – maybe because, like in international relations, it does not offer the possibility to arrive at 'grand' theories.

90 Paarlberg & Grindle, 1991: *passim*; Lindert, 1991: 46.

91 FAO/CFS, 1986/2: 13 a.f.

92 World Bank, 1986: 68; Gai & Smith, 1983: *passim*.

93 Elias, 1985: 9.

94 The malfunctioning of research stations, vulgarization offices, marketing boards, and so on, usually under state control (and often aid-financed) is well known. The classical contemporary solution to it also – privatize them. The problem is that the private sector in many countries, especially in Africa, is often no more efficient or present than the state. See for example Brett, 1987: *passim*.

95 'Deficient exchange rate setting largely eroded nominal improvements in producer prices:' World Bank, 1986: 67–8. For Latin America, see Valdes, 1987. See also Herbst, 1990: 950–1.

96 World Bank, 1986: 68.

97 Krueger, Schiff & Valdes, 1988: 263; see too Valdes, 1991: 94 ff.

98 China is one of the main success stories of agricultural and food policy, having increased its production of both by more than 50% over the last 10 years: Anderson, 1988: 48; Liu, 1987: 101. The increase in farm-gate prices and the liberalization of agriculture – in particular the private holding of land – are largely held responsible for this progress (World Bank, 1986; McMillan, Whalley & Zhu, 1989: 781), although some authors, *e.g.* Tissier, 1984, do point out that the conditions for this rapid success had been laid before 1979.

99 Period 1951/3–1979/81 Johnson, 1983: 7.

100 UNCTAD Handbook 1988, Table 6.5

101 Paulino, 1986: 15.

102 Etemad, 1984: 389.

103 Columns 1 & 2: Etemad, 1984: 389; column 3: Paulino,1986: 15; column 4: UNCTAD Handbook, 1988: Table 6.5.

104 FAO, 1981.

105 We will discuss this in chapter 3 and, especially, 5.

106 UNCTAD Handbook, 1985 & 1988: table 6.5. See too World Bank, 1984: 15.

107 Mettetal, 1989: *passim*. One example: the food imports of Burkina Faso in 1984 are, according to two different UNCTAD reports, respectively zero tons and 9510 tons and according to two different FAO reports for the same year 23,500 and 92,000 tons!

108 Raikes, 1988: 20.

109 Raikes, 1986: 62.

110 Egg, Gabas, & Lemelle, 1989: *passim*; according to Ndulu, 1986: 88, the figure is up to 70% for some countries; Morris & Newman, 1989: 1901–4, estimate them at over 50% for rice and around 30% for coarse grains in the case of Senegal.

111 Raikes, 1986; Schatz, 1986.

112 One example among many of this kind of automatic link comes from Hayami and Honma, 1986: 115, two prestigious agricultural production and trade policy experts: 'agricultural policies in advanced industrial countries have been characterized by strong protection of domestic producers by means of trade restrictions and direct price supports, in contrast with that of developing countries that has exploited agriculture by such means as taxes and over-valued exchange rates. *As a result* serious imbalances have emerged in world agriculture, as manifested by overproduction and accumu-lation of surpluses of agricultural products in industrial countries and by underproduction of food and *chronic malnutrition in develop-ing countries*' (my italics). Leys, 1987: *passim*, strongly argues against this common wisdom for the case of Africa.

113 Lofchie, 1987: 104; Murdoch, 1980: chapter 8; Lemarchand, 1986: 26–29.

114 See graph 1 in chapter 4.

115 Reinforced by a negative attitude of most of those involved toward small farmers, considered stupid, backward, ignorant, risk-averse – in short, not like us. See Klatzmann, 1983: 265 a.f.; McNeill, 1981: 78.

116 An intelligent, nuanced version of the 'urban bias' argument thus remains relevant. See the introduction by EEC Commissioner Pisani to Philippe, 1986: 3.

117 Bates, 1981: 95 & 126; Paarlberg & Grindle, 1991: 387.

118 Bratton,1987: *passim*; De Janvry, 1983: *passim*. In India, small and large farmers alike produce cereals: thus food production increased. In Colombia sugar, coffee, cattle, cotton and rice; as a result, the latter commodities were protected. See also Griffin, 1974: 80, 127.

119 Among them, see Barker, 1984: 19–24, on tropical Africa; De Janvry, 1981 and 1983 for Latin America; Bates & Lofchie, 1980, for a historical analysis of Kenya and Ghana; and most case studies in the volume on Africa edited by Lawrence, 1986.

120 Bates, 1984: 252; the author also discusses the overvaluation of the currency.

121 According to Bates, 1983: 176; and most authors brought together

in Adams, Graham and Von Pishke, 1984, these are deliberate constructs.

122 World Bank, 1986: 150.

123 For a good compilation, see Colander, 1985; for a critical discussion applied to Asian agriculture, Lipton, 1989: 1561–65.

124 Gonzalez-Vega, 1984: 120; Uvin, 1988: *passim*. Often the real interest rates, *i.e.* taking account of inflation, were negative: there thus was a most sizeable transfer of resources to the wealthier rural strata, often financed by aid money.

125 Richard, 1987: 305.

126 The introduction, originally in Mexico and India, of new varieties of cereals, which, combined with modern inputs (which originally had to be purchased on the international market but are now produced locally), produce much higher yields.

127 The most important books were Palmer, 1972; Griffin, 1974; Spitz, 1980 and Pearse, 1980, but the argument really became popular by the works of George, 1976 and Collins & Lapp, 1977. All contend in more or less radical terms that the effect of the Green Revolution has been to reinforce inequality and to decrease efficiency, because large farmers monopolized its benefits. Those in favour of the Green Revolution, evidently, did not see it that way. In the late 1980s, after some serious empirical analysis, a middle position has come into being: the Green Revolution has benefited large farmers most, but usually also medium and small ones, as well as landless labourers, managed to make absolute strides: Berry, 1989: 191–4; Hossain, 1988: *passim*; Nicholson, 1984: *passim*. According to Maurer, 1986, Etienne, 1986, Hossain, 1988, Patnaik, 1990 and most texts in Gourou and Etienne, 1985, relative differentiation did increase in Bangladesh, India and Indonesia, but it is wrong to conclude that the rich became richer and the poor poorer: most of the poor became better off too. Another big problem are imbalances between regions with high potential and others: Patnaik, 1990.

128 For a most interesting debate on this matter between specialists such as Griffin, Mellor, Christensen and Lofchie, see Ladd Hollist and Lamond Tullis, 1987.

129 World Bank, 1986: 80; Singh, 1983.

130 For example, Barker, 1984: 14. This is also argued by Mellor, and, at present, by those adhering to the structural adjustment philosophy.

131 OECD, 1987(c): 10; see too Nau, 1978: 218.

132 Ray, 1986: 5.

Part II

THE INTERNATIONAL ORGANIZATION OF FOOD AND HUNGER

Even after a short analysis of the contemporary world food production outcome such as the one we made in the preceding chapter, one basic paradox hits the eye: the simultaneous existence of surplus in the North and hunger in the South. Many attempts have been made, especially since the middle of the 1970s onwards, to explain this puzzle of the contemporary world system: why does hunger exist in a world of plenty? We hope this study will furnish material that is of use in solving it; yet, it is not properly speaking its subject. As said earlier, our aim is to analyze the international outcome in different international issue areas related to hunger, as well as the impact of these outcomes on the incidence of hunger.

In chapter 3, we will start by presenting and discussing what can be called the 'international food regime,' that is, the dominant norms and principles at the international level concerning the causes of and the solutions to hunger. This regime, we will see, is neo-Malthusian in nature; its norms neglect political issues in favor of technical ones. From it follow the four issue areas we will analyze in the following four chapters.

The first one – **assistance to family planning** – is generally considered part of the long-term solution to the hunger problem. Aiming not to increase the entitlements available to individuals, but rather to decrease the number of the 'entitled,' a quite coherent regime has become dominant at the international level, giving rise to a process that engages thousands of people and hundreds of millions of dollars of aid money, and yet little studied. We will discuss it in chapter 6.

The second issue area consists of aid to increase LDC agricultural production. The international regime which is dominant in this issue area at present is the liberal, export-oriented one contained in structural adjustment policy reform. This book, in chapter 7, proposes an analysis of the origins and nature of **structural adjustment** as well as its impact on poverty and hunger. Two other issue areas of crucial importance can be summarized under the heading of **international food flows**. States are no closed entities, able only to consume what they produce. They can have entitlements to food produced beyond their borders: when this happens, international food flows result. There are two kinds of such flows, corresponding to two kinds of entitlements. The first one is **food trade**, or, in Sen's terms, exchange entitlements. They account for around 95% of all the food that flows between nations and constitute a very important international issue of relevance to this study. We will study it in detail in chapter 4. The second kind of entitlement is aid-based: **food aid** (a kind of international transfer entitlements, in Sen's parlance), commonly associated with efforts to end hunger and to promote development. Its regime and process, as well as their effects on hunger, will be analyzed in chapter 5.

The outcomes in these four issue areas – food trade, food aid, population assistance and structural adjustment – constitute the essence of this study. Together, they contain the set of issues and instruments that are generally held at the international level to constitute the key to the eradication of hunger – a universally shared objective, as expressed at the 1974 World Food Conference.

In November, 1974, the representatives of most nations of the world met in Rome to discuss the world food problem. While in Asia and Africa millions were starving, the World Food Conference solemnly declared that 'every man, woman and child has the inalienable right to be free from hunger and malnutrition. . . . It is a fundamental responsibility of Governments to work together for higher food production and a more equitable and efficient distribution of food between countries and within countries.'[1] Thus, 'within a decade no child will go to bed hungry, no family will fear for its next day's bread, and no human being's future and capacities will be stunted by malnutrition.'[2]

The Conference was the result of two successive diplomatic initiatives by the group of 77, and by US Secretary of State Henry Kissinger. The decision for it had been taken by the General Assembly of the United Nations; funds had been committed by the FAO and the UN; different regional meetings on high level between officials of the participating nations had been held under the leadership of Marei;[3] working documents had been written. The general atmosphere at the Conference, as well as its final resolutions, were considered by all participants as being of a rare quality and degree of consensus – all the more surprising as at the time the North-South conflict and the NIEO debate were at the height of their intensity.[4] The solutions set out at the Conference belong exactly to the four just mentioned issue areas. As such, this study also constitutes a partial assessment, 20 years later, of the impact of this conference on the international outcomes in key issue areas, as well as on the incidence of hunger in the world.

One final caveat. Many other international processes exist, in other issue areas, which indirectly affect the incidence of hunger, by creating entitlements for nations and people: primary commodity trade, for example, or other forms of development aid, or the end of the Cold War. They are no part of this thesis. Yet, it could well be that their impact is more important for the incidence of hunger than those outcomes that are intended to affect it. This, then, is an important limitation of this study.

THREE

UNDERSTANDING HUNGER

We will study four topics in this chapter. First, we will briefly analyze the available data concerning hunger: where do they come from? What is their value? Second, we will present the basic international hunger regime, *i.e.* the set of principles and norms concerning hunger that is dominant at the international level. Third, we will critically analyze the fundamental tenet of this regime, pointing to the way it neglects political factors and favors technical ones. Finally, we will present Amartya Sen's entitlement concept, which supplies us with a framework capable of placing hunger squarely where it belongs: at the intersection between economic, social, biological and political factors. But before starting, we should define some key concepts.

Undernutrition refers to the chronic situation of insufficient intake of essential nutrients, manifested mainly in a loss of weight; *famine* is an extreme version of that situation, with people actually starving to death as a result of undernutrition. *Malnutrition* is a larger term, covering also the inappropriate and unbalanced consumption of nutrients.[5] *Hunger* is the sentiment people feel when deprived of food: it is as much physical as psychological in nature. This study deals with undernutrition, *i.e.* the lack of food intake by individuals, also often called 'chronic hunger.' For simplicity, we will use the term 'hunger' throughout this book, referring to both undernutrition (chronic hunger) and famine (acute, severe hunger).[6]

1 On the measurement of hunger

A The debate

Estimates of the incidence of hunger vary considerably. On the one hand there is the conforting wisdom that 'at no time in history has the world been as well fed as today'[7] and that 'there is much less hunger in the world today than is commonly thought.'[8] On the other hand, frightening scenarios are presented, as in a famous statement of Lord Boyd-Orr, then Director-General of FAO, that 'a lifetime of malnutrition and actual hunger is the lot of at least two-thirds of mankind,'[9] or in the apocalyptic projections of the Club of Rome. This diversity in estimates results from the fact that defining hunger in a more or less scientific way is more difficult than one might think. Experts do not agree on an operational definition of hunger and, as such, on the measurement of its incidence. To understand the international organization of hunger, it is worth explaining this situation in some detail.

The main organization calculating figures on nutrition and hunger is the FAO. Since Lord Boyd-Orr's statement and the publication of the First World Food Survey in 1952, much criticism has been directed against FAO's hunger figures. They are said to overestimate food requirements while underestimating availabilities, thus introducing two distortions and inflating the incidence of hunger.[10] Some say the FAO deliberately did so, as it has an 'an institutional stake in showing a relatively poor world food situation.'[11] Indeed, it has become popular among economists to suggest that the FAO's early figures were 'politically set by bureaucrats'[12] to justify the existence and growth of the organization.[13] This is at least partly untrue: these figures represented 'consensual knowledge' among most nutritionists and other specialists engaged in the field: there were but very few dissenting voices at the time (for example, the World Bank's figures were and still are even higher!). Where do these figures come from?

There are at least three ways to calculate the number of undernourished people in the world or in specific countries. The most common one, used by the FAO, the World Bank and the USDA, among others, consists of comparing minimum required levels of daily energy intake with actual energy intake.[14] This method poses many problems, four of which we will briefly present here.

The first and most important one concerns the **definition of these minimum required levels**. What amount of calories or proteins is necessary? What is the 'cut-off point' or the 'threshold' that separates undernourished people from others? Different organizations come up with different answers to this problem.[15] The FAO now uses two standards, *i.e.* 1.2 or 1.4 times the Basic Metabolic Rate (BMR), with the latter being the amount of calories needed by a healthy adult body lying at rest in a warm environment. This rate varies for age, sex, body size, physical environment and activity. The fact that there are two standards reflects a nutritional debate on what is precisely needed for a normal working life.[16] The World Bank uses another standard: the country-specific nutritional requirements adopted by a joint FAO/WHO working group in 1971. It chose two cut-off points, one of 80%, necessary for merely preventing stunted growth and serious health risks, and the other, at 90%, allowing for an active working life.[17] The Bank's thresholds are on the average significantly higher than the ones of the FAO: they amount to approximately 2060 and 1840 calories per person per day in the higher or lower version, whereas the FAO's cut-off points amount to respectively 1620 and 1460 cal/person/day.[18] Other organizations, like the USDA (for assessing the countries in need of food aid) or the Sub-Committee on Nutrition of the United Nations Secretariat, use the same method, but with again different cut-off points.[19]

These large discrepancies between thresholds – with consequent large changes in the estimates of the number of the undernourished – reflect a nutritionists' debate about the complex relation between the physical characteristics of individuals and the amounts of nutrients required by them. What is the precise influence of temperature, weight, age and activity upon the calories needed? How about disease, childbearing or lactating, when surely more energy intake is needed? A fierce debate also rages since some decades about how many proteins are essential?[20] Do women and children need more of them? And finally, does the individual's metabolic system adapt to lower levels of caloric intake, as some famous nutritionists have it, and, if so, to what extent?[21] As a result, since the 1950s, FAO's threshold has constantly moved downwards, with the last revision dating from

1985 and a new one in the make.[22] This alone accounts for a large part of the documented decline in the number of malnourished people in the world!

But problems are by far not limited to the threshold debate: much uncertainty also exists about the other side of the equation, the **overall availability of calories and proteins**. To start with, data on Third World food production are often very unreliable.[23] As we already explained in the previous chapter, they have a strong tendency for underestimating food availability, especially in sub-Saharan Africa.[24] They are also overly aggregated, badly reflecting inter-and intra-regional differences. Finally, the conversion of global food availabilities into energy is itself also the subject of fierce debate among nutritionists:[25] what is for example the caloric value of manioc? What is its value when it is boiled for hours and turned in a ball of pasta, as is common in Africa?

Third, very little is known about the **distribution** of this global availability of calories **among and within households**. Without detailed consumption studies for most countries, most organizations infer the distribution of consumption from data on income and household expenditure. The World Bank, for example, divides the population in income groups and draws their food consumption from these categories. But the problems remain: existing data on income and expenditure are scarce, often unreliable and usually too aggregate.[26] An even more difficult issue is undoubtedly the distribution of consumption within households, often held to favor males at the expense of women and girls.[27]

Finally, even data as basic as the **population size** of countries by which to divide data on availability are often unreliable. Take the case of Nigeria, for example, where the latest census (the first in three decades) showed its population to be 88 million people – whereas until then, the usual estimates were between 100 and 120 million! How to avoid that the average Nigerian will suddenly appear 50% better nourished than last year?

In short, specialists do not agree on minimum necessary intakes or on the distribution of food availability among people within countries. Moreover, the data on food availabilities or population size of which they dispose are often unreliable and usually overly aggregate. All of this renders the calculation of the extent of malnutrition an imprecise and debatable exercise,[28] whose results are extremely susceptible to the (arbitrarily chosen) cut-off points.[29]

There also exist two other methods for calculating the extent of undernutrition in the world: the anthropometric one (based on measuring the size of people's physical characteristics) and the budget one (based on measuring household expenditure on food). The former method usually compares actual weight-for-age, weight-for-height or arm circumference (the fat on the upper arm) of people in the Third World with some reference and concludes from that whether (severe) malnutrition exists or not.[30] The problem is of course the point of reference – particularly important since small changes in it have very important effects on the resulting estimates on the number of hungry people. For the past half a century, the usual reference person is a child from Cambridge, Mass., USA. Many specialists doubt his representativeness for Third World situations. As a result, other 'reference persons' have come into being, competing with the original 'Harvard' one. But a more fundamental problem is that little is known about the role of nature and hereditary factors on people's anthropomorphic characteristics (pygmees are not all undernourished), or about the influence of the environment on them.

The budget method for measuring undernutrition, finally, measures the size of household expenditure on food items and from it draws conclusions concerning the incidence of hunger. This is the method used by Poleman in the table below.[31] Among the problems with this method are that its hunger estimates are based on contestable hypotheses of household expenditure on food (even poor, malnourished, people often prefer to spend part of their money on 'prestige' items, such as cigarettes, beer and coca-cola). Practical problems include the fact that few such reliable data are available and that they are expensive to get.

Hence, outward appearances notwithstanding, uncertainty reigns among those engaging in the scientific debate about hunger. Figures on the incidence of hunger vary twenty fold, with the World Bank at the higher end and authors such as Poleman at the lower. Others, without mentioning 'precise' figures, can be safely assumed to lean towards these lower estimates.[32] Table I presents some figures. Authors and institutions can thus 'chose' a figure on the incidence of malnutrition according to their objectives and their capacity of restraint.

Surprising as this lack of precision may be, this figure-dance cannot but acquire political dimensions, with those wishing to

Table 3.1 The number of malnourished: different estimates, million people

Source	FAO 4th survey	FAO 5th survey		FAO Toward 2000		World Bank 1976	World Bank 1986		Poleman 1983	ACC/SCN 1987
Reference period	1969–71	1979–81		1983–84		1965	1980			1979–81
Method of calculation	1.5 BMR	1.2 BMR	1.4 BMR	1.2 BMR	1.4 BMR	Regional averages suggested by FAO	80% of FAO/WHO	90% of FAO/WHO	Budget method	1.2 BMR
Africa	83	70	99	105	142	190	90	150	9	80
Asia	297	210	313	191	291	736	220	510	40	197
Latin America	46	38	56	37	55	113	20	50	7	30
Near East	29	16	25	15	24	91	10	20	5	10
Total	455	334	493	348	512	1,130	340	730	63	317
Correct for China updated to 1989					685			1,045		465

Sources: FAO, 1977; FAO, 1987b: 22; FAO, 1988: 77; Reutlinger & Selowsky, 1976: 53–55; World Bank, 1986: 17; Poleman, 1983: 71; ACC/SCN, 1987: *passim*. The corrections for China and the updating for 1989 are from Chen, 1990: 6–8, whereas some of the information in the row 'method of calculation' comes from Chen & Pitt, 1991: 4–20.

mobilize people and resources spontaneously using the highest estimates and those generally in favour of the status-quo naturally advancing low figures. Hence Klatzmann recalls a publication of a French presidential candidate in May 1981 that set the number of deaths from hunger at a yearly 50 million people – while only 48 million people died in the whole world in that same year![33] Yet, statements like this remain very popular, especially in NGO circles.[34] What holds for politicians and NGOs holds for scientists as well: they also have ideologies and political preferences that influence them, as has been very well illustrated by Ellen Messer, in a study of the political and historical influences on the definition of nutritional thresholds in India and Mexico.[35]

The same process undoubtedly takes place in international politics, where the stakes are very high. The choice of nutritional thresholds is an act with important political ramifications, so it would be very surprising political considerations did not at least interfere with scientific ones. Some cases are clear. Through the 1980s, the annual list of minimum caloric requirements by country, published by the USDA to calculate food aid needs has Egypt, Afghanistan and Morocco at the top (resp. 2,510, 2,440 and 2,420 cal/person/day), while countries such as Ethiopia, Vietnam or India 'score' much lower (resp. 2,230, 2,160 and 2,210 cal/ person/day).[36] One does not really see why people in Egypt need to eat much more than those in Ethiopia, or why the bodies of Afghans have so much more need for calories than their Indian neighbors. One might be forgiven to suspect that these figures are linked to an attempt to justify large amounts of food aid to the first category of important strategic allies.

'Reputation' is also important, for most countries do not like to be described as having a large share of their population being hungry – especially not if they produce enough food to feed everybody. Thus the choice of thresholds becomes a key political exercise. A good example is Pakistan, where 'varying the nutritional norm from 90% of average requirement to 110% of average requirement increases the proportion of the malnourished ... from 0% to 90%.'[37] It will be clear which cut-off point governments of this highly inegalitarian country prefer – and scientific criteria play a small role in that choice. Similarly, the 'normal' weight of the Indian reference person is set by the Indian government and is significantly lower than in other countries, resulting in 'much lower estimates of the prevalence of lower-than-normal weights than the internationally accepted standard.'[38] Along the same lines, detailed data for countries such as China have never been made public (and, up till now, no international organization has ventured to calculate them itself – most existing data are 'excluding China'), while official data for Eastern European countries and Cuba unsurprisingly show that no one is undernourished, that infant mortality rates are constantly declining, that every one has access to full health services and so on. As most figures published by international organizations come from governments, we should be very cautious when presented with 'hard' data on the incidence of hunger, rates of infant mortality and the like.

But also international organizations themselves have their agendas and their reputations to think of. A good case concerns the definition of nutritional thresholds for children. While the normal minimum threshold for adult malnutrition is defined by the FAO, the WHO and the UNU at 1.2 BMR, *i.e.* just enough to stay alive without doing any physical activity, the threshold for children has been arbitrarily defined at an extremely high cut-off point, *i.e.* 'full growth and development' and based on a small sample of rich country children![39] This 'exceptionalism' for children seems to be linked to the powerful emotional appeal of children, and the clever way in which UNICEF has been able to push through its agenda with its sister organizations. This significantly increases the number of the malnourished in the world in most calculations.

Another example of the preferences of international organizations in the debates on the number of the hungry is the International Nutrition Conference that will be convened by the FAO in Rome in December 1992, and where new nutritional requirements will certainly be adopted again. Few people see any good reason to invest millions of dollars in this conference, which will not bring about any fundamental rethinking of the issue; it is commonly suggested that its only *raison d'être* is FAO's need to reaffirm itself on the international food/development scene, especially after the important Rio Conference on the environment.

The French agronomist Klatzmann sketches an interesting picture about the incidence of hunger, which we present here.[40] On top of the ladder, around 20% of the world population engages in excessive consumption: more than 2,800 calories and 40 grams of protein a day (less if one doubts the Eastern European statistics). An additional 5% has a well-balanced consumption – mainly the Japanese. Defining malnutrition very broadly as food intake of less than 2,500 calories and 20 grams of animal protein a day, Klatzmann counts 1,700 to 1,800 million people who could possibly be malnourished (around 35% of the world's population). The main source of malnutrition is protein deficiency, lowering the quality of diets, while maintaining sufficient energy intake. Furthermore, an estimated 1,500 million people suffer from under-nutrition, which Klatzmann defines as an intake of less than 2,000 calories and 10 grams of animal protein a day. These diets are qualitatively as well as quantitatively insufficient. Finally, around 450–500 million people suffer from serious and almost permanent under-nutrition – less than 1,500 calories and 5 grams animal protein a day – and, as such, from hunger.

Klatzmann's figures in themselves are no less debatable than those of others, but his presentation draws our attention to the gradual nature of the phenomenon of hunger: the absence of a clear drawing-line under which people are malnourished and above which they are not. Many of those who have average food intake levels above the statisticians' cut-off point, still have qualitatively or quantitatively insufficient intakes for a normal healthy diet – let alone a pleasant one. Moreover, they are often vulnerable to temporary ('seasonal') hunger, in the last months before the harvest. Vice versa, those below certain thresholds are not necessarily permanently undernourished or unable to work; it is more useful to consider them 'at risk'.[41]

Figures on the **evolution** of hunger are of much interest for any scientific analysis. Even if we are to remain fundamentally unsure of the absolute incidence of hunger, we may be able to obtain a much better idea of its trend: whatever the (biases in the) starting base, if the direction of change is similar, that would be quite convincing. Recent FAO studies show a constant increase in the ratios of human caloric consumption per day over the last decades, as can be seen in the following table. The same trend can be seen by looking at protein undernutrition of children under 5 years of age.[42] It has also been documented by organizations such as the World Food Council, UNICEF or the Sub-Committee on Nutrition of the UN.[43]

Table 3.2 Average food availability for direct human consumption, in calories per day per capita[44]

	1961–63	1969–71	1979–81	1983–85	1987–89
94 Low Income Countries	1,960	2,110	2,320	2,420	2,470
without China	2,070	2,170	2,330	2,360	2,410
–sub-Saharan Africa	2,050	2,100	2,150	2,050	2,120
–Mediterranean	2,220	2,370	2,850	2,980	3,020
–Asia	1,860	2,030	2,240	2,380	2,430
–Latin America	2,380	2,520	2,680	2,700	2,720
High Income Countries	3,090	3,260	3,370	3,370	3,420
Eastern Europe	3,160	3,330	3,410	3,410	3,420

What do these data mean? Most importantly, they show a decline in the proportion of the world that is undernourished during the 1960s and the 1970s (see graph 3.1 below). This decline, which appeared in the 5th World Food Survey, is the first one ever (with the same criteria) in the post-war period, when publication of such data began.[45] As said, this evolution is basically non-contested among specialists. Yet, there are important dark spots. First, as a result of population growth, the absolute numbers of the hungry continued to increase (see graph 3.2). Second, the 1980s probably meant a halt to this trend of declining relative incidence of hunger: most observers believe the incidence of hunger has gone up in the world recent. Third, Africa is believed to constitute the sad exception, for undernutrition has continuously increased in both absolute and in relative figures since the 1970s (graph 3.1 and 3.2). This process has probably accelerated in the 1980s: according to one source, between 1980 and 1985 all countries in Sub-Saharan Africa show declining per capita food availability.[46]

At the risk of repeating ourselves, we should note that some specialists doubt the validity of these figures for Africa, arguing not only that certain increases in food production are not recorded but also that the indirect evidence (changes in death rates or life expectancy) contradicts these estimates. According to D.G. Johnson, for example, 'the data on life expectancy cast some doubt that the improvements in per capita food supplies and nutrition were as modest as the aggregate food data indicate, and may even cast greater doubts on the estimated declines in and low level of per capita food consumption in many African countries.'[48] Evidently, the question can be asked if the data

71

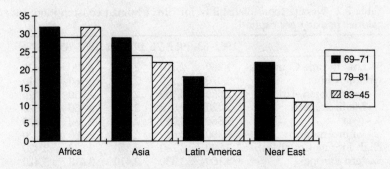

Figure 3.1. Malnourished people, in percent of total population[47]

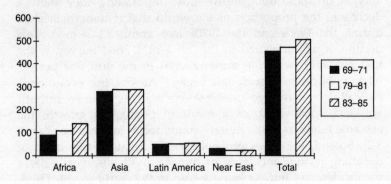

Figure 3.2 Number of undernourished, million people

on life expectancy are any more reliable than those on food consumption.

To conclude this overview, it is very hard to say what the exact number of malnourished people is. It is certain that malnutrition continues to exist on a large scale: most estimates somehow define a bottom group of at least 300 million people whose food intakes are below necessary levels. Leaving aside the discussion on the absolute figures, there is more certainty about their evolution. The trend in global food availability per capita in recent decades has probably on the average been a slowly rising one for most regions and countries except possibly for Africa; in the 1980s, this process may have been halted almost everywhere, except for South-Asia. That is all we can say with some degree of certainty.

That brings us to the relevance of all this number crunching.

All over the world – in the FAO in Rome, the World Bank and the USDA in Washington, the WHO in Geneva, the CCA/SCN in New York and in different university centers – specialists are busy cutting requirements and increasing availabilities, or *vice versa*, in short, computing 'their' numbers of malnourished and advancing their careers.[49] There are only some tens of these specialists and they work without any formal kind of coordination, even within the United Nations system, where at least four different organizations publish different data. The only type of coordination that exists is of the 'free market' kind: international commissions and colloquia are held where these specialists meet; journals exist for them to publish in[50] – so they do influence each other, usually sharing the same statistical trends (which is why, Poleman taken apart, the range of data is really only one on two). This is the dominant mode of functioning in occidental academic circles, in which the 'scientific competition' among specialists is supposed to bring about information useful for society, or, supposedly, in this case, for the hungry. In this case, most of the specialists are funded by 'development aid' destined to the same poor and the hungry. It is not sure if this use of money would get the full approval of the latter.

Indeed, is the cost really worth it? These exercises – although they are usually not really expensive in comparison to the cost of yearly calculating growth rates of GNPs, GDPs, balances of payments, and the like – tell us very little that is really important. They only supply us with aggregate and extremely contestable figures. What we really need to know remains obscured by these exercises: who is hungry? where? when? and especially why? – *i.e.* facts about seasonal, sexual, regional and socio-economic variations and their causes[51] – and, much more important, *what do these hungry people think and do about it themselves*? Extremely little is known about these questions, which involve dealing directly with the poor and the hungry themselves.

2 The international hunger regime

In our study of the international hunger regime, maybe the first observation that hit the eye was how little space it takes in the larger international development outcome. Indeed, within the international development regime and process – the set of principles, norms and actions dealing with development of Third

World countries and people – hunger is relatively neglected.[52] This is surprising given that the existence of widespread hunger is certainly one of the most typical and touching characteristics of poverty and 'underdevelopment' – whatever the latter means.

Sure, every UN Development Decade, as well as most policy statements by bilateral development cooperation agencies somewhere refer to the overriding objective of eradicating hunger. Moreover, four UN organizations, all based in Rome, have mandates that concentrate on food issues. But the World Food Council (WFC) is extremely small and has no power or even operational activities; it is merely a discussion forum, very secondary in comparison to the importance of the OECD, for example, in discussing food and agricultural policy matters.[53] The International Fund for Agricultural Development (IFAD), with its funding problems and average $ million 150 budget for the last decade, is very small too, although it is appreciated by the major countries.[54] The World Food Program (WFP) which we will study further in this book, is a large UN organization dealing with food aid for development and secondarily with combatting hunger in famine situations. The Food and Agriculture Organization (FAO), finally, is the only large organization whose primary mandate includes the eradication of hunger in the world; yet, its operational budget is small, and, most observers agree, its political importance has been declining throughout the last decades.[55]

Among the many other institutions dealing with development, few have a lot to say about hunger; even less devote a significant part of their resources to it. Their dominant objective is economic growth, or the delivery of certain services – education, health, family planning. The closest they come to hunger is through agricultural policy, rural development, or agricultural research; their usual approach is that hunger will be eradicated as a result of economic growth. Few of them give special attention to considerations of hunger in the choice or design of their development activities; none of them includes it in their standard evaluation practices.[56]

This state of affairs is also reflected in the scientific production by the 'development community'. There is no major scientific journal devoted exclusively to hunger; in the prestigious development journals, articles on hunger are very rare. Again, agricultural policy – prices, inputs, commercialization, trade, etc. –

receives very large attention, followed by nutritional matters. Apart from a decade beginning in the second half of the 1960s, few books are written on hunger in comparison to the thousands of books on structural adjustment, for example. This is important, for, given the 'low politics' nature of development and the fundamental uncertainness surrounding it, scientific production in the field has probably has a stronger impact on outcomes than in most other fields of action.

Thus, hunger is surprisingly neglected in the development outcome; its eradication is usually assumed to follow from economic growth, on which most financial and human resources are concentrated. Yet, that does not mean that no regime exists. There is a quite distinct international hunger regime, and we will now discuss its nature.

A The principles

The amount of food produced and the number of people are generally treated as the two basic variables that determine the world food situation, with changes in the growth rates of either of them causing or ending hunger. The evolution of the relation between these two variables has for centuries been the subject of considerable speculation: after all, those two seemingly unchangeable 'natural' factors lay at the basis of one of the fundamental constraints mankind, as much as individuals, faces: without food nothing can be done – *primum vivere, deinde philosophare*. The most influential thinker on the subject is undoubtedly Malthus, who believed that the number of people grows in a geometrical fashion whereas the amount of food available to feed them progresses but at an arithmetical rate. Thus, unavoidably, starvation has to occur.[57]

Malthusian pessimism has proven wrong over the last 200 years: food production more than managed to follow population growth and the heavy discrepancies between the two that the theory predicted did not materialize.[58] Yet, notwithstanding its counterfactual nature, this theory has remained popular up to our days,[59] most probably because 'it combines scientific appearance with sufficient vagueness to explain' everything.[60] But, what is more important, even the large majority of scholars who reject the scientific truth of Malthus' deterministic theory usually think in terms of a 'race' between two independent, competing variables: food on the one hand, and mouths on the other.[61] Indeed, most thinking about hunger on the international level is somehow characterized by a (neo)Malthusian principle of hunger as the outcome of the competitive relation between two essentially biological and/or economic variables, or more concretely the conflict between the food production variable and the population growth variable.[62]

This neo-Malthusian principle is the central element of the international hunger regime: the causal link between hunger on the one hand and excessive population growth or insufficient food production growth is constantly made. The dominance of this principle is reflected in the scientific production on the subject. Research on hunger is dominated by economists and nutritionists, most of whom consciously or unconsciously share this Malthusian perspective. The same principle, in a simplified form, is also propagated by the popular media, who usually present hunger as an unavoidable catastrophe hitting countries with too low food production and too high population growth rates.[63]

But a second, competing, principle on the cause of hunger also exists, and reference is often made to it. This principle, which to a large extent contradicts the first one, is that hunger is caused by poverty. People are malnourished not because of a physical lack of food, but because they lack the means to purchase sufficient food to avoid hunger. Below, we will explain in some more detail the rationale behind this principle, which we believe to be the stronger one. Suffice it for the moment to note that in international documents, both principles – hunger is caused by lack of food or too high population growth rates, and hunger is caused by lack of income – coexist on an almost equal footing: they are both mentioned in 1943, at the Hot Springs founding conference of the FAO;[64] in the Universal Declaration on the Eradication of Hunger and Malnutrition, unanimously adopted at the World Food Conference in Rome in 1974, in the Plan of Action, adopted after the 1974 World Population Conference in Bucharest, and in countless other statements. Hence, the international hunger regime is quite ambiguous, referring to two basic principles that have opposite implications. But what are the norms or solutions to hunger that this lead to?

B Norms and solutions

Just as the nature of a remedy is always linked to the diagnosis, different norms follow from different principles. The 'hunger-is-caused-by-poverty' principle gives rise to norms which stress equality, income transfers and redistribution in the short term, and increasing the income of the poor in the long term, whereas the 'hunger-is-caused-by-lack-of-food' principle logically leads to norms that give priority to increasing food production and decreasing birth rates. The processes these different norms give rise to are theoretically not mutually exclusive, but when it comes to the allocation of scarce resources, they do imply different priorities and concerns.

At the international level, the norms that are linked to the latter principle are much more dominant than the others. The principle that hunger is fundamentally caused by poverty somehow gets lost when it comes to its operationalization, while the neo-Malthusian principle gets translated much easier into standards of behavior. Of course, reference to the need for policies that favor greater equality is regularly made, especially during the second half of the 1970s, at the time of basic needs – but no real norm or international standard of behavior exists that places equality or the rapid eradication of poverty above increasing production[65] (especially not during the 1980s, as we will see in chapter seven).

Concretely, this means that at the international level the following solutions dominate the hunger regime: first, reduce population growth rates so that there are less mouths to be fed; second, increase food availabilities so as to be able to nourish more people.[66] Both are usually advocated together. The latter, it is usually held, can be done in two main ways: by increasing local food production, or, if a country has no comparative advantage therein, by importing food. Food aid, finally, can constitute a temporary third way. International assistance to any of these issue areas – family planning or food production, for example – can be, and often is, justified along the lines of this regime as leading to the eradication of hunger.

These four issue areas constitute the subject of the rest of this book: they will be analyzed in detail in the following chapters. Suffice it here to point to their dominance as the solutions to hunger. The most globally advocated among them certainly is to increase food production in the LDCs: governments stress its necessity;[67] international conferences pledge their full support to it;[68] international organizations advocate it and or actively work for it.[69] Second to the desirability of increasing food production comes increasing food trade. Also this norm is generally shared, albeit more so in the 'development community' than in the 'community of states.' Third, the need for reducing population growth rates, and the utility of assistance to LDCs to help them do so, is hardly questioned anymore: it is advocated – and often implemented – by the governments of almost all countries on the globe, while a large variety of public and private international organizations are active in it.[70] Finally, food aid is almost without exception favored at present, despite the fact that it is also very much the subject of criticism because of its potentially negative impact. It is thus usually seen as a temporary remedy, not a part of the solution.

A look at the scientific literature confirms this dominance of the 'hunger-is-caused-by-a-lack-of-food' principle. Out of 80 research reports published by the famous International Food Policy Research Institute in Washington, the largest share deals with food supply, food trade, food stocks and economic growth. Around a quarter deal with nutrition intervention programs (which is not really based on the hunger-is-caused-by-poverty principle, but at least specifically targets the poor) or with issues of inequality and poverty. The same holds for the articles published in the *Food Policy* journal: the largest share deals with agricultural research or production policy, followed by food aid and food trade. Nutritional interventions and issues of inequality in the access to food arrive much lower. When the other major academic journals treat development and food issues, by far the largest share of the articles published deal with agricultural production policies, technological innovation, agricultural research, population growth, etc. Very few deal with the mechanisms of access to food, or with local institutions coping with food and hunger issues.

This situation is undoubtedly linked to the different political implications of both principles and the norms they lead to: the first ones are technical and economically non-interventionist in nature, whereas the others are political and redistributionist, with socialist overtones. The latter are thus politically much more difficult to implement for international development agencies as well as for Third world governments, if they wished to eradicate hunger. Moreover, the poverty of individuals is essentially a matter that belongs to the domestic affairs of countries: the degree of equality within countries is not easily influenced from abroad, as the cases of Brazil or Zambia, for example, show – especially not if many of the most inegalitarian countries happen to be allies of the major powers (the Philippines, Pakistan, El Salvador, for example). Important political processes thus militate against the operational translation of the 'poverty principle' on the international level.

The Malthusian principle, on the other hand, is easy to understand to most of the experts that man the development community: engineers, agronomists, economists, medical doctors and the like. It allows them and the institutions they work for to do research and consulting funded by the many international development agencies, while being politically neutral, not offending the sensibilities of elites and governments in donor or recipient countries. In short, it pleases everyone that has to be pleased in the development community: financing institutions and donor governments, experts and specialists from all over the world, Third World governments and the elites that back them, industrial and commercial interests, and the like. The opinion of the poor and the hungry in the Third World, who might supposedly prefer the 'poverty' principle, is of little or no importance in this matter.

Before we analyze in detail the functioning of the four dominant issue areas that are globally considered to be the solutions to hunger, we will briefly discuss and criticize the neo-Malthusian principle, and present a pluridisciplinary concept for the study of the problem of hunger, which we will subsequently use throughout this book.

3 Neo-Malthusianism: a critique

In this section, we will present arguments in favor of the thesis that hunger and starvation are essentially distributional and political matters and not primarily of technical or technological concern. Hunger is a political economy problem, and the poverty-principle, to which not much more than lip-service is usually paid, is crucial for understanding hunger. Hence the neo-Malthusian principle and the norms based on it constitute serious misrepresentations. This is no trivial or purely theoretical matter: it has important effects. First, the dominant regime creates and reinforces a perception of hunger as a natural given almost beyond human control, rendering it 'rational' not to expect anything to change fast and 'realistic' not to get too upset about starvation and malnutrition. This misrepresentation thus adds to the legitimation and prolongation of the existing situation. Second, as suggested above, the approach to a problem conditions the solutions ('norms') that are advocated and implemented:

> If climate is the problem, weather modification is the answer. If population growth is the problem, then family planning is the answer. (...) If economic and political relations have within them the causes of the problem, then it is those relations that must be altered.[71]

If hunger is not primarily an agronomic or demographic problem, most efforts undertaken to end it based upon the dominant perspective are doomed to fail. Throughout this study, we will see over and over again that this is the case. In the words of Nicole Ball, a radical critic of contemporary food politics:

> world hunger is a political problem. It can only be solved by political means. The history of post World War Two aid, particularly aid to the rural sector, has been one of attempting to resolve political and social problems by technical means.[72]

What are the reasons that allow us to affirm that hunger is primarily a political problem and not, as it is usually treated, a technical/natural one? We will present five of them below. None of them are new or unexpected, but that does not diminish their basic validity; they merit restatement.

The most common argument supporting the assertion that hunger is primarily a political phenomenon points to the fact that the aggregate availability of food in this world is at present largely sufficient to feed everybody. Even during the famous years of the 'world food crisis' of the 1970s, when famines ravaged parts of the Third World, food prices quadrupled, and the Club of Rome's predictions of doom were widely discussed, world food supply actually diminished only once, by 1.9%![73] Moreover, the potential production of food in the world is much larger than the actual production. Clark holds that 'the world's agricultural capacity to produce food is vastly in excess of the needs of any expected world population.'[74] Not everybody would be that optimistic, but it is now generally agreed that the world can feed many more people than it does.[75] Estimates vary considerably, with the world being able to increase production 2,5 times, 3 times, 5 times, and much more.[76] This is not to suggest that these potentials are in any way easy, cheap, politically evident, or environmentally desirable – but they exist. If hunger continues to exist, then, it is not a matter of some unavoidable necessity, but of choice about the allocation of scarce resources, a societal choice that is essentially political.

This perspective becomes all the more plausible when one considers that what is needed to change this sad situation is little: for the 15 million children who according to UNICEF die prematurely every year from hunger or hunger-related illness to survive on an adult diet, it would take 3,6 million tons of cereals. In 1980 this number represented a mere 0,2% of world cereal harvests![77] According to a World Bank economist, 2% of all world grain would provide enough food for over a billion people who need it.[78] The cost, in money, of this amount of cereals was calculated to be approximately seven billion dollars, equivalent to 0,3% of the world's GNP.[79] According to Insel, financing the cereals shortfall that caused the African famine of 1984, would 'cost perhaps $500 million, barely a footnote to US export credits and food aid totalling $7 billion.'[80] According to a WFC report, the creation of international emergency stocks totalling 150.000 tons, to guarantee food availability in times of crisis, would cost 1% of present food aid.[81] All these figures represent only part of the story: they should not be taken to point to the existence of easily attainable, cheap solutions that are just waiting to be implemented. Reality is much more complex. Yet, what they do hint at is the same as what A. Sen hints at when he states:

> Hunger in the modern world is more intolerable than past hunger not because it is typically more intense, but because it is now so unnecessary. The enormous expansion of productive power that has taken place over the last few centuries has made it possible, for the first time in history, to guarantee adequate food for all. It is in this context that the persistence of chronic hunger and the recurrence of violent

famines must be seen as morally outrageous and politically unacceptable. If politics is 'the art of the possible' then conquering world hunger has become a political issue in a way it could not have been in the past.[82]

This argument becomes even stronger when the above cited figures are compared to the expenditures for other activities. This point is often made by contrasting expenditures for armament with those for any other, morally desirable purpose – in this case, eradicating hunger. In UN fora, it became habitual practice to pass resolutions that make this comparison and condemn excessive arms expenditure – after which all countries go on with business-as-usual.[83] But it remains a fact that, according to the prestigious Stockholm International Peace Research Institute, in 1985 the military expenditures of NATO countries accounted for $ 327 billion, those of the Warsaw Pact for $ 160 bn, Asia $ 43 bn, Africa $ 12.7 bn and Latin-America $ 17 bn. According to Sivard's authoritative overview of world's military expenditure, the 1987 figures were $ bn 450 for the NATO and $ bn 297 for the Warsaw Pact; $ bn 123 for Asia, of which $ bn 62 in the Middle East, $ bn 15 in Africa and $ bn 12 in Latin America – figures that are disproportionately large compared to the ones cited above.[84] As UNICEF points out in its 1990 report, the annual military spending in developing countries ($ bn 145) is 'enough to end absolute poverty on this planet within the next 10 years.'[85]

Clearly, all this is not meant to suggest that there would not be a great many political and technical difficulties to overcome in order to implement any ambitious plan to end hunger, nor that the solution to the problem of hunger in the world lays in such massive operations of transfer. The previous references only serve as indicators; what they signify is that in light of the different uses societies make of the resources at their disposal, the amount needed to try seriously to end hunger is high but not prohibitively high. They prove that hunger is a matter of distribution, preference, power and choice – and not one of technical necessity or unavoidable doom.

Another link between hunger and politics resides in the fact that acute starvation often occurs in countries which are at war. At the time of writing, people in Ethiopia, Afghanistan, Sudan, Liberia, Mozambique and Somalia suffer from starvation, while their country is engaged in either domestic or international wars.[86] Certainly four out of these six countries can easily feed their own populations: Sudan was once called the wheat loft of Africa! In these and other ases, willful withholding or destruction of food has been used as a weapon.[87]

Yet another way of pointing to the political nature of hunger is to disaggregate the figures on food consumption, looking at which individuals are malnourished, and what their socio-economic position is. They show there is no direct link between food production and hunger: neither for countries nor for people. On the one hand, even within low income food deficit countries not everyone suffers from hunger: many people actually have diets quite like those common in the rich countries: they always are the rich, never the poor. The US Department of Agriculture calculated that, in food-deficit Africa, 4% of the population consumes more than 3000 calories a day, a very 'Western' diet, while another 22% enjoy a sufficient diet; all others suffer from undernutrition.[88] Even if the absolute figures are wrong (it is improbable that 75% of all Africans are undernourished), the proportions are indicative.

But also within food-surplus countries, not all residents have enough food: often large proportions of the population are under-nourished. The most famous case is undoubtedly Brazil: its average food availability is 108% of all needs, and it is a large food exporter; yet, the majority of the people suffers from hunger.[89] The same situation, less dramatically, characterizes much of Latin America, but also countries such as Zimbabwe, India, etc., with the profound political, economic and social reasons for this being different in each case.

An illustration among many of the link between poverty and malnutrition is supplied by the comparison between Sri Lanka and India, two countries with similar per capita GNP's, but different historical patterns of policy and income distribution. As can be seen from graph 3.3, although their average caloric intakes per capita are very close, a much smaller part of the population suffers from hunger (defined here as intake below 1900 kcal) in Sri Lanka than in India. Similar comparison has been made by Sen between India and China.[91]

This implies that the distribution of food within countries is at least as important as the distribution of food among them. This point should be obvious when we consider that in the richest and most food-abundant countries in the world, the United States

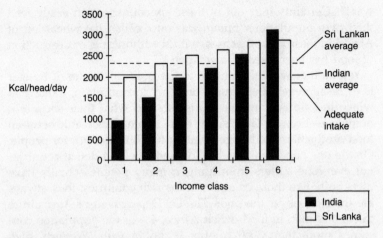

Figure 3.3 Income and caloric intake in India and Sri Lanka[90]

and Canada, there is still hunger and malnutrition.[92] It becomes only reinforced when one knows that among countries which are most unable to feed themselves with their own production, we find most OECD countries.[93]

Poverty, then, and not failing food availability, explains the incidence of malnutrition.[94] Yet, the reasoning should not stop there: poverty itself is the outcome of the interaction between different social, economic and political processes.[95] It is the latter that constitute the real causes of hunger – and it is these that have to be analyzed and changed in order to eradicate hunger. That is the key vision underlying the rest of this book.

4 Entitlements

We have seen that hunger is the result of, among others, war, the distribution of food and income, societal spending preferences and local food availability, most of which are man-made and man-maintained, and as such subjects of political economy *par excellence*. The best methodological approach to grasp this large and heterogeneous variety of factors can be found in the work of the Indian economist Amartya Sen, starting with his famous 1981 book Poverty and Famines. In it he develops the notion of *entitlement*, *i.e.* a person's ability to command food. Such ability depends on economic as well as political processes, on cultural and social organization, on domestic and international factors.[96] The concept of entitlement is a pluridisciplinary 'cornerstone' notion, allowing us to integrate the large variety of factors and disciplines needed.

In a simplified form, three fundamental categories of entitlements can be distinguished:
1) production-based entitlement: people are entitled to what they make themselves;
2) exchange-based entitlement: people are entitled to what they can obtain by trading their labour or something they own; and
3) transfer entitlement: people are entitled to what is willingly given to them by another who legitimately owns it.[97]

Starvation occurs whenever one's entitlement set, *i.e.* the total goods one can command, contains an inadequate amount of food. Hunger and starvation, in this approach, are 'a function of entitlements, not of food availability as such'[98] – implying that hunger is not primarily a problem of production, but rather one of access. 'If starvation and hunger are seen in terms of failures of entitlements, then it becomes immediately clear that the total availability of food in the country is only one of the several variables that are relevant.'[99] Increasing food production thus does not necessarily bring about a decline in hunger. Changes can be needed in any of the variables that determine entitlements, which include, amongst others, employment opportunities, the possibility to sell export crops at a reasonable price, the system of land tenure and social security, etc. Most of these variables are related to policy and distribution: they are political in nature. In Sen's words: as 'the food problem is not just concerned with the availability of food but with the disposition of food, . . . there is indeed no such thing as an a-political food problem.'[100]

The above discussion implies that one should guard against what Sen has called 'Malthusian optimism'. It is not because the per capita food availability in a country is sufficient that hunger does not exist in that country; similarly, it is not because the food production growth rate of a country exceeds its population growth rate that hunger is disappearing.[101]

This is not to say that increases in food production are a bad thing – on the contrary – but only that they do not necessarily eradicate hunger. They only do so if at the same time they create entitlements to the hungry. This will mainly happen if it is the poor that produce these increased quantities of foodstuffs, either for auto-consumption, or to sell them, or as labor in the case of landless farmers. In that respect, food production is on the same level as any other agricultural production: it is the entitlements that come from its production and exchange that matter, not its availability itself. John Mellor, one of the world's leading specialists on rural development, has stressed in all his works that 'boosting overall food production' is necessary for improving food security 'because of the dominant role of agricultural production as a source of employment'[102] – and thus income. Hence, food production increases, as any other economic change, will decrease the incidence of hunger if they create entitlements to the poor and the hungry; if they do not, hunger will stagnate or might even increase. History sadly shows the latter to be all too much the case.[103]

5 Conclusion

The Earth is capable of feeding many more human beings than it actually does: estimates vary from 10 to around 40 billion people. As the world population is projected, even in the worst scenario's, to stabilize at the very low end of this range, 'it is . . . clear that physical and technical problems do not set the limits to food production and will not set such limits in the foreseeable future for virtually all of the developing world.'[104] Some countries, or regions within countries, are technically unable to feed their population from their own soil, but this more the exception than the norm; moreover, this does not by itself imply there should be massive hunger. If millions of people are hungry, this is mainly caused by poverty, policy, power and preference – all changeable givens. Thus the neo-Malthusian perspective is misleading, mistaking symptoms for causes.

The concept of entitlements will be central to this study. First, it fundamentally incorporates the principle that hunger is caused by poverty, or, more generally, by failing access to food – and not by lack of food per se. Second, it is open to such sociological/cognitive factors as principles and norms, which are central elements of our theoretical framework as described in chapter one. Third, it draws our attention to the interplay between economic, political, cultural and natural factors in explaining hunger. The concept of entitlement thus allows us to link a variety of disciplines, including the main one of this study: international political economy.

Notes

1 From the 'Universal Declaration on the Eradication of Hunger and Malnutrition:' UN, 1975: 1.
2 From resolution I: 'Objectives and Strategies of Food Production:' UN, 1975: 4. E. Martin, s.d., 51, US ambassador at the Conference, later commented: 'it was an eloquent statement of a goal for the nations of the world, ambitious yet realizable – at a price – if mankind wished.'
3 See for his own account: Marei, 1978.
4 Martin, s.d.: 5; Weiss & Jordan, 1976.
5 FAO, 1987b: 17, 23; Srinivasan, 1983a: 105. The distinction between malnutrition and undernutrition can be, but is not usually, made: see for example Srinivasan, 1983a: 105 and Srinivasan, 1983b: 23. Malnutrition thus also includes *overnutrition*, a serious problem in many HICs: see FAO, 1987b: 18. For the definition of famine, see Johnson, 1970.
6 The Brown University World Hunger Program distinguishes between food shortage, food poverty and food deprivation. See Chen, 1990a: *passim*; Millman, 1991: *passim*, Newman, 1990: *passim*.
7 Poleman, 1983: 41; Johnson, 1975: 17.
8 Avery, 1991: 27 (for the Hudson Institute).
9 *Scientific American*, August 1950.
10 Srinivasan, 1983: 101; Poleman, 1981: 1–58;
11 Simon, 1981: 57.
12 Poleman, 1983: 52.
13 Thus *The Economist* on August 25, 1952 described FAO already as 'a permanent institution devoted to proving that there is not enough food in the world'; quoted in Clark, 1970: 10. Revelle, 1968: 374, qualifies FAO's figures as 'propagandistic and self-serving' and 'a rather bad guess.'
14 Also vitamins and minerals are important, but, for easiness' sake, we will neglect them here.
15 For an interesting discussion, see Millman & Chen, 1991: *passim*. The following pages profited from discussions with Robert Chen, Robert Kates and Ellen Messer.
16 FAO, 1987b: 18–20. In the Fourth World Food Survey (FAO, 1977), the cut-off point was set uniquely at 1.5 BMR.
17 World Bank, 1986: 17. See too Reutlinger & Selowsky, 1976, for the World Bank
18 Chen, 1990a: 6.
19 See, for example, USDA, 1990: 20, 59 and UN ACC/SCN, 1987: 6.
20 Foster, 1992: 70 ff.; Warnock, 1987.
21 Sukhatme, 1982; Sukhatme & Margen, 1982; Srinivasan, 1983(b) and the excellent Messer, 1987.
22 This process has inter alia been described by Millman & Chen, 1991: *passim*, Millman, 1991: 3–4., Poleman, 1983: 42 ff. and Warnock, 1987: 5: since 1950, the 'reference man' (the ideal food consumer with whom people are compared to establish if they are undernourished)

consumes 500 calories and 21 grams of protein less! According to data shown in Avery, 1991: 31, the decline since 1946 is even around 1,000 cal/day.

23 See also Lipton, 1983: 6.

24 Svedberg, 1991; Schatz, 1986, Raikes, 1988.

25 Foster, 1992: 63 ff.

26 Chen & Pitt, 1991: 25- 26; FAO, 1987b: 20–1.

27 Sen, 1981(b).

28 Indeed, strictly spoken, *average* dietary intakes do not mean very much. Srinivasan, 1983(b): 24, provides the following image: 'it is as if one tried to establish if a group of soldiers can cross a river by comparing the average length of the soldiers to the average depth of the river.' (translation by me) For an excellent presentation of the different data concerning Africa as well as an analysis of their scientific value, see Svedberg, 1987.

29 Millman & Chen, 1991: 32–33 and Millman, 1991: 3–4 discuss how in some 1990 FAO data, a new and lower cut-off point was used, most notably dropping a 10% allowance for food losses. As a result of this simple (and arbitrary) modification, the figures on world under-nourishment drop from 1,368 million to 152 million persons, an almost tenfold decrease, basically eradicating hunger with one little assumption. This new assumption is not upheld in the forthcoming Sixth World Food Survey.

30 For good overviews, see Foster, 1992: 19–60 and Svedberg, 1987.

31 Poleman, 1983: *passim*; Avery, 1991: 33–4.

32 For example Johnson, 1983; Svedberg, 1987.

33 Klatzmann, 1983: 29.

34 Simon, 1981.

35 Messer, 1987: *passim*.

36 USDA/ERS, 1990: 59. In 1990, for unclear reasons, these requirements are changed in favor of new, regional ones.

37 Scandizzo & Knudsen, 1979, quoted by Sen, 1980: 3. A similar reasoning for the case of Indonesia is presented by Millman & Chen, 1991: 39–40: depending on the threshold chosen (FAO or USAID) as much as half of the population of Indonesia may or not be considered undernourished.

38 Millman, 1991: 11.

39 See Millman & Chen, 1991: 13, 28–9.

40 Klatzmann, 1983. In another book 15 years later, the same author states that he still stands behind his earlier estimates, but that, if he had to redo them, he would make the ranges of the different categories even wider.

41 Such as the conclusion of Millman & Chen, 1991: 45.

42 WFC/1988/4: 5.

43 WFC/1987/2: 3; UNICEF, 1988, 1989; UN ACC/SCN, 1987: *passim*.

44 FAO, 1988: Table 2.1 and FAO, 1992: Table 3. Also FAO, 1987b.

45 Walton, 1989: 15.

46 See Svedberg, 1987: 16.

47 WFC/87/2: appendix 1.

48 Johnson, 1983: 9. For a detailed analysis of the contradiction between the FAO/IBRD figures and the available anthropometric and clinical evidence on Africa, see Svedberg, 1987: *passim*.

49 We can speak of an 'epistemological community of hunger', as defined in the issue of *International Organization* edited by Peter Haas, 1992.

50 *e.g.* the *Food and Nutrition Bulletin*, published by the United Nations University in Tokyo.

51 Chen & Pitt, 1991: 48 – 58; Foster, 1992: 95 ff.

52 I owe this observation to Robert Kates, director of the World Hunger Program, Brown University.

53 Although its secretariat publishes interesting documents, more critical and less inhibited by diplomatic constraints than those of other international organizations – proving its marginal status in the international system. For a good analysis, see Talbot, 1990: chapter 4.

54 Talbot, 190: chapter 5,

55 Again, see Talbot, 1990: chapter 2. This is in part due to the controversial behavior of its long-time Director-General, Edouard Saouma.

56 For a plaidoyer to do so, see Lipton, 1988.

57 Malthus, 1960.

58 Birdsall, Fei, Kuznets, Ranis & Schultz, 1979.

59 Few contemporary books feature titles such as 'The Population-Food Collision is Inevitable' (Paddock & Paddock, 1967: chapter 1), but the perspective remains popular. For an excellent overview of this perspective in recent literature, see Warnock, 1989: 29 a.f.

60 Wilber, 1977: 1–2.

61 Murdoch, 1980: 2 ff.; Pethe, 1990: 59; Hunger Project, 1985: 22. Almost all the works previously referred to, as well as as good as all specialists on th issue, share this perspective. The OECD, 1984 talks about a 'race', while the UNFPA, 1990: 6, writes about the 'struggle' and the 'battles' between food and population. The *World Bank News* of November 8, 1990: 2 holds that 'rice production is in a race with population growth.' A recent WFP brochure concerning its activites in Africa, starts with the question: what are the causes of hunger in Africa? The first answer is: 'the fastest population growth in the world.' This, by itself, is considered enough to explain its crisis and hunger.

62 See too Vaughan, 1987: 4–8. Even the Global 2000 Report to the President, directed by Barney, 1982 and containing 930 parameters in a complicated set of equations, deals with food, population and hunger in the same basic manner.

63 Also the high-quality ones, such as *Le Monde*, 27 mars 1990; *The Economist*, January 20, 1990 or the *New York Times*, May 10, 1992: E4.

64 Walton, 1989: 15.

65 See too Lemaresquier, 1986: 11: 'Dans les [organisations internationales] les ressources sont davantage consacrées aux questions de production et de commercialisation qu'à celles, politiquement plus complexes, de sécurité et d'autonomie alimentaire.'

66 See *inter alia* the introduction by R. Bolosage to George, 1984. He talks

about 'three prevailing assumptions on hunger:' hunger is caused by over-population, hunger can be alleviated by food trade and assistance, and hunger is a scientific problem, to be solved by technological innovation.

67 See for example the Special Reports by the U.S. Department of State on the subject of hunger in 1974 and 1975(a).

68 World Food Conference; World Population Conference; World Agrarian Reform Conference, etc.

69 UNCTAD, FAO, 1981 (also aware of institutional constraints); World Bank, 1981, 1984(b) and the WFC/1984/2: 8. See too George, 1988: 110.

70 See the declaration by the Ministers of Development Cooperation of all OECD Development Assistance Committee members in OECD, 1990(a). Among the organizations active in this field, we find the World Bank, UNFPA, UNICEF, WHO, USAID, SIDA, ODA as well as IPPF, Pathfinder and many other non-governmental organizations.

71 Franke & Chasin, 1980: 130.

72 Ball, 1981: 17.

73 And this decrease was strongly linked to the US' massive set-aside program of the previous years! For figures, see Hathaway, 1987: 9, 12–13. Supply is defined here as production plus carry-over stocks. Actually, over the last twenty years, the growth in food supply was below the growth of population only 4 times; all other times, it was much higher.

74 Clark, 1985: 123.

75 For interesting overviews, see Warnock, 1989; Srinivasan, 1989; Revel, 1981.

76 Respectively De Hoogh e.a., 1977; Klatzmann, 1983; Murdoch, 1980: 130 (and this without adding new land!) and Clark, 1985: 123. See also Buring, Van Heemst & Staring, 1975.

77 See George, 1984: 4, who wrongly arrives at 0,002%. I owe this point to J. Forster.

78 World Bank, 1986. See too Avery, 1991: 29 and Murdoch, 1980: 95: this is less than 10% of the amount of grain fed to livestock in the rich countries.

79 Mönckeberg, 1979.

80 Insel, 1985: 905.

81 WFC/1986/10.

82 Sen, 1987: 5.

83 At the World Food Conference of 1974 Resolution XIII was devoted to this argument. It represents a strong case of what Donnelly, 1986 calls a 'declaratory regime.'

84 SIPRI, 1986: 233–7 (in 1980 constant dollars); Sivard, 1991. See too UNICEF, 1990: 1.

85 UNICEF, 1990: 1. It adds that the debt and interest payments in the latest year for which data were available, 1988, amounted to $ bn 178, an even higher figure than the one of military spending, and three times the total development aid received during the same year!

86 This – 'man made disaster' – is the only way that the dominant

regime accounts for the fact that hunger, or more precisely, starvation, is a political phenomenon. See for example The Independent Commission on International Humanitarian Issues, 1985.

87 Messer, 1991: *passim* for a most interesting study.

88 Charvet, 1987: 11.

89 Lamond Tullis, 1989 and 1986, *passim*; and Warnock, 1989: 17–18.

90 Roche, 1976; UN, 1975; cited in Murdoch, 1980: 71.

91 See Dreze & Sen, 1989.

92 Brown, 1977 and Physician's Task Force on Hunger in America, 1985 for the U.S.; Warnock, 1989: 181–2 on Canada.

93 Of course, one should be aware that OECD countries could produce much more if they abandoned feedgrain production for animals and replaced it by foodgrain production for human consumption.

94 Although this is fundamental economic wisdom, certain economists and most policy makers display a tendency to forget it.

95 Dreze & Sen, 1989: 179.

96 'The entitlement approach concentrates on the ability of different sections of the population to establish command over food, using the entitlement operating in that society depending on its legal, economic, political, and social characteristics:' Sen, 1981(a): 162.

97 Sen, 1981(a): chapter I. It is clear that the extent of these entitlements differs by society and social class to which one belongs.

98 Sen, 1981(a): 7, also Sen, 1987: 7: 'the real issue is not the over-all availability of food, but its acquirement by individuals.'

99 Sen, 1982: 19.

100 Sen, 1983: 459.

101 Sen, 1983: 111.

102 The quotation comes from Mellor, 1988: 997, but all his other works, and especially Mellor, 1976, develop the same argument. See too Timmer, 1991: *passim*.

103 The case of Brazil must be the most striking one in this respect: its agricultural production growth rate has been very high over the past fifteen years, but the incidence of hunger increased.

104 Murdoch, 1980: 131.

FOUR

ON WARS FOUGHT WITH BUTTER, NOT WITH GUNS: THE INTERNATIONAL FOOD TRADE OUTCOME

The EC will shortly sell a large part of its beef and butter stocks to the Soviet Union at rock bottom prices, EC sources said on Friday. A French businessman has signed a contract with the Soviet union to sell 200,000 tons of beef and 100,000 tons of butter from the Community's intervention stocks, a senior official told Reuters. He said the EC Commission had approved the deal, under which the butter will be sold at one-fifteenth of the price of 3,132 ECUs a ton (3,5 dollars a kilo) which the Community pays its own producers. The official gave no price for the beef deal, on which the contract has not yet been finalized. (...) Commission sources said the EC executive had wanted to sell only the beef to the Soviet union, but Moscow had refused to sign the contract unless butter was also included. The introduction of dairy production quotas in 1984, and sales of nearly 500,000 tons to the Soviet Union in 1987, have reduced the EEC's butter stocks to 350,000 tons, from 1,5 million tons two years ago. The sale of a further 100,000 tons to Moscow will take stocks below sufficient levels to cover large-scale EC programs to incorporate old intervention butter in animal feed. But the Community agreed to sell the butter in order to get rid of a large part of the 760,000 tons of surplus beef currently lying in cold storage warehouses.

Reuters cable, 15–1302, July 15, 1988.

International food flows constitute one of the most important processes in the international food/hunger outcome. Indeed, the fact that countries are not closed, but that they can exchange food, allows their consumption to differ from their domestic production. Countries and people can use this possibility in order to increase consumption, or simply to diversify diets.

This chapter deals with commercial international food flows; concessionary ones (food aid) will be studied in the next chapter. Commercial food flows constitute around 95% of the international flow of food, with concessional flows accounting for the other 5%. These figures become 90% and 10% respectively if we look at food flows to developing countries only.

To many specialists in the international development community, food trade constitutes one of the main solutions to the problem of hunger: Third World countries should produce whatever products they have a comparative advantage in (which is rarely assumed to be food, but often other agricultural products or minerals) and import food with the proceeds. This should ensure the most efficient use of resources and diminish the incidence of hunger in society. This assertion that food security is not necessarily served by food self-sufficiency and that comparative advantage and trade are the most efficient way of tackling the hunger problem is regularly affirmed, as well in the 'development community,'[1] as in the 'international community of states.'[2]

But how does the international food trade system work? What is the regime applying to it? What does the process look like? What are its main effects? What does this say of the capacity of the international food trade system to deal with the problem of hunger? These are the questions we will address in this chapter. First, we will briefly present some basic data on international food trade, necessary to understand what follows. In sections two, three and four of this chapter, we will resp. analyze the international food trade regime and process as well as its principal effects. The implications of all this on the incidence of hunger will be discussed throughout.

1 Some data

Food-and feedgrains taken together constitute the second largest internationally traded item, preceded only by petroleum. Yet, as table 1 shows, the volume of food traded is only a small part of total world food production – much smaller than similar shares for other agricultural primary commodities, or for petroleum for that matter. For other staples, such as manioc, potatoes and the like, recorded international trade is negligible.[3]

Table 4.1 Shares of production traded, 1980s[4]

coffee	68%	wheat	19.5%
cacao	61%	coarse grains	11.9%
sugar	30%	rice	2.6%

Hence, most food consumed in the world is produced domestically; only a small share of it is the object of international flows. Of course, averages hide exceptions. Indeed, some countries, such as Egypt and Japan, are dependent for an important share of their aggregate food supply on imports.

The volume of world cereals trade has expanded significantly over the last decades, and especially so during the 1970s (see table 4.2). The largest share of this growth was accounted for by developing countries, who tripled their food imports over the last twenty years. By the 1980s, developing countries had overtaken developed countries as the main food importers. This is mainly due to their dominance in foodgrain imports, for in all other food trade sectors, such as meat, dairy and feedgrains, the developed countries remain the main importers.[5]

Table 4.2 Volume of world grains trade 1960–85, mio tons[6]

	World	OECD	LDCs		World	OECD	LDCs
1960/61	72			1980/81	206	109	97
1964/65	95			1981/82	212	115	97
1970/71	106	64	42	1982/83	196	90	106
1971/72	108	65	43	1983/84	203	93	110
1972/73	133	83	51	1984/85	218	109	109
1973/74	135	75	60	1985/86	181	82	99
1974/75	134	72	62	1986/87	184	78	106
1975/76	150	95	56	1987/88	197	81	16
1976/77	148	90	58	1988/89	205	89	116
1977/78	163	90	72	1989/90	209	88	121
1978/79	171	89	82	1990/91	203	83	120
1979/80	195	105	90				

Increased Third World food imports equal diminishing food self-sufficiency. As we can see from graph 4.1, Third World food self-sufficiency is negative and continues to decline. The

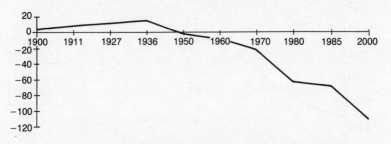

Figure 4.1 LDC cereals balance, 1900–1985, million tons[7]

same graph also shows that this process is not new: it has gone on for more than half a century, beginning long before independence.

Interpreting these figures, though, is not as easy as it looks like. The only thing the above figures indicate with certainty is that effective, *i.e.* monetary, demand in all LDCs together outstripped their domestic availability of food; but they tell us nothing about the *causes* of this decline in food self-sufficiency. Increased effective demand for imported foodstuffs can be caused by many factors: population growth; declines in domestic production; income increases; changes in relative prices between domestically produced and importable staples; taste changes in favor of imported foods; increased meat consumption, necessitating feedgrain imports, etc. The relative importance of all these factors differs from country to country, and so do their effects on the incidence of hunger.

Hence, contrary to common wisdom, these figures tell us little or nothing about hunger. Indeed, the foremost feature of international food trade is that its direction is decided by monetary, not by dietary demand. In other words, 95% of food flows across borders do so on the basis of the ability to pay for it – not on the criterion of need. Hence, the richer countries or persons are, the more food they import. As the hungry are also the poor, commercial food flows by themselves have little relation to the incidence of hunger: an increase in any country's food imports thus can coincide with an increase as well as a decrease in the incidence of undernutrition. Similarly, decreasing imports do not mean hunger is on the decline: it actually often means the opposite.

This is clearly demonstrated when we look at the developing countries whose food imports rose most dramatically: they are

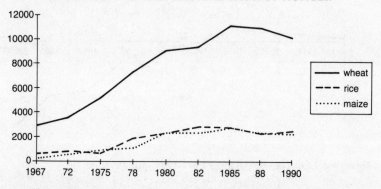

Figure 4.2 Imports in sub-Saharan Africa, 1965–1985, in 10,000 tons[10]

all middle income countries. Some ten small countries, accounting for only 3% of the Third World population, import close to half of all Third World cereals imports by now.[8] This evolution is largely due to their increased wealth and taste changes in favor of imported food. Of particular importance are the Maghreb countries – Egypt, Libya, Tunisia, Algeria, Morocco – which, during the last three decades, have consistently known the highest growth rate in food imports of all regions in the world. Placing high priority on industrialization and sufficiently rich to pay for importing food, they have been expanding their imports very fast, at least until the 1980s, when the debt crisis hit them. Since 1982, their imports have stagnated, but they still account for over one third of all Third World food imports.[9]

We now turn to the widely discussed case of sub-Saharan Africa. Over the last 3 decades, its food imports have gone up significantly, even on a per capita basis (see graph 4.2), be it that on a world scale they are still insignificant (fluctuating around 5 million tons in total). This is held to be primarily due to increased need: it is considered one of the main proofs that sub-Saharan African food production per capita has dramatically declined.

But as we have seen in chapter 2, serious doubts can be cast on this interpretation. Rather, as different authors suggest, Africa's increased food imports are mainly due to urban demand and the political imperatives behind it;[11] they are quite unrelated to domestic food production or hunger: again, those who buy commercially imported food are rarely the poor and the hungry. During the 1980s, Africa's commercial food imports declined significantly: the most dramatic case is Nigeria, once close to importing 3 million tons of cereals, which almost stopped importing altogether.[12] The main reason for this change is lack of financial means, not increased domestic food availability.

A few Third world countries, which implemented policies favorable to agricultural development, have increased their domestic food production per capita and have contracted their commercial food imports, sometimes even to the point of becoming small exporters. Among them we find relatively small countries such as Saudi-Arabia and Turkey, but also very important ones, such as China, India and Indonesia, all of which *grosso modo* achieved cereals self-sufficiency in the 1970s. This still only means that effective demand in these countries is satisfied, which is not the same as saying they know no more undernutrition.

Apart from the LDCs, there is one other group of countries which significantly increased its food imports: Eastern Europe (see table 4.3). Among the latter, the USSR is most important. Although its import behavior has usually been quite erratic, the long-term trend is clearly upwards. The other Eastern European countries have always been net food importers, with the trend being upwards during the 1970s and downwards during the 1980s. If these countries do not import more, this is mainly because of financial constraints: for most of them, their imports are a balancing act between their lack of foreign currency and the length of the queues at their stores. By the beginning of the 1990s, their financial predicament has increased dramatically, making it very difficult for them to import food commercially;

Table 4.3 USSR and Eastern Europe, net imports of wheat and coarse grains, mio tons[13]

	USSR	Eastern Europe		USSR	Eastern Europe
1960/61	−6.24	5.08	1979/80	30.03	13.30
1965/66	3.69	6.65	1980/81	33.50	13.72
1970/71	−7.54	9.84	1981/82	45.80	9.28
1971/72	1.10	7.90	1982/83	32.80	2.84
1972/73	20.87	5.72	1983/84	31.60	2.38
1973/74	5.11	5.61	1984/85	54.58	−0.15
1974/75	0.23	7.09	1985/86	28.90	3.47
1975/76	25.15	8.74	1986/87	19.00	1.20
1976/77	7.30	10.55	1987/88	31.50	2.90
1977/78	16.36	9.49	1988/89	37.00	4.70
1978/79	12.54	12.90	1989/90	36.50	6.00

some of them have become major food aid recipients. In most of these countries, the level of food production achieved is far below their potential: as such, if they manage to reorganize their economies, it is quite probable that this will be accompanied by heavy increases in food production.

Let us now turn to the food exporters. As can be seen in table 4.4, rich countries are by far, and increasingly so, the main exporters of food – as, contrary to common assumption, they also are for almost all primary commodities.[14]

Table 4.4 % share of world food exports, LDCs–OECD[15]

| | 1967 | | 1980 | | 1990 | |
	OECD	LDC	OECD	LDC	Dev.ed countries	LDC
meat	62.1	22.3	78.9	10.4	n.a.	n.a.
dairy	91.0	1.5	95.4	1.5	n.a.	n.a.
foodgrain	68.7	14.4	79.4	14.4	90.9	9.1
feedgrain	63.8	25.1	88.7	6.7	90.7	9.3

Since the Second World War, the most significant change in the international food trade system at the export side is the emergence of a new large exporter: the EEC, who, as a result of its protectionist policies, reached self-sufficiency in major cereals during the 1970s.[16] This hurts other exporters in two ways. The first one is the decline and eventual disappearance of the EEC as an export market for their cereals; the second one the reduction of their third country markets, as the EEC becomes an exporter itself (graph 3). As a result, the market share and the income of the other 'traditional' exporters decrease (table 4.5).

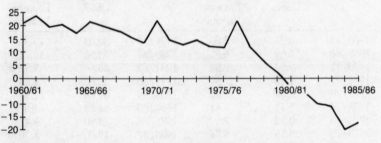

Figure 4.3 EEC net cereal imports 1960–1985, mio tons[17]

This situation was tolerable until the 1980s, when, mainly due to expanded Third World demand, the world food market was in constant growth. But it has become source of great conflict among food exporters since the early 1980s, when, due to the financial crises facing large parts of the Third World and Eastern Europe, world food imports stagnated and even declined.[19] This situation is unlikely to change soon, for none of these groups has a very strong economic outlook. With stagnant population growth and full bellies, also the OECD countries are not likely to augment their food imports very much. Only the food and

Table 4.5 Market shares, major exporters, 1970–86, in %[18]

| | Wheat | | | | | Rice | | | |
	71/2	75/6	80/1	85/6		71/2	75/6	80/1	85/6
Australia	16.1	11.8	9.9	16.6	Myanmar	10.0	6.5	5.1	5.0
Argent.	1.8	4.3	4.0	6.3	China	15.3	17.0	22.9	18.8
Canada	21.1	16.6	16.8	17.5	Italy	3.1	4.2	3.6	5.2
EEC–12	10.3	19.6	22.4	28.9	Pakistan	2.2	7.5	8.8	9.0
US	35.8	43.1	42.5	26.6	Thailand	18.7	18.4	23.0	34.1
					US	17.3	17.0	22.9	18.8

| | Coarse grains | | | | | Wheat and coarse grains | | | |
	71/2	75/6	80/1	85/6		71/2	75/6	80/1	85/6
Australia	5.3	1.2	2.0	5.3	Australia	10.8	7.7	5.6	11
Argent.	16.8	7.9	12.1	10.1	Argent.	9.1	6.3	8.5	8.2
Canada	7.9	5.7	4.0	6.1	Canada	14.6	10.7	9.8	14
China	0.1	0.4	0.2	7.4	EEC–12	13	16.8	17	24.9
EEC–12	15.8	14.4	12.6	20.5	US	35	50.3	51.8	32
US	34.3	56.4	54.9	38.0					

feed imports by the NICs are likely to grow further, be it probably not very fast. It is also likely that some populous countries such as India, China and Indonesia, will, as a result of rising incomes, soon become importers again.

Hence, under present conditions of supply and demand, food trade, a large source of foreign exchange for some of the most important OECD countries has a bleak future. Export quantities will continue to stagnate, prices to fall, stocks to grow, and export competition to increase. The only factor that could modify this outlook is the event of a large-scale liberalization of agriculture in the OECD. The effects of such policy reform would be very beneficial for the traditional exporters such as the US and Australia and the inverse would hold for the highly protected European and Japanese farms. Henceforth it is only logical that liberalization of OECD agriculture is a very contested item of international politics at present.

This situation of structural food surplus and continuously lowering prices is not new. Stocks of the major traded staples have been consistently large since the Second World War, reflecting the rapid increases in production in many OECD countries, caused by protectionism (table 4.6; compare with table 4.2).

This, of course, could but have a negative effect on prices, which have constantly declined. According to recent World Bank research by its acting specialist on terms of trade, Enzo Grilli,

Table 4.6 Stocks of the world and major exporters, mio tons[20]

	72	75	78	81	84	87	88	89	90/91
what	92	76	97	99	134	171	145	117	131
coarse grains	95	74	102	108	98	231	213	144	118
rice	30	29	39	44	49	55	44	45	50
developed countries	154	110	146	148	157	318	277	184	172
developing countries	62	68	93	103	124	135	122	122	127
major exporters	127	77	129	124	136	277	232	137	n.a.
World cereal stocks	216	179	239	251	281	452	400	305	299

food commodities are the only ones for which a secular decline in the terms of trade (à la Prebisch-Singer) really exists (see graph 4.4).

The main exception to this old scenario of rising stocks and lowering prices was the 1972–74 period, when world prices for the major food items suddenly skyrocketed. This was due to the simultaneous occurrence of different factors: bad harvests in some large countries (USSR, US, India, much of sub-Saharan Africa); a successful policy of reducing stocks the US government had begun some years before; sudden and massive USSR imports;[22] and the taking off of NIC food imports. At the time, this was considered by many the beginning of a period of chronic world food shortages: urgent action was needed if the world would not go down in Malthusian doom. Such was, for example, the atmosphere that pervaded the 1974 World Food Conference. For exporting farmers, on the other hand, this was seen as the

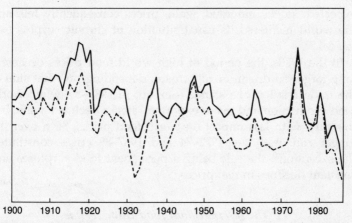

Figure 4.4 Evolution of world prices for cereals, 1900–1986, constant prices[21]

Table 4.7 Food import value, food production and food supply, 1970–86 (annual % change of indices)[23]

	Index of value of world food imports	Production index	Supply index*
1970	5.1	2.6	0.7
71	3.3	7.1	2.7
72	8.0	−0.1	0.4
73	43.8	9.5	6.4
74	35.8	−3.5	−1.9
75	12.2	6.3	5.6
76	−3.9	4.5	5.3
77	7.6	2.7	4.0
78	15.6	4.2	6.9
79	20.2	0.8	4.0
1980	16.8	0.8	−0.9
81	2.9	9.0	4.0
82	−5.9	2.6	5.5
83	−5.2	−0.2	−0.9
84	4.3	5.2	4.7
85	−4.2	2.7	4.3
86	4.3	1.7	5.7
87	9.3	0.4	
88	12.4	1.5	
89	6.0	3.6	
1990	9.6	1.4	

beginning of a period of unprecedented wealth. Both were wrong: world production (continued to) increase(d) faster than expected, stocks mounted again, prices consequently fell, and the world reentered its usual situation of chronic surplus (see table 4.7).

In the 1980s, the period of high world food prices became a long-forgotten dream or nightmare, depending on what side of the trade relation one stands – except in 1987–89, when world food production and major exporters' stocks declined again, but this time with less impact on world food prices. Seen over the longer run, both the 1972–74 and 1987–89 crises constituted the exceptions, the rule being a permanent food surpluses and constant declines in real prices.[24]

2 The international food trade regime

There is no real international food trade regime as such, but rather an international agricultural trade regime, applying *inter alia* to internationally traded staples. This international agricultural/food trade regime is to a large extent codified. Indeed, the General Agreement on Trade and Tariffs (GATT) contains different provisions which apply only to agricultural trade, distinguishing it from other items of international trade, which are governed by the 'ordinary' GATT regime. The special treatment of agriculture in the GATT rules revolves around two main issues. Article XVI prohibits the use of export subsidies, but makes an exception for primary commodities (agricultural and other).[25] Article XI, prohibiting quantitative restrictions and quotas, allows export and import restrictions for 'agriculture and fisheries' products.[26] Moreover, in 1955, the US asked for and obtained a 'waiver', freeing it from its remaining obligations under Articles II and XI, allowing for quantitative trade restrictions in support of domestic agricultural policies.[27] The continued existence of this waiver has greatly undermined the credibility of the US in its later attempts to liberalize agricultural trade.[28]

This special regime for agriculture results from the strong preference of the US for special treatment of agriculture in the period after the Second World War – against the preferences of many other countries. Hathaway distinguishes two sources of opposition:

> on the one hand, certain countries, such as Australia, whose agricultural policies did not require the use of exports sub-

sidies, vigorously opposed special treatment for agriculture. On the other hand, a number of important developing countries, which were largely agricultural and had a substantial interest in developing domestic manufacturing, were opposed to special treatment for agriculture unless they, too, could have similar rules to protect and develop their domestic manufacturing industries.[29]

It testifies to the power of the US at the time, as well as to the biased nature of the GATT regime, that special treatment for US agriculture was accepted in the GATT framework, but not for any other sector or country. As Paarlberg notes, the objectives of the US in this field differed markedly from its preferences in other issue areas:

> while pushing trade liberalization for industry early in the 1950s, the US has taken the lead in *excluding* agricultural products from the liberalizing rules of the GATT.[30]

All through the 1960s and the 1970s, agriculture has been kept outside the ordinary GATT framework. During the Dillon Round, the EEC did agree to a 'zero-duty binding on EC imports of oilseeds (such as soybeans), oilseeds meals, and some other non-grain feed items such as corn gluten feed,'[31] but this did not represent any adherence to liberal norms whatsoever, but a simple deal with the US, in return of which the latter agreed not to contest the CAP. The EEC has scrupulously adhered to this concession, notwithstanding the important distorting effect it later proved to have on the CAP. In 1973, the statement of intent opening the Tokyo Round explicitly affirmed the 'common acceptance of the special status of agriculture.'[32] After 6 years of negotiations, two slightly liberalizing agreements on bovine meat and on dairy products saw the light in Tokyo, but they had little if any concrete effect.[33]

The illiberal nature of the post-war international agricultural trade regime made it possible for member-states to develop formal domestic regimes, which, while being formally in line with the rules of GATT – bastion of free trade and international cooperation – were protectionist in nature (*i.e.* in the objects they promoted). As Wolf comments: 'once discrimination has become a norm, further and progressive increases in protection are virtually inevitable.'[34] The Common Agricultural Policy (CAP) of the EEC is the prime example of this, its cornerstone, variable levies, being sanctioned by GATT. But also the trade legislation of states such as Japan, the other European countries, the Asian NICs and some OPEC countries became highly protectionist.

Yet, together with this illiberal formalized regime, the international system regularly engages in rhetoric which stresses its attachment to liberal principles concerning agricultural trade. International organizations – the OECD, IMF, UNCTAD, WFC, and the World Bank – advocate agricultural production and trade liberalization so as to promote global economic development.[35] At times, even the concert of states solemnly declares its adherence to these norms – but continues its policies unchanged afterwards. The 1974 World Food Conference, for example, in Resolution XIX,

> calls upon all Governments to co-operate in promoting a steady and increasing expansion and liberalization of world trade with special reference to food products (. . .); accordingly, requests all Governments to co-operate, inter alia towards the progressive reduction or abolition of obstacles to trade and all discriminatory practices . . . [36]

More generally, OECD countries often use liberal principles and norms to justify their policies of the moment – including their protectionist ones. Examples of the latter include the EEC's repeated insistence that the CAP is in accordance with GATT rules and that it is committed to the liberal trade regime, although it manifestly is not;[37] or the US which, over the last two decades, has been very vocal in prefessing its commitment to liberal agricultural trade principles, while at the same time doing the opposite.[38] Yet, this rhetoric has done little, if anything, to change the written norms and rules concerning international agricultural trade. Because of this incongruence between a certain international rhetoric and the written-down rules concerning agricultural trade in the GATT and in national legislations, we label the international food trade regime as ambiguous, but definitely illiberal in nature.

This ambiguity has been explained by some authors by the fact that the US was genuinely committed to a liberal agricultural trade regime, but did not vigorously pursue this objective because it 'was more concerned about diplomatic solidarity within the Atlantic Alliance than it was about threats to US farm interests.'[39] This explanation passes over the lack of real interest of the US in agricultural trade liberalization: various forms of agricultural protectionism have always existed in the US itself, and its commitment to making the 'normal' GATT rules apply to agriculture has always been small. The ambiguity of the world food trade regime can better be explained by referring to the concept of 'nesting' as used by Aggarwal for the textile and apparel trade,[40] where the norms and principles of the general liberal international trade regime 'shame' states into justifying their illiberal agricultural trade acts in liberal terms.

Hence all through the 1960s and 1970s, the most powerful actors agreed to largely illiberal principles and norms, notwithstanding some occasional rhetoric to the contrary. It is only in the 1980s that a change of regime became a real subject on the international agenda. A conflict-ridden 1982 GATT session triggered off a series of initiatives and declarations in fora such as the OECD, UNCTAD and the G–7, expressing the 'urgent need to bring more discipline and predictability to world agricultural trade.'[41] The launching of the Uruguay Round in September 1986 constituted the first serious attempt to change the nature of the agricultural trade regime. The Punta del Este Declaration includes standstill (no increases in protectionism to start with) and rollback (dismantle barriers afterwards) clauses concerning agriculture.[42] This evolution is largely due to a change in preference of the US, which, confronted with stagnating export demand, has taken the lead in pushing for the creation of a liberal agricultural trade regime, based on the twin beliefs that this will create new markets and wipe out the EEC as a competitor for them. In this it has been partly supported by the so-called Cairns group, a group of both rich and poor food exporting countries, who consider themselves hurt by the existing situation and joined their forces in GATT in favor of such a regime change.[43] Both these groups have been opposed by the EEC, Japan, and other European and Asian countries, who do not want to radically alter the present agricultural trade regime and process. This constellation of preferences and power has ensured a ten-year deadlock in the GATT negotiations, which have been prolonged already two times, but without success.

The norms of the regime will probably change. Yet, it is doubtful that such change will take the form of a genuine consensus in favour of liberalism, rather than a series of measures, destined to bring under control the costs of current policies. Indeed, to the extent that any acceptance exists of the need to renegotiate the agricultural trade regime, this is only due to the skyrocketing cost of present practices – not to any generally shared domestic preference in favor of free agricultural/food trade.[44] It is thus likely that changes will be made in the regime only so as to decrease its cost to more manageable proportions, but not so as to create a world free market in agricultural products. This means that the EEC, for example, would adopt measures that bring its self-sufficiency down to around 100%, decreasing the cost of its protectionism and creating trade benefits to other participants.[45] This is quite close to the nature of its GATT position since 5 years.

Theoretical interlude

We saw that the regime applying to international food trade is the same one as the one for international agricultural products trade. Its written part (the GATT norms and rules, as well as domestic legislation), is distinctly illiberal, reflecting US preferences. According to Hathaway:

> not only did agriculture receive special treatment in the GATT, but the special treatment also appears to have been tailored to the US farm programmes then in existence[46]

From the 1960s onwards, as a result of the growing dependence of its agriculture on international markets, the US' perception of its interest began changing, and it feebly attempted to change the nature of the regime in a liberal direction. Yet, it lacked both the will and the power necessary to impose this on the large variety of OECD states who preferred the continuation of the existing regime. Hence, some rhetoric to the contrary, the dominant norms and principles remained essentially illiberal.

Hence, the food trade issue area presents us with the interesting case of the hegemon – the US in the 1940–50s[47] – holding distinctly illiberal preferences, with a largely illiberal regime following from this. Afterwards, while being a 'declining hegemon,' its preferences change in a more liberal direction (which does not mean that they were any less self-interested), but it is not capable anymore of changing the nature of the regime – witness the now 15-year-old stalemate on this matter. Hence, the association often made in the literature between hegemony and liberalism is unjustified.[48]

In 1979, Hopkins and Puchala wrote one of the first (and only) articles about food within a regime framework. Their first principle of the food regime goes as follows:

> *Respect for the free market.* Most major participants in the international diplomacy of food between 1948 and 1972 adhered to the belief that a properly functioning free market would be the most efficient allocator of globally traded food commodities and agricultural inputs. They therefore advocated such a market, aspired towards it, at least in rhetoric, and assessed food affairs in terms of free market models. Actual practice deviated rather markedly from free trade ideals.[49]

This analysis of the nature of the regime is surprisingly contrary to ours. The reason for this difference resides in the problematic nature of the concept of regime, well exemplified in the above quote. In it, they state that 'major participants' 'adhered to a belief,' that they 'aspired to it, at least in rhetoric' but that 'actual practice deviated rather markedly.' The problem here concerns the operationalization of regimes. Concretely, what do we derive regimes from? 'Beliefs?'; 'aspirations?'; 'rhetoric?' or 'actual practice?' Based upon their quote, it is not clear what the choice of Hopkins and Puchala was, giving fuel to Susan Strange's charge of 'wooliness' to the concept of regimes.[50] Their analysis seems to be drawn from US rhetoric combined with the liberal values which are dominant in the Anglo-saxon academic circles to which they belong.

In chapter 1, we have discarded the 'actual practice' option for reasons of circularity. Kratochwil and Ruggie, in an excellent article, do the same and advocate the development of an 'interpretive epistemology,' which should be capable of grasping the essentially 'intersubjective' nature of regimes.[51] While agreeing with their diagnosis, we argue against their 'belief' solution. At the present state of social sciences, there are too many unresolved issues with this approach. How do authors know what 'most major participants in the international diplomacy of food' believe? Do these participants know it themselves? Which participants' beliefs do we look at? And if some participants disagree publicly? Or privately?

In order to avoid these problems, we have previously argued in favor of operationalizing regimes as those principles and norms which are expressed by the major actors in a given issue area as governing their behavior – through codified, written rules and procedures, and through their authoritative discourse.[52] In practice, this signifies that, first, we look for written international norms (international laws, treaties, charts of international organizations) to derive the regime from. Second, we add to this the authoritative statements of powerful actors in the issue-area: the principles and norms they refer to when justifying their behavior – any behavior, not just the one in accordance with the regime the analyst thinks is the 'true' one. This amounts to replacing the intersubjective ontological status of regimes with an easier-to-handle positivist one. This way, we avoid not only imputing beliefs and values to policy-makers, or, worse, to states, but also the danger of circularity, for regimes are constructed in a way different from the process. It is this method we used for analyzing the food trade regime in this chapter, which might explain the differences with Hopkins and Puchala's interpretation.

3 The international food trade process

We will not present here a full technical review of quantitative import and export restrictions, variable and fixed tariffs, import and export subsidies, direct and indirect income transfers, escape clauses, regulatory reliefs, insurance and guarantee funds, compensatory measures, voluntary export restraints, preferential export or import agreements, sanitary-and phytosanitary barriers etc., for these are not properly speaking subject of our analysis.[53] What is clear, though, is that the food trade process has unambiguously and continuously been illiberal. Barriers to trade, whether allowed by the GATT or not, are the norm; free trade the exception. This holds for almost all food products and countries. As table 4.8 shows, the frequency of protectionist measures is much higher for agricultural products than for manufactures, showing a congruence between the respective regimes and processes.

Two practices which characterize the food trade process specifically need to be mentioned here. The most common one

Table 4.8 The frequency of application of various barriers in industrial countries, in %, 1984[54]

	Tariff quotas and seasonal tariffs	Quantitative restrictions	Minimum price policies all	variable levies	Total
meat and animals	12.3	41.1	26.0	23.8	52.2
dairy products	6.9	29.6	28.6	25.6	54.6
cereals	1.7	10.9	21.7	21.7	29.0
other food	0.8	16.3	13.5	13.2	27.0
tea, coffee, cocoa	0.4	4.0	2.5	2.5	6.6
other beverages	18.5	22.9	18.4	0.4	42.3
raw materials	0	7.5			7.8
all agriculture	8.2	17.2	11.5	8.2	29.7
manufactures	2.2	6.7	0.6	0.0	9.4

is state trading. Most of the world food trade is done between companies at least one of whom is a state trading company. McCalla and Schmitz calculated that private trade (private exporter to private importer) accounted for only 4.4% of world wheat trade during the period 1973–77.[55] According to Hathaway:

> the use of state-trading agencies as a method of controlling all imports and exports of agricultural commodities provides a convenient way to restrict imports or control exports without imposing quantitative restrictions under Articles XI and XIII . . . It is estimated that as much as 90% of world trade in wheat passes through such governmental agencies, and about 70% of trade in coarse grains. Countries using such agencies range from China and India to Japan, Canada and Australia.[56]

Another, less widespread but more damaging, practice is the use of export subsidies. The US has consistently used them whenever market conditions necessitated it: from 1949 to the mid–1960s,[57] for example, and then again from the beginning to the middle of the 1970s (even for sales to the USSR); and, of course, during the 1980s. The EEC subsidized some exports from the beginning of the CAP onwards,[58] but only started using them on a large scale from the end of the 1970s onwards, when the size of its stocks and the low world prices rendered it inevitable. This led to the prolonged trade wars we will discuss further.

The fact that the international food trade process is illiberal should not be taken to mean that it is centrally managed or anyhow regulated. Indeed, in a paradoxical way, the process is also **unregulated**.[59] No international regulation exists in food trade – neither a liberal (GATT-type) one (as must be abundantly clear by now) nor an interventionist (UNCTAD-type) one.[60] International food trade can be properly labelled anarchic in its organization.

At the 1974 World Food Conference, the international community of states solemnly adhered to the necessity of international food trade regulation for world food security purposes.[61] Yet, very little has been achieved. Notwithstanding much talking in international organizations, no international grain trade management system has come into being. Similarly, all proposals implying international food price coordination through stocks, quotas or mere consultation have failed.[62] UNCTAD's Integrated Programme for Commodities and the Common Fund – the only regulation of commodity trade accepted, but not implemented, by states in the 1980s – does not include food items, for the major exporters are not LDCs, and prices are low, benefiting them.[63] The immediate cause of this lack of progress is the existence of conflicting interests between importers and exporters (a North-South conflict) as well as between exporters (a US-EEC conflict) concerning the desirable level of prices and stocks. But the fundamental cause is that any international regulation threatens to intervene with the domestic policies of the rich countries and is thus unacceptable to them.[64] The same factors that bring these countries to protect their farmers do not allow them to create world food security mechanisms in the food trade issue area.

Progress has been made on two points. One is food aid, which we will discuss in detail in the next chapter. The other one is an IMF facility, created in 1981, that allows countries to draw on their quota to compensate for exceptionally high cereal import bills, whether caused by increased imports or high prices or both. This new facility, referred to as the Food Financing Facility or the Cereal Import Facility, is part of the Compensatory Financing Facility (CFF), created by the IMF in 1963 and destined to compensate overall balance of payments shortfalls of LDCs. It has not been used much, mainly because world prices have been generally low.[65] Between May 1981, when it came into operation, and 1986, there have been 13 drawings under the FFF amounting to SDR 1.1 billion, all designed to compensate for bad weather-induced exceptional imports.[66]

Hence, of the different international trade mechanisms agreed upon at the World Food Conference for achieving world food security, only those which leave rich countries free to pursue their domestic policies, but repair some of their damaging effects on LDCs, have known some success: food aid and compensatory financing, both mechanisms well-liked by exporters. The others, implying a regulation of agricultural trade along liberal or managed models, have not been realized, for they were in contradiction with the domestic production policies of powerful countries.

In the absence of any international regulation, the process is necessarily strongly **bilateral**.[67] Indeed, one of the most important features of the present international grain trade is the presence of a large number of bilateral trade agreements. They are usually long-term contracts, averaging 5 years, in which an importer commits himself to an agreed-upon minimum volume of imports at floating, but favorable, terms.[68] Since the 1960s, their number has multiplied fast: at present, more than half of all world annual food trade is covered by them.[69] They allow surplus countries to buy importers' loyalty in an oversatisfied market, by offering security of supply, advantageous price conditions, and, usually, long-term credit.[70]

As the largest share of international grain trade is done by means of export subsidies and long-term agreements associated with favorable credit conditions, the notion of a 'world market price' has become largely devoid of significance.[71] In 1986 and 1987, for example, according to Philippe Chalmin, the ' "effective price" of wheat was around 30% to 40% lower than the official Chicago price.'[72] Similar gaps exist for secondary cereals and rice.[73]

In conclusion, with many other authors, we can characterize the contemporary international agriculture trade process as **residual**.[74] By this is meant that the international market is the left-over of domestic policies and preferences, and not the result of real international competition.[75] 'The world market, whether in time of surplus or shortage, is treated as a residual, used by producers and consumers alike as a means of stabilizing their own supplies and not as a price mechanism indicating the required adjustment in either supply or demand.'[76] This explains why its nature is so illiberal, non-regulated and bilateral: any other form would be in conflict with the domestic production policies of the major countries.[77] Or, in political science terms: 'foreign policies in agriculture, because of the political imperatives behind them, have tended to serve domestic interests ahead of international ones.'[78] This, then, is the biggest constraint on progress in the Uruguay Round: given the absence of commitment to domestic agricultural production policy reform, nations are unwilling and incapable of changing the international food trade regime or process more than marginally.[79]

This residual nature of agricultural trade helps us to understand that in a very real sense the international food trade outcome is the **unintended result** of decisions taken on other levels and for other reasons. Many of the present-day features of international food trade were never planned nor desired. The food surpluses of OECD countries are the unintended consequences of policies designed to protect farmers' incomes; the effect of domestic policies designed to protect against international instability has been more international price instability;[80] the effect of the zero-duty binding on corn substitutes, allowed by the EEC to buy US compliance with its CAP, has resulted in a heavy and costly structural imbalance in the CAP and in a phenomenal increase in the exports of cereal substitutes to Europe (from below 5 million tons to above 30 million tons), to the greater benefit of the US and Thailand;[81] etc. This phenomenon – that important outcomes are the unintended result of policies made for other reasons and with often diametrically opposed objectives in mind – is difficult to deal with in international relations studies, which are used to working with a simplifying 'rational state' model.

4 The effects of the international food trade outcome

The international food trade process has three important effects: it brings about food trade wars, especially between the US and other countries, often allied ones; it lowers and destabilizes food prices; and it allows a handful of grain trading companies to play a large and profitable role. The impact of these phenomena on the incidence of hunger is small.

A Trade wars

The first effect of the food trade outcome up to the 1980s has been the existence of intense trade wars, mainly between the US and the EEC. In the 1960s, the world had become familiar with the existence of 'chicken wars' and 'pasta wars.' The 1970s, as a result of increased export possibilities for all exporters (and mainly the US, profiting from a low dollar), had been a relatively peaceful era. But in the 1980s, stagnating import demand all over the world coincided with a sharply increased dollar exchange rate. As a result, the US saw its share of the world market (see table 5), and its export proceeds dramatically tumble. Tens of thousands of American farmers went bankrupt. The blame was laid on unfair EEC competition. Unfair competition there certainly was, but this was not the only reason for the loss of US export markets. First, the US share at the end of the 1970s was artificially high, and, second, the role of currency instability – in particular, the rise of the dollar until 1985 – was at least as important but consistently neglected by the US administration.[82]

Hence the 1980s became the decade of an increasingly aggressive and expensive agricultural trade war between two military allies: the U.S. and the EEC. The whole world, but especially the Mediterranean zone, was to become the theatre of this tit-for-tat trade war, fought with lavish export subsidies, subsidized credits, long-term bilateral agreements, diplomatic pressure, and the like.[83] At present, the major share of world cereals trade is done with the help of such weapons. The EEC routinely subsidizes as good as all agricultural exports (it has no choice for they are produced at costs above the world market price), but, since the 1980s, the US increasingly did the same again, with the proportion of agricultural exports subsidized reaching 75% in 1985/6.[84] The fight is not limited to cereals only: also butter, milk and meat are involved.[85]

The US also uses the threat of trade sanctions to directly open up third markets which, for one or another reason, are closed to them. Japan had to give in in recent years on beef, citrus and, to a lesser extent, rice; South Korea on rice; Nigeria, which ended all wheat imports because of its debt crisis, is under strong US pressure to import again its wheat,[86] etc.

In all this, domestic considerations have preceded over other ones. This can best be seen in the history of US grain sales to Russia. In the beginning of the 1960s, President Kennedy's attempt to sell farm products to the USSR met with violent domestic opposition, from the anti-Communist AFL/CIO as well as from within the Republican Party[87] But in 1971, Nixon made it possible for the USSR freely to import grain.[88] As a result, the USSR managed to supply itself with 19 million tons of subsidized US cereals, by negotiating different contracts simultaneously and secretly with different grain trading companies.[89] This 'great grain robbery' ended up costing the US Treasury $ 300 million in subsidies,[90] and, along with bad harvest elsewhere and the continuation of the acreage-reduction scheme in the US, was instrumental in pushing up world prices to unprecedented levels[91] – the so-called 'world food crisis.' In the aftermath of this, President Ford concluded a long-term agreement with Moscow in October 1975. The minimum limit for annual Soviet sales was set at 6 million tons annually and the upper limit at 8 million tons.[92] On January 4, 1980, after Russia's invasion of Afghanistan, President Carter announced an embargo on USSR grain sales, and asked befriended nations to do the same. This embargo did not touch the 8 million tons the Soviets were allowed to import under the 1975 agreement.[93] In April 1981, newly elected President Reagan immediately lifted the embargo: not only had it had no effect whatsoever – the Russians simply turned to other suppliers – but also had the US farm sector entered in a heavy crisis, with the latter being the main reason for lifting the ban.[94] In 1983, 'under intense domestic pressure from export-conscious US producer lobbies,'[95] his administration renegotiated a 5 year agreement, in which the level of imports the USSR could yearly freely make from the US was raised to 20 million tons, with a minimum of 9 million. In 1988, the long-term agreement was, not without difficulty, renegotiated as it was for 2 more years.[96] Apart from the foregoing, from 1985 onwards, with the trade war with the EEC at its height, a real battle to feed the Russians began between the US and the EEC, who aggressively competed by offering always higher subsidies on USSR food imports.[97] As the quote at the beginning of this chapter shows, the USSR played this ridiculous game as well as it could.

It is doubtful if the US satisfied any of the preferences that motivated its behavior. Its use of export subsidies did not create many new export opportunities. What it won in one market, it lost elsewhere, because of the targeted counteractions of the EEC.[98] The only ones to gain are those who receive the subsidies, which have mainly been the USSR and China.[99] US behavior in the food trade issue area was against its interests in other issue areas, in particular foreign policy. As early as the 1960s, 'friction within the NATO was the diplomatic cost associated with promoting US commercial grain exports through export subsidies.'[100] At present, the heavy-handed use of threats against the Asian NICs and Japan, to make them buy more American wheat, rice and soybeans, does not add to its standing in the region, while the EEC-US trade war remains a constant source of painful friction among allies.

But the sales to Russia in the 1980s are the ones that damaged America's credibility most. While the 1972 sales could still be explained by Destler as 'a convergence of farm and foreign policy interests,'[101] by the 1980s, under Reagan's hardline anti-communist presidency, this had definitely ceased to be the case. According to Paarlberg,

> Reagan's decision to continue to promote grain sales to the Soviet Union in 1982–1983 was more than a little disconnected from the rest of his foreign policy. It actually did significant damage to that policy, as it stirred resentment among allied governments.[102]

The extensive use of subsidies to sell wheat to the 'empire of evil' greatly hurt America's foreign policy credibility – witness Secretary of State George Schultz's comment about 'the American taxpayers making it possible for a Soviet housewife to buy American-produced food at lower prices than an American housewife.'[103] These subsidized sales also added to the resentment felt by third, befriended exporters, such as Argentina and Australia. The latter country in 1986 even questioned its continued commitment to US defence installations because of this.[104]

The fact that 'the United States and its allies must. . . . compete for the privilege of selling to our chief adversary,'[105] not only shows that US interests are not always served by its behavior, but also that domestic farm interests did effectively outweigh the foreign policy interests of the US. According to Paarlberg, this has almost constantly been the case over the last forty years.[106] This observation directly contradicts Realism's fundamental assumptions about the hierarchy between security issues and other issues and the unitary nature of the major actors in international relations.

B Effects on prices

The second important effect of the world food trade outcome is on food prices: they have become lower and increasingly unstable. Rich countries, by making adjustments through trade, rather than through changes in domestic production and consumption, amplify the natural weather-induced instability of world food markets; 'they are "exporting instability" into the world's agricultural marketplace.'[107] According to different studies, protectionist policies account for between 33% and 48% of the variability of world wheat prices.[108] The effects of the CAP are considered the most pronounced: according to a recent overview of a large number of studies, the variability of world prices is in large part due to the CAP, especially in wheat and milk products.[109]

This increased instability of world prices is at the least paradoxical, given that it is caused by policies, one of the objectives of whom is to stabilize prices.[110] This makes the 'need' for defensive action against international market instability become even stronger, which consequently increases instability, etc.[111]

But world food price instability is also exacerbated because of a second factor: speculation. At the big food markets in Chicago, New York, London, Paris and Amsterdam, food prices skyrocket and tumble on the basis of mere rumors and fears. The prospect of a small decrease in US harvests, or of a change in the relative prices between any food commodity and any other traded product, such as petroleum, or gold, can bring about in some days the doubling of the prices of basic staples such as wheat, maize, soja or corn. This is certainly a potential source of great enrichment for those who know the subtle game of playing the markets, but Third World countries are not usually among them. General worldwide oversupply of food has circumvented problems until now (apart for the 1972–74 period), but in the absence of any international mechanism of price control, there is no guarantee this will remain so.

It is often held by agricultural economists that the instability of world food prices is not to the disadvantage of LDCs: the variability in LDC food import bills is largely due to variations in their domestic production rather than in world prices.[112] This is at the least doubtful. First, as the same economists' calculations show, for some large importers, world price fluctuations have accounted for more than 30% of the variability of food import costs during 1961 – 1976.[113] Second, for the poorest food importing countries, big price shifts imply serious economic burdens – especially in the 1980s, with the financial crisis many of then face.[114] LDCs by definition have few financial resources to cushion themselves from shocks: they are thus much more vulnerable to food price variations than other countries, which puts them in a weak position vis-à-vis the international market.[115]

C The merchants of grain

A third consequence of the unregulated nature of the international food trade outcome is the central role which a handful of trading multinationals play in the day-to-day management of food trade.[116] These 5 companies – Cargill, Continental, Louis Dreyfus, Bunge and Born, and André – together are said to be engaged in around 80% of all international cereals trade[117] (see table 4.9). Even in state trading countries, private companies play an important role: the former are often dependent on the latter for transport, storage or information facilities.[118]

These companies share some special characteristics. All five 'merchants of grain,' as Morgan called them in his famous book[119] are privately owned, and hardly anything is known about them.[120] Discreet, neutral and worldwide present, these firms live on information and its interpretation.[121] None of them owns land, *i.e.* they only engage in the activity of commerce (they do own large amounts of storage capacity for that reason). Yet, since the 1970s, all of them have diversified, mainly in the agribusiness sector (drinks, meat, seeds) but also in shipping, banking and transportation. The most advanced is Cargill, the number one trader, which also became the number one agribusiness company in the world.[122]

Governments have usually created a climate favorable to them. They have been left largely free to act as they wish; at times, they have been actively helped to expand their operations, par-

Table 4.9 % share of trade done by the five largest companies, 1973–4[123]

Canada		Argentina	
wheat	20	wheat	80
barley	90	com	50
rye	90	sorghum	70
oats	90	Australia	
EEC		wheat	40
wheat	90	barley	5
com	90	sorghum	90
US		oats	20
wheat	42	Brazil	
feedgrains	59	soybeans	30
		com	30

ticularly by the US.[124] Most food aid as well as the commercial transactions made by governments – the long-term bilateral agreements for example – are carried out by these companies, who are handsomely paid for their services.[125] They even profit from the US-EEC trade war: it has been calculated that Cargill received around $ 100 million of subsidies under the EEP (the main subsidized export program of the US) between May 1985 and December 1986, while Continental and Dreyfus both pocketed $ 50 million.[126]

The international trade outcome, then, is undoubtedly very 'benign towards their interests.'[127] Yet, contrary to the theses of certain authors,[128] the power of the merchants of grain (*i.e.* their capacity to make other international actors act against their will) is quite small. This is due, according to Seevers, to their absence of control over transport, the fact that they only own a small part of total supply, and the competition among them.[129] Indeed, according to most authors, there is no collusion among the merchants of grain, but intense competition.[130] As such, 'the grain market ... remains competitive, but the distribution of gains is concentrated.'[131] Similarly, their direct effect on hunger is negligible too: they do not sell to hungry people, for the latter have no effective demand. They neither create, nor eradicate, hunger – they make money.

Hence, the five merchants of grain have a rather limited power to shape or influence the international food trade regime and process. The latter remains strongly within the power of national governments and is motivated by domestic preferences. Like any other industry, they undoubtedly can make their voices heard with governments (and at times, particularly in the Third World, they use doubtful means to do so[132]), but they are not the main actors in the international food trade outcome. States are, and are likely to remains so. These corporations' freedom of manoeuvre is the one states gave them – not the one of those who control.[133]

5 Conclusion

The international food trade process is fundamentally unregulated. It is neither organized on the basis of liberal, free market, competitive norms, nor along centrally managed, interventionist ones. It is totally ambiguous, with attempts for liberalization going hand in hand with protectionist policies. During the present round of GATT negotiations, for example, while committing themselves to a standstill and rollback of market-interfering measures, most countries increased their illiberal policies dramatically. This situation is mirrored in the ambiguous nature of the regime.

Among the preferences that shape their nature, world food security or hunger-related ones are largely absent from the food trade regime and process. The few mechanisms for world food security that materialized – food aid and compensatory financing – serve 'to stop LDCs from drowning, not to help them out of the water.'[134] The main, if not only, objective promoted by the international food trade outcome is the accommodation of the domestic production policies of the major industrialized nations. The strength of this preference in favor of the continuation of protectionist food production policies is such that it largely dominates all other objectives states usually have, be they of a foreign policy of or a general economic nature. The international food trade outcome is in a very real sense only the residual of their domestic production outcomes. The concrete form this takes is often unintended and undesired – as in the case of greater international price instability or declining farm incomes.

World food prices are far from being the indicators of real scarcity and comparative advantage among countries they are supposed to be. They are the outcome of the protectionist policies of rich countries and the speculative behavior of the players in the main markets. As a result of these factors, food prices have generally been low – but nothing guarantees they will remain so, and indeed they have suddenly exploded in the past on several occasions. On such occasions, there exist very few international mechanism to protect LDC food importers from the disastrous effects of such shocks.

Hence, some basic points should never be forgotten in any discussion of international food trade and its role in the elimination of hunger. First, in the fixing of world food prices, and in the general functioning of the international food trade issue area, considerations of food security or hunger are fully absent. Second, world food prices bear little relations to real comparative advantage; they are, moreover, artificially fluctuating. Third, it is never the poor and the hungry who import food, but at the most their governments or elites. All this should place considerable doubt on the dominant theories and declarations which treat food trade as the most efficient way to combat hunger.[135] The problem is not the 'bad motives' of food trade companies, as is often suggested by radical authors, but rather the nature and functioning of the world food markets themselves and the distribution of power and preferences that underlies it.

As for our theoretical preoccupations, the international food trade regime constitutes an interesting case of the preferences of a powerful actor being against his interest, even in the security issue area. Indeed, the original US preference for an illiberal food production and food trade regime allowed other countries to increase their production far beyond what would have happened had they adopted more liberal production and trade policies, thus eventually seriously affecting US economic market share and export revenue. This was at the detriment of the US' issue-specific power, for its relative capabilities in agriculture certainly declined as a result. Hence protracted and inconclusive trade wars with the EEC and the Asian NICs. As we saw, all this also had negative spill-overs in the international political issue area.

All this goes to question the standard precedence Realism attributes to international over domestic issues, as well as its usual hierarchy among issue areas, with security concerns at the top. These observations accord well with Keohane and Nye's analysis of complex interdependence. Indeed, together with the limited usefulness of force (trade wars are fought with butter, not with guns), the two other characteristics of complex interdependence seem also to be united in this issue area: multiple channels connecting societies (the predominance of some large trading companies) and, as said, the absence of hierarchy among issues. Yet, some of the consequences of complex interdependence which are often predicted did not take place: international organizations do not play a central role, nor does cooperation prevail. This fits with the view of a neorealist such as Gilpin, whose work notes the 'paradoxical' fact that 'governments have responded to the growth of global economic interdependence by enhancing their authority over economic activities,'[136] and whose book constitutes an interesting attempt to document how this is done: mercantilistic competition, economic regionalism and sectoral protectionism- all features which have long existed in the agriculture issue area.

Notes

1 See, among many others, Reutlinger, 1977 for the World Bank, Valdes, 1981 for the International Food Policy Research Institute; and Valdes & del Castillo, 1984, for UNCTAD. The only mentions in OECD documents of hunger in the Third World are in connection with agricultural and food trade and food aid.

2 Kissinger, for example, in his opening speech at the World Food Conference, mentions five fronts of cooperative action needed to eradicate hunger, with the first one being 'increasing the production of food exporters.' (US Department of State, 1975(b): 12) This assumption that increased food exports by the major exporters – foremost among them the US – is part of the solution to hunger constitutes an important element of the global food rhetoric: it is the object of one of the unanimously adopted resolutions at the same conference.

3 This is not to say that they are not the object of intense intra-country trade, but that subject is outside of the scope of this work.

4 1st column: Charvet, 1987: 80; second column: own calculation, based on figures from 1979/80 to 1988/89, drawn from *Food Outlook Statistical Supplement* 1989, and *Food Outlook*, May 1989. The figure for wheat in 1946–7 was 13,8%: Madaule, 1990: 33.

5 OECD, 1984(b): 14 & 16.

6 Sowell, s.d.: 12 for 1960–1970; *Food Outlook Statistical Supplement*, different years, for 1970–1990. Figures for 1989/90 are estimates; for 1990/91 previsions.

7 Data from 1900 to 1980, based on Etemad, 1984: 392 and Heidhues, 1977: 6. Data for 1983/5 and 2000: FAO, 1988b: table 3.12.

8 Calculated from FAO *Trade Yearbook* 1989: Table 38. These countries are Hong Kong, South Korea and Singapore, the five Maghreb countries and Turkey; and finally Panama and Venezuela.

9 FAO *Trade Yearbook*, 1989: Table 8.

10 Based on FAO, 1985(c) and FAO, 1992: appendix. See too World Bank, 1986(a): 77.

11 Raikes, 1988: *passim*. See too Byerlee, 1987: 319, 323 and Schatz, 1986.

12 FAO's *Food Outlook*, different years.

13 Hathaway, 1987: 10–1. A more detailed table can be found in Paarlberg, 1985: 88 and Sowell: 56–7. For 1987–1990, own calculations based on *Food Outlook*, April 1989: 23 & August 1990: 30.

14 Out of the 10 largest primary commodity exporters, 8 are OECD countries; only China and Malaysia figure on the list: GATT, 1986(a): 49. But LICs are much more dependent on primary commodities for export earnings than HICs. The so-called '2/3 rule' still holds: two thirds of the LICs are dependent for 2/3 of their income on primary commodities: Delmas, 1983: V & 182.

15 Based on OECD, 1984(b): 14 & 16. For 1989/90, own calculation, based on *Food Outlook*, August 1990: 30. Note that the third series of figures compares LDCs to developed countries, with the latter including the communist ones. That accounts for the difference as to the developed countries; the figures for the LICs, however, are comparable.

16 See chapter 2, table 3.

17 Derived from Hathaway, 1987: 10.

18 Based on Cathie, 1989: 43 and Hathaway, 1987: 46 a.f.

19 Daviron, 1990: 12.

20 *Food Outlook Statistical Supplement*, various issues. For 1990/91, forecast from *Food Outlook*, August 1990.

21 Grilli & Yang, 1988: 18–21. The two lines reflect the use of two different deflators.

22 Many leading authors concluded that the USSR was largely responsable for world food price instability in the early 1970s: for example, Paarlberg, 1979: 96. Only D.G.Johnson, 1975: 25 a.f. argues that the price effect of Soviet purchases in the 1970s has been overstated.

23 Based on Hathaway, 1987: 9 (column 3); FAO, 1988b: annex table 9 and FAO, 1992: annex table 9. *production plus beginning of year stocks.

24 Solagral, 1989: 1.

25 In 1979, at the end of the Tokyo Round of GATT negotiations, a Subsidies Code was adopted, laying down more explicit and restrictive conditions under which art. XI subsidies were allowed. Yet, the Code has had no liberalizing effect: it still legitimized illiberal practices, and did not influence the actual policy of states. Hathaway, 1987: 106 ff.; Paarlberg, 1988: 51 ff.

26 Hathaway, 1987: 108ff. and Paarlberg, 1988: 44 ff. provide excellent short descriptions.

27 Johnson, Hemmi & Lardinois, 1985: 66; OECD, 1987(3): 21 & 77.

28 'This waiver, which provides different sets of rules for the US than for other countries, has been a source of continuing resentment by other countries and is regularly used by others to argue that the US is not serious about trade liberalization in agriculture': Hathaway, 1987: 109.

29 Hathaway, 1987: 103 a.f.
30 Paarlberg, 1985: 113; italics in the original.
31 Paarlberg, 1988, p. 47.
32 Butler, 1986: 118. Hence, the Uruguay Round does not bring agriculture back to liberalism, as some have it (*i.a.* its director), but rather attemps to introduce liberal norms to it (*i.e.* make the other GATT norms apply to agriculture). This amounts to a fundamental change in the regime.
33 See different articles in De Haen, 1985.
34 Wolf, 1986: 7.
35 For example: OECD, 1984(a): 8; Rosenblatt, Mayer e.a., 1988, for the IMF; UNCTAD, 1987: 18; WFC/1985/5; WFC/1986/7; and World Bank, 1986, *passim*.
36 UN, 1975: 16. See too the 1987 declaration of the Council of Ministers, reprinted in OECD, 1990(c): 167–71
37 EEC, 1983; 1985(a): *passim*; 1985(b): 16. Similarly, European academics writing on the subject often take a CAP-justifying attitude, in contrast to their US counterparts, sticking to a more 'EEC-bashing' style. For an example of the former, see Philippe, 1986: *passim* and Madaule, 1990: 56–7.
38 As Reagan said it nicely: the US is committed to 'open trade and the reduction of trade distortions, while adhering to the principle of reciprocity' *25th Annual Report of the President of the United States on the Trade Agreements Program* 1980–81, cited in OECD, 1987(3): 20.
39 *Morgan Economic Quarterly*, 1985: 22–3; Paarlberg, 1985: 120; Butler, 1986: 115.
40 Aggarwal, 1985: 4.
41 *Ministerial Declaration on he Uruguay Round*, Punta del Este, Uruguay, September 1986.
42 GATT Focus, 41, October 1986: 2–5.
43 The Cairns group was created on Australian initiative just before the launching of the Uruguay Round; its members are Australia, New Zealand, Hungary, Brazil, Argentina, Canada, Colombia, Chile, the Philippines, Malaysia, Thailand and Uruguay.
44 Anderson & Hayami, 1986: 5, formulate the hypothesis that 'assistance is constrained not by political pressure from consumers but rather by limitations on direct budgetary support from the government.' Otsuka and Hayami, *ibid.*, then proceed to prove this hypothesis true in the case of Japan. Concerning the EEC, *Financial Times*, December 2, 1988.
45 Paarlberg, 1988: 29 ff.
46 Hathaway, 1987: 105.
47 It is usually agreed nowadays that the US was hegemonic during at least the first 15 years after the second world war; whether the US also was hegemonic in the agricultural trade issue area is less sure. Hopkins & Puchala, 1979: 27; Talbot, 1990: 132, and George, 1988: 230 hold that the US was hegemonic while Seevers, 1979: 160, writes that there was no hegemon whatsoever. As there are no precise criteria for deciding where hegemony begins and ends, the case is

not easy. It seems that the US was indeed an issue-specific hegemon, at least in food trade. Its enormous post-war surpluses, combined with its financial and logistic capacities, made it the world's prime food supplier in the immediate post-war period. But even later, during the first half of the 1960s, the US still accounted for more than half of all world cereals stocks and trade and 90% of all food aid – a proportion which is generally considered hegemonic (compare, for example, to Aggarwal, 1985: table 3).

48 This observation has *i.a.* been made by Strange, 1987: 560.

49 Hopkins & Puchala, 1979: 22.

50 Strange, 1982.

51 Kratochwil & Ruggie, 1986: 764.

52 *i.e.* in public fora, representative of the level at which they address themselves: e.g. the UN General Assembly, the US Congress, the assembled press at the World Food Day, etc.

53 In the EEC, 'there are around 2000 different tariff regimes relating to agricultural trade with more than 100 partner countries:' OECD, 1987(a): 26. The best and most up-to-date information is published by the OECD. See OECD, 1987 (a), (b), (c), (d); 1988(b), 1989, 1990(c).

54 World Bank, 1986a: 117. Note the absence of tariffs on industrial countries' imports of raw materials and tropical beverages. The category 'other beverages' refers mainly to wine and fruit juices.

55 McCalla & Schmitz, 1982: 64.

56 Hathaway, 1987: 110–11. The US has no state trading agency. See too Seevers, 1979: 160–1.

57 Paarlberg, 1985: 114–15; Paarlberg, 1988: 78.

58 Paarlberg, 1979: 85, documents that in '1970 the Community subsidy for soft wheat exports was actually larger than the world price to which it was being added.'

59 'In common with international agricultural trade in general the grain trade has been ... immune to suggestions of international management. (...) The trade remains illiberal, erratic and unmanaged:' Butler, 1986: 74–5.

60 Charvet, 1987: 242 ff.

61 UN, 1974: 16, Resolution XIX.

62 An FAO proposal in the 1950s proposed the creation of facilities for the financing and organizing of food transferts to countries in need – without, in ordinary times, actually physically transfering anything to them. Although accepted by the General Assembly, it remained without effect: Matzke, 1974: 96 a.f. During the 1970s, after the World Food Conference, and at the initiative of the U.S., negotiations were held for the establishment of a new International Wheat Agreement (I.W.A.): the previous one, dating from 1932, had no effect whatsoever on members' behavior. These were to last for 120 weeks but did not yield any agreement concerning the size of the stocks and the acquisition and release prices. The I.W.A. has been defunct ever since, apart from a London-based secretariat which publishes information all specialists know already. For more details, see Hopkins and Puchala, 1979: 33; Hathaway, 1981: 455 a.f.; Paarlberg, 1988: 78.

Parallel to the failed IWA negotiations, the FAO and the Secretariat of the WFC advocated all through the 1970s the creation of international stocks or nationally held, but internationally coordinated stocks, *i.e.* stocks held by the exporters, but whose release in times of crisis would be done according to internationally-agreed rules to the benefit of low-income food-deficit countries. This failed to materialize. Still another proposal of the WFC was to transfer part of exporters' surpluses in good years to DC stocks. There has been no follow-up on this proposal either. At present, nobody talks anymore about any kind of internationally negotiated stock mechanism – a sign of the times. See WFC/1982/5: *passim*; WFC/1984/2: 26 a.f. and Swank, 1979: *passim*.

63 Seevers, 1979: 159. Among staples, the proposal only included meat and vegetable oils. Paarlberg, 1988: 79.

64 WFC/1984/2: 31: 'it has proven very difficult to bring the main importing and exporting countries to agree on adjustments in their agricultural product production and trade policies. The exigencies of the domestic policies of the important countries, which are geared to maintain producers' revenue by regulating prices, have constituted fundamental obstacles;' see too OECD, 1984(a): 28: 'efforts at the international level aimed at stabilizing certain agricultural markets have yielded only very partial results, mainly as a result of the divergence of domestic interests.' (translations are mine)

65 World Bank, 1986a: 139.

66 The Facility, originally intended for 4 years, has been reconducted in 1985. Among the countries which made use of it until 1985, we find Malawi (3 times), Bangladesh and South Korea (each 2 times); Ghana, Jordan, Kenya and Morocco. FAO/CFS, 1986/2: 20.

67 Butler, 1987: 86–7: 'For both exporters and importers bilateral deals have become an extension of the system of national protectionism. . . . In the absence of wider agreement, bilateralism is also the central feature of trade negotiations.'

68 Lerin & Tubiana, 1986: 265.

69 Madaule, 1990: 29.

70 Lerin & Tubiana, 1986: 266. For many countries in financial problems this has become the only way to import cereals at present.

71 According to Charvet, 1987: 104, the 'increased fragmentation of the international market' has a s a result that the 'world price has lost its reference function'. Studies indicate that 'the price of cereals is at present less important than the conditions of their financing, conditions which vary from one importer or exporter to another': Lerin & Tubiana, 1986: 266.

72 Chalmin, 1986: 220–1; Chalmin, 1987: 21.

73 Chalmin, 1987: 27.

74 OECD, 1984(b): 11; Philippe, 1979: 704; Philippe, 1986: 41.

75 Philippe, 1986: 103; Bourrinet, 1982: 14; Simantov, 1982: 254; Seevers, 1979: 152; WFC/1986/7: 1.

76 Butler, 1986: 73; see also 8, 76, 81, 113.

77 Butler, 1986: 86 a.f.

78 Hopkins & Puchala, 1979: 37; Paarlberg, 1985: *passim*; Insel, 1985: 909.

79 Paarlberg, 1988: 71; Fitchett, 1987: 170.

80 Philippe, 1979: 723: 'the chain of effects of agricultural support which we have described is not always deliberately sought for: they are a side-effect of policies which have purely domestic objectives, without fully taking into account their effects on third countries.' We will come back to this later.

81 On the one hand, cereal subsitutes (soybean; different kinds of gluten) enter duty-free in the EEC market; on the other hand, as a result of the protection afforded to the cereals sector, the ordinary cereal animal feeds are artificially expensive. As a result, European cattle farmers massively turn to these substitutes, thus greatly increasing the cost of the CAP (less demand for domestically pro- duced cereals, thus more surplus; more imports from outside the community . . .) Philippe, 1986: 34. This feed-food-animals link is the key to the whole complex issue of the agricultural trade nego- tiations: we will not discuss it here, for it does not belong to our subject. For data, see RAMSES, 1986: 138. Since 1982, 'voluntary export restraints' negotiated by Thailand, Indonesia, China and Brazil limit the imports of manioc in the EEC.

82 According to many authors, the phenomenal rise in the value of the dollar, due to President Reagan's deficit spending policies, was the primary cause for the US loss of market share. See Lewis, 1986: 44: 45; Fitchett, 1987: 162; Paarlberg, 1988: chapter 1, 124 & 136. Hathaway, 1987: 14 a.f. and Ramses, 1986: 139, provide excellent figures. Similarly, as the Government Accounting Office suggests, the fact that the US managed to get back most of its share of the world market, might be due as much if not more to the decline in the value of the dollar after 1985 than to its export subsidy pro- gramme: *Financial Times*, April 19, 1989.

83 Jacquet, 1986: 304 a.f.; Lerin & Tubiana, 1986: 265 a.f.; Butler, 1986: 125; Paarlberg, 1988: 92; 126

84 Charvet, 1987: 185.

85 Chalmin, 1986 and 1987; Paarlberg, 1988: 96.

86 *International Herald Tribune*, 27/6/88; Reuter, 18/10/88.

87 See Nixon's argument that a wheat sale would be 'the major foreign policy mistake of this Administration, even more serious than foul- ing up the Bay of Pigs:' quoted by Paarlberg, 1985: 115.

88 Paarlberg, 1985: 124.

89 Paarlberg, 1979: 96.

90 Paarlberg, 1985: 125; Sanderson, 1975: 3.

91 'Purchases in 1972–1973 were the principal factor in the decline of carryover stocks in the major exporting countries . . . grain prices rose sharply.' See too Destler, 1979: 47

92 Paarlberg, 1979: 99–100.

93 Paarlberg, 1985: 131.

94 According to Alexander Haig, this decision was 'viewed almost exclusively as a domestic issue.' Quoted in Paarlberg, 1985: 134.

95 Paarlberg, 1985: 136.
96 Moscow, in line with its drive for self-sufficiency, wanted to commit itself to buy only about eight million tonnes and this, of course, at the lowest possible price. *Reuter*, 6–7–8 July, 1988.
97 See among many others, Paarlberg, 1988: 5, 9, 96; *Libération*, 9 avril 1990; *Le Monde*, 28/12/1988; *Financial Times*, 24/2/89 and 27/4/89
98 Butler, 1986: 126–7; Paarlberg, 1988: 93 & 126.
99 In 1988/89, for example, both gained $ 250 million in discounts over and above the already low world prices from the US – as well as around $ 350 mio from the EEC: *Libération*, 4 avril 1990.
100 Paarlberg, 1985: 115.
101 Destler, 1979: 47.
102 Paarlberg, 1985: 135.
103 quoted by Paarlberg, 1988: 95.
104 *International Herald Tribune*, August 9–10, 1986; *Le Monde Diplomatique*, November 1986: 25; Hathaway, 1987: 4, 17 & 84; Paarlberg, 1985: 138.
105 Insel, 1985: 892.
106 This is the main tenet of Paarlberg, 1985. The main exception was PL480 food aid at the end of the 1960s (see chapter 5) and Carter's embargo against the USSR.
107 Paarlberg, 1988: 19. See too Ritson, in De Haen, 1985: 118–21; Butler, 1986: 74: 'unpredictability is enhanced by the lack of international organisation or regulation of the trade.' This is also one of the main points made by international organizations: WFC/1984/5: 10; OECD, 1984(b): 11.
108 Schiff, 1985; World Bank, 1986: 131. See too an excellent article by Hazell, 1988.
109 Rosenblatt, Mayer, e.a., 1988: table 46: depending on the products covered, the base period and the model used, the CAP accounts for up to 50% of the variability in world prices. All through the 1979s, on the contrary, most models calculated that it was the USSR which accounted for 80% of all deviation from trend in world wheat imports (e.g. Paarlberg, 1979: 96). It is interesting to observe how 'independent' economic literature manages to calculate that the US 'enemy' of the moment is at the basis of all the mess the international food trade is in. This might not be independent of the American hegemony in the discipline, and the strong desire of many economists (and, for that matter, international relations scholars) to influence, or even make, US policy. Paarlberg is member of the Council on Foreign Relations. See too footnote 37.
110 OECD, 1984(b): 63; Johnson, 1983: 18; Viatte, 1985: 266–270; and Fitchett, 1987: 162;
111 For an exellent analysis of this 'externality' of domestic stabilization policies, and its perverse feed-back, see Philippe, 1979: *passim*; Philippe, 1986: 28–34.
112 Valdes & Konandreas, 1981; Morrow, 1981: 232; Reutlinger, 1977; Reutlinger & Knapp, 1980; Adams, 1983: 550–51.
113 Valdes & Konandreos, 1981. This is the case for countries such as

Egypt, Ghana, Guatamala, Lybia, Nigeria, Peru, the Philippines, Senegal, Sri Lanka and Zaire.

114 Valdes & Del Castillo, 1984: 4.

115 Hoffmeyer, 1982: 12; also Hopkins & Puchala, 1979: 11: 'price instability tends to skew rewards from market participation toward those participants who can best afford to speculate. Conversely, it imposes penalties on those who can least easily and least quickly adjust to fluctuation, namely lower income countries in general and lower income consumers in particular.'

116 'In the absence of international control, much of the management of the grain trade has devolved to the international grain traders – the 5 major companies:' Butler, 1986: 85.

117 They do not control domestic trade in cereals, which is managed by a large number of often small, local, companies. The first two companies are USA based, the others French, Argentinian-American, and Swiss, respectively.

118 Davies, 1986: 105; Butler, 1986: 91.

119 Morgan, 1979, is still the only serious source of facts on the topic in English; in french, there is Fottorino, 1988 and Chalmin, 1984.

120 Seevers, 1979: 164; Davies, 1986: 93.

121 Charvet, 1987: 117–18. It might be no acccident that they all do much of their trading management in Switzerland, where they have large offices: id., 116.

122 Fiottorino, 1988: 199 ff.; see also Bombal & Chalmin, 1980: 36; Davies, 1986: 101–3.

123 Based on Davies, 1986: 91 and Seevers, 1979: 91. I found no more recent figures.

124 See Paarlberg, 1985: 101; 125. Food aid has at times served as a vehicle of aid to them.

125 See too Hopkins & Puchala, 1979: 35.

126 Charvet, 1987. 116.

127 Hopkins & Pucala, 1979: 36.

128 Most notably radical authors such as Moore-Lappé and Collins, 1977; George, 1976, 1981; Dinham & Hines, 1983 and many others, but also Bradley & Carter, 1989: 113.

129 Seevers, 1979: 165.

130 Davies, 1986: 95, 108.

131 Davies, 1986: 98.

132 As documented *inter alia* by Dinham & Hines, 1983; George, 1976; Mirow, 1982: 138 a.f.; Morgan, 1980; and in a stimulating book by Tudge, 1979.

133 See the argument of Gilpin, 1971.

134 Delmas & Guillemin, 1983: 2.

135 See for example Reutlinger, 1977, for the World Bank.

136 Gilpin, 1987: 408.

FIVE

REGIMES, SURPLUS AND SELF-INTEREST: THE INTERNATIONAL POLITICS OF FOOD AID*

Food aid is the transfer of food (mainly cereals, as well as oils, dairy, and other products) on concessional terms from one country to another.[1] It comes in three forms: emergency food aid, given in cases of famine and natural or man-made catastrophes, project food aid, administered within development projects and targeted feeding programs, and program, or structural, food aid, consisting of bulk transfers of food to governments, to be used for sale on the local market.

This chapter will first present and criticize the usual interpretation of food aid giving, and, second, develop an alternative explanation, based on the existence and increasing impact of a developmental international food aid regime. Finally, some theoretical implications of this case study for the analysis of international politics will be briefly discussed. Part of the originality of this chapter resides in the use of the 'development literature,' and especially the excellent analyses produced by scholars at the Institute for Development Studies at Sussex, Great Britain,[2] the world's leading center on this subject, in supplying the information for a case study written within the discipline of international relations. Moreover, there is a deliberate attempt to draw from both francophone and multilateral primary sources, to avoid the excessive concentration on the US that characterizes most of the literature.

* This chapter benefited from comments by James Ingram, Raymond Hopkins, Robert Kates, Robert Chen, Ellen Messer and two anonymous referees. A slightly different version of the first part has been published in the September 1992 issue of *International Studies Quarterly*: Uvin, 1992.

PART 1 THE POLITICS OF FOOD AID

1 Some facts about food aid

In 1954, the US Congress passed the Agricultural Trade Development and Assistance Act, better known as PL480 or, later, 'Food for Peace.' It was the world's first law institutionalizing international food aid. Currently, the law includes three parts. Title I offers concessional sales to LDC governments for sale on their domestic market.[3] Its proceeds ('counterfunds') are to be used in ways agreed upon with the US and are increasingly directed towards agricultural development.[4] Title II donates food to NGOs based in the US and to the UN World Food Programme. These donations are intended either to provide emergency aid in the case of famines, or support targeted feeding programmes for children, mothers, the very poor etc.[5] Title III, changed in 1990,[6] concerns food donations to low-income food-deficit countries,[7] with the exclusive aim of contributing to food security, defined as 'access by all people to sufficient food and nutrition for a healthy and productive life.'[8] Until 1990, US food aid was managed by the Food Aid Subcommittee, located within the Development Coordination Committee, and composed of representatives of the Departments of State and Agriculture (USDA), the Agency for International Development (USAID), the Office of Management and Budget, the Department of Commerce and the National Security Council.[9] At present, Title I is managed by the USDA, and Title II and III by the USAID.

The EEC started donating food aid in 1968. Its aid was administered by both the Directorate-General of Development and of Agriculture; no specific law governed it until the 1980s. The decision-making structure was complex and slow, with the Council of Ministers deciding upon all food aid allocations, and the Commission implementing these decisions. Since 1985, the Council only makes an annual decision about the available budget, while the Commission has the authority over the global distribution and day-to-day management.[10] Thus, at the beginning of the year, the Commission's Directorate-General of Development (and not of Agriculture), on the basis of the budget adopted by the Council, fixes the overall quantity of food aid and the list of products concerned; throughout the year, it approves specific 'standard food aid' donations and 'emergency' food aid to specific countries.[11] All EEC member-states also have their own food aid programs, which together have the same approximate total size as the EEC program.

Other long-standing donors are Canada – donating since the beginning of the 1950s and in the early years the second donor – and Australia and Argentina, all major food exporters. Since the end of the 1960s, most other OECD countries, including those who are not food exporters, also began giving modest quantities of food aid. In the 1980s, the last new donors appeared on the scene: Spain and Greece, upon joining the EEC, as well as China, Saudi Arabia, India, Turkey and the OPEC countries have all given food aid for most years of the past decade. Besides India, though, none of them have ever donated 1% of world food aid.[12] Since the last decade, around 25% of global food aid has been channeled through the UN World Food Programme (WFP – see below), which bi-annually receives food from around 100 countries all over the world, making it the second largest single agency providing food donations after the US.

Data about the USSR are difficult to get. In 1973/74, at the height of the 'world food crisis,' the USSR loaned 2 million tons of wheat to India and 200.000 tons to Bangladesh, to be repaid in kind.[13] According to unofficial sources, the USSR also gave to different Asian countries 200.000 tons of emergency food aid in 1977/78 and 1978/79, and 400.000 tons in 1978/79;[14] under international pressure, it also donated food and some trucks to Ethiopia in 1984/85 and in 1987/88, but the precise amount is unclear;[15] the effort has continued until 1990.[16] According to the WFP's Food Aid Monitor, in 1989 and 1990 the USSR donated respectively 51,000 and 62,000 tons to Madagascar, Afghanistan and Nicaragua, but nothing in 1991; according to Arefieva, in 1990 food was also donated to Ethiopia, Mozambique and the SWAPO.[17]

There are two ways of presenting how much food aid is given: in value or in volume. The following table does both. The left side supplies us with information about the donor – how much did the food aid 'cost' its budget?[19] The right side is the more important one for the study of hunger: how much food is concretely transferred? For the recipient economy, both sides are important, pointing respectively to the approximate transfer of scarce foreign exchange and to the transfer of food products.

As can be seen from table 5.1, the size of food aid donations

Table 5.1 Food aid by major donors, in million dollars and in thousand tons[18]

	Million dollars				Thousand tons, grain equivalent				
	1971	1975	1980	1985	1970/71	1974/75	1980/81	1985/86	1989/90
Australia	12	61	64	51	226	340	370	345	305
Austria	1	1	3	8	–	–	32	30	18
Canada	88	263	165	263	1,608	594	600	1,216	930
Finland	0	8	4	12	14	24	29	5	27
EEC	78	412	716	827	1,287	1,413	1,291	1,562	3,293
Japan	134	15	261	53	729	182	914	374	430
Norway	4	8	22	27	14	–	40	16	31
Sweden	6	75	47	39	54	316	94	69	82
Switzerl.	4	12	28	29	32	29	15	22	35
USA	805	126	130	1,859	8,321	4,712	5,212	6,675	6,147
Total DAC	1,131	2,129	2,618	3,151	12,285	7,610	8,525	10,314	11,390

varied significantly among donors and between different years, both in volume and in value; the US by far surpasses the other donors in both categories, but its predominance is declining (see too table 5.2).

Table 5.2 Major donors' % share of food aid, by value[20]

	USA	Canada	EEC + member countries
1965	94	4	1
1970	71	8	11
1975	61	12	19
1980	50	6	27
1985	59	8	20
1990	54	8	29

Yet, these differences among donors are less important than they look at first sight. Actually, as table 5.3 shows, there is a remarkable similarity of outcomes if one takes account of what can be labelled 'relative effort.' Indeed, as a proportion of cereal production or of cereal stocks ('surpluses'), the US gives no more food aid than the EEC, Japan, Australia, Canada or even Sweden. The reason the US donates half of global food aid is that it is a huge country and food producer. Hence, in studying the global food aid regime, its particular preferences should not be over-stated. For that reason this article will treat the US as only one among the two dozen or so donors – albeit the most important one.

Table 5.3 'Relative effort' of donors[21]

	Food aid as a % of cereal production		Food aid as a % of cereal stocks	
	1985	1990	1985	1990
U.S.	2.1	2.1	7.6	10.0
EEC	1.5	2.0	8.5	10.4
Canada	1.7	1.9	7.0	8.6
Australia	1.8	1.4	5.3	9.2
Japan	1.8	3.0	6.5	8.4
Sweden	1.6	1.5	n.a.	n.a.

2 The classical interpretation of food aid

The food aid outcome is usually explained as a combination of economic and political self-interest, give or take some humanitarian impulses.[22] It is generally considered to be a perfect case of the self-interested behavior Realists expect states to display.[23] A simplified but conventional account of the usual analysis broadly goes as follows.

Economic self-interest is considered by most authors to be the primary objective of food aid. Food aid is considered to satisfy the economic interests of the donor in two general ways. On the one hand, there is the surplus disposal function: food aid reduces storage costs and increases market prices by removing stocks which have a depressing effect. On the other hand, food aid is considered to have positive long-term effects for commercial food exports, bringing about taste changes in favor of the donated food and opening up potential markets.[24] This is its market creating function. The effectiveness of food aid in achieving both these objectives is regularly stressed by policy-makers.[25] Hence, food aid is considered to be a favorite of the agricultural producers' lobbies and the Ministries of Agriculture of the donor states.

Political self-interest is considered to be the second basic preference behind food aid. Food aid serves both as carrot and stick in inducing recipient countries to comply with the foreign policy objectives of the donor. Evidence seems easy to come by. At the end of the 1960s, in the midst of the Cold War, the largest share of US food aid went to Vietnam, South Korea, Cambodia and Taiwan, leading many critics to label PL480 'Food for War' rather than 'Food for Peace'.[26] The mid-seventies, characterized by high oil prices and North-South tension, saw policy-makers in the US become very vocal about 'food power.'[27] And today, the massive amounts of US food aid accorded to Egypt and Central America are clearly motivated by strategic policy considerations. The Foreign Ministries of donor countries are thus supposed to be the second major initiators of food aid.

Last and least, there is a third preference, **humanitarian** in nature. This one is considered secondary, however, just as those who hold it are not the most powerful.[28] Mention is often made of the general public support for food aid,[29] mainly arising from the appeal of emergency food aid. At the policy-making level, supporters include the development cooperation agencies within governments as well as a large variety of non-governmental organizations (CARE, CRS, Caritas, Euronaid) that act as lobby groups.[30]

In short, almost all international relations scholars and development specialists explain food aid up to the present by reference to a most 'Realist' coalition of economic and foreign policy interests in the donor country. Humanitarian or developmental preferences play a background role, creating conditions which render food aid 'popular.' A mechanical conception of self-interest is the main feature of this interpretation; it can be found in two fundamental assumptions. One, on the input side, is that non-self-interested preferences are unimportant for explaining the food aid process; the second, on the output side, is that food aid does satisfy the self-interested preferences that underlie it. At first glance, these assumptions seem to be well supported, by political declarations as much as by the 'hard facts.'

3 A critique of the classical interpretation

But closer analysis reveals both assumptions to be incomplete, if not counterfactual. On the input side, a significant part of food aid is not motivated by self-interested preferences, especially if countries other than the US are included in the analysis. On the output side, most food aid does not serve the economic or political interests of the donors in any significant way. In a dynamic analysis, where the feedback between output and input is of central importance, this observation constitutes a problem which must be addressed.

Food aid fulfills no surplus-disposal function. Quantities donated are too small – for no country does food aid constitute more than between 5 and 10% of its stocks or exports[31] – and the cost of giving too high to have any significant positive effect on exporters' stocks or budgets. The surplus disposal function held true in the first 15 years of massive US food aid, when it accounted for up to 25% of its agricultural exports[32] (and much more for selected commodities), or in the first years of EEC food aid, when it donated mainly dairy and dairy-related products, of which it had big surpluses; but it is no longer applicable.

Moreover, an increasing share of food aid (at present above 10%[33]) is given in the form of triangular aid, whereby the donor buys food in neighboring developing countries, or in different regions of the same country, and transports it to the recipient.[34] Most cases of triangular aid are found in Southern Africa and the Sahel, where the need for such aid is highest.[35] This practice is very costly to donors, not only because the food donated is bought in third countries and not drawn from domestic surpluses, but also because of the heavy logistical costs involved in transporting it from one developing country to another.[36] Among similar lines, the EEC started in the 1980s with so-called 'alternative operations', by which in the event of an exceptionally good harvest the Community accords recipients under the standard programme the financial counterpart of the food aid they would have normally received. Beneficiaries of this scheme include Burkina Faso, Chad (two times), Haiti, India, Mali (three times), Niger, Senegal, Tanzania and Zambia.[37] For the donors such types of food aid really constitute a form of financial aid: they draw from their treasuries, not from their storehouses.

As for the market-creating function of food aid, the large commercial food imports of many of the so-called success stories of early food aid – Japan, West Germany, Taiwan, South Korea and Portugal – are the result of the sharp rise in their income, not of PL480 aid.[38] Among the main recipients of US food aid from 1964 to 1980[39] we find India, Vietnam, Yugoslavia, Brazil, Spain and Poland: none of them is a significant importer of US cereals now; on the contrary, some of them have even become competitors on the international food market. Only for a handful of countries such as the Philippines, Morocco, Pakistan and Egypt a direct relation between food aid and commercial food import dependence from the US can be supposed (but there might be other, political, reasons too). Most present recipients of food aid, such as sub-Saharan Africa, which receives between 25 and 40% of all food aid, cannot be expected to become significant commercial importers in the foreseeable future.[40] Hence, food aid is extremely limited as a means of conquering new markets. It is probably no accident that references to the market-creating capacities of food aid usually come from the donor agencies or policy-makers who have to pass the aid budget, suggesting that political opportunism rather than factual accuracy is the main objective of these declarations.[41]

Food aid has been used to promote American trade and investment abroad. The Cooley amendment, in force from 1957 to

1972, allowed the use of counterfunds to promote US private investments in recipient countries.[42] Dan Morgan describes in detail the cooperation between American policy-makers and private companies to use food aid for the advantage of the latter.[43] This suggests that the political and economic power of big business is large and that powerful private interests often manage to bend things to their advantage – not that all food aid is given for the economic self-interest of the donor.[44] As political scientists know, *any* policy, whatever its 'raison d'être' is likely to be lobbied by interest groups so as to bend it to their perceived interests.[45] Moreover, the practice of using food aid to create commercial markets has predominantly been documented for the US, and to a lesser extent for France;[46] for other donors, there is little such information.

As to political self-interest, for most donors, including some important ones, such as Canada, Australia, the EEC and most of its member states, and the Nordic countries, there is little proof that it underlies their giving.[47] Edward Clay, one of the world's foremost specialist on food aid, notes:

> paradoxically ... and contrary to commonly held views, a number of important donors are not channeling food aid in relation to narrow bilateral perceptions of geo-political advantage.[48]

To be sure, donors tend to give food aid to significant, *i.e.* politically befriended, countries, or, at least, they donate more to those with whom they are befriended than to the others, who might be as deserving. Thus the US gives much more generously to its African and Asian friends than to others, while the EEC and France donate at least a bit to all ACP countries, so as to avoid that any one of them feels neglected.[49] Given a larger demand for, than supply of, food aid, this may be expected in a world of independent states where no compulsory redistribution mechanism exists.[50] That, however, still does not allow us to explain the reality of food aid only by political self-interest: governments could have chosen to give no food aid at all, or only to a handful of really important client states!

Moreover, food aid, like development aid in general is most inefficient as a means to attain specific foreign policy objectives.[51] As for the famous recipients of the 1970s, food aid did not stop Vietnam and Cambodia from falling into the wrong camp;

present relations with South Korea, Taiwan or Israel are quite good, but all political scientists would agree that this is not caused by the food aid those countries received. For Egypt, the case *par excellence* at present, detailed research shows just how little effect aid, and particularly food aid, has had on its behavior and the capacity of the foreign policy makers to influence it.[52] Paarlberg, after a comprehensive analysis, concludes that food aid consistently had more foreign policy drawbacks than advantages.[53] Moreover, as the number of donors is growing, the scope for exerting leverage through food aid is becoming even smaller:[54] recipient countries, depending on their skill and on the resources at their disposal, can play one donor against the other.

The danger of the use of emergency food aid for the political objectives of the donor is often discussed. This case seems strong, for the resource donated is very scarce, and its impact should thus be very large. Bangladesh in 1974 is the case that is always referred to. Despite obvious famine, the US delayed food aid shipments in order to force Bangladesh to end its export of jute to Cuba.[55] But this seems to be the only recent case of the abuse of emergency food aid by donors. This suggests the existence of a constraint on its use, which we hold to be a generally shared international norm against famine and acute starvation.[56] This norm causes donors to give emergency food aid and at the same time constrains them from using it for their political self-interest.[57]

To conclude this brief discussion: large amounts of food aid are given to a broad variety of countries without any apparent self-interested motivation; moreover, the effects of food aid are most inefficient in furthering the political and economic self-interested preferences which are supposed to underlay it. All of this casts serious doubts on the validity of the classical interpretation. A different explanation, which can account for these contradictions, is needed.

Such analysis is now presented, centering on the operational existence of a non-self-interested regime. It divides into two propositions: first, there exists a food aid regime, which is predominantly non-self-interested in nature; and, second, this regime matters, *i.e.* it influences the international process to a significant extent. Both of these propositions will be presented in the next sections.

4 *The changing food aid regime*

With the US supplying 90% of global food aid, the early international food aid regime can be said to have been the one set down in PL480, the US law governing its food aid program. This law reflected the constellation of preferences favoring food aid in the US at the time. These preferences were of a commercial and a foreign policy nature.

After the second World War, as a result of high domestic prices guaranteed to US cereal producers, government-owned surplus stocks of wheat and corn had grown dramatically. If the US wanted to continue its protectionist policies, it needed a vehicle for disposing of such surpluses. At the same time, the success of the Marshall Plan had convinced the foreign policy establishment of the importance of aid. All this led to a 'marriage of convenience' between food surpluses and foreign policy considerations: the creation in 1954 of the Agricultural Trade Development and Assistance Act, better known as PL480.[58] Its stated objectives are:

> to expand international trade; to develop and expand markets for US agricultural commodities; to combat hunger and malnutrition and to encourage economic development in the developing countries (. . .); and to promote in other ways the foreign policy of the US.[59]

This regime was still dominant at the time of the first, modest engagements of European states in the field of food aid in the 1960s. It was characterized by two basic norms, and they were fully in accordance with the classical Realist interpretation.

First, food aid was to reflect only the changing political and economic goals of the donor:[60] as such it was to be given totally bilaterally, to politically befriended nations, on an ad-hoc, annual basis. There were no international legal or practical constraints on its use. Second, food aid was to be additional to the commercial food flows of any given country – this in order to prevent it from displacing the commercial exports of US farmers. The latter preoccupation became formalized at the international level by the establishment by the FAO in 1954 of the Committee on Surplus Disposal (CSD), significantly located in Washington D.C. The CSD developed a procedure of consultation and rules of donation: food aid should be additional to the yearly set 'Usual

Marketing Requirements' (UMRs), which denote the minimum commercial food import volume any potential recipient has to satisfy before receiving food aid.[61]

But the international food aid regime has changed significantly since those early days. It has become developmental in nature: food aid is now seen as an important element in a strategy of world food security,[62] while the smaller but most visible part – emergency aid – strengthened its humanitarian character.[63] This coincided with an increase in multilateralization. This regime change was triggered by an acute global awareness of the problems of hunger and malnutrition in the world following the 'world food crisis' of 1972–1974, and the World Food Conference – both of which represented, in the words of Clay and Singer 'a watershed in the history of food aid.'[64] In the US, still the largest actor in the issue area, other factors also played a role, such as the decline of the Cold War, the backlash against 'dirty politics' following the Vietnam War and the export boom of agriculture, rendering food aid superfluous as an instrument of export promotion.

Resolution XVIII, appropriately called 'An Improved Policy for Food Aid' and unanimously adopted at the World Food Conference, 'codified' the emerging developmental nature of the international food aid regime.[65] According to Minear, this resolution 'articulated a new international consensus on key policy issues such as the need for continuity of supply, forward planning, higher commodity levels and larger grant and multilateral shares of total food aid levels'[66] – all notions that conflict with the original norms of politically useful flexibility, surplus disposal and additionality to commercial flows. During the following decade, donor countries repeatedly restated their commitments to these objectives in the Committee on Food Aid Policies and Programmes.[67]

The change in the international regime was mirrored in changing national food aid legislation, starting with the US.[68] In 1975, the US Congress decided that three fourths of all food aid should go to the poorest countries[69] and the possibility of using counterfunds for military purposes was abolished. In 1977, Title III 'Food For Development' was added to PL480; in 1979, Congress passed the Bellmon amendment requiring the Secretary of Agriculture to provide assurance that food aid would not be a disincentive to domestic marketing or production in recipient countries – a requirement which has been made more stringent in the 1980s.[70] Finally, US Title I food aid is prohibited from going to countries that systematically violate human rights.[71] During the Reagan presidency, a 4 million tons Food Security Wheat Reserve has been established, so as to guarantee the availability of wheat for humanitarian food needs under the PL480 program, 'without regard to the domestic supply situation.'[72] As Clay comments: 'these modifications of PL 480 have been designed to give a developmental and humanitarian focus to the US food aid programmes.'[73]

The EEC legislated that its food aid be exclusively in the form of grants and that it should go primarily to the poorest countries.[74] In 1981, it adopted the 'food strategy' approach, in which food aid is used to support integrated self-sufficiency programmes in recipient countries.[75] This involves a commitment to coordination of EEC food aid with the development policies of the recipient, as well as pluri-annual planning[76] – features which were inconceivable only one decade ago.

All this denotes the integration between the overall development regime and the food aid regime.[77] Since the middle of the 1980s, much has been said about linking food aid to structural adjustment. Hans Singer, probably the world's foremost authority on food aid, has written on it, as have other experts,[78] and his thoughts have been taken over by the WFP and even the World Bank, traditionally lukewarm about food aid.[79] Over the years, the US has attempted to impose structural adjustment-type agricultural policy changes on food receiving countries such as Bangladesh, Ethiopia and Egypt;[80] the same aim underlies such showcase initiatives as the 1987 Presidential Initiative to End Hunger in Africa or the 1985 Food for Progress clauses.[81] At the same time, the EEC has developed and implemented its so-called 'food strategies', starting with four African countries (Mali, Rwanda, Tanzania and Zambia), which basically consists of agricultural production and trade liberalization along World Bank lines.[82] Whatever one's opinion is about structural adjustment and its impact, the increased integration between it and food aid goes to show the developmental nature of the latter.

In 1991, on French initiative, a longstanding international discussion in the CILSS[83] led to the adoption of a Code of Good Conduct for food aid, codifying its use as an instrument of development and food security.[84]

141

The extent of multilateral institutionalization has increased significantly in the last two decades. In 1964, the World Food Programme (WFP) was created, a UN organization responsible for project and food emergency aid, and fed by voluntary contributions. It grew rapidly during the 1970s and now disburses approximately 25% of all food aid donated. It is the second largest source of development assistance within the United Nations system, after the World Bank.

In 1967, the major cereals trading nations signed a Food Aid Convention.[85] The FAC constituted an attempt by the US to persuade other rich countries to contribute more and on a regular basis, *i.e.* to share the burden of food aid;[86] it signalled the beginning of EEC engagement in food aid. Donor countries committed themselves to providing 4.5 million tons of food aid. 'The FAC was a milestone in international food aid, since for the first time, it represented an assessed contribution, to be honored by the signatories.'[87] A new Convention was signed in 1971 and extended in 1974 and 1979. In 1981, 22 donors increased their minimum engagements to 7.6 million tons; this was extended in 1986 and again in 1991. Among the signatories to the FAC we find countries which are not surplus food producers. The FAC, if respected, thus weakens the link between world food aid and the fluctuations in the surpluses of donor countries, especially the US.[88]

In 1976, an International Emergency Food Reserve (IEFR) was established, under the control of the CFA, with a target pledge of 500,000 tons. Its goal was to make sure there would always be multilateral food aid available for rapid responses to emergencies; it is managed on a day-by-day basis by the WFP.

To conclude this section: the food aid regime has undergone a significant evolution over the last two decades, primarily triggered off by the general perception of a 'world food crisis' in the early 1970s, but also by ideological changes within the major donating country. Food aid donation is increasingly governed by multilateral institutions, norms and procedures. The objectives the regime now promotes changed from economic and foreign policy interests to developmental and some humanitarian preferences. The commitments agreed upon in Resolution XVIII at the World Food Conference have to an increasing extent been incorporated in the food aid legislation of the donors. A developmental international food aid regime has come into being, but has the process followed suit? That is the question that will be dealt with next.

5 The outcome: 1975–1990

In this section, it is demonstrated that the largest share of food aid follows the above described international regime. Specifically, it argues that food aid donation is increasingly independent of donor surpluses; that the UMR's are no longer applied; that triangular food aid and other innovative mechanisms which are considered superior to ordinary food aid from a development perspective are on the rise; that food donation is increasingly multilateral; that the international commitments donor countries made through the FAC and IEFR are almost always met, even in years of bad harvests and declining stocks; that by far the largest share of food aid goes to the Low Income Food Deficit Countries, who are not foreseeable commercial food importers; and that emergency aid is on the increase.

As can be seen in table 5.4, the extent to which variations in food aid follow variations in carryover stocks or prices declined significantly (but still exists) for the major donors; for the majority of small donors this link is absent.[89] After the 'world food crisis,' while stocks in the OECD countries grew at an impressive speed, food aid quantities donated remained stable at around 9–10 million tons, until the 1984/85 famine years, when they jumped to around 12 million tons, mainly as a result of the increase in emergency aid. The EEC held stable its donations of dairy aid during the 1980s, although its stocks grew dramatically during the same period;[90] at the same time, it began donating vegetal oils, although it has no surpluses of that product.[91] Moreover, many donor states do not donate surplus food for the simple reason that they do not have them: Germany, Japan, Italy, Sweden, Switzerland, the UK or Saudi Arabia and others have to buy at least part of their food aid in other countries or simply donate money to the WFP, which will buy the food itself.[92] Finally, triangular food aid, or 'alternative operations' such as those of the EEC, now accounting for more than 10% of all food aid, are totally unlinked to stocks in donor countries.

Surpluses (or, more positively, availability), then, appear to be mainly influential in accounting for the *commodity composition* of food aid of the large donors, *i.e.* the mix of different cereals and

143

non-cereal products.[93] That explains why the EEC is the world's largest dairy aid donor and the US and Canada give mainly cereals; why Denmark and the Netherlands like to donate some meat products, and Switzerland . . . cheese! But that is nothing but logical: one has to have something in order to give it away; the surprising facts are that several countries actually give food aid without having surpluses, and that surplus-countries do not give more of it.

Table 5.4 Cereal food aid, cereal stocks in developed countries and world wheat prices[94]

	Total food aid mio tons	DC stocks mio tons	Wheat prices current US $		Total food aid mio tons	DC stocks mio tons	Wheat prices current US $
1977/78	9.2	156	113	1984/85	12.5	200	148
1978/79	9.4	188	139	1985/86	11.0	289	128
1979/80	8.9	171	170	1986/87	12.6	320	109
1980/81	8.9	148	179	1987/88	13.5	275	122
1981/82	9.1	188	169	1988/89	10.2	183	166
1982/83	9.2	235	158	1989/90	11.4	167	169
1983/84	9.8	157	153	1990/91	11.4	190	118

The UMRs – the rules that serve to guarantee that food aid is additional to commercial exports – are no longer applied.[95] According to Singer, 'the CSD continues its regular meetings in Washington even though nobody takes it very seriously.'[96] As a result, much food aid displaces commercial imports.[97] The fact that food aid is increasingly governed exclusively by the development agencies of the donors illustrates the same evolution. Evidently, the donors still have the power to enforce UMRs if they so desire: the world remains a Realist one, lacking an authority to force powerful actors to be 'morally good.' But this rather confirms the point: if even in such a situation donors do not act in their myopic self-interest, there must be a regime constraining them.

As Clay and Benson point out, by 1987/88, triangular food aid, local purchases and similar innovative practices, accounted for 1.4 to 1.5 million ton – around 12% of global food aid, which becomes 20 to 25% if the US, which gives only 0.2% of its assistance in these forms, is left out[98] – from nothing a decade ago.

More specifically, such triangular operations represented the quasi totality of the food donations of donors such as the Netherlands, Switzerland, Denmark, Norway and especially Japan, which has a policy to buy all the rice it gives in developing countries (Pakistan, Burma, Thailand). Also the EEC, which has large food surpluses of all kinds, often engages in triangular transactions.[99] The justification for this is developmental.

Table 5.5 Multilateral institutionalization of food aid[100]

	Multilateral food aid as % of total	% IEFR fulfilment	% FAC fulfilment
1965	1.00		
1969	7.60		
1972	12.90		
1976	15.20	16	
1980	24.70	85	
1981	21.40	126	105
1982	24.70	102	109
1983	24.30	101	121
1984	23.10	124	138
1985	22.00	149	157
1986	23.30	97	156
1987	27.10	133	169
1988	23.70	93	166
1989	28.30	83	150

Table 5.5 demonstrates that the share of food aid that passes through multilateral channels has increased from around 15% in 1975 to 25% ten years later. Through the FAC the donors legally tied themselves to supply certain amounts of aid, at any price. The present and substantial minimum commitment of 7.6 million tons has always been fulfilled, even in 1988–90 (two years of bad harvest and increased prices).[101] Clay cites the performance of Australia, which in 1983, in order to fulfill its FAC commitments in a year of bad harvest, bought the grain needed on the world market.[102] Also the IEFR targets have quite consistently been fulfilled since 1980. All this contrasts favorably with financial aid, where similar targets – for example the 0.7% of GDP aid target – have never been met by most donors.[103]

Table 6 indicates that, in accordance with the resolutions of the CFA, around 85% of food aid at present goes to the so-called Low Income Food-Deficit Countries. Moreover, more and more of this goes to sub-Saharan Africa, where needs are high and donors' economic interests comparatively low. This has always been the case for other donors' food aid allocations, but also is becoming increasingly true for the US.[104]

Table 5.6 Cereal food aid to LIFDCs, to sub-Saharan Africa and for emergencies, as a percentage of total[105]

	LIFDC	SSA	Emergency		LIFDC	SSA	Emergency
1975	82.14	n.a.	n.a	1983	91.03	25	12
1976	78.26	n.a.	n.a.	1984	85.18	31	15
1977	79.90	n.a.	n.a.	1985	84.97	40	25
1978	78.11	n.a.	n.a.	1986	84.38	38	30
1979	78.89	n.a.	10	1987	82.67	26	21
1980	81.21	15	10	1988	80.00	28	19
1981	79.20	21	14	1989	84.70	27	
1982	80.19	24	21				

This does not imply, though, that food aid is allocated exclusively according to nutritional need, or, in Sen's terms, that it has become an international transfer-based entitlement mechanism. First, the total quantity donated is too small to help all those who are in need;[106] second, its allocation is not proportional to nutritional need. Some countries, foremost among them Egypt, Pakistan and the Philippines, receive food aid far above their nutritional needs, while others, such as Bangladesh, India and China are in the inverse position.[107] As to the first point, however, it should be pointed out that the stagnation of total food aid quantities during the last fifteen years (in a period of increasing surpluses) is to a large extent due to the fact that most actors in the 'development community' do not favor food aid. As we will see in part two of this chapter, food aid is the subject of virulent criticism, both from scientists and from aid practitioners, especially in Europe and Australia. This unpopularity of food aid is based on its supposed pernicious long-term effects on recipient countries' capacity to feed themselves. As such, the stagnation in food aid donations, surpluses notwithstanding, can be considered a demonstration of the extent to which it is governed by a developmental regime.

Finally, commercial and political calculations are absent from emergency food aid (10–25% of the total), which closely follows the occurrence of famine, making it probably the only inter-

national transfer-based entitlement mechanism. That the threat ⌉
of famine is a powerful motive for food aid donation has been
repeatedly proven in recent years, with food aid from all donors
flowing to the Sahel countries during the 1984–86 drought, to
China after typhoons hit its Northern provinces in 1988, to the
USSR after the Armenian earthquake of 1989, to Iran after an
earthquake in 1990, to Vietnam to help refugees, to Bangladesh
and Sudan after floods, and to the Marxist regimes of Mozambique, Angola and Ethiopia where famine threatened mainly as
a result of war.[108] The most interesting case is probably the one
of the US donating large quantities of food aid to Ethiopia,
although the latter was governed by a Communist government,
and the US supported the separatist rebels fighting that
government.

According to Jack Shepherd, before October 1984, when the
BBC showed images of massive starvation in the Ethiopian
countryside, the Reagan administration actually refused to send
food to government-controlled areas, notwithstanding clear
knowledge of famine conditions there, while sending large
amounts of food to rebel-controlled areas in Tigray and Eritrea.[109]
This cynical policy was made possible because of the absence of
public knowledge about the famine in Ethiopia, and because
of the visceral anti-communism of the Reagan administration.
Yet, it changed dramatically after the public outcry that followed
the October 1984 television images: US food aid multiplied by
thirty in some months, and the country became the largest single
emergency food aid donor to Ethiopia.[110]

During the immediate aftermath of this famine, the US put in
place a Famine Early Warning System (FEWS) which publishes
monthly reports on eight African countries, including Ethiopia
and Mozambique, so as to avoid famine through timely and
targeted strategies of food delivery.[111] When famine conditions
have broken out again from 1987 onwards, the US was and still
is consistently amongst the first and biggest donors to Ethiopia.

One could speculate as to whether American emergency food
aid to Ethiopia (and to other 'unfriendly' nations such as Mozambique in 1984/85 or Iran in 1990) presents a problem for the
Realist approach to international political economy. The US
seems to act in this case against its myopic self-interest, for in
the amoral system of power politics, Realism posits that surely
massive starvation in an enemy country would be most welcome.

The anomaly is not removed by suggesting that food aid is motivated solely by an American desire to enhance its international standing. Even if this were true (which it is not, for the pressure of the American public is at least as important),[112] it presupposes that states care about such things as having a good reputation. What constitutes a 'good' reputation or a 'bad' one must be defined somehow – it does not blow in the wind. This points to the operational existence of an international regime, in this case one that puts a high premium on avoiding starvation.[113]

This anti-starvation regime, which has long historical origins in all cultures and religions,[114] it is quite universally shared, *i.e.* in our terms, it is a rare example of a consensual norm. Its strength can be gauged from the fact that emergency aid, unlike project or program food aid, is not linked to policy conditions of any kind, or that, when governments cut their development assistance to countries, they always exempt emergency aid. The latter has been the case recently for Myanmar, Sudan, Somalia, Liberia and Ethiopia among others.[115]

Approximately one quarter to forty percent of all food aid can be said to be donated only for the reasons the traditional interpretation would expect: manifestly self-interested ones. A small part of this is made up of the use of food aid as an instrument of export promotion. This seems to be the best explanation for the EEC food aid to Egypt – 14% of the member states', and 24% of Community grain aid[116] – and to the Mediterranean countries in general.[117] This constitutes part of the trade war that has erupted in the 1980s between the US and the EEC in the Mediterranean.[118] Yet, such use is much lower than in the 1950s–1960s, when it was indeed one of the major objectives of US food aid; for most donors other than the US, food aid fulfills no such function.[119] The present trade war is mainly fought with other weapons, ranging from the common discounting of food prices via various subsidies to the granting of other products by exporters to importing countries. To quote Clay again:

> most donors are no longer using food aid as a marginal instrument for managing their surpluses of wheat and coarse grain. Other forms of concessional export credits, managed by agriculture and exporting ministries and agencies, now play this role of surplus management. Developmental

priorities now have a much greater weight in the decision-making process concerning food aid allocations.[120]

Another part of food aid can be explained only by political considerations. The disproportionate amount of food aid given to Egypt by the US constitutes the main example;[121] the cut-off of food aid to Nicaragua after the fall of Somoza and the subsequent dramatic rise in donations to neighboring countries is another.[122] Although it is true that all these recipients were LIFDCs and can make good use of food aid, it is equally obvious that the aid they received was motivated by political rather than developmental considerations.

Finally, we should note what can be labelled 'apparent multilateralism;'[123] whereby formally multilateral food aid is manipulated in such as way as to serve bilateral objectives. This can be done in different ways. One is the 'multibi' option, whereby multilateral donations are earmarked by the donors to specific uses in specific countries: for example, in 1985, 150,000 of the 250,00 tons of food aid donated by the US to the IEFR were earmarked to Afghan refugees.[124] The other option derives from the fact that food aid donations to the WFP and the IEFR are not actually physically donated to them but remain in donor countries' storehouses; whenever the Director-General of the WFP needs them, he has to contact the donors and ask them to liberate the food. Certain donors, and especially the US, use this to delay or block food aid for particular countries or projects – even if they have formally approved these uses of food aid in the CFA, the governing council of the WFP! All this evidently decreases the real multilateral nature of WFP food aid. On the other hand, all through the 1980s, the WFP has given food aid to countries such as Cuba, Vietnam, Nicaragua and Iran, against explicit US desires;[125] for the first two countries, the WFP was respectively the largest and second largest donor of any kind of development assistance.

6 Conclusion and implications for the study of international relations

Our analysis has discerned three basic factors that are needed to understand the actual food aid outcome. The first is **availability**: one cannot give away what one does not have. For most large donors, this primarily takes the convenient form of drawing on surpluses; for the other donors, availability is mainly obtained by purchases on the market. Yet, even for the large exporters, who hold large surpluses, food aid represents only an insignificant share of their stocks or commercial exports; moreover, many of the countries receiving food aid are in no position to become commercial importers anytime soon. Hence surplus is a necessary, but not sufficient condition of much, but not all, food aid.

The second factor is the existence of a **regime** that causes all rich states, and even some others, to give food aid. This accounts for 60% or more of total food aid donations. It goes to explain the remarkable similarity of food donation effort between all OECD countries, small and big ones alike (see table 5.3). The objectives promoted by this regime are mainly developmental in nature, with a strong humanitarian component; it is increasingly characterized by commitments to international organizations. Yet, also the regime is a necessary, but not sufficient, condition for the explanation of present food aid practice. Part of food aid is still given for economically or politically self-interested purposes, particularly by the US; moreover, even the food aid given for developmental preferences is often influenced by the specific economic or political preferences of powerful lobby groups in the donor countries. Hence, the third factor needed to explain the contemporary food aid outcome is **self-interest**: not some generalized national self-interest, but rather the changing perceptions of their interests by different groups, lobbying, with varying degrees of success, aid administrators and policymakers.

The 'traditional' interpretation cannot account for more than half of all food aid donations. The divergence between the dominant explanation and the contemporary food aid outcome can partially be explained by the fact that, until now, most of the literature within the classical interpretation is based solely on the case of the US before 1975:[26] what happened afterwards, as well as the behavior of other countries (whose food aid giving has never been as linked to economic and political interests), has not been analyzed by political economy scholars. Another part of the problem stems from the selective blindness of radical and Realist authors alike for those facts that contradict their usual 'self-interest is the motor of all state behavior' approach.

The relative importance of these three factors – availability, self-interest and regimes – has changed over time, with a multilateral developmental regime becoming more important after the World Food Conference at the expense of bilateral self-interest and, to a lesser extent, surplus.[127] The central issue for our theoretical concerns is the relationship between the former two factors: regime and self-interest. We have found three ways in which regimes play a role in an anarchic international system where self-interest constitutes the central force.

The first has to do with the fact that policymakers continue to use food aid for economically and politically self-interested preferences, even though it is most doubtful that food aid is useful in bringing about the desired results. Two explanations are possible. One is that policy-makers suffer from chronic misperception; the other is that they do not, but for some reason cannot change their behavior. The first explanation asserts that the groups supporting food aid believe that it serves their interests while it actually does not. This explanation is compatible with Realism and the hypothesis of (bounded) rationality that underlies it. Yet, one cannot stop there. The question immediately arises: 'why do policy-makers not perceive that food aid is a useless tool in achieving their self-interested goals?' A plausible answer to that question is: 'because a regime stops them from doing so.' This answer can be tested: every time the 'errors' in perception go in the direction of the nature of the regime, it can be speculated that the regime is causally linked to the misperception. The second explanation was that politicians give food aid for different reasons; the self-interested preferences come only later into the picture, as policy-makers want to or are lobbied to use the food aid, which is given anyway, for some specific interest. This implies that food aid is not motivated by the interests it is often (ab)used for. Whatever the motive, when food aid is given, pressures will exist to ship it in American vessels, to give it to befriended countries, to use the counterfunds to promote American business, etc. Aid is very prone to such pressures, not only because of the absence of a strong domestic constituency for it but also because aid administrators often share the values and ideology of those lobbying them.[128]

This brings us to the next mechanism, which deals with the definition of interest. What constitutes one's interest or one's good reputation in a certain issue area is not given nor always evident: it must be defined somehow. The choice that politicians end up making, out of a wide range of possible options – including, for example, the cheapest option of giving no food aid – is influenced by the norms and principles that apply to the issue area. This argument helps explain why so many states engage in food aid, and why the US gives emergency food aid to Ethiopia.[129]

It can be argued that, even if self-interest is defined through regimes, states still only act in their self-interest, and, hence, there is no need for the concept of regime. If, for example, the use of food to help other nations is somehow (for reasons of international standing, or of political stability, for example) considered by politicians in donor countries to be in the interest of their country, there is no reason to speak about a developmental regime governing food aid: the concepts of long-term self-interest and enlightened self-interest are readily available to deal with this. But in that case, self-interest becomes so large a category that it comes to apply to everything and thus to mean nothing;[130] neither can this practice analyze how the content of such long-term self-interest changes over time, and why it does so.

The first and second mechanism described above assume the Realist postulate that actors prefer to act in their self-interest. The third and last mechanism, on the contrary, simply allows for the fact that actors' preferences can consciously be of a non self-interested nature. Certain actions, of policy-makers as well as of groups of citizens, can be, and are, motivated by charity or solidarity. This is reflected in the existence of norms and principles inducing actors to behave in certain charitable or altruistic manners. It explains why donors give large amounts of food aid to African states which are largely devoid of any political or economic interest to them, as well as the rapid responses to (known) famines.

Some might still argue that the operational existence of a developmental regime is denied by our very own case study: after all, a serious share of food aid is still given for blatantly self-interested purposes. But it could hardly be expected that all international actions would always be in accordance with the norms and principles that apply to the issue area. After all, domestic norms are often violated – which is precisely why law-enforcing mechanisms exist. In the international system, no such mechanism exists. When states act according to norms, they do so voluntarily, without the threat of enforceable sanctions. Hence, if it cannot be expected that all individuals within a society always conform

152

to the norms of that society, states (or, more precisely, statesmen) can be expected to do so even less. Thus, the test of the operational existence of international regimes should be less stringent, *i.e.* a larger amount of violation is compatible with claims regarding the existence of norms and principles in international relations than in domestic societies.

One could also interpret the discrepancies between the regime and the process in the following way. The process is 'behind' the regime in allocation, especially to the extent that a significant share, mainly of US food aid, is still allocated for political reasons. Another part of food aid is 'in advance' of the regime, most notably the fact that the largest share of food donations substitutes for commercial imports by the recipient countries, thus violating the still existing additionality principle. But most of the time, and to an increasing extent, the food aid process is in tune with the regime.

In guise of conclusion, we saw that a developmental international food aid regime exists and clearly influences the actual outcome of the issue area. At least three ways have been distinguished in which this happens. First, the international food aid regime influences policy-makers' perceptions of the costs and the benefits of food aid giving; second, it constrains their margin of manoeuvre in the definition of their interests; and third, it encourages them to display non-self-interested behavior. All this is consistent with the Realist view of the nature of the international system: the absence of a central authority or enforcement mechanism, the central role of power, etc. It does not question the importance of these structural realities. Yet, it is inconsistent with some of Realism's basic claims, *e.g.* that states are the only relevant international actors, and that they only seek power or the enhancement of their self-interest. We have seen this to be false, both for fundamental factual reasons – self-interest is not the only motor of state action; international institutions do play central roles – and for methodological ones – the nature of self-interest is not God-given: hence, the answers to the questions of who defines it? in what manner? based on what perception of reality? are crucial. All of this gives credit to what have variously been labelled neo-institutionalist, reflectivist, sociological or cognitivist approaches.[131] They do not render Realism superfluous, but impose important complements and modifications on it – the research agenda of the 1990s.

Two final remarks concern the relation between food aid giving and the Cold War and the role of the media. According to some authors,[132] the Cold War was beneficial to food aid giving inasfar as it was to the interest of the donors countries to woo Third World nations with surplus commodities. According to others, the end of the Cold War is positive for food aid giving because it puts developmental issues higher on the agenda, creating an interest for states to follow suit. What precisely, might one ask, is the value of speculations about the impact of the Cold War on the food aid process, if both its existence and its demise lead to the same outcome? The problem is, of course, the attribution of interests to states, which is a very subjective activity, based on preconceived ideas, such as Realist expectations, and backed up by politicians' words – which, if one searches long enough, one can usually find to back up basically any position. The concept of 'interest' is just too imprecise to be very useful. Take the example of Vengroff, who posits that US food aid allocation to sub-Saharan Africa is motivated by US foreign policy interests and serves to reward friendly regimes, and subsequently goes on to analyze the existing data. What these data show him, though, is that 'the greater the voter disagreement with the US in the United Nations, and the greater the level of arms trade with communist nations, the more US food aid a country received'[133] – *i.e.* exactly the opposite of his expectations. Instead of considering that food aid might be allocated in sub-Saharan Africa according to need, and that it is especially self-styled communist countries that suffer from hunger in that region, Vengroff draws the conclusion that 'apparently, rather than using food aid as a reward to friends, it is being employed to try to win support from, or increased trade with, those nations that are most opposed to the US.' This interpretation constitutes a typical *'fuite en avant'* of a Realist confronted with disturbing facts: the author could not conceive of the fact that a non-directly self-interested objective might be behind the US action, so he looks desperately for some other self-interest he might ascribe to US behavior. What this example also shows us, again, is that 'self-interest' is extremely imprecise a category, by far too subject to preconceptions and manipulation to merit being the cornerstone of a scientific theory – be it a social science one. More is needed, and the interaction between regimes, preferences and interests seems more promising to us.

As the food aid issue area also shows, the media, and especially television, have become increasingly important in shaping international processes. This is very clear in the case of emergency aid: publics respond massively to images of famine, morally obliging their governments to do the same, even to enemy countries, such as Iran or Ethiopia. The other side of the coin is that people do not respond to famines they do not see on television – such as the Ethiopian one before the BBC images, or the Sudanese one in 1992, when all attention was going to Somalia – allowing their governments to do the same and let starvation occur. Moreover, as the media – and again, especially television – usually give only superficial information, most people do not know the difference between emergency food aid and the rest of food aid, which is 5 to 10 times larger; this creates a kind of artificial favor for all kinds of food aid, based on emergency aid's popularity. This central role of information and the media in triggering off international processes fits very nicely with the premisses of the interdependence school of thought. Yet, its effects only partially confirm the positive expectations generally associated with increasing interdependence. On the one hand, human solidarity has indeed become increasingly global, and actions are undertaken that concretize these new bonds between peoples and countries; but on the other hand, these processes of solidarity are dependent on the mode of functioning of a handful of occidental, superficial, mostly privately controlled media, as well as on the willingness of governments to let them work and film in their countries!

PART II FOOD AID AND HUNGER

It should be clear that the argument which has been made until now, *i.e.* that food aid donation is increasingly governed by a developmental international regime, does not imply that food aid actually serves that purpose and brings about development in recipient countries – just as the argument that food aid is given for self-interested preferences does not automatically entail it retards development, as many radical authors have it. Many factors intervene in the explanation of the impact of food aid on recipient countries, and donor motivation is but one, and probably not the most important, among them. It is these points we

155

will now discuss: the direct and indirect effects of food aid on the incidence of hunger.

It is impossible in the next few pages to present a full review of the state of the art on the effects of food aid on hunger, food security, food production and economic development. Such venture has already been successfully undertaken by IDS scholars, most notably Maxwell and Singer in 1979, Clay and Singer in 1985 and Clay and Stokke in 1991. In this chapter, we propose to think through some selected items from a political economy point of view, a discipline rather neglected in the above mentioned overviews, as the authors themselves admit.

Much criticism has been voiced against food aid. As Clay and Singer note, 'food aid has become one of the most controversial and emotional subjects within the total aid picture.'[134] Here, we will discuss some of the most commonly made criticisms against food aid. The first one refers to the question whether food aid actually relieves hunger or not. This debate on the **direct impact of food aid on hunger** applies to all forms of food aid: project, structural and emergency. Three other critiques apply only to structural and project food aid. They deal with the **indirect**, longer-term impact of food aid on the agricultural and social development of the recipient countries, and ultimately on the incidence of hunger. They hold that food aid (1) has a negative influence on agricultural production in the recipient countries (the so-called disincentives debate), (2) keeps repressive and inegalitarian governments in power (that do not combat hunger), and (3) brings about changes in consumer taste and dietary demand in favor of imported foodstuffs (thus increasing dependency). These three criticisms are often used to argue that food aid should be ended, for it perpetuates hunger rather than alleviating it.

One final remark before beginning. Also in this field, the absence and the low quality of data combine with fundamental methodological problems of causality and attribution and greatly varying project design to render extremely difficult and debatable any general conclusions.[135] For that reason we will have to be very careful all through this chapter, thinking through the issues rather than pretending to dispose of general truths. In the process, we hope some commonly held wisdoms might suffer a serious blow.

1 The direct impact of food aid on hunger

We will not try here to calculate how many lives food aid saves: as should be clear by now, judgments of these matters should be extremely nuanced and based on in-depth case studies on the direct and indirect, short-term and long-term effects of different types of food aid. Schubert, based on a detailed study of nutritional data for 89 countries receiving food aid from 1962 to 1975, concludes that 'a modest, positive, significant association is observed for the impact of food aid on nutritional status in less developed countries.'[136] Yet, such analysis is too general and contestable; hence, we will briefly discuss the three basic types of food aid and their direct impact on hunger: structural, project and emergency food aid, accounting respectively for approximately 60%, 30–20% and 10–20% of global food donations.

To begin with, structural food aid, *i.e.* government-to-government transfers of food which is usually sold on the local market, at first sight has very little or no direct impact on the incidence of hunger, for, as we saw in chapter three, those who are able to buy food on the market are usually not the hungry. As a Congressional Research Service briefing points out concerning US Title I food aid to Central America, it 'is being distributed through the marketplace to those who have the money to purchase it rather than through grant aid to needy individuals.'[137] But structural food aid can also be used for the creation and renewal of national or regional food security stocks, allowing constant food availability and food prices. This has been the case in countries as diverse as India, Mali or Botswana. Structural food aid's impact on hunger then occurs to the extent that these stocks fulfill their function, which is a debate development economists have not as yet settled.[138]

Project food aid, as we saw, mainly concerns supplementary feeding programs and food-for-work projects. The latter's direct impact on hunger depends on the extent to which it is the hungry that participate in them, which seems quite likely. People do not like to be paid in food if they can avoid it: it is unpractical and humiliating: thus only desperate people are willing to work in such projects.[139] The impact on hunger of supplementary feeding programs, usually targeted at school-children and mothers, is generally considered limited, because of difficulties in targeting the needy and possible substitution effects: parents might just give their schoolchildren less to eat at home, knowing that they will get fed at school. This kind of problems, which applies to all kinds of project food aid, really reflects the fact that food aid is too simple and unidimensional an answer to the complex problem of hunger, involving political, economic, social and health factors.[140]

Finally, we will briefly discuss the impact on hunger of emergency food aid, *i.e.* 'the provision of food aid as a response to short-run food system problems, causing hunger, increased morbidity, and the breakdown of socio-economic institutions.'[141] Emergency food aid is not only by far the most popular with the general public, it is also the only type that finds acceptance in the eyes of most food aid critics. Yet, its efficiency is still often questioned.[142]

First, it suffers from the limits imposed on external donors in a world of sovereign countries. Indeed, emergency aid donors can only intervene after governments acknowledge the existence of a famine.[143] This 'acknowledgment problem' poses itself first of all at the side of the less developed country, who often admit being faced with a famine only when starvation is already well under way. In China in 1959–60, Ethiopia in 1974 and the Sudan in 1990/91, governments refused to acknowledge famine and made help nearly impossible.[144] But also donors have to acknowledge the existence of an urgency and commit the necessary resources. They systematically tend to underestimate the extent of the problem, based on the attitude that recipient governments or NGOs always exaggerate the problem so as to capture more of their scarce resources;[145] also political reasons can incite donors to close their eyes to the existence of famine conditions. Given the fact that all the actors in the system – international organizations such as UNICEF or the WFP, NGOs such as CARE, CRS, ActionAid or the ICRC, and the emergency desks within bilateral agencies – depend on governments giving them the food and other governments allowing them to bring it in, preventive action against famine is almost impossible, and remedial action can be very difficult, if governments are unwilling to help. Hence, many thousands of people die each year of deaths that could have been prevented if the barriers of sovereignty were not that high.[146]

A second important limitation on the efficiency of emergency food aid is of an administrative nature, and also exists both at the donor and at the recipient side. At the donor side, it has to do with the long delays which characterize the arrival of aid which by definition should be fast. The literature is replete with references to the EEC, the most inefficient actor in this respect, whose emergency aid has been shipped as late as three years after a famine broke out! But even if the food aid arrives in a timely way in recipient ports, many administrative problems still persist. Given failing infrastructure and missing human resources, enormous logistic and management problems of storage and distribution usually exist.[147] Moreover, corruption, inefficiency, official passivity and incompetence intervene as much in the process of emergency food aid as in any other domain of Third World politics and development aid.[148] All kinds of food aid, once arrived at the country's border, have to be unloaded, stored, transported inland, restored, protected against theft and predators, repackaged and weighted; beneficiaries have to be selected, distribution to be monitored, etc.[149] In the case of emergency aid, this has to be done urgently. Hence there is ample scope for loss, delay, misappropriation or theft. Under those conditions, emergency food aid can lose much of its utility for those in dire need.

After the African famine of 1983–4, which had mobilized the whole international community in an unprecedented way, most donors engaged in lengthy and critical reviews of the quality of their management: large donors such as the WFP, USAID and the EEC all published evaluations in the following years[150] and tried to streamline their procedures and improve their capacity of response. According to Clay and Stokke, they have learnt from then and have been able to respond faster and better to the 1988 African crisis.[151]

Its limits notwithstanding, emergency food aid has known successes. According to most authors, most of it gets to those people who are really in need and as such can be said to avert starvation. According to Schubert, food aid 'has played a significant role in most successful efforts to relieve famine', bringing down mortality rates from highs of 15 to 30% to 1–3%;[152] a recent detailed study by Minear et. al. of Operation Lifeline in Sudan concludes similarly that food aid has prevented death for hundreds of thousands of people.[153] Emergency aid is also very useful in fighting hunger in the paradoxical case of 'structural' emergency aid, *i.e.* the distribution of food among populations suffering from long-term man-made disasters: refugees and displaced persons. This work is done by the WFP, UNHCR, UNICEF, the International Society of the Red Cross and the League of Red Cross and Red Crescent Societies. According to the Food Aid Monitor, for the last three years 1989 to 1992 this activity involved respectively 1,365,000; 623,000 and 801,000 tons of food aid; it has fed millions of displaced people.[154]

At best, food aid can play a preventive role. After the 1984–5 African famine, for example, the WFP has acquired the experience and infrastructure which allowed it to avert famine for millions of people in the following years – and, what is as important, to avoid the disruption of the social and economic fabric of the threatened societies by preventive action.[155] Food aid is said to have also prevented famine in India in 1965–67, in Bangladesh after the floods of the second half of the 1980s, and in many other African countries at present.[156] Thus emergency food aid has made a positive impact on the incidence of hunger and especially acute hunger, and can even do so on longer-term development.[157]

2 The disincentives debate

The main debate concerning food aid centers around its supposed disincentive effects on food production in the recipient country. There are two such effects that are discerned, and both hold that food aid takes away the incentive to produce food in the recipient country. The first one is economic in nature. It argues that food aid depresses domestic prices in recipient countries and as such decreases domestic production, making recipient countries even less able to feed themselves. The second one is *political* in nature, and it holds that inasfar as governments policies are the causes of the inability of countries to feed themselves, the granting of food aid will remove the incentives to change these 'bad' policies, thus perpetuating avoidable hunger.

These arguments are dominant within the academic community, within most of the development community and in certain policy-making circles. They are made by authors from both the left and the right. In the US, for example, the Heritage Foundation voices these critiques, as do a significant number of Congressmen, such as Rep. Jack Kemp and the majority of development economists.[158] In Great-Britain, people as different as Tony Jackson, writing for Oxfam, and Francis Pym, a Thatcher

Foreign Secretary, are publicly highly critical of food aid.[159] In the France, all 'Third-Worldism' is anti-food aid based upon the same criticism, as is much of the right.[160] In short, within the development issue area, there are few, if any, points on which the 'left' and 'right' find each other so closely in agreement as on food aid. It is thus all the more worthwhile to scrutinize the disincentive argument in detail.

A The economic disincentive argument

The economic disincentive argument has been presented for the first time in 1960 by the Nobel-prize winner Theodore Schultz.[161] It holds that food aid increases the availability of food on the market of the recipient country and thus puts downward pressure on prices. This discourages local farmers from producing these food crops and will consequently diminish domestic food production. The 'emergency' food aid following an earthquake in Guatemala in 1974 presents a typical example of this critique.[162] The food aid which arrived months after the earthquake, came in competition with food from the local harvest in neighboring regions of the country. Thus food prices went down, bringing hardship to farmers and ending up by decreasing domestic food production in Guatemala in subsequent years. It would have undoubtedly been much better to move food from the other, food-surplus regions to the earthquake-stricken region of Guatemala.

This argument of typically economic nature has been taken over with much passion by the Left. In typical fashion, this side often imputes intentions to the observed effects: food aid then becomes an instrument of agricultural interests in the donating countries to destroy LDC food production, so as to turn the latter into commercial importers and into a general state of dependency.[163]

Although the economic disincentive critique is 'widely accepted as an established and inevitable product of food aid,'[164] it is one of the many cases in which common wisdom is too simple. On a theoretical level, it has been argued that if prices went down as a result of food aid, consumption would consequently increase, which would strengthen prices: finally, the two effects could balance out each other – at higher consumption levels.[165] In practice, the conditions under which Schultz' argu-

161

ment holds (existence of perfect information, perfect mobility, high supply elasticity, etc.) are very unrealistic in most LDCs: food prices are often not set by the market, but by public bodies, dual structures of distribution tend to exist,[166] there usually is a large amount of unmet (non-monetary) demand, commercial food imports are high anyhow, etc.[167] All these factors make the automatic manifestation of the disincentive argument doubtful. Many of the empirical studies that have attempted to quantify the disincentive effect of food aid on prices and production, did not find very much of it.[168] The *prima facie* evidence that many big food aid receivers of the early days – India, Japan, Spain, Portugal, South Korea, Taiwan – all have flourishing agricultural sectors rather hints at the opposite. A more detailed analysis by Bachman & Paulino of 18 LDCs which achieved particularly high growth rates of food production from 1961 to 1976 reveals that these countries also received on the average 80% more food aid per capita than other countries.[169]

Moreover, recent evolutions in the way food aid is given act as brakes on the occurrence of the economic disincentive effect. First, for US Title I food aid (around one third of global donations), the Bellmon and Gillman/Solarz amendments require specific, concrete and measurable self-help measures, additional to ongoing agricultural policies; their explicit objective is to avoid the disincentive effect. Yet, their application is problematic, both because of the inherent difficulty in measuring and monitoring such measures and because of the fact that, whenever food aid is donated for political purposes, such requirements tend to be only formally fulfilled.[170] Second, more and more aid is given in the form of project aid, *i.e.* to very poor people in the framework of some project (rural development, food-for-work, pre-school feeding and the like) or emergency aid. Both these forms of food aid are exempted from the disincentive critique, for food given to those who had no prior monetary demand does not influence the market price of food.[171]

Third, as more and more program food aid becomes balance of payment support, *i.e.* replaces commercial food imports the country would have made anyhow, it does not increase the total quantity of food on the recipient country markets and, as such, its disincentive effect disappears.[172] According to recent calculations by Saran and Konandreos, around 60% to 70% of total food aid substitutes for commercial imports,[173] meaning that the largest share of food aid escapes from the economic disincentive charge. The large donors go at great pains to convince the development community of this fact, which puts them in a difficult position, for they have to keep the farmers' lobby, which does not particularly like this notion, happy too. Thus the rhetoric of food donating agencies displays the most curious inconsistencies and contradictions.[174]

Finally, policy innovations such as the one of the EEC discussed earlier – where food aid is replaced by financial transfers in the case of good harvests in recipient countries – are designed to avoid the economic disincentive effect.[175] In the summer of 1990, the same happened with Poland, which asked the EEC to end its food aid deliveries, because the local harvests were good, and the risk existed that prices would decrease.[176] All this does not yet happen enough: most recipients do everything to inflate their needs and hence their food aid receipts,[177] while donors are too often locked in bureaucratic procedures and considerations of convenience – but these are signs of progress.

To conclude, inasfar as low food prices are a problem in LDCs, the cause is not food aid, which is usually small in quantity, but rather commercial food imports (seven times bigger than food aid for the Third World) and the agricultural and/or general macroeconomic policies followed by LDC governments,[178] which have been studied elsewhere in this thesis. The economic disincentive effect of food aid, although a possibility and in the case of Guatemala undoubtedly a reality, is avoidable. Its occurrence depends mainly on the agricultural, macroeconomic and social objectives of the recipient and his administrative capacity to ensure them as well as on the management quality and the flexibility of the donors.[179] As to the latter, recent evolutions such as the ones outlined above go in the right direction, although far too much inflexibility and instability still exist. As to the former, in countries such as most sub-Saharan African ones, it can be doubted whether local administrative and political capabilities to avoid the disincentive effect of food aid exist.[180] But this problem is not caused by food aid – as Maxwell concludes 'the possibility of disincentive effects is modified by government policy, which is not normally determined primarily by the flow of food aid.'[181]

B The political disincentive argument

This argument starts from the usual diagnosis on Third World agriculture we presented in chapter 2: it is the 'bad' agricultural policies of LDC governments that are at the root of their food problems. Continuing from there, the argument holds that food aid, especially program food aid, fills the production shortfall caused by these wrong policies and thus allows for their continuation. Thus food aid should be stopped, so as to oblige recipient country governments to reform their agricultural policies. This argument has been popular with the Reagan administration, and partially accounts for its very delayed reaction to the Ethiopian famine.

In order to judge if the withdrawal of food aid will change bad policies, we need to know if food aid *causes* these policies. For, if food aid did not cause these bad policies, *i.e.* if other, independent factors were responsible for them, another argument is necessary to explain why the withdrawal of food aid should change these bad policies.

The research of Bachman and Paulino mentioned above evidently does not support the assertion that food aid causes bad policies – as does much other empirical economic work on food aid.[182] Food aid represents a very small part of total food availability or imports for most recipient countries, for most of the time. During the 1980s, it constituted on the average less than 10% of LDC food imports, and less than 1% of their food availability. Those figures become higher when one leaves out the middle-income countries – although also in some of them 'bad' policies have been pursued. As noted in chapter two, the origin of 'bad' Third World agricultural policies are to be found in a large variety of social, historical, political and economic factors; food aid might be among them, but it is far from being the central variable.

If there is a link between 'bad' agricultural policies and food aid, it is rather the other way round for many countries: 'food aid is sucked in by poor agricultural policy rather than itself being responsible for the vacuum which it fills.'[183] Food aid is then a **consequence** of 'bad' policies, but not their cause. Our own calculations support this argument. The 15 countries with the lowest (negative) growth rates of food production per capita during the period 1979/81 – 1987/89 received an (unweighted) average of 14.2 kg of food aid per person – two times more than those with the highest growth rates.[184] Yet, in the previous period (1972–76) these badly performing countries had received only 5.6 kg of food aid per person. This, then, would tend to supply evidence for the above argument.[185]

Hence, as there seems to be no causal link between food aid and bad agricultural policies, the argument in favor of the suppression of food aid in order to change these bad policies can only be based upon some notion that, in the absence of 'palliative' food aid, governments will be forced to reform their policies under the pressure of internal forces due to the bankruptcy of their agriculture and the revolt this incites among the population. The logic behind this 'polarization' argument[186] presents serious ethical problems. Is it moral to 'create' misery for people, even for 'their own good?' Is not the solution worse than the problem? Particularly because those who are bound to suffer most from this solution are not those that caused the problem.[187] Moreover, it is not at all certain that the change of government policy that ensues will be beneficial or in the right direction! Given the constraints and the preferences which led to the 'bad' policy in the first place, the result of suppressing food aid might as well be increased poverty, famine or repression![188]

To conclude: the political disincentive argument is a typical case of a seemingly evident economic reasoning which is transposed to political situations. Such transposition often does not survive the test of political inquiry. Arguments in favor of suppressing food aid because this would force governments to change their 'bad' policies are hard to defend: food aid did not usually cause these policies and the 'conflictualization logic' poses very serious ethical and practical problems. Suppressing food aid thus only amounts to some kind of cruel punishment for 'bad' governments or populations, but not to a policy reform inducing tool.

3 Food aid and political stability

Another effect of food aid is often considered to be its influence upon the survival or the capacity to remain in power of recipient governments. Many authors state that food aid 'forestalls major social upheavals'[189] and thus keeps governments in place. As described before, part of food aid has been and still is given in order to achieve exactly this purpose, at present especially by the US in Egypt and Central America. Above, we have attempted to distinguish what share of food aid is motivated by such political interests of the donor and what share is not. In this section, we will examine the *effect* of food aid on the stability of governments.

We will first analyze if food aid contributes to keeping governments in power. At first sight, there could be two reasons for this to be the case: (1) the financial value of food aid constitutes a significant resource to recipient governments, which they can use to buy off strategic groups so as to stay in power, or (2) food aid significantly increases food availability, thus avoiding popular unrest and major social upheavals.

If it can be shown that food aid is effective in keeping governments in power, then, second, we will assess the effects of the maintenance of these governments in power on the incidence of hunger. The latter question boils down to the one of the 'quality' of these governments, *i.e.* what is the effect of the government's policies upon hunger? Is the eradication of hunger a government priority or is it not?

To start with the first point, theoretically spoken, food aid, especially in its structural form, can be an important foreign exchange support to recipient governments if the latter would have imported the food anyhow (as we have seen, this might be the case for as much as 60% of global food aid). Food aid then amounts to balance of payments savings allowing governments to import other products instead. In the 1980s, with the financial and economic crisis facing most of Africa and Latin America, every dollar saved as a result of food aid was more than welcome: even 'richer' countries, such as the three Maghreb ones or Brazil and Mexico became very interested again in receiving more food aid. Moreover, the proceeds of the sale of the food on local markets constitute local currency revenues, which can be used, with the agreement of the donor, for other purposes. Usually, these 'counterfunds' have to be devoted to agricultural development projects or programmes, but in practice, as a result of the fungibility of money, as well as of methodological and political difficulties in donor control on the real use of counterfunds, recipient governments basically do as they please with the revenues of the food aid they received.[190] Hence, it seems theoretically quite possible that food aid, intentionally or as a

166

by-product, helps governments to spend additional money on staying in power.

But in reality, the financial value of food aid to individual recipient governments is quite low. According to Von Braun and Huddleston,[191] food aid reduced the total cost of cereal imports by around one third for LIFDCs, but only by 2–5% for other developing countries – and food imports usually are only a small part of government expenses. Hence, the only countries where food aid might have a significant financial impact are those which import much food and which are very poor. Table 5.6 below is based on a sample of 35 countries, including most of the biggest food aid recipients; it includes *all* food aid, not only structural. As it shows, apart from Bangladesh, the additional spending allowed to recipient governments as a result of the food aid they received is low, even in the case of Egypt.

Table 5.7 Value of food aid a percentage of value of government expenses, 1980–84[192]

Middle East	1.3%	Far East	0.5%
Egypt	2.5%	Bangladesh	8.4%
Africa	1.2%	India	0.6%
Ethiopia	2.4%	Latin America	0.2%
Sudan	0.3%	Bolivia	2.4%
Tanzania	1.0%	Peru	0.7%
All regions	0.5%		

The second way food aid could help recipient governments to stay in power was by increasing food availability, thus decreasing popular unrest. Also here, at first sight, a strong case can be made in favor of the argument. Historical examples suggest that an important factor to incite popular revolt is food price increases: the last ten years have seen food riots in a large variety of LDCs on all three continents, especially in the Mediterranean countries and in Latin America:[193] they often directly followed dramatic increases in food prices. Other forms of unrest are not specifically triggered off by food price hikes but by the more general discontent about the erosion of purchasing power, in which food prices play a crucial role. Thus many authors trace ideological radicalization and religious revolt back to such factors: see for example the revival of Islam fundamentalism in Northern Africa and Nigeria. It thus seems that the lack of food, or the price level of food is an important source of political instability.

But, as Bienen and Gersowitz and Furlong have argued, few, if any, governments have ever fallen as a result of food riots;[194] more cynically, Schubert, among others, argues that lack of food actually renders people politically passive rather than active.[195] Moreover, emergencies apart, food aid usually represents only a very small share (less than 5%) of domestic food availability in recipient countries. Hence, the argument that food aid, through its impact on food availability, forestalls major social upheavals seems most unlikely; it certainly cannot be held as a general rule.

On the other hand, the argument gets reinforced if one takes into account the generally accepted fact that it is only potential *urban* unrest governments are afraid of. It is then politically meaningful to look not at what share food aid constitutes of total domestic food availability in a recipient country, but only what share it constitutes of the food availability of the politically relevant population, which usually signifies the urban population. It is hard to generalize and surpass the level of mere speculation,[196] but it can be held that food aid often makes up quite a large share of urban food availability, making it possible to keep cheap food available on urban markets without too high a budgetary cost. Food aid can also be used to advantage specific client-groups, such as the military, the population of the presidents' region or more generally any group whose support the powers-that-be consider necessary. Such is said to happen in Egypt and Bangladesh, the two biggest recipients of programme aid, where the food received allows their respective governments to serve the urban poor and middle class in the one, and the military, the bureaucracy and the rest of the urban middle class in the other;[197] it has also been documented for other countries, such as Ghana and Peru.[198] Even emergency food aid can be, and at times is, used for this purpose: Cambodia at the end of the 1970s, and Ethiopia, Mozambique and Sudan in the second half of the 1980s constitute painful examples of this.[199]

In short, it is unclear to what extent food aid helps keeping governments in power. Notwithstanding the apparent logic of the arguments in favor of this assertion, closer analysis reveals that it is hardly supported, neither by the available data (see too table 5.7 above) nor by political economy inquiry. The most we can say is that it is possible, for some countries that receive large quantities of food aid, displacing commercial imports, and that target it efficiently to specific groups of their population, might be increasing their legitimacy as a result of it. As an evaluation by USAID states it: 'the availability of U.S. food aid, *if it is as substantial as in the case of Egypt, probably* contributes to domestic stability and thus to the continuation in power of a friendly government.'[200] But apart from this case and maybe a few others, food aid's impact does not reach as far as to keep governments in power.

This also argues against overestimating the political benefits to be derived from food aid by the donor or the 'dependence' food aid entails for recipient countries: if food aid represents only such a small share of recipient governments' expenses and food availability, granting or withdrawing food aid confers only a limited capacity for leverage to donors. For years, the US has attempted to bring about agricultural policy reform in large food aid recipients such as India in the 1960s, Bangladesh in the late 1970s and Egypt in the 1980s, going as far in each case as to threaten the withholding of aid, but success has been very limited. The same holds for Ethiopia, where the US, the EEC and the World Bank all through the 1980s put strong pressure on the government to change its agricultural policies, but to no avail.[201]

For those countries where it can be proven that food aid helps governments to remain in power, we still need to answer the question of the effect of this on the incidence of hunger. This judgment will depend on the quality of the governments which are thus helped: what is the record of recipient governments in eradicating hunger? The situation is not particularly impressive in that respect: the largest share of the countries that receive much food aid have repressive, highly inegalitarian, war-fighting and often economically inefficient governments. The US legislation that prohibits Title I assistance to countries that engage in consistent violations of human rights, is consistently violated itself, partly because of the political motives behind it, but partly because there really is little choice! Consistent application of this norm – on the basis of *Amnesty International* reports, for example – would exclude all but a handful of countries from receiving food aid.

As to the indirect impact of food aid on the incidence of hunger, among present big recipients, we find countries such as Ethiopia, Sudan, Mozambique, Angola, Zaire and the Philippi-

Table 5.8 Recipients of food aid, 1988[203]

1,000 tons	Country	Political system	Political stability
1,523	Egypt	legal but limited opposition	sporadic urban unrest
1,227	Bangladesh	totalitarianism or one party system	
1,112	Ethiopia	totalitarianism or one party system	civil war
606	Mozamb.	totalitarianism or one party system	civil war
550	Pakistan	legal but limited opposition	religious unrest
548	India	legal but limited opposition	religious and regional unrest
531	Sudan	totalitarianism or one party system	civil war; genocide against Christians
375	China	totalitarianism or one party system	political unrest
350	Sri Lanka	legal but limited opposition	ethnic war
350	Tunisia	legal but limited opposition	sporadic urban unrest
346	Indonesia	totalitarianism or one party system	ethnic unrest; genocide in Timor
320	Morocco	totalitarianism or one party system	sporadic urban unrest
295	Jamaica	pluralism	
215	El Salvador	pluralism	civil war
199	Domin. Rep.	pluralism	
188	Philippines	pluralism	guerilla
175	Honduras	legal but limited opposition	
175	Guatemala	legal but limited opposition	guerilla
140	Nicaragua	recently pluralist	recent civil war
135	Vietnam	totalitarianism or one party system	?
129	Uganda	totalitarianism or one party system	recent civil war
127	Ghana	totalitarianism or one party system	
127	Zaire	totalitarianism or one party system	urban unrest
125	Malawi	totalitarianism or one party system	

Table 5.8 continued

124	Kenya	totalitarianism or one party system	urban unrest
123	Somalia	totalitarianism or one party system	civil war
123	Angola	totalitarianism or one party system	civil war

nes, in which war and the policies of the government are to a large extent responsible for their hunger problems – but also India, Indonesia, China, Bangladesh or even Egypt, countries which are considered to have done a serious job of eradicating hunger (whatever their record on human rights).[202] Hence, food aid intervenes in countries of all kinds, some of whom have governments committed to eradicating hunger, some of whom do not. There certainly is no proof of a grand design to use food aid to keep in power governments that starve their people – nor of the opposite: the 'quality' of governments and the priority they attach to the eradication of hunger seem not to be a criterion of global food aid allocation.

4 Taste changes

Another negative effect often mentioned in discussions on food aid is the taste change that results from it. In its most clever, non-paternalistic form, the reasoning is not that food aid imports new desires – there is really nothing wrong with liking cereals more than cassava – but that this creates inefficiency and dependency, for the new food is not the most adapted to local climatological and technological conditions and it has to be imported from abroad.[204]

There are two problems with this critique of food aid. First, as Byerlee has shown among others, the domestic pricing structure in favor of these foreign foods is the main cause of the fast increasing demand for them – not the existence of international food flows by themselves.[205] Second, there is often a high social prestige attached to these imported foods, symbolizing occidental habits and sophistication.[206] These predispositions in favor of imported foods are more often than not cleverly and incessantly reinforced by advertisement campaigns of mainly occidental companies. White bread, rice, white sugar and red meat, just like Coca-Cola, Benson and Hedges cigarettes and instant baby formula, belong to these goods: they can be found up to the smallest village in Africa, Asia and Latin America alike. Moreover, often these foods are easier to prepare and cook than local staples – a feature women surely appreciate.[207] Hence large parts of rising (and not so rising) incomes are spent on acquiring these products, whose nutritional value is often not superior to local staples. Food aid, by lowering the price of imported cereals, can facilitate these taste changes but cannot usually be said to create them.

Hence, the policies of local governments and foreign companies, and the psychological and practical conveniences of imported foodstuffs all combine to bring about taste changes which are not to the interest of Southern farmers, or the development of their agriculture[208] – but, as usual, to the benefit of the rich and the North. Yet, this is not due to the giving of food aid, but rather to the structure and the functioning of the global world political economic system.

5 Conclusion

Food aid constitutes an international mechanism to combat hunger and promote development, and it does so more and more efficiently. Most of the negative effects for which food aid is so often criticized do not stand the test of political economy inquiry. They either find their origins in other processes, most important of which are the recipients' government policies, or they apply to all forms of aid.[209]

On the other hand, the same arguments that defend food aid against unjust charges also limit its potential impact on starvation and the incidence of chronic hunger. For one, food aid is but a small element in the global picture, greatly conditioned by third factors, most notably the domestic policies and the power structure in the recipient country. Moreover, if inappropriately used by either the donor or the recipient, it can even have a negative impact on agricultural production and, ultimately, on hunger.

At the donor side, the contemporary international food aid outcome has gone some distance in avoiding some of the important critiques against food aid: more stable quantities, more project and emergency aid, the displacement of commercial imports by food aid, the improved use of counterfunds, greater emphasis on regional procurement, etc. Yet, much greater administrative flexibility, forward planning, and coordination are still needed. This – and not the self-interest supposedly served by food aid – is the most important defect of food aid: as it is managed by complex bureaucracies, lacking flexibility and freedom of action, food aid is an inherently unstable, uncertain and non-responsive source of supply of food for poor countries and poor people alike.[210]

To conclude this discussion on the impact of food aid on the incidence of hunger, we could usefully restate the question in Sen's entitlement terms: does food aid constitute an entitlement to the hungry, to those whose total entitlement set is below the level needed to avoid occasional hunger or, worse, starvation? At the outset, it is clear that food aid does not really constitute an international entitlement mechanism to poor and hungry people or even nations. Its donation is still entirely at the mercy of the major rich countries' governments, and most of its distribution is at the mercy of recipient governments' intervention. There is no automatic international redistribution/transfer mechanism, no legal or even moral claim poor hungry people can make to food aid in sufficient quantities to allow them to increase their entitlement sets above hunger level. Only in the field of starvation, when entitlement sets go below survival levels, does there come into being a transfer entitlement to food transfers. Yet, these mechanisms are still not fully internally institutionalized or automatic, depending to a certain extent on the vagaries of rich country citizens' and their governments' commitment; the entitlements they create, while real, are shaky and uncertain.

Program food aid does not constitute an entitlement to the hungry, for it only creates possibilities for those with money to buy food at ongoing market prices. The hungry by definition lack the exchange entitlements to buy this food; if not, they would not be hungry. Only to the extent that food aid stabilizes or even lowers food prices can it be held to improve the capacity of the poor to acquire sufficient food. Much will depend, though, on such technical matters as: who has access to such rationed food? Project food aid to a certain extent feeds hungry people, although the extent to which this is the case is still the subject of intense debate. Yet, again, it is a most uncertain and shaky transfer: there is no automatic or even intentional link between its granting and the incidence of hunger; rather, it is an unstable resource used in development projects, which happens to take the form of food.

One final remark: most North-American students of international relations, and, for our purposes, especially Raymond Hopkins, the main scholar to have studied food aid, write a lot about so-called 'consensual knowledge'. In fact, recently, a whole issue of *International Organization* has been devoted to this issue, in which Hopkins published an article on the changing consensual knowledge on food aid.[211] It seems to us that the term 'consensual' is inappropriate to describe the state of knowledge concerning food aid. As we have seen throughout this chapter, debates rage on the motives and objectives underlying its giving, its disincentive effects, its impact on hunger, and the like. No single aspect of the current food aid picture, both at the input and at the output side, is uncontested, and often strongly so. The only thing we can talk about, in line with our thinking exposed in chapter one, is *dominant* knowledge, voiced by an increasing number of scholars and food aid administrators alike. Those are indeed the kind of people usually invited to the conferences Hopkins talked about in the above mentioned article,[212] thus creating the illusion that other, contesting, knowledge simply does not exist. If such conferences were attended mainly by Third World scholars and administrators, or by radical First World authors, dominant knowledge would certainly be defined very differently. One should not stretch the meaning of the term 'consensual'.

Notes

1 Apart from Title I U.S. food aid and some Japanese assistance, all food aid actually comes in the form of grants: Clay & Stokke, 1991: 11.

2 Clay, 1983, 1985; Clay & Everitt, 1983; Clay & Singer,1983, 1985; Clay & Stokke, 1991; Maxwell & Singer, 1979; Singer, Wood & Jennings, 1987; Singer, 1987, 1989; Stevens, 1985.

3 Loans may be for up to 40 years with a 10 year grace period on capital and with a minimum interest rate of 2% during the moratorium period and 3% afterwards: OECD, 1987: 82. In the best case, this amounts to a grant element of about 70%.

4 In the past, the counterfunds have also been used to purchase US military equipment: Cathie, 1989: 33; Singer, Wood & Jennings, 1987, appendix; Moore-Lappé & Collins, 1977: 381. But even if that is not the case, as a result of the fungibility of resources, it is hard to monitor what the counterfunds are 'really' used for: Blott, 1984: 168.

5 Garst & Barry, 1990: 98–9.
6 The original Title III was introduced in 1977 and was designed to support agricultural and rural development programmes through multi-year commitments (OECD, 1987: 82–3). Recipients included Bangladesh, Sudan, Bolivia, Honduras, Senegal and Egypt.
7 LIFDC is a UN term, denoting countries, most of whom have a PNB per capita below the threshold that qualifies for concessional World Bank aid through the International Development Association (US$ 580 in 1990), and who have serious food deficits, as measured by their caloric consumption per capita, food imports and rate of infant mortality. This category includes Egypt.
8 WFP, 1991: 14.
9 USAID, 1985: 16; Talbot, 1990. 141.
10 Stevens, 1985: 11.
11 EEC Commission, 1987: 321. The commission has to submit for advice – and not for decision – all food aid decisions to the Food Aid Committee, composed by representatives of the member-states: EEC Comission, 1991. See too Shapouri & Missiaen, 1990: 21.
12 WFP, 1988: 37.
13 FAO, 1982: 17.
14 FAO, 1985a: 42.
15 U.S. House Committe on Hunger, 1987: 17; Financial Times, May 26, 1989.
16 Arefieva, 1991: 309.
17 *Ibidem.*
18 The monetary value of food aid as represented in the donor statistics does not represent the value to the recipient. Food aid donors present the cost of their donations on the basis of domestic prices, which are often far above the world market price. But the foreign exchange savings the recipient makes have to be calculated on the basis of the price it would have to pay for commercial imports in the absence of the food aid received, *i.e.* the world market price. Recent calculations by Saran and Konandreos, 1991: 57, conclude that the value of food aid to recipients is about half of the budgeted value.
19 Columns 1 to 4 compiled from data from OECD DAC Reviews and WFP, 1988: 36; columns 5–9 from different issues of FAO's Food Outlook Statistical Supplement.
20 Calculated by FAO on the basis of OECD figures published in FAO, 1985a: 43. Figures for 1985 and 1990: own calculation, based on FAO, 1991a.
21 Own calculations, based on FAO, 1991a.
22 To my knowledge, there is only one fundamentally different analysis, which has repeatedly been made by Hopkins (1983, 1989, 1992) and which holds that a developmental regime came to govern food aid.
23 This might be one of the reasons that it has actually rarely been analyzed by international relations specialists as such. The few exceptions include Wallerstein, 1980; articles in Hopkins & Puchala (eds.), 1979 and the works of Hopkins referred to above. But there

is a large literature on the politics of food aid, written by radical and mainstream development specialists alike. See for example Alaux and Norel, 1985; Bessis, 1985; Cathie, 1982, 1989; Crow, 1990; Doyle, 1990; George, 1976; Insel, 1985: 897 and Moore-Lappé & Collins, 1977: ch. 42 and 1984. Although these authors do not use the international relations jargon, their approaches and conclusions are perfectly Realist in nature, along the definition of Osgood, 1964: 8, who defines Realists, with capital 'R', as those who 'believe that nations, as a matter of fact, are moved by self-interest' and Realism as 'the approach to international relations which is *inter alia* based upon this assumption.'

24 For some examples, see Acker, 1987 & 1991; Cathie, 1989: 41; Erard & Mounier, 1984: 52; Garst & Barry, 1990: 52–3

25 See for example President Ronald Reagan on the occasion of 40 years of PL480: 'Eight of our top ten agricultural markets are former recipients of Food for Peace aid . . . And this has not only been good for the American farmer and the American economy; it's been good for our international relations.' Department of State, 1984: 47. See too quotes from the french Center for External Trade, cited in Erard & Mounier, 1984: 31.

26 Moore-Lappé & Collins, 1977.

27 For some famous and often repeated quotes from Secretary of Agriculture Earl Butz, see George, 1976; see too Wallerstein, 1980: *passim*.

28 Peterson, 1979: 310; see also Doyle, 1987.

29 In the US, it is the only form of aid which consistently scores positive in opinion polls. In most European countries, it scores higher than all other forms of aid. This might partially be caused by the fact that food aid seems almost costless to the taxpayer. Singer, 1987: 331–2.

30 Hopkins, 1983: 74. See also articles in *Le Courrier*, 1989.

31 Own calculations. *Le Courrier*, 1989: 55, arrives at 4%. According to Wood, 1982: 111–12, in Canada, a major donor, farmers 'derive only some 2% of their total income from food aid spending.' According to calculations by Shapouri & Missiaen, 1990: 9, 13, 15, the share of food aid in the grain exports of the US, the EEC and Canada, the three major surplus donors, never exceeded 10% over the last fifteen years, and on the average fluctuated around 6%.

32 For figures, see *inter alia* Hopkins, 1989: 10 and Cathie, 1989: 44.

33 FAO, 1988; for 1989/90, *Food Outlook*, April 1990; Clay & Benson, 1991: 153.

34 Triangular food aid is considered by development specialists to be a superior form of food aid, because it encourages Third World food production and South-South food trade. See Clay & Benson, 1991: 167–8 for an overview.

35 Jost, 1986: 15–19; Clay, 1987.

36 Clay and Benson, 1991: 144.

37 EEC Commission, General Report, various years.

38 Only if food aid would be a major factor in promoting economic growth, could it be held responsible for subsequent commercial food imports. But most economists agree that food aid has been marginal

in doing so. For exceptions, see Cathie, 1989: conclusion, concerning South-Korea or Orville Freeman, representative of the Agricultural Coucil of America, before the House of Representatives, 1987: 86.

39 Cathie, 1989: 32.

40 Hopkins, 1992: 254.

41 As Talbot, 1986: 179, states it nicely: 'understandably, given present economic conditions, US policymakers respond enthusiastically to the often stated belief that US food assistance builds cash markets in recipient countries.' Duane Acker, for example, was Agency Director for Food and Agriculture of USAID, while all quotes refered to in footnotes 25 and 27 were made for much the same reasons. It is important for scholars to be aware of this function of the rhetoric of statesmen. Otherwise, the danger exists of a convenient but inappropriate harmony between Realists' expectations and the rhetoric of statesmen. See Russett, 1975: 97 a.f.

42 Moore-Lappé and Collins, 1977: 370; Cathie, 1989: 51.

43 See too George, 1981; Wallerstein, 1980.

44 As Mosley, 1987: 171 remarks about aid in general: 'the industry lobby is only . . . a lobby, not an arbiter.'

45 The most typical example of this is the famous cargo preference on US food aid, presently stating that 75% of US food aid has to be shipped by American vessels, which are more expensive than others. It is clear food aid is not given to support the marine transport sector, but has been lobbied to do so. Note that it is the US government that pays for the cost increase this entails. For more information, see U.S. House, 1987: 52.

46 Alaux & Norel, 1985: 105; Erard & Mounier, 1984: *passim*.

47 Wallerstein, 1980: 74, 76, 78, 79, 80.

48 1985: 22.

49 Cathie, 1989: 52.

50 Indeed, in a 'Realist' world, we would be very surprised if the US gave food aid to Ethiopia, Mozambique, Angola etc. See for example Barbara Insel, 1985: 897, writing in Foreign Affairs that 'PL480 credits . . . are explicitly political in their orientation, giving priority to shipment of aid to countries considered friendly to the United States, and posing serious obstacles to aid for such nations as Ethiopia.' Similarly, Doyle, 1987: 327, states categorically that 'any LDC that does not respond positively to US demands, or that has been tagged with the 'Marxist' label, or that is of no strategic importance to the US is unlikely to receive direct [food] aid, regardless of need.' Statements such as these can be tested: if they are wrong (which they are), that should make us doubt the (Realist) assumptions underlying them.

51 Kegley & Hook, 1991.

52 Weinbaum, 1983: 654; Burns, 1985: 210.

53 1985: 108 ff.

54 Clay, 1983: 6.

55 Although the case is constantly referred to in the literature, perhaps due to a lack of information, the concrete result is unclear: Wall-

erstein, 1980; Sobhan, 1982: 44; and Crow, 1990: 35, only mention the attempt. Parkinson, 1981: 98–100, suggests that the attempt was not successful: Bangladesh only stopped exporting only after the contract was fulfilled.

56 The existence of such 'consensual' norm has been noted by Hopkins & Puchala, 1979b: 24. See too UNICEF, 1989: 13.

57 This norm has been violated too, as the cases of Sudan and Ethiopia in 1988 and 1990 – when both the governments and the guerilla tried to abuse the famine situation and the resulting food aid – show. See *International Herald Tribune*, August 31, 1988: 2; *Newsweek*, Oct. 24, 1988: 26; *Time*, Dec. 21, 1988: 25 and 28; *Le Monde*, Dec. 20, 1990: 8.

58 Half of all Marshall Plan aid was in the form of food: Singer, Wood, & Jennings, 1987: 5; see too Cathie, 1982 & 1989, p. 19. In the words of Secretary of State George Marshall 'food is a vital factor in our foreign policy: quoted in Paarlberg, 1985: 106.

59 Blott, 1984: 162 ff.

60 This analysis draws heavily from excellent analyses by Hopkins, 1983: 74 and 1992: 229 ff.

61 Cathie, 1989: 45 ff.

62 WFC/1984/2: 24 ff.

63 Clay & Singer, 1985: 17.

64 1985: 1; see also Hopkins, 1983: 74 ff.; Thompson, 1981: 194–8.

65 UN, 1975.

66 Minear, 1983: 63.

67 Especially important are the 'Guidelines and Criteria for Food Aid,' adopted at its 7th session in 1979. The Committee on Food Aid Policies and Programmes (CFA) was created at the World Food Conference of 1974. Its task is to coordinate of all bilateral and multilateral food aid, not just WFP.

68 USAID, 1985: 1.

69 *i.e.* IDA-elegible countries. This effectively limited food aid to recipients like Israel, Jordan, South Korea, Lebanon, Syria and Portugal.

70 The 'Gilman-Solarz amendment requiring self-help measures to be both 'specific and measurable' and 'additional to the measures which the recipient country would have anyhow undertaken': Blott, 1984: 169.

71 Garst & Barry, 1990: 9–10.

72 U.S. House, 1987: 48. It has been drawn upon during the 1985 African famine.

73 1983: 5.

74 Gueydan, 1982: 129; EEC, 1977.

75 EEC, 1983.

76 EEC, 1983: 10; *Le Courrier*, 1989: 56–9. See also the following publications by the Commission of the European Community, 1982a, 1982b, 1986(a); and the EEC Commission General Reports of 1987 to 1991. For a mid-term evaluation of the food strategy approach, see EEC, 1986(b): also Madaule, 1990: 94–8. The food strategy approach has also been adopted as a central point of action in the latest Convention of Lomé between the EEC and 65 LICs.

77 Clay, 1985: 7.
78 Singer, 1991: *passim*; Mellor, 1988b: *passim*; Stewart, 1988: *passim*.
79 World Bank, 1986c, 1988e; for the debate, see Hopkins, 1992: 263; Mellor, 1988b: *passim*, and Sukim, 1988: *passim*.
80 See Clay, 1991: 21See part 2, section 4 of this chapter for a brief discussion of its effectiveness.
81 U.S. House, 1987: *passim*. The carrots are increased and multi-year food aid commitments by the US; little is known at present about their implementation or effectiveness.
82 EEC, 1982a, 1986b.
83 The 'Permanent Inter-State Committee for Drought Control in the Sahel' is an international coordinating organization, along the lines of the OECD (in whose structure it is included), created after the 1974 famine. It is composed, apart from the Sahel countries, of 6 donors, including France and the US. The CILLS has been innovating in the food aid issue area since the beginning of the 1980s, as Erard & Monnier, 1984: 111 point out.
84 Ministry of Cooperation, 1988; WFC/1991/9: 8.
85 Gueydan, 1983: 122.
86 Parotte, 1983: 11.
87 Singer, Wood & Jennings, 1987: 73; Parotte, 1983: 11.
88 Maxwell and Singer, 1979: 229–30; Clay and Singer, 1985: 10.
89 FAO 1985b: 45 a.f.; Clay, 1983: 8; Hopkins, 1992: 249; FAO, 1987a; Clay & Stokke, 1991: 27; Chapouri & Missiaen, 1990: 26.
90 Klatzmann, 1988: 101; Mbius, 1987: 25.
91 EEC, 1988: 4.
92 Clay and Benson, 1991: 166; Hopkins, 1992: 249; Shapouri & Missiaen, 1990: 21.
93 Clay, 1983: 5, 17, 28–9, 55–6.
94 FAO, 1989, 1991a, 1991b.
95 USAID, 1985: 15.
96 Singer, 1987: 326.
97 Singer et al., 1987: 6 & 40.
98 Clay & Benson, 1991. 153 and own calculations.
99 *Idem*: 166.
100 Table on IEFR from FAO's *Food Outlook Statistical Supplement*, 1982: 16 and 1990: 46 and FAO, 1988: 40. Table on multilateral aid: period 1960–1975: Wallerstein, 1980: 232; afterwards, own calculation from WFP, 1988 and FAO, 1990: 43. FAO, 1988: 41, has different figures. Multilateral aid consists of contributions to the WFP, which also manages the IEFR, and small donations to UNDRO, UNICEF, and some other organizations: Singer, Wood and Jennings, 1987: 30–1. Only data for FAC fulfillment from 1981 onwards are presented: beforehand, the quantity to which donors were committed – 4,7 million tons – was low and easy to fulfill, even during the 1972–4 crisis. The 1989 drop in IEFR fulfillment rate is mainly due to the US: Clay & Stokke, 1991: 27; eee Shapouri & Missiaen, 1990: 7 for different data.

101 The EEC, because of administrative problems, has the worst record. For comprehensive charts, see FAO, 1985(b:) 53 a.f.

102 1985: 17. But, as Saran & Konandreos, 1991: 40, point out, in 1986, Australia revised its FAC commitments from 400,000 to 300,000 tons.

103 Singer, 1987: 329.

104 Maxwell and Singer, 1979: 227; Hopkins, 1992: 244; Clay and Stokke, 1991: 11.

105 WFP, 1988; FAO, 1991a.

106 Note however, that there is little agreement between different sources on the precise extent of these needs. Projections of food aid needs for the 1990s vary between 32 and 74 million tons: Bender, 1990: 45.

107 The USDA itself publishes figures on this: for example, USDA/ERS, 1990. See too Bender, 1990: 42–3; Hopkins, 1992: 247.

108 According to the Food Aid Monitor, September 1990: Table 2, Iran received 29,000 tons in 1989 and 42,000 tons in 1990; food aid donations to Vietnam for the same years totalled respectively 43,000 tons and 30,000 tons.

109 Jack Shepherd, "Some Tragic Errors": American Policy and the Ethiopian Famine, 1982–85', forthcoming. See too Doyle, 1987: 330 and Rau, 1991: 106. It is clear that the official US version is different. See testimonies in House, 1987a: *passim*.

110 The US refuses to give any developmental food aid to Ethiopia, though; but European countries do.

111 The information for this system comes from a large variety of sources, including US government ones, such as different desks within USAID, the NASA, or the National Oceanic and Atmospheric Administration's National Environment Sattelite; US NGOs, and UN organizations, such as FAO, WFP and FAO's own Global Information and Early Warning System! One might discuss the appropriateness of putting into place a system parallel to the FAO's, but one cannot deny the existence of a network here.

112 The same holds for food aid to Iran after the 1990 earthquake. For a good overbiew of the fast and strong reaction of US NGOs, the public and government, see *Monday Developments*, an InterAction newsletter, 8, 12, July 9, 1990: supplements.

113 Talbot, 1986: 180; Talbot & Moyer, 1987: 281. This is also the case for the USSR, which, according to Arefieva, 1991: 308–9 gave food aid to Ethiopia, Afghanistan and Southern Africa for humanitarian considerations coupled with 'ideological and political ones': it 'fit well into the new international image the USSR is establishing'.

114 See Newman, 1990 for an interesting discussion of the existence of different norms against starvation throughout history. Over the last centuries, the world has witnessed the globalization of such norms which have come to apply to larger entities – as Robert Kates has it, from 'kin to kind'.

115 For the US, see *Le Monde*, November 3, 1990, June 24, 1991; *The*

Economist, July 27, 1991; for the EEC, see the *Bulletin of the European Community,* 24, June 1991: 17–18.

116 Möbius, 1987: table 3.

117 Alaux et al., 1985: 103–105.

118 Lerin, 1986.

119 Cathie, 1991: 460 argues that for the EEC there is no link between food aid and surplus. For other countries, see too Shapouri & Missiaen, 1990: *passim.*

120 1985: 5. See too Clay & Stokke, 1991: 11.

121 During the period 1980–85, it received between 21 and 40% of all bilateral cereals aid.

122 Garst & Barry, 1990: 1, 12, chapter 2.

123 James Ingram, personal communication, Providence, May 13, 1992.

124 See table in Singer, Wood & Jennings, 1987: 232 – 234. During the same year, another 207,786 tons of cereals donated to the IEFR, coming from ten countries, were specifically designed for the African emergenc,. This included 100,000 tons from India, 5,000 tons from the US, and 50 tons from . . . Egypt!

125 James Ingram, lecture on the 'Future Archictecture of International Humanitarian Assistance,' Thomas Watson Jr. Institute for International Studies, Brown University, May 8, 1992, to be published in *'Humanitarianism Across Borders'* edited by T. Weiss and L. Minear, forthcoming; see too Talbot, 1990: 61.

126 Clay, 1983: 3, 6; Clay & Singer, 1985: 18; Clay & Stokke, 1991: 3.; Cathie, 1991: *passim.* This is partially due to the fact that, as a result of the Freedom of Information Act official data on US food aid, and even critiques of it, are much easier to get at than those of other countries.

127 Singer, Wood and Jennings, 1987: 35.

128 White, 1974; McNeill, 1981.

129 If there were no developmental international food aid regime, statesmen would not consider it to the interest of their country to give 5 million tons of food to sub-Saharan Africa every year. Similarly, if there were no strong norm against famine, American policymakers would not consider emergency aid to communist Ethiopia necessary or beneficial for the reputation of the US.

130 With some imagination, practically every action (giving food aid as well as not giving it, for example) can be interpreted as being in the long-term or the enlightened self-interest of an actor – just as, for Liberals, 'common interests' can be found everywhere.

131 Among many, see Keohane, 1988: 381 ff.; Nye, 1988; and Ashley's, 1986: 273 ff. for treatments of a sociological position. See too Kratochwil & Ruggie, 1986; E.B. Haas, 1982; P. M. Haas, 1992 and Haggard & Simmons, 1986 on cognitivist approaches.

132 Doyle, 1987: 315.

133 1982: 39

134 Clay & Singer, 1983: 1; Clay & Everitt, 1983: 58; Clay & Singer, 1985: 27.

135 Cathie, 1991: 91; Garst & Barry, 1990: 107; Jost, 1991: *passim*; Schubert, 185.

136 Schubert, 1986: 191–12; Cathie, 1991: 6, arrives at the same conclusion for Botswana.

137 Quoted by Garts and Barry, 1990: 19

138 Cathie, 1991: 114 concludes that Botswana's stockpiling policy has effectively succeeded in stabilizing food prices, but most classical economists would disfavor food stocks, arguing that they are too expensive and intervene with the market.

139 They are thus what development specialists call 'self-targeting'. See Garts & Barry, 1990: 132–40 for a critique; for the standard overview of the literature, see Clay, 1982: *passim*

140 See too Garts & Barry, 1990: 107–8.

141 Definition used by Clay & Singer, 1985: 57.

142 For interesting literature on the topic, see Fryer, 1981; Jackson & Eade, 1982; Clay & Singer, 1985.

143 Schubert, 1986: 187; Green, 1977: 77.

144 Wood & Jennings, 1987: 14; Millman e.a., 1990: 321; *Le Monde*, 20 dec. 1990. Even in the 1984 famine, although the Ethiopian government recognized the famine quite early on (this time before the international organizations did, but it took until the famous BBC television images for the latter to get in action), it still made it impossible to give food aid to its population in the rebel-controlled areas. It took continuous lobbying by aid organizations (public and private) and governments to change this position. This cynical and paradoxical situation, where donors have to fight for the right to feed starving people, is well exemplified in the following newspaper quote: 'for the first time, the aid given to the Addis Ababa regime nourishes people on the other side of the front line. . . . This was the result of months of negotiations . . . the authorities could not afford anymore the luxury of bad publicity with the international opinion which is becoming increasingly firm towards it. Fully playing its new strategy of overture, the government even *allowed* the United Nations to repair two bridges on the road [to Tigre] which allows the sending of food aid to the north of Wollo and Tigre . . .'. *Libération*, May 21, 1990: 24 (italics are mine).

145 This strongly came out strongly at a high-level discussion of managers of emergency aid, held by the 'Humanitarianism and War Project' at the Thomas J., Watson Institute for International Studies on April 8, 1992, and directed by Larry Minear and Thomas Weiss. See too chapter one of Hancock, 1990. In general, the role local governments and people play in fighting famines and other emergencies is often not adressed: it looks as if only the international community – and especially the famous NGOs such as CARE and Mdecins sans Frontires – does anything about it. For that reason, it is useful to quote Clay & Stokke, 1991: 20 on the African 1983–4 famine 'the relief operations were financed, in order of significance, by the domestic ressources of affected countries, by aid donors, and last, and very much least, by NGOs and media-centred fundraising.'

146 James Ingram, personal communication and lecture on the 'Future Archictecture of International Humanitarian Assistance,' *op. cit.*

147 For a good and recent example, see *The Economist*, May 13, 1989. For a detailed analysis of the problems involved, see Singer, Wood & Jennings, 1987: *passim*. On the African famine, see Clay & Stokke, 1991: 19, Clay, 1991: 225–9 and Borton, 1989: *passim*. According to a study by the US Government Accountig Office, 1986: 8, US 1984 emergency food aid to Africa arrived on the average six months after the request, during the rainy season, making its distribution to the needy exceedingly difficult.

148 Such 'leakage,' as political scientists know, is nothing but expectable and hardly avoidable; it is not a feature which only food aid displays. See Clay & Singer, 1985: 86.

149 Singer, Wood & Jennings, 1987: chapters 8 and 9; Garst & Barry, 1990: 103. The recent case of Somalia highlights these problems in a dramatic manner.

150 WFP, 1986a and 1986b; USAID, 1986a and 1986b; USGAO, 1986.

151 Clay & Stokke, 1991: 23; see too Clay, 1991: 223 ff..

152 Schubert, 1986: 189; Clay & Stokke, 1991: 20,

153 Minear, 1991: *passim*.

154 *Food Aid Monitor*, September 1990: Table 2; September 1991: Table 3. For a good overview, see Chen, 1990b: *passim*.

155 See *The Economist*, October 14, 1989.

156 Personal communication, Gilbert Etienne.

157 The latter question constitutes a big debate among food aid specialists and practitioners at present: how to use food aid (and, for that matter, all emergency aid) in such a way as to maximize its positive impact on longer-term development. See WFP, 1986c: *passim*; Clay & Singer, 1985: chapter 5; Hagman, 1987.

158 In August 1988, the Heritage Foundation published a Report, written by James Board, which was highly critical of US food aid, mainly because of the disincentive argument: see *Financial Times*, August 17, 1988; also conversation with Michael Johns from the Heritage Foundation. For a strong example of 'scholarly' attitude, see Melvyn Krauss, 1989: *passim*.

159 Jackson & Eade, 1982; Pym, 1982, mentioned in Clay & Singer, 1985: 14; The Independent Group on British Aid: see Elliott, 1982: 26.

160 For a short overview of the position of different authors from both sides, see the commented bibliography of Klatzmann, 1987.

161 Schultz., 1960.

162 Jackson & Eade, 1982; see too Clay & Singer, 1985: 82.

163 See for example: *Cahiers Nord-Sud*, 1983: 23.

164 Maxwell & Singer, 1979: 224.

165 This has been argued *inter alia* by the famous agricultural economist John Mellor, 1980, 1982. Also Bhagwati, 1985: 296, argues that food aid almost always has a positive welfare effect.

166 When, apart from the 'normal' commercial market, there also exists a low-price food distribution system, through ration cards, low price shops, etc.

167 Dandekar, 1965; Bhagwati, 1985.

168 For an overview of some hundreds of studies on the subject, see Maxwell & Singer, 1979: 225, Clay & Singer, 1985: 33–9 and Jones, 1989, *passim*. On Bangladesh, a big recipient, see Nelson, 1983: 52. For US food aid, see USAID, 1985: 3–5, that synthesizes five evaluations of Title I programs.

169 Bachman & Paulino, 1979; referred to in Von Braun & Huddleston, 1988, who share this vision.

170 U.S.A.I.D., 1985: 13, 14, 17.

171 To the extent that there is 'leakage,' *i.e.* people selling (part of) the food received on the market, in order to buy other items with the proceeds, the disincentive effect still holds. But, if the distribution of food aid is well targeted to those in need (and such mechanisms of self-targeting, such as the use of 'inferior' foods, exist nowadays), leakage represents only a small fraction of total food aid and *a fortiori* availability.

172 Clay & Singer, 1985: 31. Funnily enough, this substitution effect takes place especially in the case of large amounts of politically motivated food aid to strategic countries, which is allowed to replace commercial imports, such as Egypt and Central America: Garst & Barry, 1990: 62. We here have a case where 'bad' political motives can have 'good' developmental effects.

173 Saran & Konandreos, 1991: 56–7.

174 See Hopkins, 1983: 78. Especially the WFP, being a multilateral agency funded by voluntary contributions, does all it can to avoid hurting any possible preference of its member states. One has to be extremely careful in interpreting its Annual Reports: little can be 'demonstrated' by referring to them: at the maximum, one can hope to uncover trends and novelties in its discourse, and thus its changing perception of what the preferences are of the different publics it caters to. This does not hold for the technical studies it publishes: these are done by and for the development experts; they are usually of a very high quality: see for example the 1983 Seminar on Food Aid as well as Clay and Singer, 1985.

175 EEC, 1989: 7. Note that this report of the commission to the Parliament on the 1985 food aid exercise is effectively being published in 1989!

176 *Financial Times*, July 7, 1990; see also July 6, 1990. Note also that the EEC had to *buy* part of this food (meat and milk) on the international market, for its food stocks are too low! *Libération*, July 17, 1989.

177 Cour des Comptes . . . , 1988: 4.

178 Dawson, 1985; USAID, 1985: 4–5; Clay, 1991: 215, 217.

179 See Clay & Singer, 1985: 29, 38 & 42, with numerous references to the specialized literature. Also USAID, 1985: 5 & 15; Hopkins, 1992: 255, Erard & Mounier, 1984: 55; and Jones, 1989: *passim*. For a most interesting overview of the extreme bureaucratic complexity of the procedures involved in the allocation of food aid in the case of the US, see Wennergren e.a., 1989: 196 (appendix 2.10).

180 Indeed, the impression I got from the literature, as well as from conversations with Professor Hans Singer, is precisely that it takes political commitment and administrative capacity to avoid the disincentive effects of food aid by targeting measures, dual market systems, the efficient use of counterfunds, and the like. Yet, if they existed in India for example, these conditions are often absent in Africa. That poses a problem, necessitating greater donor flexibility and stability: Von Braun & Huddleston, 1988: 253 & 263; Singer, 1989: 200.

181 Maxwell, 1991: 86.

182 This is also the conclusion of older research by Isenman & Singer, 1977; Kern, 1968; and Merrill, 1977.

183 Maxwell & Singer, 1979: 226; Shapouri & Missiaen, 1990: 31–7.

184 The 15 countries with the biggest increases in per capita food production during the period 1979/81 – 1987/89 received only 7.3 kilo of food aid per person – half of the other group. Then again, among them, we find Egypt, the biggest per capita food aid recipient in the world, and Morocco, also in the top league.

185 Note also that 6 out of the 15 countries with sharply declining food production per person were plagued by civil war.

186 This is a surprisingly 'Marxist' reasoning, reflecting a 'Verelendung der Massen' logic.

187 See for a reflection on this matter: Deers, 1973: *passim*. To a certain extent, the debate about solutions for the debt crisis presents the same moral problem. Concerning food aid, see too US House of Representatives, 1987a: *passim*.

188 See also Singer, Wood & Jennings, 1987: 42. This has been the case, for example, in Ethiopia at the beginning of the 1980s.

189 George, 1984: 48. See too Dumont, 1985.

190 USGAO, 1987: 28–30; USAID, 1985: 14.

191 1988: 256

192 Figures drawn from FAO, 1987: tables 3.16 and 3, 18.

193 Only for Northern Africa, Richards, 1987: 307 mentions Egypt in 1977 & 1984; Morocco in 1981 & 1984; Sudan in 1981 & 1985; and Tunisia in 1984. We would add at least Egypt in 1986, Algeria in 1988, and Jordan in 1989.

194 Bienen & Gersowitz, 1985: *passim*; Furlong, 1989: 141–5.

195 Schubert, 1986: 194–6.

196 If, for example, food aid represents 5% of the food available for feeding the strategic groups needed to keep governents in power, then most would agree that food aid is not causally linked to their remaining in power. At 50%, evidently, that would be different. Then again, even a 5% decrease can cause hardship for those close to the border and declining legitimacy for governments. On the other hand, governments could make that up quite easily with commercial imports. How about 15%? Or 25%? Where do we draw the line?

197 For Egypt, see Burns, 1985 and Weinbaum, 1983, as well as press

reports. For Bangladesh, see Parkinson, 1981, as well as Moore-Lapp and Collins, 1980.

198 USAID, 1985: 9.

199 For Cambodia, see Shawcross, 1985. A controversial description of the Ethiopian case can be found in Glucksman & Wolton, 1986. In the 1988 Sudan famine, and again in 1991, the government used the inpouring food aid to support the Muslim, northern minority of the country and neglected the Christian, Southern population. The abuse of food aid for political purposes is no privilege of governments: rebels and guerillas, if they get the chance, will often do the same. Thus in the Sudan famine, the rebels tried everything to stop food aid from going to government-controlled regions, going as far as shooting down the relief planes. This now happens in Somalia too.

200 USAID, 1985: 10. Underlining by the author.

201 See the testimony by USAID's assistant administrator for Africa, M Love, before the House subcommittee on Hunger, 1987a: *passim*; also USAID, 1985: 6, 7, 12; Faaland, 1981: *passim*; Hopkins, 1992: 260.

202 Note that many of these recipients are self-declared communist countries!

203 First column: WFP, 1988; third column: *L'Etat du monde*, 1988–89.

204 For a good example, see Charvet, 1987: 14 ff. and Garst & Barry, 1990: 55. For a bad example, see Erard & Mounier, 1984: 84.

205 Byerlee, 1987. See also Clay & Singer, 1985: 39, with references to studies on Bangladesh, Indonesia and Sri Lanka.

206 Often dating from the colonial period: Dawson, 1985.

207 See too Madaule, 1990: 75 a.f.

208 See Clay & Singer, 1985, chapter 2, for a good discussion of this; also USAID, 1985: 8.

209 Maxwell and Singer, 1979: ftn. 196; see too James Ingram, Executive Director of the World Food Programme, in WFP/Government of the Netherlands, 1983: 18: 'sometimes the problems inherent in all aid are identified with food aid, as if it alone had problems in working through weak administrations in desperately underdeveloped countries.'

210 See too Von Braun & Huddleston, 1988: 255–60 and Hopkins, 1992: 255–7. As Clay & Stokke, 1991: 27, and Clay, 1991: 221 point out, food aid has not yet become *countercyclical*, which greatly limits its use.

211 Haas, P., 1991: *passim*; Hopkins, 1991: *passim*.

212 Hopkins, 1991: 237–9; the proceeds of this conference have been published in WFP/Government of the Netherlands, 1983.

CHAPTER SIX

THE UNBEARABLE LIGHTNESS OF BEINGS: THE INTERNATIONAL ORGANIZATION OF POPULATION

The dominant hunger principle treats undernutrition and rapid population growth as causally linked; recently, environmental stress or degradation has been added. In chapter three, we analyzed the international regime applying to hunger; in this chapter, we will study the population side of the equation.

We will start with a very brief overview of the main facts and the recent evolution of the issue area. In the second and third part of this chapter, we will analyze the content and origin of the international population regime (an issue not analyzed by international relations specialists[1]); in the fourth part we will discuss the international processes it gave rise to. Finally, more general theoretical remarks will be addressed. They discuss the role of power, norms and principles and international organizations in the international politics of population. We believe these issues to be of interest, not only for specialists of international relations, but also for those working on development matters and North-South issues.

1 Some facts about people, land and food

Forecasts of population growth rates or population size display serious weaknesses.[2] For one, they have a very mechanical character, neglecting the feedback of economic and social change. Given the state of rapid social and economic change that characterizes most LDCs, this makes their long term results very uncertain.[3] Second, their results are extremely dependent on the underlying assumptions: thus, changing the predicted fertility rate from the replacement level to 5% above it increases the population forecast for the year 2150 from 11.5 to 28 billion people![4] Moreover, they are subject to a considerable margin of error, resulting from unpredicted, if not unpredictable, facts. Take the case of China. During the 1980s, its population growth rate was estimated at 1,18%; it was predicted to fall to 0,53% in 2020–2025 – the level of HICs. But according to recent data from China itself, this tendency has been arrested in the countryside, where the desire for children is great and the means of control less efficient.[5] The resulting increase in world population is likely to be significant – 100 million people by 2000.[6] The sad phenomenon of AIDS is another case in point. If, as some reports suggest at present, around 2 million Africans have the disease, and some 6 million more are seropositive, this is bound to have significant effects on African population growth rates – at least for some countries and some groups of the population.[7]

As if to prove this, in the 1970s, what all specialists termed an 'incredible' decline in population growth was said to have taken place. This unprecedented[8] and unpredicted decline resulted from a decrease in birth rates in almost all LDCs, implying that more and more countries are leaving the transitional phase.[9] As a result, long-term population forecasts were significantly downwards revised. According to estimates, then, total world population was to stabilize at around 11 billion people by the year 2050 – 4 to 9 billion less and 50 years earlier than demographers predicted some years before.[10] In the second half of the 1980s, the opposite process took place: as preparations for the new World Population forecast advanced, it became accepted that the previous forecasts had to be upwards revised. In 1990, a highly publicized United Nations Fund for Population Activities (UNFPA) report predicted the world will hold up 14 billion people by the middle of the 2100s – a significant increase. Of course, also these figures have little more scientific certainty than the previous, and the same critical approach should be taken to them.

Hence, population forecasts are to be adressed with utmost care. Forecasts of less than 20 years are mere extrapolations of present trends, while those on more than 20 years are doubtful and arbitrary.[11] The utility of the investment in producing these figures, then, is probably much more political than scientific in nature. When they are higher than predicted, they serve to legitimize increased family planning activity and consequently resources; when they are lower, they are taken to prove the effectiveness of family planning, and hence the necessity to increase the ressources for it.

2 The international population regime

As explained before, neo-Malthusian principles and norms domi-nate the international hunger regime. Following different periods in the writings of Thomas Malthus himself, we can distinguish between 'first-edition' and 'second-edition' Malthusianism.[12] The former sees both population and food production growth rates as unchangeable and leading to a catastrophic confrontation; the norms it leads to are those of non-interference with so-called natural processes and passive euthanasia.[13] The latter, on the contrary, believes that population growth rates can be lowered. Its normative tendency is that population control coupled with the expansion of agricultural output are necessary for avoiding disaster.[14]

It is the latter one which has become dominant in occidental academic and policy-making circles as well as in an increasing number of LDCs. It is one of the main principles in the hunger issue area and a central pillar of the international development regime. Hardly any study, policy statement or speech on hunger or development can be found that fails to refer to the need for lower population growth rates.[15] Among the scholarly literature on the subject – not only demographers and economists[16] but also practitioners of the other sciences – those arguing that population growth is not a major cause of hunger are but a small minority.[17] The press, drawing attention to famines and starvation, reinforces this vision. And according to a recent poll com-missioned by the Population Crisis Committee, 'more than 90% of Americans think that poverty and other social problems will get worse if the population of developing countries continues to grow rapidly, and that these countries will increasingly rely on US famine relief and other aid.'[18] Often we are shown a famous figure which graphically represents the long-term population size of the world, since, say, the year zero, or 2,000 B.C., or 1,000 A.C. As shown below, this yields a curve which strongly resembles the one of the amount of nuclear weapons in the

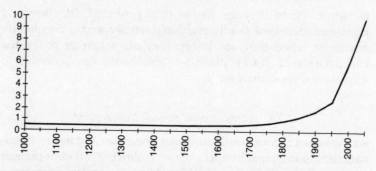

Figure 6.1 World population, 1000–2050, billion people

world, and is surely every bit as threatening.[19] In and of itself, this is supposed to show us the impending menace of the world population explosion. Nobody, though, adds to this the long term curve of world food production or income, although both increase even faster than the population curve.

Second-edition Malthusianism is usually based on either of two principles.[20] The first one, held by most economists for example, is that *high population growth retards or annihilates development*. In its most simple version, this is a matter of arithmetic – per capita indicators increase when population decreases. More scientifically, it is held that high population growth decreases the resources available in a society for savings and investment, thus slowing economic growth and creating or perpetuating poverty and hunger.[21] This argument is also at times applied to the level of the individual family.[22]

In the development community, it is the World Bank which is most active in strengthening the 'high-population-growth-decrease-economic-growth' principle – as well as, of course, the norms in favor of population control. The most important recent expression can be found in its *1984 World Development Report*. Published just before the World Population Conference in Mexico, it argues that 'rapid population growth (at rates above 2 percent, common in most developing countries today) acts as a brake on development'[23] and consequently advocates population control as a necessary condition for development. The four important reports the World Bank devoted to sub-Saharan Africa in the 1980s all include population control as a priority.[24] And over the last years, successive World Bank presidents repeatedly declared that the Bank would intensify its population control efforts, especially in sub-Saharan Africa. Because of the central position of the World Bank in the development community, this constitutes an important reinforcement of the regime.

The second principle holds that food production cannot be expanded in line with expected population growth, particularly not if the quality of the average diet must increase. This principle, bordering on first-edition Malthusianism, came to the fore in the beginning of the 1970s in the Reports to the Club of Rome and has remained alive ever since. It has found its application in many more or less scientific arguments about the 'carrying capacity,' *i.e.* the food production potential of the land, of the Earth, or of individual countries.[25] It is often voiced by the FAO, the World Food Council (WFC) and the UN Fund for Population Activities (UNFPA) – the UN organizations directly engaged in the food/population business. At the end of the 1980s, it got new breath, for it became a central element of the emerging international environment regime, as applied to developing countries.[26] In that version, population is not only linked to the limits of food production, but also to all kinds of environmental damage. Hence, it has become commonplace among international policymakers and intellectuals interested in development and the environment to connect issues as diverse as the incidence of hunger, the burning of the rainforests, acid rain and sewage disposal in the Ganges to the necessity of cutting population growth in the developing countries.[27] In its most official, the Director of the UNFPA and the Executive Director of the WFC, respectively, point out that.

> population growth and development patterns not only affect the demand for resources but also generate environmental changes which will have repercussions on the future carrying capacity of the earth[28]

and that

> the pressures resulting from overpopulation tend to provoke or aggravate the bad utilisation of lands ... which leads to their desertification. ... If Africa does not undertake a massive effort to render its lands 'healthy' (sic) again, chronic famine will replace periodic famines[29]

This 'population-growth-puts-too-heavy-a-burden-on-the-

Earth's-capacities' principle is shared by people at the highest levels of policymaking, especially in the US[30] – which is surprising as the 'limits to growth' body of principles has in general not been very popular among the earthly powers. Decision-makers (businessmen and politicians alike) have always excelled in their certitude – based either upon their blind belief in the market and technological progress or upon mere disinterest in the matter – that the world is not as finite as the Club of Rome predicted. But this optimism does not seem to hold when it comes to the poor people in the Third World.

The reason for this might be a more or less unconscious image of poor people as mouths to be fed, as liabilities rather than assets.[31] Starting from this Eurocentric[32] image, population contol policies indeed become evident solutions to the hunger problem. In this respect Franke and Chasin note:

> It is assumed by population theorists – though rarely stated – that people are primarily mouths and stomachs to be fed. That they are also hands to work and minds to think and create is rarely mentioned. (. . .) It is just as logical to assume that population growth should have been a major cause of *overcoming* droughts.[33]

Indeed, the latter is what Julian Simon does, for example, when he writes that:

> the most important positive effect of additional people – improvement through the contribution of new ideas and the learning-by-doing resulting from increased production volume – happen in the long run and are cumulative.[34]

The 'limits to growth' principle is also often voiced in a more nuanced version, which points out that, as it is precisely in the poorest and most food-deficit countries that population growth rates are predicted to be highest, family planning is an absolute necessity for them. Reference is usually made to sub-Saharan Africa, where population growth rates are projected to start decreasing only after the year 2000, implying that the largest relative increase will take place on the poorest continent, which already has most problems feeding its population.[35] Bangladesh and Ethiopia are other cases which are often referred to. People who use this argument implicitly assume that carrying capacity problems only exist in the poorest countries – not in the rich ones. Take a typical example: 'indeed, given the fact that the present technologies cannot expand because of capital constraints, most areas of Africa have reached or exceeded their carrying capacities of human and animal populations.'[36] This suggests that, somehow, the notion of carrying capacity is a relative one, and the real factors behind both hunger and carrying capacity problems are to be poverty and technology.[37] This is also the conclusion we will arrive at in the next section.

3 Neo-Malthusianism: a critique

As said, the basic tenet of the contemporary second-edition neo-Malthusian regime is that high population growth leads to hunger. This is argued in a variety of ways: directly, because of the finiteness of the world's (or of poor countries') physical capacity to produce food;[38] and indirectly, through the effects of population growth on an individual's or country's savings, income and ultimately, economic growth. In all cases, this leads to norms in favour of family planning: through lowering population growth rates, the above mentioned factors will increase and hunger decline.

There are thus two different but related sequels to the dominant body of thought: (1) family planning policies lead to lower population growth rates; and (2) lower population growth rates bring about a decrease in the incidence of hunger. We will argue that both are incomplete if not wrong, empirically as well as theoretically. We will start with the second.

A Population and hunger

Population related variables do not cause hunger. There is no statistical correlation between population growth and food production. Abercrombie calculated that 'there appears to be no correlation between the rate of population growth and whether the increase in food production has been above or below it.'[39] Klatzmann even concludes that there is no link between population growth and growth of food production *per capita!*[40] This comes as no surprise to anyone with some historical knowledge: it is exactly during its phase of unprecedented population growth, that Europe made the greatest advances in feeding its population.

Table 6.1 Population, carrying capacity and nutrition in Africa[44]

	Actual population mio people	Potential popul. low input (mio people)	Potential popul. medium input (mio people)	Average dietary consumption (cal per day)
	1987	1980	1980	1985
Algeria	23.1	7.0	24.6	2.677
Benin	4.3	6.3	28.4	2.173
Botswana	1.1	0.9	4.8	2.219
Burkina Faso	8.3	5.5	26.5	1.924
Burundi	5.0	0.9	4.6	2.166
Cameroon	10.9	76.8	209.2	2.098
C.A.R.	2.7	44.8	211.8	2.050
Congo	2.0	40.4	162.4	2.549
Egypt	50.1	61.1	61.6	3.263
Ethiopia	44.8	17.0	60.5	1.691
Ghana	13.6	20.3	88.5	1.747
Guinea	6.5	15.0	54.0	1.728
Ivory Coast	11.1	48.0	164.7	2.505
Kenya	22.1	3.7	12.1	2.151
Lesotho	1.6	0.6	1.4	2.358
Liberia	2.3	9.5	47.8	2.311
Lybia	4.1	1.8	3.7	3.612
Madagascar	10.9	48.3	192.1	2.469
Malawi	7.9	6.7	24.3	2.448
Mali	7.8	7.8	35.1	1.788
Mauritania	1.9	0.5	2.0	2.078
Mauritius	1.0	0.6	1.2	2.740
Morocco	23.3	12.6	26.9	2.678
Mozambique	14.6	38.2	156.7	1.678
Niger	6.8	0.8	2.6	2.250
Nigeria	106.6	54.1	218.2	2.038
Rwanda	6.4	0.7	3.6	1.919
Senegal	7.0	4.4	19.4	2.342
Sierra Leone	3.8	5.1	27.8	1.817
Somalia	5.7	1.3	2.3	2.072
Sudan	23.1	59.4	238.7	1.737
Tanzania	23.9	35.2	144.3	2.335
Tchad	5.3	13.6	69.8	1.504
Togo	3.2	3.9	18.4	2.236
Tunisia	7.6	2.5	6.3	2.836
Uganda	15.7	11.0	44.0	2.083
Zaire	32.6	291.9	1,281.0	2.154
Zambia	7.2	48.9	215.9	2.137
Zimbabwe	9.0	10.3	48.7	2.056

Similarly, there is no correlation between population density and the incidence of hunger[41] – nor even, as table 6.1 shows for the case of Africa (the continent with the highest proportion of undernourished), between carrying capacity and the incidence of hunger: some countries with potentials far above their actual population size know hunger, while others in the opposite situation do not.[42] As Robert Repetto concludes: 'there is ample room for communities and countries facing natural ressource pressures to maneuver. Historically, many nations with extremely limited natural ressources have built successful economies. The key is managing available resources wisely.'[43]

The conclusion of all the above is clear: natural resources are important, but not sole, determinants of food availability, and even less so of hunger. Many countries produce food far below their potentials, and this for political and economic reasons; there is no necessary or direct link between land availability, food production and the incidence of hunger.

As far as the indirect link goes – where higher population growth decreases economic growth and as a result increases the incidence of hunger – according to two UN overviews of the literature on the matter, in 1973 and in 1988, and a World Bank review of 1984 no theoretically significant or certain effect between population growth and depletion of natural resources, growth of GNP, savings and investment or hunger has yet been proven.[45] It is telling that after twenty years of intensive research, this seemingly evident relation, which is at the root of a large part of the development community's adherence to population control norms, has still not been established, neither in inter-country comparisons, nor with any methodological certainty at the household level.[46] The fact that no such statistical correlation has been established brings Julian Simon to conclude that

> because the studies persuasively show an absence of association in these data, they imply the absence of a negative causal relationship ... Absence of correlation between two variables can usually be considered a strong indication that neither variable is influencing the other – in this case, that slower population growth does not cause faster economic development.[47]

Hence, the commonsense affirmation that decreasing population growth directly or indirectly reduces hunger is false. The scientific origins of hunger are different and more complex, having to do, as said before, with distribution and entitlement failures, levels of technology and economic development, management of natural resources and the like. It is perfectly possible to have lower population growth rates together with a stationary incidence of hunger. Such could be the case if those who have enough to eat are the ones who have less children, or if the decrease in population growth rates coincides with an increasingly unequal distribution of the available food.[48] A similar message emanates from a study by a National Research Council study in 1986, concluding that

> globally slower population growth *may* delay the time at which a particular stage of depletion of an exhaustible resource is reached. *This effect does not necessarily increase the number of people who will have access to that resource.*[49]

At maximum, the statements we can make about the relation between population and hunger are of the following kind. One, it can be said that **if nothing changes**, it is likely that there will be more hunger in the future. This is evident, but, by itself, insignificant. In 1984, the FAO published a booklet under the title *Land, Food and People* – the non-specialist version of an important joint FAO-UNFPA-IASA study.[50] According to it, by the year 2000, 64 LDCs will be unable to feed themselves. For that reason, the study advocates population control. But the same study also documents the potential for food self-sufficiency in most (but not all) countries, even if population growth continues at the high predicted rates. Technological and social progress is possible: more intensive use of better inputs, more adapted seeds, improved irrigation and land reclamation, improved agrarian structures through land reform, conservation measures, and a more equitable distribution of food availability.[51] The study concludes: 'there is no reason to assume that the world could not produce, or many developing countries afford, the required amounts, given sufficient investment in agriculture.' Hence, what the study establishes is that there will be a population/food imbalance *if nothing changes*. The task ahead is thus to bring about the above needed technological and social changes – not to decrease population growth rates. If these changes do not materialize, and if present technologies and social structures continue unchanged, then population pressure is indeed likely to become a problem, through the intervening variable of environmental degradation.[52] And even if they reach that catastrophic situation, that, still, will be a problem of technology and policy, and of the factors that cause the adoption of a technology, and not of population growth as such.

Two, there is **arithmetic**: as most commonly used indicators of development (economic growth, food consumption, income or access to certain services) are expressed in *per capita* form, lower populations by definition imply higher development – all other things equal, of course. For example, under conditions of a population growth rate of 2,5%, common in Africa, a 4% growth rate of GNP, very common also, becomes a per capita change of 1,5%. If the former were only 1,5%, the latter would jump up to 2,5%. Such difference becomes highly significant if one compounds it over many years: after 12 years, given stable 4% absolute GNP growth rates, income per capita would be 25% higher with a 1,5% population growth rate than with the 2,5% one. This is simple algebra, which is always 'true' – but it is not a scientific proof of a causal relation between two variables. Yet, it is this simple arithmetic which constitutes the great seductive force of neo-Malthusian thought. One encounters it often, even in the most serious documents. Consider the following statement, from the previously mentioned FAO study: 'In cases of deficit [of food production], the imports or the increase in agricultural effort required to meet food needs are lower for the low population projection. For surplus regions, the potential surplus for export is greater.'[53] This cannot be contradicted: the arithmetic fact pointed out by FAO (if there are more people to feed, there is more food needed to feed them) is by definition and always true.[54] This is pleasant to know, but can hardly be called a strong scientific argument to prove that high population growth rates cause hunger. In its most absurd version, it would imply that we would achieve the highest rate of development and/of eradicating hunger by actually . . . killing people.

Third, it has been held that lowering population growth rates is useful, because it **offers governments a breathing space to change policies**.[55] This is politically uncertain, given that the existence of these policies-to-be reformed is in no way linked to prevailing population growth rates; moreover, many other measures exist which can provide breathing-spaces to governments in need of oxygen – massive transfers of food for example.

In this argument, there is no direct link anymore between rapid population growth and slow economic growth or hunger: rapid population growth perhaps exacerbates existing problems, or 'reveals them sooner and more dramatically than would otherwise have been the case, but it is either not the cause, or is only an indirect cause.' Indeed, 'many of the "problems" previously associated with population are now clearly established as not primarily demographic in nature: they are caused largely by other factors, and population growth serves primarily to reveal their symptoms sooner and more dramatically.'[56] We are then left with an argument or 'realpolitik' – not of demography.

Such a realpolitik argument could be quite meaningful, be it on a very general level. It would hold that in this world, being as poor as it is, with access to technology and land as unequally distributed as it is, and with serious institutional, economic or political change as is unlikely as it is, the small quantity of resources available to the poor would be distributed on fewer people if they had fewer children. This argument implicitly assumes that the productivity of poor people is zero: if this were not the case, fewer people would mean less production, and less to distribute on the remaining ones.[57]

To conclude: there is no direct or necessary relation between population related variables, such as population growth or population density, and the incidence of hunger. The incidence of hunger can decline with a stable or increased population growth rate, and vice versa. The relation between the two variables at best is a mathematical truism. Family planning can be justified on many other grounds, such as improving mothers' and children's health,[58] or the right of all human beings to have access to means of deciding upon their family size – yet, just as distributing condoms will not end hunger in the US, decreasing population growth rates does not constitute the key to ending hunger in the Third World.

B Family planning and population growth rates

We now turn to the second sequel, which holds that family planning policies lower birth rates (and as such, given stationary mortality rates, population growth). This is a complicated issue, which we will treat only superficially here. The central problem is, in the words of Barbara Herz, whether birth rates are 'affected primarily by availability of effective family planning services and information ("supply") or by social, economic, and cultural conditions that affect how many children people want and how intensely they try to limit their childbearing accordingly[59] ("demand")'? Supply factors are important variables, but it seems that demand factors are much more important. To explain this, we will use Herz's distinction between three components of a completed family:

– minimum desired family size: the number of children the parents would want if they felt entirely free to choose, without fear that any would die.

– insurance births: additional children they would want to ensure survival of the desired minimum.

– extra births: additional children that they might not have chosen to have, at least consciously, but nonetheless do have, because they lack access to effective birth control, know little or nothing of the birth control option, follow cultural or religious tradition, just do 'what is natural' in the biological sense; or resign themselves to a fate that in this respect as in others they feel unable to control.[60]

Over the years, as organizations and agencies have learned to effectively design and manage family planning programs and policies, they have become increasingly capable of responding to the unmet demand for contraception. The available data seem to indicate that, in many but not all, cases, contraceptive adoption rates increase after such programs have been functioning for some years; fertility declines often follow.[61]

But it is only this last, and smallest, category of births that is directly prevented by most family planning programs; the others are mainly sensitive to changes in demand. Demand does not increase automatically when the supply of contraceptives improves; it is primarily conditioned by poverty and well-being, or the absence of it – and, of course, by the social and religious values of society.

Different explanations have been advanced for this: we will mention them very briefly here. In many traditional societies, (male) children are very highly valued: poor is he who has no children even if he has much money. It is now also generally held that in poor households, for a variety of reasons, 'having a large family is the economically rational decision for poor parents to make' – they add to the labor force, and eventually act as an oldness and sickness insurance. The richer societies become, the more it makes economic sense to have small families.[62] Moreover, parents want surviving children: with high infant mortality, more births are needed to guarantee the minimum desired family size. Finally, development entails a variety of socioeconomic and cultural changes – income, food consumption, hygiene, female education, employment – which all work in favor of smaller families.[63] Hence, the higher level of development of a country, the lower its population growth rate. But that does not explain everything.

The relation between poverty and population growth becomes even stronger when we disaggregate the analysis and look at the level of individuals. The more equally income is distributed within countries (i.e. between people), the lower their population growth rates.[64] In other words, the fact that some countries at low levels of GNP have low population growth rates (such as China and Sri Lanka), is caused to a large extent by the fact that they managed to create entitlements for poor people, i.e. access to the above mentioned advantages of development: income, health services, education, and the like.[65] According to calculations by Murdoch, the distribution of income within countries, added to the distribution of income between countries, explains 73% of the differences in population growth rates in the world.[66]

Hence, family planning policies by themselves are unlikely to make much of a difference on population growth rates. The central forces behind declines in birth rates are individual well-being (implying economic growth and redistribution) and the values of a society. Family planning policies are of use to help satisfy what is often called 'unmet demand': when there is a demand for lower birth rates, the availability of effective family planning techniques at the individual's level is bound to speed up the decline of these birth rates (under given social, cultural and religious constraints). This is probably the explanation of the success of family planning policies in countries such as Mexico and Morocco, where rising incomes had created an unmet demand for fewer children: the availability of contraceptive techniques resulting from the introduction of a national family planning policy had rapid effects.

To conclude our discussion about the effectiveness of family planning programs, we quote from the conclusion of Robert Cassen's detailed review of the literature:

the prospects for fertility reduction are limited in a world where people are poor, illiterate and subject to high mortality, and their most urgent need is undoubtedly to find a way out of deprivation itself. But even the deprived may benefit from family planning, and might wish to adopt it if they knew more about it. And once real development does take place, there should be an increasing demand for contraception.[67]

Development and well-being decrease population growth rates significantly, at any level of GNP, just as they decrease the incidence of hunger. The wise management of scarce human and natural resources by governments can stop and reverse environmental degradation and increase food production and economic growth. Family planning programs are certainly of use to satisfy unmet but existing demand for decreasing births, for women empowerment and childrens' and women's health improvement. But they will not eliminate world hunger nor reverse trends of environmental degradation.

Yet, as said, notwithstanding its doubtful scientific validity, the international hunger, development and population regimes remain characterized by neo-Malthusian principles and norms. This has not always been the case. Moreover, this has some important consequences. The rest of this chapter will deal with these points.

4 Population and the international system[68]

Because of its strong link with religious and national sentiments, population has always been a very sensitive issue in international relations. In the words of Richard Symonds:

The population question has not only aroused stronger emotions than any other activity in the economic and social field; it has also cut right across familiar international divisions, producing strange coalitions, and, at times, more than usually equivocal resolutions.

Some Northern countries, most notably the Nordic ones, and some Third World countries such as India, Pakistan, South Korea,

China, Egypt and Sri Lanka, early on expressed preferences for population control measures and UN involvement in the issue.[69] But the main advocacy of population control in the beginning came from a small but vocal minority of scientists (organized *i.a* in the International Union for the Scientific Study of Population) and international NGOs such as the International Planned Parenthood Federation. They acted as pressure groups, which were highly successful in influencing official attitudes.[70] But they were also of operational importance. According to the authoritative interpretation of Symonds and Carver, as a result of their actions,

> a network of specialists came rapidly into existence, ready when needed to help governments or private groups either formally or informally. They were able to fill, to some extent, the void left by the UN, WHO and UNESCO.[71]

On the other side representatives of Roman Catholic countries and of the Holy See have tried every means at their disposal to retard discussion, let alone activity, in the field of population control. Ireland, Belgium, Italy and France (for the rich countries), the French-Speaking African countries as well as most Latin American ones (for the LDCs) vehemently opposed population control measures. Their position was based upon religious and sociological preferences, although some Third World countries also considered themselves underpopulated rather than overpopulated. They found strange bedfellows in the Eastblock countries, who, although domestically very 'liberal' on family planning and abortion, consistently obstructed international discussion on these issues. Marx himself repeatedly expressed anti-Malthusian arguments, but it is probable that the fact that population control was mainly advocated by rich Western countries and attacked by LDCs was not alien to the communist position. This combined front of catholics and communists managed to abort most international discussions of the population question for nearly two decades. As a result, and unlike other issue areas, the different organizations of the UN system – and especially in the organization within whose mandate it fell, the World Health Organization – mainly tried to avoid engaging themselves in the population issue.[72]

In the middle of the sixties, the domestic regime of many rich countries on population issues began to change. The influence of the Catholic Church decreased. More and more people began using birth control methods themselves; the general atmosphere towards such issues became one of tolerance if not encouragement. This relaxation of taboo's opened up the way for specialists, lobbyists and eventually politicians to publicly take a more positive stance on the issue – first of all in the US.[73] At the same time that population control (re)became popular among rich country elites, the intellectual atmosphere among development specialists (mainly economists) also became favourable to it. Hence, when in the 1960s 'economic development became a major UN objective, population growth was increasingly and publicly linked to it.'[74]

Although the Scandinavian countries had advocated for more than a decade such measures and had started to implement them in their bilateral development cooperation policies, it was not until US, with the most extensive resources and the largest academic community, began favoring population control, that things really started moving on the international level.[75] In 1967 the United Nations Fund for Population Activities (UNFPA) was created. Initially very small, mainly funded by the US, its importance and income grew all through the 1970s. The World Bank was the first important UN-related organization to officially adhere to population control. In a famous speech before the Board of Governors in 1968, McNamara marked the beginning of World Bank involvement in the issue.

In 1974, on the initiative of the US, the first World Population Conference was convened in Bucarest. It was characterized by heavy resistance of the Third World to the proposed population control policies. The issue was linked by the Group of 77, then at the height of unity and anti-Western sentiment, to the New International Economic Order, under the slogan 'development is the best contraceptive.'[76] The fact that family planning was advocated by the Western countries was certainly not alien to this resistance. As a result, the final Plan of Action adopted at the Conference made little reference to family planning, contrary to US desire. Yet it did formally link the population issue to development concerns, and brought about the legitimization of international involvement in population issues.[77]

Thus, by the middle of the 1970s, the official international principle had become that increased development would cause decreasing birth rates, and the norm that population assistance was a necessary activity of the international community. This situation was most ambiguous, for, if taken literally, the former is in conflict with the latter; it presented but a shaky legitimation of the international involvement in the population control. Most UN organizations tried to remain verbally close to the principle, while at the same time having family planning policies based on the opposite one; many development specialists and rich country policy makers never adhered to the principle but acted along the lines of the norm in favor of population assistance.

Throughout the years, those in favor of family planning, most prominent among whom are the multitude of private mainly Washington-based organizations and the World Bank, tried to strengthen the international population regime by establishing the opposite relation (that lower birth rates increase the pace of development) as its central principle. Still others, in the quest for international legitimacy, also linked population control to women's health when they were popular; to human rights[78] and to national security[79], when addressing occidental fora; and presently, as explained above, to the latest discovery of the international system, the environment.

Spending on family planning thus becomes legitimized by linking it to other desirable and internationally accepted issues, foremost among them 'development' or 'women's health'; it testifies to the increased acceptability of population control that spending on other activities is now justified by linking it to population. Hence, at present, the Population Crisis Committee, for example, tries to legitimize more resources for family planning by 'demonstrating' that more family planning and lower population growth rates will 'cut three million deaths among Third World children'; at the same time, UNICEF, trying to justify spending on children's health, proves exactly the opposite relation, namely that lower child mortality rates will bring about lower population growth rates.[80] Hence, all through the 1970s, there existed a strong ambiguity as to the central international principle concerning population, with two diametrically opposite ones – development causes declining population growth and vice versa – being used interchangeably by different actors, both searching to legitimize international involvement in population issues.

In 1984 a second World Population Conference was held in Mexico. This time the principle that high population growth causes development problems, as well as the norm in favor of family planning, were generally adopted. There were but two negative votes: the Vatican[81] and, surprisingly, the US. Indeed, so as to please the 'new' right in the US, its official preferences on the issue had changed again.[82] Under the Reagan administration support for UN engagement in the field of population control ended[83] – all the more interesting as its vice-president had previously been a major advocate of birth control, in Congress as well as in the UN.[84] In 1985, the US stopped funding the UNFPA (down from 25%) as well as the International Planned Parenthood Federation, officially because of their support of abortion, but in reality for reasons of domestic politics.[85] Note that, according to Crane and Finkle, since the US ended its funding of UNFPA, no Department of State or White House official ever mentioned the abortion issue to China itself during the last decade. Moreover, USAID continues to spend almost as much money as before on population assistance to many countries, in all of whom abortion evidently exists. This brings us to conclude, as Crane and Finkle did, that US foreign policy on this issue was not unitary, and that domestic factors were much more important to explain this international policy outcome than any clear notion of self-interest.[86] Yet, this decision has not led to any change in the international regime on the matter. Other donors, most notably Finland, Germany and Japan more than compensated for the decline in US funding, and, by the end of the 1980s, the UNFPA budget, after a period of stagnation, is on the rise again.[87] Moreover, the causal link between population growth and hunger, and since recently also environmental degradation, has become more and more accepted among all those engaged in the international development community, while the advocacy of family planning by the highest levels of policymaking goes on unabated. In their joint declaration on development cooperation in the 1990s, for example, the Ministers of Development Cooperation of the OECD affirmed that 'it [will be] of crucial importance to create an awareness of the imperious necessity to slow down population growth rates in the many countries where they are too high to allow sustainable development.'[88] All through 1990, the President of the World Bank incessantly stressed that curbing population growth is a precondition for development, and that it will be an absolute priority for the Bank for the next decade, being worth as much as 500 million $ a year by 2,000.[89]

In summary, we saw the slow and difficult emergence of an international population regime based on the principle that population growth retards development and causes hunger, and leading to the norm that the international community should finance family planning policies all over the Third World, so as to curb population growth rates; parallel to that, a variety of other principles and norms are also fighting for recognition. But what form did this regime take in practice? What activities did it lead to? That is what we now turn to.

5 Population assistance

Notwithstanding the ambiguities of the regime, by the middle of the 1970s, and 'fueled by concern over the world food crisis',[90] nearly all actors in the international development community were active in the field of what is euphemistically called 'population assistance', i.e., 'the aid response made by donor agencies to requests from developing countries who wish to effect some change in the demographic characteristics of their population (primarily, though not exclusively, a reduction in the rate of population growth)[91] – which amounts primarily to aid to developing countries for the design and implementation of family planning programs and policies.[92]

As can be seen from the next two tables, the size and origins of the funds for population assistance closely follow the changes in the regime and the underlying preferences. Throughout the 1950s and the 1960s, population assistance was very small; its major funding source were private organizations, such as the above mentioned IPPF, Pathfinder, but also the Ford Foundation[93] and some governments, especially the Nordic ones.[94] It is only at the end of the 1960s that the developed countries, and in particular the US, became engaged in the issue. As a result, the available funds increased twentyfold (although high inflation rates during the same period account for part of that), with the US initially donating around 80% of all population assistance.[95] The entry of the World Bank on the scene is also important: in the 1980s, it will become the second source of population assistance worldwide. Other UN organizations, such as the WHO, UNICEF, UNESCO, ILO, FAO and others, also spent part of their budgets on population matters.[96] At present, the position of predominance of the US has declined: it accounts for around 30–40% of all funds for population assistance.

Table 6.2 Sources of commitments for population assistance, 1952–89[97]

	1952–59	1960–69	1970–79	1980–89
Developed countries	0.4	114	2,123	4,506
Private foundations	6.3	192	394	355
UN organizations (not: UNFPA)	–	–	–	230
World Bank	–	–	197	685
Total	6.7	306	2,714	5,775

Table 6.3 Donor commitments 1952–89, million $[98]

	1969–81	1983	1986	1989
Developed countries	3,036	380	484	561
Canada	n.a.	15	27	32
Denmark	n.a.	8	12	18
Finland	n.a.	2	6	16
France	n.a.	0.2	0.3	0.7
Germany	160	16	22	31
Japan	136	40	50	60
Norway	230	20	41	44
Sweden	265	18	23	34
United Kingdom	n.a.	19	22	29
United States	1,734	215	238	248
World Bank	350	18	139	125
Private Foundations	437	29	35	39

The UNFPA was not mentioned in the previous tables, because it is a channel, not a source of funding. Yet, all the above actors except the NGOs channel at least part of their funds through the UNFPA. The table below shows us the evolution of its resources over the last two decades. As can be seen, the cut-off of US funds has been fully recovered by other countries increasing their own contributions. Yet, as with total population assistance, in real terms, the budget of UNFPA has stagnated all overt the last decade. Around 95% of its budget comes from ten donors, who are the same states that provide most bilateral population assistance;[99] the other hundred or so nations contributing to the UNFPA provide the rest.

Table 6.4 UNFPA expenditures, 1969–89[100]

Year	$ million	Year	$ million
1969	3.9	1981	136.4
1971	8.9	1983	122.0
1973	34.7	1985	135.9
1975	71.2	1987	136.5
1977	72.1	1989	179.5
1979	131.6	1991	

The fact that family planning was still a sensitive issue had two important effects. First, global population assistance never became larger than around 1–2% of total development aid. Second, many countries – in particular the Nordic ones but also some of the very small donors, such as France, Belgium and Austria who, mainly for religious reasons, are not really motivated into giving population assistance but who do not want to not give anything – looked to the United Nations as a way to legitimatize their involvement in population matters. As a result, assistance for population planning policies has long been dominated by the UN system, with both the above mentioned categories of countries channelling 80% to 100% of their assistance through the UNFPA.[101] Over the last decades, around 40% of all population aid went through the UN,[102] foremost the UNFPA, followed by the World Bank, and, to a much lesser extent, almost all other existing international organizations.[103] An additional one third of all populations assistance, a comparatively very large share, has been channeled through private organizations,[104] in particular by the US: this is far above the average 10% of all development aid channelled through NGOs. The remaining third – a small share in comparison with other aid sectors – is bilaterally administered. This situation differs markedly from usual development assistance, both in the proportion passing through international organizations and through non-governmental organizations.

Thus came into being a network of population assistance, consisting not only of international organizations but also of hundreds of private organizations as well as the family planning desks within bilateral development cooperation agencies.[105] The different rules and procedures that govern the actions of these different actors, as well as the activities they undertake and the way in which they do and do not cooperate are not the object of our study. Yet, they are certainly most interesting to the international relations scholar who is weary of the usual narrow security interest focus of the discipline – witness phrases like 'thus, when Indonesia wanted condoms from Japan, which could not be provided under the programme of USAID, UNFPA agreed to supply them.'[106]

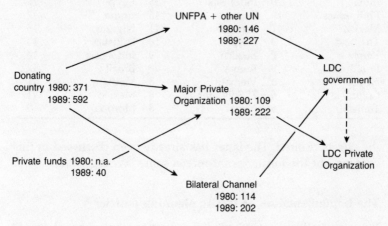

Figure 6.2 The population assistance system, 1980 & 1989: channels and volume, million $[107]

Looking at the recipients' side, it can be observed that few countries in the world do not receive some kind of population assistance, often from a large variety of bilateral, multilateral and non-governmental donors (see the following two tables). Apart from World Bank loans, population assistance is totally in the form of grants and very concentrated on the poorest and largest countries, partly by design and partly because the first countries to request population assistance happened to be among the world's poorest (India, Indonesia, Pakistan, and later Kenya and Bangladesh).[108] Also note from these tables the usual variations in aid from year to year, rendering difficult any forward planning in the recipient countries.

Yet, implementing effective population control policies has been an extremely difficult affair, for at least two major reasons. One is the attitude of the LDCs on the matter; the other is the difficulty and low effectiveness of family planning policies in themselves. The first one renders it unlikely that population policies will be implemented; the second one for them to have

Table 6.5 Major recipients of population assistance 1982, 1985, 1989, million $[109]

1982		1985		1989	
Bangladesh	36	Bangladesh	51	Bangladesh	50
Indonesia	27	India	45	India	32
China	21	Pakistan	21	Kenya	20
India	20	Indonesia	15	Egypt	17
Philippines	19	China	15	China	17
Mexico	11	Senegal	11	Nigeria	15
Thailand	9	Egypt	10	Pakistan	14
Kenya	7	Mexico	9	Indonesia	14
Brazil	7	Kenya	9	Brazil	12
Nepal	6	Vietnam	8	Vietnam	11
Colombia	6	El Salvador	8	Mexico	11
Tunisia	5	Nepal	8	Morocco	9

the effects desired. The latter has already been discussed in this chapter, but the former point merits some investigation.

The implementation of family planning policies

It is politically very difficult for donors to impose or otherwise strongly pressurize population control on unwilling governments, or attach it as a condition to other forms of aid.[110] This is due to the sensitive nature of population measures, combined with the fundamental norm of sovereignty in international relations: no state can afford to look like it wants to limit the size of another people.[111] The international system thus fully depends on the willingness of LDC governments to engage in population activities before it can begin to function.[112] Yet, as the following figures show, many LDC elites did not, and still do not, perceive population as a problem: according to UN sources, while the percentage of governments that considered their population growth rates to be too high increased from 30% in 1976 to 45% in 1986, there were still in 1986 45% that considered their population growth rates to be satisfactory (same percentage as in 1976) and 15% too low (25% in 1976).[113] Subsequently, at least half of all countries in the world had no, and still have no, coherent policy to decrease fertility and population growth.

The situation has changed from the second half of the 1970s onwards, and more and more LDC governments began considering the fertility rates of their countries too high and subsequently set up population control policies and programmes. Two researchers constructed a Family Planning Program Effort Index, synthesizing the *official* effort undertaken by countries to lower population growth rates. Comparing the data of 1972 with those of 1982 reveals that the general tendency is for family planning effort to increase over time in the LDCs.[114] At present, there is only a handful of countries left which did not include family planning among the stated objectives of their public health system.

This kind of positive 'we-are-making-progress' messages is constantly heard from the defenders of family planning, be they in the UNFPA or in the many private organizations concerned with population issues: versions of the above figure abound. But, as table 6.6 shows, all this means that around 40% of developing countries still have governments that have no population policy; moreover, among those who declare they have one, such policy remains very limited, and in no way denotes any real enthusiasm or serious political commitment toward limiting births! Governments 'play the game', adding family planning objective to their public health programs, and receiving increasing amounts of international funds for these activities, but they do not consider family planning as a priority or allocate substantial human, financial and educational ressources to it. As Dorothy Nortman, a famous specialists on family planning policies, observes:

> it is difficult to reconcile the frequent rhetoric on the importance of family planning practice with the budget proportions governments allocate for this purpose – a small fraction of 1%.... Just as health is typically a minor part of the total budget, family planning is typically a small part of the health budget. Notable exceptions are Bangladesh, India, Indonesia, Pakistan and the Philippines.[116]

This holds especially for sub-Saharan African and Arab countries, as well as some Latin American ones.

As a result, population assistance, although only 2% of all development aid, was probably the only area in the development aid issue area where 'supply' for a long time exceeded 'demand'![118] Faced with the lukewarm engagement of many potential recipients, and unwilling to push the issue beyond the level of rhetoric, donors have not increased their funds for

Table 6.6 Government policy on fertility levels, 1989, in percentage[117]

	Lower fertility	No policy	Maintain or raise fertility
Developing countries	47	39	14
Africa	49	38	13
Asia	38	41	21
Latin America	56	38	6
Developed countries	0	22	17

population assistance in real terms, notwithstanding their favorable discourse. Indeed, in constant dollars, present levels of population assistance are only equal to the levels of 1975: there has been a continuous decrease in the real availability of international resources for family planning since the middle of the 1970s.[119] Other issues – structural adjustment, the environment, protection of the poor – have come to dominate the agenda.

Hence, population assistance has remained small, certainly in comparison to the importance attached to it in the dominant development ideology. A number of countries persist without any real commitment to family planning, especially in the Middle East and sub-Saharan Africa; they hardly receive any population assistance (see table 6.7). Donors cannot push the issue more than rhetorically, so the key to changing this situation resides in the preferences of the governments of Third World countries. The distribution of family planning assistance between countries seems to be unlinked to the political, strategic or economic interests of donor countries; instead, it follows very closely recipient government policy preferences and activities. Population assistance, in a certain way, might be among the most 'recipient-need oriented' fields of development assistance. The recent sudden rise to predominance of the environment on the international development community agenda has relaunched population as a priority issue in the discourse of the donors and the international institutions, but it remains to be seen how much will really change in the field.

Table 6.7 Twelve smallest recipients of population assistance, 1982, 1985, 1989, million $; mini-states (population below 2 million) excluded*

1982		1985		1989	
Chad	0.000	Saudi Arabia	0.003	Kuwait	0.000
South Korea	0.000	South Korea	0.020	Lybia	0.000
Iran	0.000	Algeria	0.050	Saudi-Arabia	0.000
Saudi Arabia	0.002	Chad	0.080	Myanmar	0.020
Algeria	0.004	Kuwait	0.090	Iraq	0.200
Venezuela	0.010	Iran	0.100	Lao	0.300
Myanmar	0.040	Venezuela	0.200	Chad	0.400
Lao	0.070	Iraq	0.200	Congo	0.400
Kuwait	0.070	Myanmar	0.200	Guinea	0.400
Niger	0.100	Angola	0.300	South Korea	0.400
Burundi	0.200	Argentina	0.300	Venezuela	0.500
Ivory Coast	0.200	Congo	0.400	Argentina	0.500

* UNFPA, 1991(a).

6 Conclusion

High population growth or density are commonly considered important causes of hunger; such a principle is a central element of the international hunger regime. Following this principle, a strong international norm in favor of reducing population growth rates has come into being. This norm has brought about international involvement in family planning from the end of the 1960s onwards. Yet, such population assistance has remained small and has not grown during the last fifteen years. There are a variety of reasons for this: limited recipient country enthusiasm, up till now (some exceptions apart); sensitivity of the issue, bringing about a certain donor 'shyness' to push it; passivity by a number of countries, such as France, Italy, Belgium, Austria, that donate almost nothing; and a general perception of inefficiency of family planning programs.

That is regrettable, for family planning programs have many uses. Foremost among them, they respond to the unmet demand for birth control, the size of which differs by country, but probably exists to some extent everywhere. Moreover, family planning has important health benefits for both mothers and infants: it decreases morbidity and mortality rates among these groups.

Yet, family planning has very little impact on the incidence of hunger. The reason for this is simple: the incidence of hunger is independent of population growth rates or densities. A strong

213

biais among development specialists in favor of the dominant regime notwithstanding, an overview of the scientific literature and the available data shows little link between population growth rates or densities and the incidence of hunger. To the extent that there is a relation between the two, population growth rates decline when human welfare, including freedom from hunger, increases. The relation between hunger and population growth rates is thus rather the inverse than the one often assumed, which partially explains the limited effectiveness of family planning programs by themselves.

7 Theoretical relevance of the case study

How does all this relate to international relations theory, and more particularly to the debate between classical Realism and such a pre-theory as we outlined in the first chapter of this thesis? Do all these states constantly act in their self-interest, as Realism professes? Are norms and principles unimportant enough to neglect them as Realism does? And finally: are international organizations the powerless fora Realism tells they are?

As to the first question: the behavior of the rich and poor states alike in this issue area seems to be largely guided by preferences which are non-self-interested in nature.[120] Originally, most LDC governments' preferences were pro-natalist – apart from a limited number of Asian countries, such as India and Sri Lanka. Although they can be said to have an objective interest in holding down their population size (less social expenditure needed, welcome arithmetic of faster growth per capita, etc.), their preferences differed, reflecting the religious, social and political principles and norms of their powerholders. It is only later, influenced by the international population regime, and then still reluctantly for many of them, that their preferences changed (apart from China, whose dramatic conversion was probably independent of the international regime).

As for the wealthy countries, it is hard to see what self-interest they would be trying to satisfy through their activities in the population field. It has been suggested that it is to the industrialized countries' interest to keep the Third World population down, in order to keep its domination intact.[121] But the North's dominance surely is not based upon numbers but upon goods and technology. Others invoke the typical North-American policy establishment argument that high population growth causes political instability in the Third World, rendering it to the interest of rich countries to promote family planning.[122] But this argument is counterfactual. There is no link whatsoever between population growth rates or densities and the occurrence of civil or international war. Civil wars are taking place in both Angola, Mozambique, Sudan, Peru and Yugoslavia, where population densities are very low, as well as in Rwanda and El Salvador, where they are high. Recent international wars were fought between Iran, Iraq and Kuwait, and there again, population was not the issue. Finally, the rich countries do not *have* to engage in population activities to formulate preferences about them: if only self-interest were their motive, passivity about the population issue would surely have been as good and, given the sensitivity of the issue, certainly more expectable.

Some might wonder why such simplistic neo-Malthusian regime became dominant. As suggested above, part of the answer resides in the fact that it fits with classical prejudices in HICs about 'primitive' and 'underdeveloped' people. This **euro-centric** view of poor people is as much engrained in the mentality of most development experts as it is common wisdom among the general public. Second, there is attractive **arithmetic**: confronted with the magnitude of greatly increasing the food output and the well-being of large masses of poor people, population control (diminishing the size of these masses) looks like the easier alternative. Third, the regime presents the convenient advantage of placing the **locus for action** with the poor and the hungry themselves (or their governments). If anything has to change, it is the poor's reproductive behavior[123] – not the actions of rich countries or rich people. This characteristic applies to all dominant development strategies – to basic needs in the 1970s as well as to structural adjustment in the 1980s.[124]. Fourth, such regime is caused by and reinforces the dominant occidental **technical-productivist approach** to hunger as to all other development problems. To reduce people – in whose name development is sought – to just another variable in the great technical equations and to cut their numbers if necessary, must be the ultimate symbol of the dominance of this approach. The regime, finally, **removes attention from the political nature of hunger**, replacing it with a technical image, which is much more comfortable for powerholders – wherever they are.[125]

Without doubt these factors increase the appeal of these principles and norms in (occidental and Third World) policy-making circles: such population regime is easy to understand, poses no threat to their perceived interests, and it is not inimical to their vision of the world. This undoubtedly explains the great popularity of neo-Malthusian ideas with the most conservative sections of the establishment. Indeed, and contrary to other new ideas, the population control lobby from the beginning had close ties with the military and economic establishment,[126] implying that, even if the latter did not consider these ideas in its direct self-interest, it certainly did not see them as inimical to it either. This longstanding appeal of population control principles and norms to the powers-that-be is one of the main factors explaining the subsequent rapid development of what was to be euphemistically called 'population assistance'.[127]

This is not to say that the regime has been deliberately developed for this purpose by rich country elites. Rather, the enthusiasm with which they defend it, initially against the desires of most LDCs, is not independent of its convenience or neutrality towards their preferences and values. This convenience is fundamentally political in nature, as much for the questions it does not raise as for the solutions it does not advocate. This mysterious capacity of dominant ideas to be convenient to the powerful is nothing new, at least not for political economy scholars. The fact that more and more LDCs adopt the dominant regime (changing its nature from imposed to consensual) does not contradict our analysis, but merely documents one possible dynamic of regimes.

As for the second question – on the importance of norms and principles – our analysis showed that the international regime did influence the concrete process. Following the dominance of a neo-Malthusian regime, more and more actions went on in the real world based on these principles and norms. International organizations engaged their often considerable resources for actions based on neo-Malthusian norms. A new organization was created, the UNFPA, which has developed increasingly sophisticated family planning techniques. Family planning programmes spread from a handful of Asian countries to almost all LDCs in the world. The Family Planning Effort Index increased consistently over the last two decades, for almost all countries.

Yet, some limits exist to this rosy picture. First, the international

population regime is not entirely homogenous: there exists conflicts on certain principles, even among adherents to the basic
tenets of the regime. Among them, we can mention the conflict
between proponents of family planning as one aspect of health
care and those for whom it is an absolute priority, and conflict
on the methods of family planning, involving extremely sensitive
issues of the acceptability of sterilization and abortion. Hence,
proponents of family planning have not been able to agree on
what should be done, and even less of how it should be done;
the process reflects these divisions. Second, the international process has not displayed the same intensity as the regime.[128] Notwithstanding the rhetoric about the urgency of the population
problem and the need for international action by all actors in
the development community, there are still many LDCs without
systematic or well-integrated family planning policies, while
international population assistance has stagnated for 15 years.
The reasons for that situation include the highly sensitive nature
of the subject as well as the low effectivity of population assistance and the high complexity of developing an efficient family
planning policy. Hence, although the regime strongly influences
the process in the issue area, by itself it cannot explain it. In
order to account fully for the population process over the last
decades, one also needs to include political and social constraints
as well as the dynamics of the population issue area – which,
ultimately, boils down to the reproductive behavior of poor
people, a variable about which little is known. All of these limit
the *strength* of the outcome, as defined in the first chapter of this
book.

We now turn to the third and final question, about the influence of international organizations. It is generally agreed that
the UN has had an outstanding influence on the population
issue. The UN system as a whole was central in bringing the
population issue onto the agenda of international politics. Its
world population censuses greatly influenced the perception of
the seriousness of the 'population problem' over the decades.[129]
The UN was the only source of such figures and had the authority
that derives from its international and 'objective' position. Particularly the 1960 census came as a shock in most of the countries
concerned, as its results were higher than the worst scenarios
made in the 1950–1 census, the first ever for many LDCs;[130] the
forthcoming census might have the same effect. But also the other

population studies published by the Population Division[131] are widely respected and are one of the major sources of scientific information on population in the world.[132]

Moreover, the development of an international population regime devoted to family planning was also made possible by the international organizations acting as fora for discussing such novel ideas, adding what Symonds calls a 'seal of respectability' to the question, as well as to the personal commitment of some of the Director-Generals to draw attention to the issue.[133] As a result of its enormous resources and prestige in the development aid system, the World Bank's 1968 conversion and continued commitment to the cause of population control was of particular importance.

Hence, the UN system has undoubtedly significantly contributed to the development of the international population regime, which, as we saw, has strongly influenced the actual process in the issue area. But international organizations also influenced the process in a more direct way. They have been very important operational actors in population assistance over the last two decades, designing, managing and financing a large number of family planning programs and policies. In the early days, apart from some Asian countries, most of the financial and intellectual resources needed for implementing effective family planning policies in LDCs originated on the international level.[134] During the 1970s, international funds for family planning constituted half of all expenditures by LDCs for this activity.[135] By the middle of the 1980s, the UN estimated that 'on the average, developing countries are ... spending $ US 2 for every $ US 1 contributed by international sources. According to the UNFPA, for projects sponsored by it, countries spent $ 4.60 for each $ 1 contributed by it.'[136] Among the same lines, one can find data on individual countries – Columbia, India, Indonesia, Taiwan, etc. – showing the increasing extent to which their governments devote resources to family planning, both in absolute financial terms as in relative ones, as a share of total such expenditures.[137] Hence, the conclusion seems unavoidable that international organizations are crucial operational actors in the population process; the fact that their position of exclusiveness is declining can only be proof of their effectiveness.[138]

Yet, as we said above when discussing data on national attitudes and policies towards fertility, these optimistic statements emanating from population organizations should be qualified. The examples they refer to are basically always the same: the main Asian countries without Bangladesh, and one or two African or Latin American countries. Looking closer at the other data, one can see that the dependence of most countries on donor funds does not decline, but on the contrary most of the time increases, especially in Africa.[139] There is thus no increased commitment of national governments to family planning, certainly not relatively as a proportion of total such expenditures, but often even not absolutely. This, then, means that, apart from the handful of success stories of high government commitment and financial engagement for family planning policies and programs, most of what goes on in family planning is the product of the international system, designing, managing and funding population activities in a large number of countries, without any real implication by recipient governments. This increases the crucialness of the international system on the one hand, but makes us doubt its long-term effectiveness on the other.

Hence, as our analysis suggested, the concrete effect of international organizations (crudely spoken: the amount of births prevented as a result of their activities) is quite limited, certainly when compared to the perceived magnitude of the problem – or to the expectations of population assistance defenders. As said above, this is due both to the low enthusiasm of many LDC governments and to the low effectiveness of family planning programmes in isolation. Indeed, the implementation of potentially effective family planning programmes depends above all on the government's commitment to reduce fertility: in the absence of that, only lip-service will be paid to these objectives, but little will be done.[140] International institutions and bilateral donor agencies are uncapable and/or unwilling to impose such policies on unwilling governments.[141] Moreover, even if elaborate and well-financed family planning programmes and policies are adopted, their actual capacity to reach their goals – *e.g.* significantly decrease fertility rates – is very limited: the reproductive behavior of people is conditioned by a complex set of social, cultural, economic and psychological factors which international organizations and national bureaucracies have a hard time to influence, let alone fundamentally modify.

To my knowledge, Krueger and Ruttan are the only authors to have studied the question of the general impact of population assistance (*i.e.* not related to a specific program). According to them, international population assistance had a substantial impact on national population policies, a varying impact on family planning programmes, and only a small, indirect impact on fertility, with socio-economic factors being more important.[142] The previous analysis fully supports this conclusion.

One final remark. We consider the employment of the theoretical approach of this thesis to have been useful, leading to a more nuanced understanding of the issue than classical Realism allows for. But it should be clear that by doubting the usefulness of the rigid application of the standard Realist 'interest' and 'power' explanation, we did not suggest that conflicting interests and power are mysteriously absent in this issue area. We have seen that the dominant regime was, and remains, largely Western-customed, based upon a Eurocentric, productivistic approach to development. Second, it can be claimed that the nature of the regime is particularly convenient for those with an interest in the economic and political status-quo. This convenience applies, it seems, as much to Third World elites as to vested interests in the North. This undoubtedly explains the support the population lobby has consistently received from the highest levels of conservative policy-making in the US. Indeed, the development of the international regime is clearly most influenced by powerful actors, individuals as well as states. When it became internationally dominant, the regime was mainly of US origin; it became dominant against the will of most LDCs. It has become gradually accepted ('internalized') by LDC elites. It is clear that in this issue, as in others, the values of powerful individuals are much more important in the development and spread of a regime than those of the others – and that poor peasants are very absent in the development or acceptance of such regimes. Hence, the use of the concepts of norms, principles and preferences should not and need not distract us from the realities of power, interest and conflict.

Notes

1 The only article in an international relations journal I know of is by Roger Revelle, published in *International Organization* in 1967; the author is a geochemist by training. In the more specialized demographers' journals, authors such as Finkle, Crane and Berelson have

written quite extensively on the political aspects of family planning. Finally, authors such Johnson, 1987, Piotrow, 1974, Symonds & Carder, 1973 and Menken, 1986, often with first-hand experience from within the UN, have published interesting books on the international politics of population.

2 See Keyfitz, 1975 and Haub, 1987 for interesting discussions.

3 Srinivasan, 1987; *passim*; Haub, 1987: 38. Extrapolating present growth rates, one can as well predict the end of the world because of underpopulation, as the famous French demographer Bourgeois-Pichat did in 1988.

4 UN, 1992: VII-VIII.

5 In a reversal of policy, two children were allowed in villages, if the first one is a girl: *Financial Times*, Febr. 4, 1989. Before, since 1979, China officially had a one-child policy.

6 The population of China is predicted to be 1,3 billion by 2000, exceeding the original target of 1,2 bn with 100 million – more than unified Germany, or 10 times the population of Belgium: *ibid*.

7 Most touched are Burundi, Kenya, Uganda (with 30% of pregnant women seropositive), Rwanda, Tanzania and Zaire. According to specialists, the population growth rate in those countries is predicted to decline by 20 to 30%: *Le Monde*, June 2, 1990. Some AIDS researchers go as far as predicting that Africa's population growth rate by the year 2000 will be 1% (it is above 3% per year now): *The Economist*, November 25, 1989. Others, on the contrary, argue that the AIDS epidemic, no matter how tragic, will have only a negligeable impact on overall population growth rates: 50 million deaths make little difference when compared to a predicted population increase of more than 1 billion for the next decade.

8 Until then, all successive world population forecast had to be revised upwards. In 1945, America's foremost demographer though that by the year 2000 the world would carry 3 billion people: *The Economist*, January 20, 1990.

9 The transitional phase is the period in which death rates have declined significantly but birth rates have not yet followed, resulting in high population growth rates. Europe passed this phase from 1750 to 1950. During this period its share of world population increased from 16% to 32%. From the beginning of this century onwards, as a result of improved food intake, medicine and hygiene, all LDCs successively entered their transitional phase. As a result, and combined with declining population growth rates in Europe, the latter's share of total world population dropped back to 20% and is predicted to fall to 10% by the middle of the next century. The LDCs are passing the transitional phase in a much shorter time-span than Europe did, but the population growth rates they display in the meantime are considerably higher than those of Europe.

10 United Nations, 1986(a); UNICEF, 1989: 18, United Nations, 1992: VIII.

11 The latter has been observed by Leon Tabah, former director of the

U.N. Population Division, at a speech at the Institut Universitaire d'Etudes de Développement in Geneva, Oct. 1990.

12 Birdsall, Fei, Kuznets, Ranis & Schultz, 1979: 212. See too Woods, 1989: 165.

13 Hardin, 1974; for an interesting discussion of the moral implications of his argument, see Aiken & La Follette, 1977, which also contains a reprint of Hardin's article.

14 See for example Abercrombie & McCormack, 1976: 495: 'The Malthusian specter is still with us.... However, the specter will not materialize inevitably, as was believed by its inventor. What happens can be very much influenced by what is done in such fields as population policy, agricultural production, and income distribution. If the right policies are followed, there is some hope that, even with the greatly enlarged population that must be expected by the year 2000, at least the worst manifestations of hunger and malnutrition can be eliminated.'

15 Also, Rau, 1991: 98. Indeed, the most important policy or research documents of the major development institutions, such as the World Bank, the FAO or the OECD, all stress the crucial importance of curbing population growth as a condition to development and the eradication of hunger. See the important statement by the Ministers of Development Cooperation of the OECD for the 1990s, 1990(a); the four programmatic World Bank reports on the African crisis as well as its important 1990 *World Development Report* on poverty. At FAO's side, see the three major studies of the 1980s: *Horizon 2000* in 1981, *Land, Food and People* in 1984, and *World Agriculture Toward 2000* in 1988. The titles of some of the publications of the major development actors on the topic are also telling: among many others, see World Bank president McNamara's (1984) 'The Population Problem: Time Bomb or Myth', the U.S. Department of State's (1978) 'Silent Explosion' or 'Oxfam's (s.d.) 'Already too Many. An Oxfam Special Report on Population, Family Planning and Development'. See too the famous Brandt Report, 1980.

16 A typical example of this catastrophe talk, is given by the 1989 Nobel Prize winner in economy, Maurice Allais: 'modern societies are subject to different threats, of which the biggest is the demographic explosion in the third world. The second one is the atomic bomb, which, if used, will be used because of the effects of the demographic explosion.' (translated by the author) Interview in *Figaro Magazine*, 1 juillet 1989.

17 Some of the few exceptions are Colin Clark, 1970 and Franke & Chasin, 1980. Some scientists have even argued that population growth is a necessary condition for agricultural innovation and progress. Simon, 1981, and Clark, 1970, make this point as economists, whereas the Danish anthropologist Ester Boserup, 1965, 1981, explains it with a historical analysis of Africa.

18 *Monday Development*, the InterAction biweekly newsletter, 10, 6, 30 March 1992: 6.

19 For similar observations, Avery, 1991: 70.

20 See Herz, 1984: 26, for interesting work along similar lines.
21 The debate started in 1958, with the article by Coale & Hoover, followed by Kuznets, whose essays have been reprinted in 1974. See quote from the Dutch minister of development cooperation in the 1991(b) UNFPA report.
22 As in Lipton, 1983.
23 World Bank, 1984: 79; p. 105. For a critical discussion of the Report by some well-known experts, see Review Symposium, 1985.
24 See World Bank, 1981, 1984b, 1986b, 1989.
25 At its worst, this takes the form of Hardin's 'Lifeboat Earth' argument: we should not help countries such as Ethiopia or Bangladesh, for they are exceeding the carrying capacity of their land. More scientifically, this takes the nature of the Institute of Applied Systems Analysis (FAO, 1984a) computation of the maximum food production of thousands of ecological zones under different conditions of technological input.
26 The Third World environment regime, in its turn, is then linked to the general development one: higher population leads to environmental degradation leads to lower economic growth leads to more hunger.... Thus the two principles justifying population concerns become linked.
27 N. Sadik, director of the UNFPA, in the *International Herald Tribune*, May 14–15, 1988. See too His Royal Highness Prince Phillip, International President of the Worldwide Fund for Nature, who synthesizes nicely: 'it should be glaringly obvious that as the number of people increases, so does damage to the global biological and physical systems.' *Population, UNFPA Newsletter*, May 1990: 1.
28 Salas, 1985: 63. This most interesting book, filled with quotes from the numerous speeches, lectures and documents prepared by Mr Salas during his period as Director of the UNFPA provides the reader with an excellent overview of the process of international regime-building. See too his successor, Mme Sadik, on the cover of the 1990 UNFPA report for the same message.
29 World Food Council, 1988/5: 4–5.
30 Barney, 1982; U.S. Department of State, 1978; Secretary of State Cyrus Vance, in *US Dept. of State Bulletin*, 80, 2036, March 1980; and McNamara, 1984. See also Ivan Head, former foreign policy advisor to Canadian Prime Minister Trudeau, in *Foreign Affairs*, 1989: 77. 'from now to the turn of the century, then, the world will grow by the equivalent of one new Bangladesh every year.' One Bangladesh – not two Germanies, or less than one Indonesia ...
31 See too Wood, 1986: 203: 'the dominant imagery stresses the isolation and passivity of the poor.' More generally, see Chambers, 1982 and Boiral, Lanteri & Olivier de Sardan, 1985.
32 See the definition by the Caribbean historian Addo, 1986: 12: 'Eurocentrists tend to believe that the non-European world is merely underdeveloped Europe; and they tend to believe that, given time, non-Europeans will come to understand concepts just as Europeans do.' The Indian demographer Pethe, 1990: 57, correctly considers the

current state of population theory as a 'western paradigm. Neo-Malthusianism is an inseperable part of the western approach.' This approach is becoming increasingly internalized among westernized Third World elites; yet, it remains euro-centric in its origin and nature.

33 Franke & Chasin, 1980: 114.

34 Simon, 1989: 330.

35 For example, FAO, 1984(b): 47; UNFPA, 1990: 1.

36 Green, 1980: 57.

37 See O'Neill's 1977: 155 comment on Hardin that the world resembles a 'lifeboat in which special quarters are provided for all the (recently) first class passengers, and on which the food and water for all passengers are stowed in those quarters.' A similar argument has also been made by Mamdani, 1972 when he asks: why is there a population problem in Lagos, Calcutta and Mexico City and not in London, Tokyo or Washington?

38 Which is where the international population regime overlaps with (or is identical to) the international environment regime.

39 Abercrombie, 1975: 48.

40 Klatzmann, 1983: 108–109.

41 According to figures from the UN 1986(b), table 3, out of the 36 countries with population densities of 200 and more per square kilometer, 14 are small islands (generally not known for the incidence of starvation); 11 are rich OECD countries; 5 are NICs and OPEC members. The rest are poor LICs – Bangladesh, with a population density of 699, Puerto Rico (394), Lebanon (260), Rwanda (238), El Salvador (234) and Jamaica (216) – of which two – Bangladesh and Rwanda – have average dietary consumptions below the minimum requirement. High population density is thus not in itself a cause of hunger. There are many countries which are sparsely populated and which know hunger. See too Bradley & Carter, 1989: 105–6.

42 Note particularly the fact that many countries facing famine at present are well within the limits of their carrying capacity, even at low input levels: Angola, CAR, Chad, Mozambique, Sudan, Tanzania. Others, like Burkina Faso, Ethiopia and Mali are able, with medium inputs, to feed their populations. Among those which cannot – Algeria, Burundi, Cape Verde, Comores, Kenya, Lesotho, Lybia, Mauritania, Maurice, Marocco, Namibia, Niger, Reunion, Rwanda, Somalia, Tunisia and the Western Sahara – many know no famine or even hunger! Low input means essentially that only human and animal inputs are used in agriculture; high input refers to the present European situation; medium input is somewhere in between.

43 Repetto, 1987: 38–9.

44 World Bank, 1989; FAO, 1984(b).

45 UN, 1973; 1988: 281–94; McNicolls, 1984: 61–6; see too Hammer, 1986; *passim*, in a survey on the link between population growth and savings.

46 Lipton, 1983: 6.

47 Simon, 1989: 325.

48 This might precisely be what is happening in certain Latin American countries, where population growth rates are decreasing, while the incidence of hunger does not.

49 National Research Council, 1986: 85–6; my italics.

50 See FAO, 1984(a) and 1984(b) for both versions.

51 FAO, 1984(b): 58ff.

52 It must be clear, though, as table 5.1 showed, that for most countries, that catastrophe point is far away: yet, they already know hunger now! On the other hand, certain countries, or regions within countries, seem quite close to it: in Africa, Cape Verde, Mauritania, Rwanda and Burundi are among them. Still, in all these, enormous technological progress is usually possible – which does not take away the need for other urgent action of environmental conservation, the development of non-agricultural employment, etc..

53 FAO, 1984(b): 70–1. An argument of exactly the same nature can be found in the part devoted to population growth in the World Bank's 1989(b) report on Africa.

54 Which is precisely the strength of Malthusianism: Miranda, 1983.

55 Kelley, 1986: 568: 'in conclusion . . . reducing the pace of population growth will provide countries time, flexibility, and in some cases additional resources to respond to development needs . . .'

56 Kelley, 1986: 566–7.

57 This notion – that the productivity of poor people is zero – is quite generally accepted among development economists. In cost-benefit analysis, it is very common to ascribe a zero shadow wage rate to labour, implying that the poor do not produce economic values. This judgment is simply absurd, as any one who knows the Third World from something else than economic textbooks knows. This is where we come back to Euro-centrism. See MacDonald, 1989: 200 a.f.

58 Among many publications making this point, see UNICEF, 1990: 27.

59 Herz, 1984: 40.

60 Herz, 1984: 43.

61 Among many others: Donaldson & Ong Tsui, 1990; UNFPA, 1991(b); Maudlin & Lapham, 1987.

62 Chapters 2 and 3 of Murdoch, 1980, as well as Cassen, 1982: 30 a.f. contain good presentations of this strand of explanation. The quote was from Murdoch, 1980: 26.

63 The best discussion of this can be found in Cassen, 1982.

64 For an easy introduction to this in one of the standard handbooks in the field of development economics, see Todaro, 1981: 165 a.f. Two of the main works presenting this argument are Repetto, 1979 and Bhattacharyya, 1975. Note how similiar this phenomenon is to the one mentioned in the previous chapter concerning food consumption.

65 We certainly do not suggest that cultural/religious factors are unimportant. As anybody who has been involved in field work knows, they are. They surely help accounting for the different speeds at which different populations bring down their growth rates. Yet, the remarkable fact remains, that, whatever their religious and cultural

values, when individuals' well-being increases, their reproductive rates decline. But, even under conditions of high individual well-being, contraceptive methods have to be known and available for population growth to decline: family planning policies thus are important.

66 And the author, 1980: 61–2 adds: 'this is an astonishing result considering the difficulties of measurement, the tremendous variety of nations examined, the fact that only two variables are examined, and that income does not catch all aspects of well-being.'

67 Cassen, 1982: 14. Note the remaining uncertainty in the field, as typified in the above quote by the 'may', 'might' and 'should'.

68 The next discussion draws heavily from the excellent works of Symonds & Carder, 1973 and of Johnson, 1987. Both are detailed historical analyses of the work of the United Nations in a particular issue – of which there are all too few.

69 Donaldson & Ong Tsui, 1990: 5.

70 UN, 1986(c:) 133.

71 Symonds & Carder, 1975: 107.

72 Revelle, 1968: 381.

73 From Eisenhower, stating in 1959 that 'birth control is not our business. I cannot imagine anything more emphatically a subject that is not proper political or government activity or function or responsability', over Kennedy, the first Catholic president moderately in favor of birth control, to Nixon telling Congress in 1969 that '[t]his administration does accept a clear responsibility to provide essential leadership [on the population issue],' there is a constantly changing American regime and process in the population growth issue area. This is true for both the domestic and the international level. See Symonds & Carder, 1975: 89 a.f.

74 Piotrow, 1974: 200.

75 Symonds & Carder, 1975: 199, Piotrow, 1974: 199–200 and Donaldson & Ong Tsui, 1990: 10 all mention the change in the US preference on the issue as the main cause of the international regime change.

76 Finkle, & Crane, 1974. It is thus not necessary to focus on population control but rather on means to increase the pace of development – as the slogan goes: 'take care of the people, and population will take care of itself.'

77 Donaldson & Ang Tui, 1990: 11. For a detailed analysis of the Plan of Action, see Berelson, 1974.

78 There also exists a 'United Nations Expert Group on Population and Human Rights', and it meets in Geneva. It publishes around 10 documents a year.

79 McNamara, 1984, 14–17; and *Population*, a newletter by the Population Crisis Committee, Sept. 1983: 1. See also the ex-head of USAID's Office of Population, in a newspaper interview: '[the] population explosion, unless stopped, would lead to revolutions . . . [and disrupt] the normal operations of U.S. commercial interests around the world . . . ,' quoted in Green, 1982: 48.

80 *Monday Developments*, 1 October 1990: 8; UNICEF, 1991:

81 Indeed, contraception remains unacceptable to the Vatican up to our days: *Le Monde*, November 17, 1989. It is among these circles of catholic social scientists that we find some of the few dissenting voices among the chorus of neo-Malthusians.

82 Finkle & Crane, 1985: *passim* and Crane & Finkle, 1989: *passim*.

83 The Reagan administration adopted a 'free market' approach to the population problem, preconizing that no specific policies were needed regarding population; it suffices to liberalize LIC economies; the resulting growth will take care of any population problem. According to Colliard, 1988: 793, this position represented a 'deliberate provocation to the Third World.'

84 George Bush, member of Congress and US Representative to the UN, adopted the catastrophe tone in Piotrow, 1974: VII; 'Will we learn fast enough from one another and with one another to defuse the population bomb?'

85 Crane & Finkle, 1989: *passim*.

86 *id.*: 25 & 45.

87 Donaldson & Ong Tsui, 1990: 13–14; UNFPA, 1991(a): 7.

88 OECD, 1990: 132.

89 See many 1990–192 issues of the biweekly *World Bank News*; also UNFPA, 1991(b): 40.

90 UNFPA, 1990: 27.

91 Wolfson, 1983: 9.

92 Family planning aid constitutes around three quarters of total population aid. Other forms of assistance focus mainly on population censuses: see *i.a* Krueger & Ruttan, 1983: chapter 8 and UNFPA, 1991(a): 9 for data.

93 Indeed, the latter is a very important actor in terms of funding as can be gauged from the data in Nortman, 1985: 20.

94 UNFPA, 1991(a): 2 ff.

95 Nortman, 1985: 18.

96 UNFPA, 1985.

97 UNFPA, 1991(a): 20.

98 Donaldson & Ong Tsui, 1990: 29 for 1969–81, except the UNFPA and the World Bank, which is 1970–81, which is based on own calculations, coming from a variety of expenditure sources, most notably Nortman, 1985: 18. All the other data come from UNFPA, 1991(a): 20 & 24.

99 Donaldson & Ong Tsui, 1990: 14; UNFPA, 1991(b): 39.

100 Nortman, 1985; UNFPA, Annual Reports. From 1985 onwards, these are commitments, and not expenditures.

101 UNFPA, 1991(a): 5–7.

102 As Wolfson, 1983: 18, comments: 'It is surely significant that in no other field have donors chosen to provide so much of their funding through multilateral channels, in preference to financing their own aid programmes in particular developing countries.' The proportion of population assistance going through multilateral channels is 80% for the U.K., 75% for Norway, and 66% for Sweden.

103 UN, 1986(c:) 120–133 for an overview.

104 The IPPF, Pathfinder, the Population Council and other, smaller ones.

105 The size and diversity of this network is properly speaking impressive: it can be gauged by consulting the UNFPA's *Inventory of Population Projects in Developing Countries around the World* – a 900 pages small print catalogue of projects and programs in all countries of the world, implying at the very least 600 private and public organizations active in population issues.

106 To be found in the excellent analysis – be it rather descriptive – by Wolfson, 1983: 14.

107 For 1980: Herz, 1984: 14 and 22; for 1989: UNFPA, 1991(a): 22–23.

108 UNFPA, 1991(a): 12–13.

109 UNFPA, 1991(a).

110 The US has formally done it, though, *e.g* as a condition of self-help with its PL480 food aid. Also the World Bank seems to have added population control to some of its Structural Adjustment loans.

111 See too Crane & Finkle, 1989: 34.

112 See too Krueger & Ruttan, 1983: 8–30.

113 UN, 1988: 37. See UN Export Group on.... , 1989: 14. See too O'Manique & Lerner, 1984: 17.

114 Mauldin, & Lapham, 185.

116 Nortman, 1985: 12–13.

117 Drawn from Donaldson & Ong Tsui, 1990: 6, based on 1990 UN data; and UN, 1988: 36 for data on the developed countries.

118 One side-effect of this situation was that those countries that implemented family planning policies could count on much international assistance.

119 Johnson, 1987: 284; UNFPA, 1991(a): 2–3.

120 Except for some countries, such as Singapore, Iraq and Kuwait, that consider themselves underpopulated, and support accelerating population growth for economic or military reasons.

121 Speech of the Chinese delegation at the 1974 World Population Conference, as cited in Johnson, 1987: 97. See too Quincy Wright, 1958: 265–6, McNicoll, 1984: 74ff. for the World Bank and radical authors, such as Lacheen, 1986: 93; Franke & Chasin, 1980: 112–120; George, 1976: 53–68; and Moore-Lappé & Collins, 1977: 13–53.

122 See among others the September 1983 issue of *Population*, published by the Population Crisis Committee.

123 More precisely, it should be like ours – which is where the eurocentrism comes in again ...

124 Wood, 1986: 205 & 222.

125 Davis, 1975: 31.

126 Lacheen, 1986: 99–100; Green, 1982: 48. One of the earliest and most outspoken lobbyist for population control was General Draper; at present, maybe the most well-known one is former US Secretary of Defense McNamara; McGeorge Bundy, former US Secretary of State, is president of the Population Council, which was founded by John D. Rockefeller III; ambassador E. M. Martin and former senator R.

Taft represent the Populaton Crisis Committee. President Bush used to be very much in favor of the population lobby.

127 This was the case already in Malthus' own time, as Perelman, 1985: *passim*, documents in detail. One quote: 'Malthus' simplistic formulation served admirably as a political weapon. Malthus proved to the satisfaction of the ruling classes that they had no responsibility for the existing state of affairs. They were not about to raise questions about subjects such as the effect on private property on the availability of resources; it was enough for them that Malthus showed that '. . . the real cause of continued depression and poverty of the lower classes of society was the growth of population.' "

128 Herz, 1984: 37 a.f.

129 Johnson, 1987: XXII; Bourgeois-Pichat, 1990: 358.

130 Symonds & Carder, 1975: 123. The U.N. Demographic Yearbook is published since 1948. From the 1970s onwards, other organizations also made world population forecasts, *e.g.* the World Bank, U.S.A.I.D., the United States Bureau of the Census' International Demographic Data Center, and individual scholars: Haub, 12987: 32–34; Donaldson & Ong Tsui, 1990: 31.

131 The Population Division is part of the Department of International Economic and Social Affairs within the United Nations Secretariat.

132 UN, 1986(c): 120–122.

133 Symonds & Carder mention B.R. Sen, director-general of FAO from 1956 to 1967. The engagement of these personalities can also be retarding rather than advancing change, as is the case with Julian Huxley's outspoken but premature defense of population control. This suggests that there are certain conditions that have to be met for individuals to directly influence international outcomes: Symonds & Carder, 1975: 126 a.f. and 198.

134 Donaldson & Ong Tsui, 1990: 16.

135 For most interesting data, see Johnson, 1987: chapter 8.

136 UN, 1986(c): 135. Given the fact that the former calculation applies to all UN population activities, including, for example, refugees and migration, the latter figure is probably closer to the truth as far as family planning goes. See too Salas, 1985: 100 a.f.

137 Donaldson & Ong Tsui, 1990: 27; Nortman, 1985: 7; UNFPA, 1991(b): 38.

138 Among others Donaldson & Ong Tsui, 1990: 27–28.

139 As admitted by Nortman, 1985: 10–11.

140 This comes back all through the literature, *e.g.* UNFPA, 1990: 18.

141 We will come back in detail to the conditionality issue and the role of external aid in imposing policy changes in chapter seven, on structural adjustment.

142 Krueger & Rutman, 1983: chapter 8, in particular pages 1, 16 &22.

SEVEN

THE YEARS OF ADJUSTING DANGEROUSLY: ON POVERTY AND AGRICULTURAL POLICY REFORM*

Since Independence, the international community has had strong ideas and small amounts of money for increasing Third World agricultural and food production. As usual in the development community, there have been major swings in dominant ideas on how to do this, espoused every time with strong enthusiasm and little hindered by knowledge of previous policy prescriptions or local conditions by the major institutions. Schematically, in the 1960s, agriculture was rather neglected in favor of industrialization; to the extent that special attention was devoted to it, it consisted of the 'economic infrastructure' type: roads, credit, research, markets, provision of inputs, etc. In the 1970s, absolute poverty and the satisfaction of basic needs came to the fore; consequently, the countryside, where the majority of the world's poor lives, gained in importance, and with it the strategy of (integrated) rural development, a larger term than agricultural development, englobing social services, small-scale agriculture, artisanat and commerce.[1] In the 1980s, finally, following the financial and economic crisis of most of the Third World, the dominant development strategy became the one of 'structural adjustment', stressing the necessity of liberalization and state withdrawal from agriculture as from all other sectors of economic activity so as to increase productivity. It is the latter strategy, as it applies to agriculture, food and poverty, that is the subject of this chapter.[2]

The above categorization does not mean that at the beginning

* This chapter benefited from comments by Christian Comeliau, Just Faaland, Jacques Forster, Laurent Monnier, and, especially, Marc Hufty.

of the decade, all projects based on the previous strategy are closed down and new ones, in line with new thinking, started. It rather means that as the new thinking acquires predominance and more brains (desirous to advance their careers by writing about popular subjects) and money are drawn into it, its share as a proportion of total development spending increases, but never wipes out the previous strategy. Thus poverty alleviation projects still exist, as do the institutions, such as IFAD, created to deal with it; similarly, the strategy of the 1960s still is around, as are the CGIAR researchers and rural infrastructure builders; to a certain extent, moreover, structural adjustment signifies a return to it. But it is beyond doubt that the structural adjustment strategy has come to dominate not only the development debate in the 1980s, but also the ones about agriculture, food and poverty that interest us in this book.

The term 'structural adjustment' covers both a development strategy, *i.e.* a set of policy prescriptions, and a lending instrument of the Bretton Woods institutions. As a lending instrument, SA consists of program lending, *i.e.* medium-term loans not linked to specific investments or projects in return for macro-economic policy reforms negotiated with the lender. The implementation of such reforms constitutes the condition for the disbursement of the funds: hence the term 'conditionality.'[3] As a development strategy, structural adjustment signifies a wholesale adoption of neo-classical liberalism, with its belief in the virtues of the free market, trickle down, comparative advantage and the merits of export-oriented growth. This is not new for the IMF, which always adhered to the 'bitter medicine' approach, but it is a fundamental change for the World Bank, which previously stood for a more reformist brand of capitalism.[4]

Starting from the conventional liberal diagnosis of Third World agricultural problems as presented in chapter two, one of the crucial elements of SA is the reform of Third World agricultural policies, desired both to produce more agricultural products, including possibly food, and to stimulate general economic growth. Moreover, an important indirect objective – or justification – of SA is the eradication of poverty. Hence, SA policy reform is doubly important for our analysis of the international organization of hunger: it is the dominant international development policy prescription of the 1980s, seeking to influence as well the amount of food produced as the number of the poor in Third World countries.

In part I of this chapter, we will mainly analyze structural adjustment as a lending instrument, *i.e* we will focus on the nature and effectiveness of its conditionality. This analysis is of importance, not only for theoretical reasons (the case of international institutions 'imposing' behavior on states is a quite fascinating one for the international relations scholar), but also because it helps us to understand the interactions between internal and external factors in the explanation of state policy, and the structural constraints the global political economy imposes on states, *inter alia* as far as their agricultural, food and social policies go. In part II, we will discuss SA as a development strategy, focusing especially on its effects on the incidence of poverty and hunger. Given the impossibility of arriving at any general and/or precise conclusions on this subject, we will rather present a framework that should allow us to comprehend the multiple factors involved in bringing about the impact of structural adjustment.

PART I. STRUCTURAL ADJUSTMENT AND CONDITIONALITY

Structural adjustment spread swiftly, becoming the dominant development strategy of the 1980s. Between 1980 and 1990, the IMF has signed agreements with 85 Third World countries; the World Bank group has given more than 220 adjustment loans to 63 countries. SA financing now accounts for over 25% of its annual lending, from nothing 10 years ago.[5]

Moreover, many bilateral aid agencies, such as the EEC, France, Sweden, Japan, and the US, to mention but some of the more significant ones, linked part of their development aid to SA policy reform undertaken by the recipient country with the guidance of the BWI. More generally, a tendency has been observed for good pupils of the latter institutions to receive more development aid and easier loan reschedulings than other countries.[6] Yet, bilateral donors only play a secondary role in comparison to the WB and the IMF. They make money available for countries implementing SA policy reforms with the BW institutions, but, apart from the US,[7] rarely 'impose' such reform themselves.

From the very beginning, the International Monetary Fund

and the World Bank group have been criticized for their conditionality. According to some, the nature of SA conditionality
should be hardened:[8] stronger free market policies should be
imposed; no funds should be disbursed to countries that are not
serious about opening up. Other critics, adhering to a structural-
ist diagnosis of the causes of the debt crisis, want a more 'growth-
oriented conditionality.'[9] Still others, especially radical critics and
Northern NGOs, lobby for an 'alternative conditionality:' the
resources of the Bretton Woods institutions (hereafter BWI)
should be conditional on policies that protect the poorest, respect
human rights, improve the environment, or oblige Third World
elites to repatriate their flight capital.[10]

All these critics have very different visions of debt, development and aid. Yet, they all have in common a similar vision of
conditionality and the role of the BWI therein. This vision, which
constitutes common wisdom up to the current day, incorporates
two basic assumptions. These are not typically explicitly
expressed, but they underlie much of the criticism of SA conditionality, as well as most proposals for change. First, it is
usually believed that the *nature* of SA conditionality, *i.e.* the
objects promoted by it, is developed and imposed by the BWI.
This would imply that, in order to change SA conditionality, one
should concentrate on changing the policies of the BWI. Second,
it is commonly held that the *effectiveness* of conditionality, *i.e.* the
degree of success in changing the behavior of governments, is
high. This implies that, if one managed to change the BWI's
policies, indebted Third World countries would be forced to
follow suit.

We argue in this chapter that both these assumptions are
wrong. To do so, we will present a comprehensive, three-layered,
international political economy framework. Our aim is to create,
drawing on the extensive existing literature, a coherent and
nuanced general framework, allowing a better understanding of
SA and its conditionality. This venture is of practical importance,
for proposals about alternatives to SA or about alternative conditionality, such as those developed and lobbied for by a large
variety of citizen's groups, both in the North and in the South,
are often unrealistic because of a failure to grasp the complex
realities involved.

We will begin by presenting a short overview of the economic
and political context in which SA came about. Afterwards, in

sections two to four, we will construct a three-layered framework, successively analyzing the role of the global political economy, the Bretton Woods institutions, and the recipient governments in defining the nature of structural adjustment. In part five, finally, we will discuss the effectiveness of conditionality.

1 The debt crises

At the onset of the 1980s, three different debt crises, with different origins, existed, although they were not necessarily recognized. One was the crisis of almost all sub-Saharan African low-income countries. Their debt was quite small in absolute figures: in 1983, it amounted to US$ 44.1 billion;[11] in 1987, it was billion $ 120, compared with a total Third World debt of billion $ 1,200 or billion $ 125 of Brazil. Approximately three quarters of it was owed to official creditors – OECD governments and the BWI – and usually on better conditions than commercial debt. Yet, for various reasons, the capacity of these countries to serve their debts was dramatically small and stagnating. Most of these countries have, for a large variety of reasons, hardly managed to build up any foreign currency earning capacity, notwithstanding large amounts of development aid.[12] By the middle of the 1980s, the interest payments on their debts often represented more than all their export earnings for several years. Their debt crisis represented the failure of their development models, usually consisting of, as Durufle calls it, 'collective enrichment sheltered by the state'[13] – a strategy taken over from colonisation and reinforced by development cooperation.

The second crisis was the one of 17 middle-income countries, mainly in Latin America.[14] They account for three quarters of Third World debt. Commercial banks, and HIC governments, by means of export credits, had increased their lending to these countries over tenfold during the decade of the 1970s: from $ 31.5 billion in 1970 to $ 350.6 billion in 1981.[15] These loans were often short-term, with floating interest rates, linked to the euro-currency interest rate, bringing about the 'transfer of risk from the ultimate lender to the ultimate borrower.'[16] In the early 1980s, as a result of the 'dear money' policy of the US, reinforced by the Reagan administration's budget deficit and the deflationist policies of most other rich countries, the cost of money increased dramatically. At the same time, the value and volume of world trade began to fall. As a result, the debt service ratio's of these MICs rose from a reasonable 10–20% to a dramatic 50% and more by 1982. These are the immediate causes of the second debt crisis. But its structural, long-term origins are different. For various reasons, such as capital flight, corruption, white elephant projects, expensive import-substitution strategies, and the often unfavourable evolution of the world trading system, the money they had borrowed had not generated the resources necessary to repay principal and interest.[17] All through the 1970s, an increasing gap existed between the rate of growth in the debt service burden of these MICs and the growth rate of their export earnings.[18] Their debt crisis can be said to amount to a 'consumption crisis,' as many fast growing countries – or, more specifically, certain groups within them – systematically consumed more than they earned.

The third crisis consisted of the threat of the breakdown of the international banking system as a result of widespread defaults of highly indebted countries. By 1982, many large banks, mainly in the US, had become so exposed to the above-mentioned middle-income countries that the latter's default was generally perceived as a threat to their existence.[19] The risk was generally perceived that the Third World debt-induced bankruptcy of one of them would spread to all others – a dreadful possibility reminding many commentators of the 1930s.[20]

Understanding the development of the modern international financial system is crucial in explaining this crisis. From the end of the 1960s onwards, commercial banks, particularly US, had begun exploiting international market failures and operating offshore to avoid the constraining regulations of their national markets.[21] Following the advent of the Eurodollar market and the collapse of the Bretton Woods monetary arrangements, they began to shape the world financial system (whereas the earlier system was mostly based on governments and public institutions).[22] The post–1973 recycling of petrodollars, instead of being done through the BWI or through national public banking authorities, was entrusted to the private banking system, more by non-choices[23] than by purpose. This provoked a speculative rush on various new markets, and among these, Third World countries figured prominently. Under the assumption that sovereign debtors cannot go bankrupt, internationalized banks, without carefully investigating their creditworthiness, 'forced money on the less-developed countries'[24] using new techniques such as syndication, cross-default clauses and floating interest rates. No regulatory body existed to stop them from doing so.[25] Finally, in 1982, when Mexico announced it could not reimburse its huge debt anymore, the game – and the profits associated with it[26] – ended.

2 The reaction of the commercial banks

The banks attempted to cope with their own debt crisis; they did so in five, related ways. In the beginning these policies were individual and chaotic, but over time they became coordinated, under the leadership of the big banks, and especially Citicorp. The first and immediate reaction was an almost total decommitment from the debtor countries. The banks 'got cold feet.'[27] The net flow of new finance under concerted bank lending fell from more than $ 40 billion in 1983 to $ 5 billion a year for 1985 to 1988.

Table 7.1 Net flows and net transfers by private creditors to 20 severely indebted middle-income countries, 27 severely indebted low income countries and sub-Saharan Africa, bn dollars[28]

| | Net resource flows on debt by private creditors | | | Net resource transfers on debts by private creditors | | |
	SIMIC	SILIC	SSA	SIMIC	SILIC	SSA
1980	17.4	2.8	3.6	4.6	1.9	2.3
1984	10.7	0.4	0.02	–9.8	–1.1	–1.8
1986	6.6	0.4	0.2	–17.7	–0.3	–0.9
1988	4.5	0.9	1.0	–18.3	–0.2	–0.1
1990	–1.3	–0.2	–0.05	–12	–1.4	–1.2

The second one was the adoption of a 'maximalist' policy: only full reimbursement of all debts would do. Debt forgiveness, or reduction, was taboo: only rescheduling, under harder conditions, was possible.[30] Every time a country did not service its debt, this lead to rescheduling – not forgiveness. Reschedulings bring hardly any new money: they seek only 'to keep loans in performing status and have just been sufficient to refinance a fraction – around a quarter – of interest payment.'[31] The conditions of the new loans were usually harder than the original

Table 7.2 Debt restructuring agreements with commercial banks, 1980–88[29]

	1983	1984	1985	1986	1987	1988	1990
Number of agreements	27	26	14	11	17		9
Amount restructured (bn $)	48	91	23	72	92		
Spread over LIBOR (%)	2	1.8	1.5	1.3	1	0.8	

ones, increasing the total debt burden of the rescheduling country.[32]

As a result, in the second half of the 1980s, the 17 highly indebted countries faced a negative financial transfer that averaged 35 billion a year – 'a substantially larger percentage of GNP (about 5%) than Germany was supposed to pay in reparations in the later 1920s (about 3%).'[33] Some authors treat this reaction of the banks as the main cause of the second debt crisis: Susan Strange, for example, suggests to call it the 'credit crisis.'[34] This is only partially true: the credit contraction certainly aggravated the second debt crisis, but it is not its basic cause.

The third reaction of commercial banks was the adoption of a 'case by case' approach: negotiations should take place on the level of each specific country: global solutions were unacceptable. This approach allowed the banks both to better balance their differing interests between them[35] and to avoid being in a position of weakness faced with a united debtor bloc. Fourth, the banks delegated the management of the debt crisis to the IMF, based on the assumption that the latter, as a public international institution, would be able to constrain sovereign debtors. This tendency developed after a catastrophic 1978 experience with Peru, where commercial banks, acting on their own, failed to impose reforms on the Peruvian government, but became common practice after the 1982 Mexican crisis.

Finally, after some years, banks started taking steps to improve their accountancy position. They began to create reserves against losses on 'underperforming loans'; they started selling small amounts of debt to other financial institutions, thus creating a secondary market. They even engaged in voluntary debt reduction, but on a minimal scale: between 1982 and 1988, this amounted to approximately US$ 26 bn.[36]

These policies together constituted what may be called the

'international debt regime', the origins of which date from before the 1982 debt crises.[37] They were formulated to preserve the profitability of the banks: the cost of the debt crisis had to be borne by the debtors. Such a reaction was to be expected: the banks' obligations to their shareholders and depositholders leaves them little space for compassion or charity. The 'guiding principle' of the capitalist world economy constrains them to act in a self-interested way.[38]

3 The reaction of OECD governments

Faced with the three debt crises, OECD governments have constantly acted with two principle objectives in mind. The first and most important one was that the private banking system should not collapse.[39] The second one was that a public bail-out should be avoided.[40] Hence OECD policies were designed to save the commercial banks without drawing on public budgets, implying, once again, that the cost of the debt crisis had to be borne by the sovereign debtors.

This meant a rise in debt reschedulings on hard terms in the Club of Paris, the consortium for government owned debt;[41] the full backing of the SA strategy and the use of BW conditionality; and the exercise of political pressure on debtors to keep up their reimbursements to the banks.

Table 7.3 Debt restructuring agreements with official creditors[42]

	'82	'83	'84	'85	'86	'87	'88	'89	'90
Number of agreements	6	17	14	21	18	17	15	24	18
of which: SSA	5	9	9	10	13	9	9	16	9
Amount restructured (bn $)		8	5	11	5	24	8	18	17

The behavior of the USSR resembles the other countries'. Its exposure was small and concentrated in a few befriended countries (Algeria, Angola, Ethiopia, Lybia, Mozambique). According to Shatalov, 'no comprehensive debt management program has emerged from Moscow. Rescheduling is implemented on a case by case basis.' As for sub-Saharan African debt, for example, it is estimated that the debt rescheduled, refinanced and written off by the USSR from 1982 to 1988 amounts to $ 5 bn.[43]

Such reaction was to be expected. OECD governments, already confronted with a severe economic crisis and budget deficits, perceived a risk of financial crisis in their own countries. In the absence of any international redistribution mechanism, the choice between overindebted Third World countries and overexposed banks in their own countries was easy. Their obligations to their citizens and voters left them little space for compassion for the Third World.

Only when the threat of an imminent financial collapse was gone, did Western governments actively seek a more constructive response to the two sovereign debt crises. The first attempt consisted of the 'Baker plan', launched by the US in October 1985.[43] It was a failure, but paved the way for a subsequent attempt, unveiled in March 1989, by Mr. Brady, the US Treasury Secretary.[44] The strategy of the Plan-with-his-name was to use BWI resources to give a guarantee of repayment to banks in order to seduce them into stepping up their voluntary debt reduction. The plan assumed that the banks should take a loss and gave a more active role to the BWI in the resolution of the debt crisis, reducing the banks' leverage over the debt issue.[45]

The Brady Plan signified a change in the behavior of OECD governments: the costs of solving the debt crisis would be shared between debtor countries, commercial banks, and, to a lesser extent, OECD governments. What made this change possible is that the latter no longer perceived the survival of the private banks to be at risk. As a consequence, other considerations, of a foreign policy nature, moved to the fore. Governments began to fear the political repercussions of the prolonged impoverization caused by the debt crisis, particularly in client states. The evolution in the preferences of the US, but also of all other HIC governments, towards the debt crises has been synthesized by Jeffrey Sachs as follows:

> Since the early 1980s the debt crisis has actually presented US policymakers with two crises: a crisis of US banks, which had lent too much to the developing countries, and a crisis of the developing countries, which had borrowed too much. Until 1988 the concern over the banks took precedence; in 1989 the foreign policy concerns over the deteriorating situation in the debtor countries finally came to the fore.[46]

It is significant that the Bush administration announced the

Brady plan right after serious food riots in Venezuela, and that it was for Mexico, Costa Rica, the Philippines, Morocco, and recently Egypt and Poland, that it was most active. Yet, despite some successes,[47] the Brady Plan has made very little difference to the plight of most debtors.

Things are slightly, but only slightly, different for the debtors in Africa. Although OECD concessional asistance to Africa has increased, it fell far short of offsetting the debt stranglehold. Between 1975 and 1987, bilateral donors also unilaterally converted $ 1.9 billion of outstanding concessional loans to African countries to grants, representing about 6% of concessional debt outstanding.[48] Most of this entered in the statistics on development aid. After 1987, the rhythm of occasional debt write-offs increased slightly:[49] from 1987 to 1989 a further $ 1.6 bn were written off.[50] A large share of Paris Club reschedulings were with SSA countries, but they were on hard terms. It was only from 1987 onwards that SSA countries were allowed to benefit from more liberal conditions in these reschedulings.[51] Finally, at the Toronto summit in June '88, a decision was taken by the G–7 about a debt reduction menu for SSA debtors' non-consessional debt.[52] Although this signified only a modest decrease in the debt burden for SSA, it was an important development, leaving the case-by-case approach, and accepting the need for debt relief. Yet, no more international progress has been made since then.

It is under these conditions that the third category of actors, the Bretton Woods institutions, developed and implemented its structural adjustment conditionality – the main concern of this chapter.

4 Banks, debt and structural constraints

Sovereign debtors basically have three ways to rid themselves of foreign debts: they can finance them, default on them, or adjust to them.

Indeed, nations can 'finance' their debts with the inflow of fresh money from abroad (aid and credits). For most Third World countries, this was the option they had chosen all through the 1970s, so as to 'avoid timely adjustment.'[53] As explained above, the debt crises, and the reactions of commercial banks and OECD governments to it, made this option entirely impossible after

1982: no new funds were to flow to problem debtor countries for a decade to come.

Theoretically, the possibility also exists of using the national savings accumulated abroad to finance a nation's debt. But part of this money should stay abroad: it is 'normal' that a country has credits abroad. The 'abnormal' part is composed of private money which, in a standard economic context, would be invested in the national economy – *i.e.* flight capital. Its return is also unlikely, neither voluntarily nor forcefully.[54] The banks which received the flight capital (often the same ones that supplied the original loans) have no interest in sending back the money, nor is there any national or international legislation able to force banks or individuals to repatriate flight capital involuntarily. At the time, given the shape of their economies, few Third World residents were willing to do so voluntarily. This is evident: nobody willingly loses capital, neither Third World elites, nor the citizens of wealthy nations.[55] According to the logic of capitalism, flight capital only returns when the expected yield on it is sufficiently high and the risk is acceptable. Moreover, if and when it returns, it usually does so in a highly liquid and speculative way, as seen in the case of Mexico.[56] Hence the return of flight capital cannot be considered as the solution to the crisis, but only its consequence.[57]

Default, the second option, advocated by radical scholars and the nationalist and Leftist sectors within debtor countries, had too high a price to be realistic.[58] It would have entailed the cutting off of international financial and trade systems in the defaulting country, a choice only a few rigidly communist countries have made until until our days: Albania, Vietnam, China. This would have brought about a significant decline in the standards of living of the country, and its elites – as happened in some of the above mentioned countries.[59]

Under these conditions, at the beginning of the 1980s, the only option open to the LDCs was to *adjust* to their debts. As all economists know, 'debt is deferred trade:'[60] the only way for debtors to repay their foreign debts is by improving their trade balance, either by increasing their export receipts, or by decreasing their imports. The latter is only partly desirable, because economic growth necessitates the importation of investment goods. Thus *export-oriented* strategies need to be adopted. Moreover, economic growth necessitates the inflow of foreign money and trade credits. If debtor countries want to retain any chance of access to external funds, they have to behave in a way that 'restores the confidence' of the international financial system, *i.e.* in a way that convinces bankers that that there is 'an acceptable expectation that the country can pay the interest and money back.'[61] Such expectation is likely to arise only when governments follow what are generally considered sound and efficient, *i.e. liberal*, policies.

Hence, given the functioning of the global political economy, and whatever the precise causes of their debt crises, debtors had to adjust, and that adjustment had to be export-oriented and liberal.[62] Given the functioning of the global political economy, there was no other option available to them. Any different strategy, with or without the BWI, was doomed to fail. In other words, the nature of SA conditionality as applied by the BWI is in accordance with the basic constraints imposed by the global political economy, and could have been no different. SA became dominant because it follows, in the words of Michael Manley, 'the logic of productive forces'[63] – not because of the malign or cynical character of the Clausens, Delarosières, Kruegers or even Reagans and other earthly powers.[64] As a consequence, any critique of SA which is solely based on the characteristics of the BWI, or on the intentions or moral qualities of their decision-makers, is wrong. Only a realistic and critical appraisal of the functioning of the global political economy, and of the place of the BWI therein, can constitute the basis of a useful critique, and of judicious proposals for change.

When we speak about the global political economy we are refering to the outcome of the interaction between international economics and world politics. The specific form that capitalism, the dominant mode of production and distribution in the world, takes when applied to specific activities cannot be dissociated from prevailing balances of power and preference. For our purpose, the most important aspect of the post-war global political economy is the Bretton Woods organization, and more specifically the abandonment of Keynes' proposal at Bretton Woods for mutual adjustment by debtor and creditor nations in favor of unilateral debtor adjustment.[65] As Hans Singer comments:

> Although [Keynes'] vision is still partly reflected in the constitution of the IMF, enjoining it to put equal pressure on

deficit and surplus countries, in fact the IMF has proved utterly incapable of pressure on surplus countries, neither Japan and Germany today nor OPEC in the 1970s. The pressure is now entirely concentrated on deficit countries which are asked to 'put their house in order'; even among the deficit countries the pressure is selective and there is no significant impact of the IMF on the presently biggest balance of payments deficit country – the USA.[66]

Hence, when poor countries face deficits, the IMF can give some financial help, but only to facilitate their adjustment. Although both unilateral debtor and mutual-creditor-and-debtor adjustment are compatible with the functioning of the capitalist world economy, only the first is institutionalized at present (and even then only selectively)[67] This, then, is not a God-given necessity, but a political fact, reflecting realities of power and interest.

There is one category of debtor countries for which the above applies less, and it consists of those countries whose political stability is of high geo-political significance for a major power. This has allowed these countries to avoid adjustment, if not fully (Egypt; Cuba), then at least partially (Zaire, some Central American countries; the African countries which are member of the CFA monetary zone, etc.).[68] This can either happen directly, when major states, through aid and debt relief, finance part of the deficit of the country concerned; or indirectly, when the former ensure lenient conditions in the IMF agreements with their client states.[69] This, of course, reinforces what we have said about the political nature of the international capitalist system.

5 The Bretton Woods institutions as independent actors

In this part, we will argue that, although the functioning of the global political economy does impose the general constraints on the regime developed by the BWI to cope with the debt crises, the BWI still have room to manoeuvre as they formulate their policy advice. In other words, the BWI are also independent variables for explaining the nature of SA conditionality.[70] There are at least three arguments in favor of this assertion.

First, the BWI had recognized the debt cum development crises long before it became political commonsense. Given the general lack of knowledge at the time about the extent, causes, effects and solutions of the debt crises, the interpretations the BWI made at the beginning of the 1980s were of central importance in the creation of the specific response which eventually became dominant. The BWI play an important role as lobbyists to HIC governments on debt and development matters,[71] particularly advocating increased financial resources for the LDCs.[72] Northern NGOs, for example, lobby for similar policies, but their voice is not heard as easily in high places as are the ones of Mr Clausen, Delarosière, Conable and Camdessus. This is all the more the case on the level of specific countries. Most donors place high confidence in the BWI's analysis and recommendations, and use them in their own negotiations. According to Faaland, for example, 'the donors are much more inclined to pay attention to the views of the Bank than they are to those of the countries concerned.... The Bank is a powerful influence in the design of the strategies for development adopted by the developing countries.'[73] Third, the BWI played the central role in the day-to-day concrete management of the debt crises. Their centrality has increased throughout the 1980s, as a a result of their greatly increased resources and the power delegated to them by the commercial banks and OECD governments. It is through the stand-by agreements and structural adjustment loans negotiated with the BWI that the specifics of the policies to be undertaken by debtor countries are laid out and that the latter's 'good economic husbandry' performance is monitored.[74] The Baker Plan allowing the IMF to sign agreements with countries before the latter have come to terms with private creditors, is an important evolution in this respect.

Thus, although they are certainly constrained by the functioning of the global political economy, the BWI enjoy what can be called 'relative autonomy'[75] in defining their policy prescriptions. Yet, they have failed to use their room for manoeuvring in a progressive way. Their analysis, particularly during the first years, was simplistic and dogmatic,[76] paying exclusive attention to the macro-economic equilibria and the disengagement of the state while neglecting political and social considerations as well as external factors. This is surprising in the light of the experience the Bank had accumulated in previous years: during the same years, for example, it published the results of long-standing research projects, whose conclusions and policy recommendations contradicted its own SA policy in almost every respect.[77]

This goes to show that the World Bank is no monolith, but composed of different, often conflicting desks, whose predominance changes over time.[78]

One cannot help but be struck by this narrow-mindedness of the top World Bank policymakers. It is possible to distinguish two causes. One is frustration: all through the 1970s, 'wrong' government policies (especially price and exchange policies) had minimized the predicted beneficial economic effects of many of the World Bank's projects, especially in Africa.[79] This long-building frustration, already noticeable in the later MacNamara years,[80] undoubtedly laid the foundations for the kind of policy *fuite en avant* SA initially constituted. Second, the international ideological climate of the time had a self-censuring effect on top policymakers within these institutions. At a time when the Reagan administration was threatening to cut its contribution to the BWI, and conservative governments came to power in Germany and Great-Britain, it was a normal tendency of their managers to adapt to the internationally dominant ideology dominant (apart from the fact that many of them shared this ideology anyway[81]).

6 The role of debtor governments

So far we have treated debtors as passive recipients of SA conditionality. This is incomplete. The concrete nature of SA policy reform is very much indebted to the constellation of political forces within debtor countries. The latter are also independent variables for explaining SA outcomes. There are at least two reasons for this assertion.

First, given the sovereignty of states, the content of SA agreements is to be negotiated with their governments. Surely, as Loxley observes, 'the negotiations over the details of conditionality are not between parties of equal strength. Time, expertise, resources and experience are heavily weighted in favour of the multilateral institutions.'[82] Yet, even though LDCs were in a very weak position during the 1980s, the policy reform programs finally adopted in many ways still represent a compromise between the requirements of the Fund and the Bank (and their need to keep working relations with Third World governments) and the preferences of LIC governments. According to Kendall Stiles, 'bargaining dynamics' between IMF staff and country officials constitute the single most important explanatory variable of the nature of SA programs.[83]

Second, and more importantly, the implementation of agreed-upon SA programs can only be undertaken by Third World governments themselves. Effective SA policy reform strongly depends upon their capacity and willingness to do so, which in turn depends on the existence of a sufficiently strong domestic coalition in favor of policy reform. The nature and composition of such coalition varies by type of government, level and kind of economic development, political culture, popularity of the president, and the like.[85] When there is no such domestic coalition, it is likely that SA policy reform will not, or only partially, be implemented.[86] This is now also recognized by the World Bank.[87]

All this constitutes one of the main defenses of the BWI against critiques as to the regressive nature of their conditionality: it is the governments who chose the concrete policy measures by which to attain the general objectives negotiated with them.[88] While this argument is partially true,[89] the obsession of the BWI with macro-economic equilibria and their refusal (or incapacity) to take into account political factors and explicit considerations of poverty alleviation made this all the easier. But it remains a fact that statements to the effect that 'thousands of children died of cholera in Latin America because of the SA programs the BWI imposed', professed not only by radical NGOs, but also by UNICEF, for example, are gross simplifications. One needs to know what were the precise terms of the agreements between these countries and the BWI? Were all public budgets cut in the same proportion? Or were health and education cut, but not defense, for example? And even within the public health budget: what kind of activities were cut first?

7 The effectiveness of conditionality

Aid donors have always had their vision of how aid money should be used, and, more generally, how development should be promoted. Depending on their ideology and the relative importance to the recipient country of the resources of which they dispose, they have engaged in 'policy dialogues' in order to bring about recipient policy reforms.[90] Often they made the granting of aid dependent upon such reforms. This is what is known as 'aid conditionality.' The latter can be said to have been *effectively* exercised only if a recipient country undertakes a policy change it would not have undertaken by itself, *i.e.* without the pressure made to bear upon it by the donor.[91] In all other cases, policy change cannot be called the result of conditionality – common agreement maybe, or inducement.

Aid conditionality has never been very effective. There are few cases known of effective imposition of policy changes by an aid agency against the will of a recipient country government. According to Killick, for example, devaluations, constituting part of IMF conditionality, were implemented as promised in only 1% of stand-by agreements between 1971 and 1981.[92] Even in the case of a country like Bangladesh, whose development budget is largely funded by aid money, there has been preciously little effective policy reform the donors managed to impose – although they most certainly brought a great deal of pressure to bear upon its government.[93]

The BWI in the 1980s, and especially the IMF, are generally believed to be major exceptions to the limited effectiveness of conditionality. The remarkable spread of SA is taken as proof of this. According to the World Bank itself, 57% of all its conditions were fully implemented during the loan period; if one includes 'substantial progress' this becomes 77%.[94] This rate varies widely across issues (with the most succesful ones being the restoration of current account equilibria, primarily through import compression) and across countries (ranging from 20% to 95%[95]).

But closer analysis shows that most countries implementing SA reforms – for example Chile, Jamaica under Seaga, Turkey, South Korea, Pakistan – had governments already committed to the philosophy and the policies of the BW institutions.[96] As such, many of the succesfull cases are countries that had beforehand chosen policies in accordance with BW conditionality.[97] They thus constitute examples of common agreement, but not of effective conditionality. Vice versa, many of the countries where such prior political commitment was absent – Brazil before Collor, Egypt, Zaire, Argentina in 1983–4 and Zambia before 1989 and many more – are failures as far as SA policy reform goes. A recent detailed case study by Mosley, Harrigan and Toye of 14 countries, comes to the same conclusion: three of them were succesful (South Korea, Turkey and Mauritius, all with strong liberal governments); 7 of them met with substantial slippage; 2 of them were aborted in the negotiation phase (Tanzania, Nigeria in 1985).[98] Similar conclusions arise from other accounts.[99] The regularity of the non-disbursement of tranches stands as another demonstration of the limited effectiveness of conditionality. Haggard notes that, of the 32 IMF Extended Fund Facility Programs concluded between 1980 and '84, 24 were renegotiated, or had payments interrupted.[100] This implies that only 25% of them came to their expected ends (which still does not mean their policy aims have been attained). Yet, all these countries have always managed to get new IMF and WB loans afterwards if they wished.[101]

Thus, the capacity of recipient countries to resist aid conditionality is significant, even in the case of SA conditionality. There are various reasons for this. One resides in the nature of macro-economic policies themselves. It is almost impossible to make or monitor macro-economic policy reforms with a reasonable degree of certainty or within a reasonable delay. According to Paul Streeten, 'policies, like resources, are fungible, and resistant governments can yield to one type of policy while pursuing their objectives by some other policy.'[102] As a result, according to Mosley, 'it is relatively easy for a recipient to conceal a determination to do nothing in particular behind an appearance of collaboration with the donor.'[103] Second, policy reform imposed from the outside, or identified with it, causes strong political resistance in the Third World, where the dominant ideology usually is the one of nationalism[104] – a phenomenon often used by Third World politicians to blame donors, and especially the IMF, for the unpopular policies they undertake. Third, the existence of political differences between donors creates a situation of effective competition between them, which adroit recipients are able to exploit so as to avoid conditionality. Finally, the basic principle of the international system, sovereignty, renders it very difficult for donors to enforce reform, or even the execution of an agreed-to policy, against the will of the recipient country government. The only enforcement mechanism available to a donor (short of physical threat) is to withhold funds, which for bilateral donors is not very effective in the face of the competition from other donors nor, often, very likely given the political motivations behind the aid;[105] for multilateral donors, there is a strong incentive to keep on having at least 'working relations' with recipient countries, *i.e.* keeping a steady flow of money.[106]

Conditionality, then, seems to be only effective if adjusting countries' governments, and major groups within them, have a prior commitment to the policy changes negotiated. If such commitment does not exist, *i.e.* if the programs are imposed, they may 'attract token compliance in order to gain an initial transfer of resources, but they are likely to fail quickly.'[107] As Jacquemot & Assidon state it: 'a variety of strategies and counterstrategies – ranging from diligent acceptance of SA programmes to feroce resistance, and passing by provisional adaptation to attempts at sabotage of severe measures – are followed by public actors ('appareil administratif'), depending on their perception of the interest of the population as well as of their own.'[108] This is now quite generally admitted: the Bank itself states that more efforts have to be made to design structural adjustment policies with Third World governments in order to overcome their resistance.[109]

8 Conclusion

Two arguments have been made in this chapter: one about the nature of conditionality and one about its effectiveness. We have constructed a three-layered explanation, in which each level sets the constraints upon the policy options open at the inferior level. Fundamentally, the nature of SA conditionality can be explained by reference to the constraints imposed by the global political economy. Seen at this level, the BWI acted as agents of this system, and could have done no differently. But our analysis also took into account two other factors: the specific role of the BWI, and the domestic political economy within the debtor countries. Both these factors nuance the first; they are needed to avoid an overly mechanistic or reductionist interpretation of reality.

We also saw that the capacity of LDCs to resist conditionality is much larger than is usually thought, even in the case of the BWI in the 1980s. The nature of macro-economic policy change and development aid, in combination with the norm of sovereignty in international relations, gives LDCs a significant power

Functioning of the world political economy	Defines the basic constraints
Evolution of the Bretton Woods institutions	Defines the dominant policy model
Domestic political economy	Defines the concrete policy and its effects

Figure 7.1 The international political economy of structural adjustment

to resist aid conditionality – a power, in the words of Mosley, 'that has been understated both by those who see aid as an instrument of oppression and domination and by their opponents who see it as a powerful diplomatic tool.'[110]

As we said in the introduction, the foregoing has important implications for discussions about so-called 'alternative conditionality,' such as lobbied for by many NGOs. Many of the proposals for alternative conditionality are unlikely to be imposed, for their nature goes against the functioning of the global political economy and the role of the BWI therein. The spread of SA is due to its conformity with the constraints imposed by the global political economy – and not to the inherent intellectual or moral superiority of its policy prescriptions (which existed since a long time anyhow: the works of Jackson Pollack, Bela Balassa, Anne Krueger, Harry Johnson, amongst others, appeared from the 1960s onwards). If developing countries implemented SA policy reforms all through the 1980s, it is mainly because (and to the extent that) their governments recognized these constraints the global political economy imposed on their countries – and not primarily because of the effectiveness of the pressures the BWI made to bear upon them. Thus, conditionality is not a very effective means of changing Third World government policies, especially on issues with politically sensitive distributional consequences such as these touched by SA.

Postscript

Our discussion of conditionality in this chapter served the purpose of allowing us to analyze the interactions between international and domestic constraints on agricultural and food policy. This implies old political science questions such as: what is the influence of the international system on government policy? or, seen from the other side, what is the room for manoeu-vre of governments *vis-à-vis* the pressures and constraints eman-ating from the international system?

In the development literature, two basic perspectives exist: the radical one, which explains Third World hunger (and all other problems of underdevelopment) by the functioning of the inter-national system and the place of Third world countries therein; and the liberal one, which refers to the inefficiency of Third World governments and their policies. Both these perspectives are what Kuhn has called 'incommensurable' and it comes as no surprise that their adherents have very different ideological preferences.

The explanation we developed in this chapter uses elements from both perspectives, but tried to do so without repeating their usual simplifications. On the one hand, it is clear that international or systemic factors were of utmost importance for the explanation of Third World policies. Third World govern-ments are strongly (and often negatively) affected by the behavior of other countries and, in the contemporary world, of private actors, such as commercial banks. The range of options open to them in reacting to any kind of crisis is fundamentally limited by international systemic constraints (which are of both an economic and a political nature), as was clear from our analy-sis of the nature of SA conditionality. But the concrete behavior they eventually display – in the case of financial or of agricultural policies for example – cannot be explained solely by reference to these constraints.

Indeed, we observed that the room for manouevre of Third World governments towards the international system is larger than is often assumed. This observation emerges very strongly from our analysis, for the case we studied – SA conditionality for heavily indebted countries – is an extreme one, in which the prima facie evidence is strongly in favor of high systemic constraint.

In the end, what this analysis boils down to is a strong case in favor of a nuanced and balanced analysis of government policies, which integrates the analysis of international as well as domestic constraints; which, in other words, takes into account system-level as well as actor-level factors, internal and external processes. Too many analyses concentrate but one one of them, very often for ideological reasons. But reality is not so simple, notwithstanding our ideological affinities. In order to understand the complexities and intricacies of the real world, different perspectives have to be combined in a coherent framework, and in a more than ad hoc manner.[111] This does not make scientific work any easier – but it might make it better and less stereotypical.

PART II. AGRICULTURE, POLITICS, THE POOR AND STRUCTURAL ADJUSTMENT

Notwithstanding the highly formalized and quantifiable nature of the objectives and indicators of SA policies, there is no agreement whatsoever about their effects or effectiveness. There are at least four causes for this. First is the oft lamented absence of reliable statistics for many LDCs, particularly in Africa. This is caused by the absence of infrastructure to produce such data,[112] although often political expediency also plays a role.[113] This lack of reliable data is often invoked by the BWI to guard against overly harsh judgements of SA;[114] yet, it has not stopped them from attempting to imposing far-reaching policies on LDCs.[115] Second is the relative youth of SA, rendering it impossible to make definitive judgments at present. Third are the methodological difficulties involved: they would subsist even if perfect data existed. Philippe Hugon mentions in this respect the problems of delimitation in space and time as well as of imputation:[116] is the change we note (increased mortality, for example, or unemployment, or agricultural diversification) the result of SA policy reform or of policies followed prior to it – or even of third, external factors?[117]

Fourth, and most important, given its political importance, it is nothing but expectable that the available information about this issue is in no way 'objective' or 'neutral', not even if it comes in the form of economic 'wisdom,' published by experts of international institutions. This was exemplified in March 1989, by the almost simultaneous publication of World Bank/UNDP and ECA evaluations of past adjustment performance in Africa.[118] Both reports discussed exactly the same topic, using the same data; yet, their conclusions were almost diametrically opposed: positive in the former case, negative in the latter; stressing domestic policy shortcomings in the former case, international constraints in the latter.[119] As could be expected, both conclusions reinforced the preferences of the institutions who published them.

Hence, we will not 'assess' SA here – such activity would amount to little more than a quite prejudiced choice among contradictory expert opinion of the conclusion closest to our ideological and intellectual affinities ... What we will do instead is, first, briefly outline the general effect of SA on the three debt crises, and second, analyze in some detail the SA regime and process concerning agriculture and poverty, as well as its effects upon hunger.

1 Structural adjustment and the debt crises

The 'debt crisis' *sensu strictu, i.e.* the potential collapse of the world financial system as a result of widespread sovereign debtor default, has been largely solved.[120] According to Ignacy Sachs, 'the banks received most of the interest due on the old debt, while also cutting back decisively on new lending to the debtor countries. At the same time, the banks raised new capital.'[121] After a 'historic' decision by Citicorp in May 1987, banks all over the world have built up significant provisions against bad loans. By the end of 1988, West German and Swiss banks have made provisions totalling at least 50% of their Third World debt; French banks 45%, British and Canadian ones 35% and American ones 30%.[122] Hence, by the end of 1988, total exposure net of provision declined significantly for all banks except the Japanese. This does not mean that Third World debt is no longer a problem to banks, but it signifies that these loans pose no fundamental threat anymore to their survival or even, apart from a potential bad semester, to their profit prospects. At present, bad property loans certainly cause more problems to US banks.

At the same time, in the words of the World Bank: '[while] the threat to the international banking system has abated, ... , most of the indebted countries are still no better off than in 1982 – when the debt crisis erupted.'[123] Their debt has continually increased to 1990, notwithstanding that all indicators of their repayment effort have increased. To quote Papic: 'Between the eruption of the debt crisis in 1982 and 1988, indebted developing countries repaid $ 777.7 billion, *i.e.* 138,4% of their long term debt in 1982, but nevertheless their long term debt commitments grew by $ 457.5 billion'[124] – or in more demagogic terms: 'the

Table 7.4 Some outstanding debt indicators, $ bn[125]

20 SIMICs						
	1970	1980	1983	1986	1989	1991
Long-term debt	23.0	186.3	327.4	396.4	416.8	398
IMF credit	0.07	1.1	10.3	14.4	14.7	17.5
Short-term debt	–	67.3	51.4	38.4	53.6	71.7
DEBT STOCK	–	245.9	389.3	449.3	485.1	486.5

sub-Saharan Africa						
	1970	1980	1984	1986	1989	1991
Long-term debt	5.6	43.5	64.9	95.4	123.8	149.1
IMF credit	0.1	3.0	6.0	7.0	7.0	6.3
Short-term debt	–	9.6	13.2	13.6	15.0	20.3
DEBT STOCK	–	56.2	84.1	116.0	145.9	175.8

more they pay, the more they owe.'[126] Fundamental changes barren, this situation is likely to continue.[127] This holds for both groups of countries: LA as well as SSA ones.[128] It also holds as much for those countries that undertook SA policy reforms as for those that did not: for Mexico as much as for Brazil; for Ghana and for Zambia! Hence, and without stating the causes, we can affirm that the policies followed by the different actors involved – banks, governments, and the BW institutions – have totally failed to solve the two sovereign debt crises. The debt seems to have acquired an existence of its own, like a parasite feeding itself on the economies of the countries concerned,[129] with the medicine used being unable to change this situation. This is bound to influence the effects of SA on poverty and hunger.

It is remarkable to what extent the development community – policymakers and scholars supposedly engaged in improving the lives of the millions of poor in the Third World – is complacent about this outcome. There is a remarkable candor in their judgment of SA as designed and implemented by the BWI. If this were about a private enterprise in trouble, and the BWI were hired as consultants to help the company get out of its problems, their work would be called a total fiasco; if we ourselves had stakes in that company, we would be outraged by so much ineffectualness and incompetence. The only positive impact of the SA strategy after ten years is the reduction of government deficits and of inflation in many countries. But total debt has continued to increase dramatically, to a large extent due exactly to the loans of the IMF and the World Bank; both public and private investments have fallen dramatically and future growth rates are seriously jeopardized for years to come. That is surely nothing to be proud about for some of the most powerful institutions in the world, replete with thousands of doctors from prestigious universities and disposing of tens of billions of dollars of money.

To be sure, we have seen that the BWI are not the only ones to blame for this extremely bad record: the behavior of Third World governments, commercial banks, and rich country governments is crucial too. We know that. But don't we always expect of the 'experts' we address ourselves to that they can estimate the environmental constraints and not propose unreasonable (or unrealizable) solutions? Would we be as candid if our own money or our own lives were at stake?

This complacency and candor is explained by the fact that those who design the strategy and those who judge them are basically the same; moreover, they are never those who-are-to-be-developed: the poor and the hungry. Most of the evaluations done of SA are written by the World Bank and the IMF themselves. The other analyses of SA usually come from economists, most of whom share the BWI ideology and would consider it the summum of their personal careers to eventually work or consult for these institutions themselves. The only real critiques known come from some radical authors, who are by definition not considered serious by the experts, as well as from Northern and Southern NGOs (churches, popular movements, etc.). It is not always sure to what extent these reflect the opinions and preferences of the masses of the poor and the hungry in the Third World in whose names they usually pretend to speak, but what is sure is that they have little power in the development community: it is not they who publish the articles, go to prestigious conferences, advise policymakers in the North and the South, chair commissions and workshops, disburse money, etc. Thus the development community continues its good works in complacency and ignorance, proposing solutions it does not feel the costs of and will not be held responsible for in the case of failure.

2 Agriculture, poverty and hunger

As said above, the nature of SA as a development strategy is resolutely liberal, centering on state disengagement, export expansion[130] and global deregulation. Following this, financial equilibrium and economic growth should come about, which should eradicate poverty and hunger. If the dominant norm is the restoration of the free market in developing countries, the underlying principle is that it are government policies that intervene in the free market are the cause of the present crisis.[131] Indeed, the notion that 'domestic policy issues are at the heart of the crisis'[132] pervades the SA diagnostic. This principle is espoused especially strongly for agriculture: inefficient government policies are considered to be the main if not sole cause of the agricultural and food problems of many states;[133] consequently, the liberalization of their agriculture is at the heart of the SA strategy.

A The regime

Agriculture is central to the structural adjustment agenda of both the IMF and the World Bank,[134] particularly in the case of SSA.[135] Most LDCs are considered to have a comparative advantage in agriculture, and policies unfavourable to it are treated among the main causes of the dismal development record of many LDCs, if not their debt crisis.[136] As described in chapter 2, this applies not only to specific agricultural policies, but also to other macroeconomic policies which negatively affect agriculture. SA wisdom involves changes in all of them.

Concretely, this signifies liberalizing – meaning: increasing – agricultural prices in order to encourage agricultural production (the famous getting-the-prices-right argument); increasing investment in agriculture;[137] dismantling or privatizing state marketing boards and generally freeing all trade in agricultural products; abolishing other price distorting policies, like taxes and/or subsidies on agricultural inputs and outputs, etc. – all of this accompanied by devaluating the exchange rates in order to increase the competitiveness of export crops.[138] As a result, the internal terms of trade should alter in favor of agriculture (the talk is now about 'redressing the urban-rural bias'[139]) and production should increase; agricultural exports should increase, which should be beneficial for both the external and internal financial balance of the country; and, as it is in this sector that the majority of the poor live and work, all this should have positive social effects.

In such strategy no *a priori* difference exists between cash crops and food crops: any country should specialize in exporting those products it has a comparative advantage in and import the rest. In line with dominant liberal economic thinking, the solution to the food problem of the LDCs is the same as to all other problems and resides not in food self-sufficiency but in the (re)insertion in the international market.[140] This strategy is a total opposite to the nationalistic (or radical) Third World trend which considers self-sufficiency and self-reliance the solution to the food (and other) problems of the LDCs, such as the Lagos Plan of Action of the OAU.[141]

At first sight, the SA strategy has nothing explicit to say about poverty – it is preoccupied with macro-economic efficiency and growth, not with poverty alleviation.[142] Yet, the strategy advocated by the BW institutions contains some important, be it often implicit, distributive elements. Recently, these elements have come to the forefront of the legitimizing discourse of these institutions. We can distinguish at least five of them.

First, and following neo-classical economics, poverty is supposed to be eliminated by the economic growth which results from the adoption of sound economic policies and the efficient allocation of scarce resources – the return of the previously discarded notion of trickle-down notion.[143] The usual reasoning of the BWI experts is that the economic crisis of most of the Third World is the severest source of hardship for the poor; hence, anything done to end this crisis serves them.

Second, and still following basic liberal ideology, it is believed that decreasing the role of the state will free developing countries of a body of expensive, inefficient and often corrupt officialdom, creating opportunities for dynamic elements within civil society to organize and escape from poverty through private enterprise and self-help.[144] Given the corrupt and elitist nature of many Third World governments, this impact of SA should be very positive. It should benefit small traders, the informal sector and small farmers alike.[145]

Third, the liberalization of agriculture should have positive effects on the rural poor.[146] Getting-the-prices-right should signify and end to the urban bias and increase the income of the country-side, where the majority of the poor live.[147] In he absence of state intervention, rural artisanat and commerce will develop, and peasant production for domestic or export markets will increase.

Fourth, very implicit and very political, beneath the whole SA policy there is a vision of redistribution, of transfer from previously protected and advantaged groups to previously non-protected or disadvantaged ones.[148] For example, the abolition of subsidies is justified by the fact that, as it were not the poor who received them, their ending should increase relative equality in the adjusting countries. The freed resources can and should be used to stimulate growth or to install efficient and well-targeted policies to the real benefit of the poor.

In the early regime, these four processes and their positive effects on poverty were supposed to follow automatically from SA policy reform along the lines preconized by the BW institutions; no special attention was given to the reduction of poverty. But since the middle of the 1980s, in the face of grave criticism about the regressive social effects of SA policies,[149] a second phase began, in which more attention was devoted to the poor: protecting them became an addendum parallel to ongoing adjustment. By the end of the 1980s, thinking on the issue evolved further, and, in a third phase, poverty reduction became an objective of adjustment policy design.[150] Hence, and fifth, to the original regime was added an explicit concern about the short-term need and potential to protect the poor and the hungry.[151] This should be achieved either by refocusing existing social expenditure towards the poor, or by new well-targeted compensatory programs.[152]

The latter brings us to hunger, about which the original regime had nothing to say except that it would pass as a result of the greater agricultural production and economic growth that would follow liberalization – the old 'trickle down' argument. But in 1988, the World Bank published a report which reflects the changing wisdom, and advocates specific measures for eradicating hunger in Africa. A quote from Barber Conable's foreword sums it up nicely:

> a focus on agriculture and economic growth alone will not
> be enough to end hunger and ensure food security in Africa.
> Countries enjoying strong growth and surplus food will

continue to have millions of people suffering from malnutrition – the sick, urban unemployed, rural landless laborers,
and in general the poorest of the poor. Thus, while reem-
phasizing that adjustment and growth are essential links in
the food security chain, this report also highlights the need
to look beyond growth. It recommends a complementary set
of special actions to help reach Africa's poorest and hung-
riest people.[153]

Since 1988, such poverty orientation has become part of the
common discourse of not only the World Bank, but also the IMF
and all bilateral donors.

B The process

Much of the SA wisdom has found it way to structural adjustment-type agreements. Institutional reforms, trade reforms and
public investment reforms have figured predominantly in the
conditionality of at least half of all of the World Bank's SALs
over the last decade.[154] As far as agriculture goes, three quarters
of all World Bank SALs up to Jan. 1986 included agricultural
price revision; 58% included improved institutional support to
agriculture (marketing etc.); a small minority included the abolition or reduction of state marketing boards, and the reduction
of agricultural input subsidies.[155] As to getting-the-prices-right,
'the bulk of agricultural pricing conditionality has been concentrated in the LDCs, mostly in Sub-Saharan Africa.'[156] In the case
of at least 19 countries with which the IMF negotiated SA programs (out of 36 programs), agricultural price changes were also
incorporated.[157] According to the Fund, most of its programs
'are designed to facilitate institutional reforms, improvements in
investment, and technological diffusion in agriculture – usually
in close collaboration with the World Bank. . . . In the programmes of several countries exchange rate policies were
designed with particular regard to agriculture.'[158] The World
Bank tells us that 57.1% of all agricultural policy conditions were
fully implemented; the figure becomes 81.6% if one includes
'substantial progress.'[159] This is quite low – only fiscal and budget
policy score lower (78 and 78.35 resp.) – but still is above historic
trends.

The regime's original neglect of explicit social concern is also reflected in the process. In the early years of SA, only a few Latin American countries implemented policies to protect the poor from the negative effects of SA reforms they undertook: the most succesful cases being, according to the World Bank, Chile and Costa Rica.[160] As far as Africa is concerned only Ghana's programme had a built-in social dimension.[161] In the other countries, no special policies to cushion the poor from the potential negative impact of SA reforms were taken.

Since the second half of the 1980s, and also in line with the regime change, more attention is being paid in negotiations with LDCs to education and health policies and poverty issues.[162] Since 1988, 'before IMF missions part from headquarters they are to discuss explicitly the poverty issues raised by proposed stabilization measures with country economists in the IMF and the World Bank.'[163] In 1987, the World Bank created a 'Social Dimensions of Adjustment' Unit (SDA), which by 1989 had 70 employees, of which 40 for Africa.[164] It is active at present in more than 40 countries in Africa, often co-financed by bilateral donors.[165] It not only studies the social effects of adjustment programmes but also helps design measures targeted to the poor and self-help promoting measures. There is thus more attention to the social effects of SA policies, but it is unclear what, if anything, this has meant for the poor.

C The effects of structural adjustment on hunger

According to UNICEF and other critics of SA, the incidence of malnutrition has increased for a large number of countries for which recent and reliable figures exist: Burma (now Myanmar), Burundi, Gambia, Guinea-Bissau, Jamaica, Niger, Nigeria, Paraguay and the Philippines. It adds that malnutrition has also increased in some countries where aggregate figures show no decline in food availability.[166] Yet, given the youth of SA policies and the problems of imputation, it is possible that this is not the result of the SA policies, but of the imbalances which necessitated SA in the first place. The debate is very complicated[167] and, as said, most inconclusive. Instead of entering it, we will present here an overview of different forces which affect the impact of SA on poverty and hunger. In so doing, we will mainly focus on political and social processes, all too often neglected by those engaging in the debates on SA.

We have distinguished five processes which are supposed to have beneficial effects on the incidence of poverty and hunger. We argue that these processes are not automatic: they can be counteracted by other processes. This is what we will analyze in the next pages.

The first process which according to the discourse of the BW institutions is supposed to decrease the incidence of poverty and hunger is the restoration of economic growth. This return of the previously discarded 'trickle down' notion is the centerpiece of the SA regime concerning the removal of poverty, at least in the long term. But one of the main lessons to be drawn from 30 years of development experience, is that economic growth is a necessary but not a sufficient condition for the eradication of poverty.[168] The notion of entitlement developed by A. Sen and used in this thesis perfectly captures this argument. As said above, many within the World Bank are aware of this too.[169]

The second and very important counterprocess is the simple observation that, as a matter of fact, economic growth has not been restored during the last decade in almost all heavily indebted countries. As mentioned above, the debt crisis has in no way been solved for the large majority of the debtor countries. Moreover, the evolution of the international environment has been most unfavourable: absence of solutions to the debt crisis, declining terms of trade, increasing protectionism in HIC markets and insufficient concessional assistance. All this is not caused by SA; yet, SA policies cannot change it either. Moreover, by opening up their economies to the world, SA has made developing economies more vulnerable to these unfavourable external processes. To solve the problem, international changes are needed: vigorous growth in the demand for primary commodities, declining protectionism, some solution to the financial burden of LDC economies, etc. It can be debated how these changes should come about – through the free play of the market or though interstate coordination – but it is certain that they lay beyond the power of the Third World governments and the BWI alike – and that they did not materialize until now.

Little is known as yet about the precise effects of the second process – the disengagement of the state. Have new groups emerged in civil society, or have existing ones gained in importance? Which ones? Has the performance of the informal sector improved, in size and in income? In many countries, the disen-

261

gagement of the state has signified the privatization of public companies. Have they been taken over by nationals or by foreigners? Did other industries pop up downstream or upstream? With a declining state involvement come decreasing opportunities for patronage and control over civil society. Has the access of different groups to scarce resources become more equitable? Has corruption decreased? The answers to these questions are fundamental to the future evolution of these countries.

It is not at all certain that the answers are the ones intended by the BW ideologues. A near endless variety of means exist to abort, sabotage, bypass or detonate such reforms and they are likely to be used by those individuals who make up the state and who fear for their privileges. This likelihood is reinforced by two already described facts: the reforms are imposed from outside, and often do not reflect prior domestic realignments of power or preference; and the absence of any socio-political analysis by the BWI.

One certain effect of the decreased size of the state has been a dramatic deterioration in the situation of civil servants. Many of them lost their jobs; those who remained at work lost large parts of their real income.[170] Given the style of consumption to which they are accustomed and the demands made on them by their environment, this places them in a difficult position. Again, as far as the civil servants go, it is probable that they develop mechanisms to protect themselves from the negative effects which SA policy reform threaten to have on their position, by taking second jobs, buying privatized industries, entering in favored agricultural crops and so on. As they are the ones who have to implement SA policies on a day-to-day basis, this should at least be a cause for questions.

The third process – the liberalization of agriculture – is often called the most important structural change over the last decade, especially in Africa, signifying an end to the 'urban bias' which has characterized 30 years of development practice.[171] According to the Bank 'there is a clear trend toward higher food crop prices [in Africa].'[172] Yet, as the Bank's own figures indicate, this trend might not be as new as it likes to believe: aleady during the 1970s, there existed a notable trend of agricultural price increases in Africa.[173] Moreover, this has not had the effect of significantly improving aggregate agricultural growth rates, which remained on the same depressed levels as before.[174] This, then, implies that certain crops gained as a result of the price increases, but at the expense of other crops, or, in economists' terms, that the aggregate elasiticity of agricultural production towards price was close to zero.[175]

Hence, even if prices for agricultural products increased, it is doubtful that this has had the uniformly positive effects on the poor predicted. Transportation and storage facilities are very often absent, and, given their financial squeeze, governments have no money to construct new ones or even keep existing ones functioning.[176] In the absence of a market infrastructure and some measure of competition,[177] increased prices remain theoretical for the more remote – and usually poorest – sections of the countryside; without access to markets (national or international), the risk even exists of leaving them worse off than before![178] This phenomenon is known within most sub-Saharan African countries; countries such as Kenya, Mali, Benin, Burkina Faso, Zimbabwe and Zambia have exportable surpluses which they do not manage to dispose of.[179] Such a situation also exists in the USSR of 1990, where the largest harvest ever coincides with a collapse of the harvesting, storage and trade system. The end result is that there is less to eat than ever for most of the Russian population, while food is rotting in the countryside.

On the international level, the 'fallacy of composition' – the process by which all countries, having increased their production of primary commodities, see world prices tumble, and, given constant demand, their revenues decrease – has had dramatic effects, especially for small, unprotected farmers.[180] Latin American countries, such as Brazil and Chile, have concentrated on the export of primary commodities in order to reimburse their debts – effectively ending their evolution of diversification towards manufactured products.[181] At the same time, African countries have been advised by the BWI to do the same; and some Asian so-called agricultural dragons, such as Malaysia and Thailand, dramatically expanded their very low-cost production. As a result, world agricultural prices plumetted, mainly at the expense of Africa's farmers.

The concrete effects of the liberalization of agriculture on the rural poor depend crucially on the economic structure of any specific country. The more equal the distribution of landholdings, the more the poor stand to gain, for the potential gains cannot be monopolized by large and powerful landlords.[182] As such, the

African rural poor should benefit more than the Latin-American ones. But the gains to be made depend also crucially on the particular mix of crops of the region, of the question whether the prices of non-tradable, tradable-but-not-exported or exported crops increased most,[183] and, in the latter case, of the evolution of world prices for cash crops.[184] Finally, the more net food consumers there are among the poor, the less the poor will gain.[185] In the cities, all people are food consumers and lose from increased food prices – a process usually aggravated by the simultaneous ending of food subsidies. This problem is biggest in Latin America, given the existence of a large class of urban, largely unemployed poor. On the countryside, landless rural labourers, artisans and farmers that buy a significant share of their food in the short term lose from increased agricultural prices.[186] Given the initial level of poverty of many of them – particularly women, the old and children – they might be pushed below the borderline of ultra-poverty.[187]

Hence, the effects of SA agricultural policy reform on non-peasants are probably negative; for farmers, the automatic improvement in agricultural production and rural welfare most economist supposed to follow from SA did certainly not take place. The financial crisis facing Third World governments, the fallacy of composition and the distribution of assets on the countryside all militate against it. The concrete effects of SA agricultural policy reform on rural poverty and hunger depend on many factors, and no unequivocal patterns exist. The only generalization Sahn and Harris, from Cornell's prestigious Food and Nutrition Policy Program arrive at, is that whatever positive effects there are on smallholders, they are bound to be very small;[188] a detailed study by Cynthia Hewitt de Alcantara on Mexico concludes that SA has brought about only more recession and hardship on the countryside.[189]

Fundamentally, the whole SA wisdom concerning agriculture is based on a vision of the countryside as homogenous, diametrically opposed to the city and the 'state', and waiting only for price hikes and free markets to turn into small, efficient entrepreneurs. All this is dangerously simplistic and contrary to reality: it cannot but deceive when it constitutes the sole basis of policy.

The fourth process – the end of the protection afforded to certain groups – should bring about decreasing inequality if the previously protected were not the poor. The publications of the BW institutions as well as independent academic literature strongly suggest the latter generally to be the case: practically all subsidies were, intentionally or not, largely used by the better off; even if they reached the poor they were usually inefficient and regressive.[190] The most interesting case is probably the one of food subsidies, which exist in almost all LDCs. They disproportionally benefit the rich and not-so-rich, while being extremely costly.[191]

But two important counterprocesses are overlooked by the BW institutions. First, part of the subsidies did go to those in whose name they were set up: the poor, particularly in the cities: they often still signified an important help to them in many countries.[192] In the absence of compensatory measures, the latter are bound to be hurt by their simple abolition[193] – which might bring them to revolt.

Second, such distortions are no accident, although some of their effects may be. As Bates has been the first to argue, economically inefficient policies exist 'because they are politically useful.'[194] Schematically, such policies can have two origins: or they have been created as a response to the demands of specific interest groups or politicians; or they came into being for other reasons, but have acquired important political functions for those in power and their clients. Often both situations coexist: the existence of a large and active public sector, for example, certainly has historical and economic origins, but its growth and the specific activities it undertakes owe most to political expediency.[195] The same causes that gave rise to the subsidies-to-be-cut, the policies-to-be-changed, and the parastatals-to-be-abolished, make it likely that they will not be cut, changed or abolished in the required way, or that those which primarily benefit the poor will be cut, changed or abolished first.[196] The ruling elite will resist implementing policies which hurt itself, or those who back it, more than symbolically – even under heavy external pressure.[197] As Scobie states it nicely:

> there can be no presumption that those who might have gained in the destabilizing phase will correspond to those who will lose, either relatively or absolutely, in the adjustment period. One could presumably make the case that in fact, the political forces were such that those gaining in the

destabilizing phase were not the poorest; and those who did gain will resist the subsequent erosion of those gains, so that the burden of adjustment will fall on the weakest.[198]

This resistance of the privileged and the powerful is the single most important counterprocess to the implementation of SA policy reform – not the famous so-called 'IMF riots.'[199]

Generally spoken, the process of SA presents a conflict between, on the one hand, the economic crisis (the structural constraint which the world political economy imposes and which makes it impossible to continue policies as before) and, on the other hand, the political processes which gave rise to the policies-to-be-reformed in the first place. SA is only likely to succeed if ruling groups are committed to the policy change and if they are backed (or obliged) by sufficiently powerful segments of society. In the terms of this book, this can be the case either because powerful groups changed their preferences in favor of SA reform, or because previously powerless groups with a preference for SA reform gained sufficient power – or any combination of both. Especially the policy changes belonging to SA reform which are politically sensitive (and many are) are constrained by this necessity to be backed by a sufficiently powerful domestic commitment. The BWI forgot this: they wanted policy change without bothering about the coalition of interests behind the policies-to-be-changed.[200]

SA policies tend to be externally originated and conceived – most often only resulting from the necessity for ruling elites to mobilize funds from the BWI and through them from the international capital market, but not from any commitment to SA policy reform as described above. Hence, the lack of prior political and social analysis, the ultra-liberal ideology of the SA regime (alien to most reforming countries where nationalism is still the dominant ideology), and the heavy-handed way in which BW institutions 'help' those countries all decrease the chances that such domestic commitment as described above will come or remain into being.[201] All this makes it most likely that the implementation of SA will be not take place as negotiated and that SA will not have the effects desired by the BWI.

In the absence of such domestic commitment, (and combined with the low effectiveness of conditionality) three possibilities exist. The main one is that the reforms advocated by the BW institutions are formally implemented, but that they are sabotaged or bypassed as much as possible in order to avoid precisely those politically sensitive repercussions which were their objectives. Two is that the contested policy – or SA altogether – is abandoned, or not even tried, as in the cases of Zambia, Peru, Nigeria, Egypt and Argentina during most of the 1980s. Three is that the government sollicits and/or receives aid from external donors with a preference for political stability in the country concerned, as is happening in the cases of Venezuela, the Phillipines and Egypt.[202] Such aid can then be used to avoid policy reform with the BW institutions. At times such aid allows the recipient to violate those policies which the same donor through its support for the BWI attempts to stimulate.[203]

On the other hand, things are not static: it is possible that SA policy reform, once set in motion, even only tentatively, brings about domestic realignments of preferences in favor of its continuation. As Christensen has it: 'Effective support for continued reform . . . [can] emerge from the process of implementation.'[204] This could be because economic growth is restored, or because sufficiently powerful groups perceive to benefit from the changes already realized. Indeed, the powerful are not omnipotent nor monolithic: the distribution of power or of preferences can change. Yet, evidently, the opposite also holds – that groups previously in favor of policy change turn against SA because of the hardship it brought them, or because of its perceived lack of effectiveness.

The fifth process – the implementation of social policies – has been introduced from the middle of the 1980s onwards. It nuances the faith in the likelihood of the fast restoration of economic growth as well as its benefits to the poor that characterized the previous period. According to the World Bank, it is possible to device policies which are cost-efficient and effective in improving the fate of the poor; this can be advocated not only on the basis of elementary humanitarianism, but also on grounds of efficiency, as an investment in the productive asset number one: people.

But, as should be clear by now, all these sound arguments do not make these policies take place. Their implementation depends on the domestic politics of the reforming countries, which more often than not are not very conducive to them – particularly not under conditions of economic recession.[205] Moreover, given the limits of conditionality, the BW institutions can only apply persuasion on this matter (which they failed to do until the middle of the 1980s). Under these conditions, improved social policies are unlikely to be effectively implemented.

3 Conclusion

We distinguished five processes which, according to the SA regime, should benefit the poor. But we also noted the existence of a large variety of counterprocesses which render it unlikely for the former processes or to take place, or for them to have the beneficial effects on the poor predicted. This is often forgotton, by defenders and critics of SA alike.

The precise outcome – whether the poor gain or lose from SA, or whether the incidence of hunger increases or decreases – depends on the balance between these (interrelated) conflicting processes. It can only be studied on a country by country basis, and is likely to change over time, making generalizations dangerous (whether these are pro or contra SA). Yet, an indication of the direction in which the outcome is likely to go is given by a comparison of the fate of miltary expenditures with social expenditures for selected countries. If these figures are anything to go by, the fate of the poor is not bright under SA.[206]

It is impossible to conclude about the effect of SA on poverty: the available studies are as yet inconclusive and generalizations are impossible.[207] In the short and medium term, we can quite safely conclude that 1) SA policies did not improve the situation of the poor as they were supposed to do; 2) the incidence of hunger and poverty increased among certain groups, especially urban ones and 3) policies to protect the latter are unlikely to have compensated for their losses. As to the long term, the least we can say is that much optimism is not warranted.

On the level of political economy, the central problem is the one of the state. We brought to light a conflict between the implicit and explicit objectives of SA and its process of implementation, making it unlikely that the outcome is the one wished for. There are two paradoxes to discuss.

First, while, according to the SA logic, the state has to disengage, the BWI depend upon it for the implementation of SA. The same state which has to be altered, if not dismantled, is the one who has to implement that reform.[208] This makes the wished for

Table 7.5 Structural adjustment and poverty: intended processes and counterprocesses

Process	Intended effects	Counterprocess	Level of explanation
1. economic growth	–increase incomes of all	– economic growth does not necessarily lead to increased income for the poor – economic growth did not take place	–domestic
2. decreased state intervention	–create dynamics of self-help –increase relative equality	–resistance of powerful groups, most notably politicians and civil servants	–domestic
3. liberalization of agriculture	–increase agricultural production –increase income of rural poor	–vulnerability to world market –fallacy of composition –economic-agrarian structure –decreased well-being for rural non food producers –urban poor and middle class →resistance of powerful groups	–international –domestic
4. end of subvention	–declining inequality –free resources for process 1 & 5	–some of the previously protected were poor –resistance of the previously protected	–domestic
5. policies to protect the poor	–entitlements of the poor increase	–lack of political power by the poor –lack of administrative capacity	–domestic

269

reforms most unlikely, in particular those which negatively affect the position of those making up the state (and the social groups they represent).

This paradox is caused at the level of international politics. The only possible partners for international organizations such as the BWI are states. The negotiation and implementation of SA policies can only be done with states, even if the objective of these policies is to dismantle the latter. Since recently, the BWI attempt to contact NGOs within the reforming LDCs, so as to sollicit their advice and cooperation, but such activity remains marginal, incapable of fundamentally altering the bilateral government – BW institution relation.

Second, the attitude of the BW institutions to the state is unclear if not paradoxical. On the one hand, they display a most negativistic attitude vis–vis the state: its abolition is considered a condition for development to take place. On the other hand, they treat the state as a body which, if only properly informed, will further the interests of society and implement such policies as advocated by themselves.[209] This paradox is rendered possible by (and reinforces) this other important feature of the BW institutions: the absence of any socio-political analysis of the state.

The causes for this absence are multiple. On the international level, the sensitivity of such analyses goes without saying. But the BWI could have done more than they did. What stopped them is the 'econocentrism' which characterizes all their policy making and analysis. Sophisticated tools have been developed for judging the economic and financial soundness and effects of development actions,[210] but none to judge their socio-political or institutional aspects. There are no sociologists or political scientists on the teams that visit reforming countries. Hence the neglect of political and social factors.

Notes

1 For a good description of the World Bank's approach (the most dominant one throughout the 1970s), see Donaldson, 1991: *passim*.
2 The debt crisis and structural adjustment constituted the biggest growth industry for economists in the 1980s: the volume of literature produced is properly speaking phenomenal: no one could possibly read all of it. Any choice about what to read and what not, then, is usually based on a combination of chance, reputation, and ideological affinity. Within the discipline of international political econ-

omy, the functioning of the international monetary system has been studied by *inter alia* Wood, 1986; Lipson, 1981 & 1985; Cohen, 1981 & 1982; Haggard, 1985, Nelson (ed.), 1990 and others. The content of SA is best explained by the World Bank itself: 1981, 1984(b), 1986(b), 1987(b) & 1988(d). The interactions of the two Bretton Woods institutions – most notably the growing similarity in their activities and the resulting conflict this entails – have been analyzed *i.a.* by Feinberg, 1988 and in the press.

3 For discussions of the origins of conditionality, see Gold, 1979 and Dell, 1982. For a more radical interpretation, see Hayter & Watson, 1985.

4 Colclough, 1984: 28.

5 For the IMF, see Korner et. al., 1986: 209 ff.; World Bank, 1990b: 69 ss. Note that 16 of them are mini-states with fewer than 1 million inhabitants. For the World Bank, see Wohlmuth, 1985: 39; World Bank, 1991a: 57 and World Bank, 1990b.

6 ECA, 1989.

7 The US has its own so-called Economic Policy Reform Program for encouraging SA-type policy reform, as well as a special strategy for Africa: Rau, 1991: 106 – 108. As explained in chapter five, also its food aid has been linked to SA.

8 See for example Bandow, 1989: 85.

9 See for example Singer, 1988.

10 George, 1988: 238 ff.; see too Carera for a coalition of Swiss NGOs, in *IMF Survey*, April 16, 1990; the propositions of FONDAD, the Amsterdam-based organisation regrouping most European NGOs lobbying on the debt/SA issue; or the position of the Canadian Inter-Church Coalition and the All Africa Council of Churches, etc.

11 World Bank, 1990a: XI: this is composed of long-term and short-term debt (less than 1 year). The latter amounts to US$ 4 bn. The figures for all sub-Saharan Africa, which include some middle-income countries (especially Nigeria and Ivory Coast) are US$ 79.2 bn and US$ 11.3 bn respectively.

12 Helleiner, 1986; Parfitt & Riley, 1989; Greene, 1989 for cases and discussion.

13 Duruflé, 1988: 9.

14 Mainly in Latin America (Argentina, Brazil, Chile, Mexico, Venezuela) but also in Africa (Ivory Coast, Morocco and Nigeria) as well as the Philippines and finally Yugoslavia, which hardly qualifies as a Third World country.

15 World Bank, 1988(a): 9.

16 Strange, 1986: 48. For L'Hériteau, 1982: 518; Nunnenkampf, 1986: 7; and others, the problem of these countries was not the *size* of their debts: taken account of inflation, its growth was not nearly as dramatic as it looks like. Many OECD countries have debts at least the same relative size: Belgium's public debt at the time was 128% of its GDP, and Italy's 100%. (I owe this idea to Dupuy, 1990: 352; see too Reisen, 1990: *passim*). The real problem with their debt was its *terms*, which became increasingly to their disadvantage.

17 For a good and short analysis, see Husain, 1989.

18 IMF, 1989: 48, 52.

19 A dreadful possibility reminding many commentators of the 1930s. See for example the *Wall Street Journal*, Nov. 10, 1982, for a description of such catastrophy scenario. For analyses of the 1930s, see Fishlow, 1985; Kindleberger, 1978; Marichal, 1989, and Pfister and Suter, 1987.

20 See for example the Wall Street Journal, Nov. 10, 1982, for a description of such catastrophy scenario.

21 Swedberg, 1987: 365. For a comprehensive history, see Cohen and Basagni, 1981; Sampson, 1981.

22 See Friedman, 1971; Cohen 1977; Mendelsohn, 1980; Swedberg 1987: 362.

23 Makin, 1984; Frieden, 1987: 88 and 104. For the notion of non-choice in this context, see Strange, 1986.

24 Kindleberger, 1978: 24. For a discussion on whether or not banks 'pushed loans', see Darity, 1986. Fishlow, 1989: 44, calls this period a historical aberration.

25 Hawley, 1984; Kapstein, 1989; Kahler, 1985.

26 In 1977, the international profits of Citicorp were 82,2% of its total benefits: Moffitt, M. *The World's Money*, New York, 1983: 53 cited by Swedberg, 1987: 369.

27 Koht Norbye, 1988: 6. Cuddington, 1989: 31, talks about 'retrenchment'.

28 For the SIMICs, World Bank, 1990: 159–60; for the two other categories, World Bank, 1991: 125–6 and 153–4. For other interesting data, see World Bank, 1988a: XLIII and XXIV; IMF, 1988. 45; IMF, 1989: 54. Note the difficulty of comparing such data on a long-term basis, for the composition of these different classifications (and even their names) change constantly over the years and between institutions.

29 World Bank, 1988a and 1991a.

30 Reschedulings bring hardly any new money: they only seek 'to keep loans in performing status and have just been sufficient to refinance a fraction – around a quarter – of interest payment:' World Bank, 1988a: XXIV.

31 World Bank, 1988a: XXIV.

32 Showing that the term 'debt relief' the banks use for this operation is at the least misleading. Among others, see Faber, 1988. As the *Financial Times*, May 2, 1984, states it: such operations 'so far have been widely and not too unfairly caricatured as a process designed to rescue the banks rather than debtors.'

33 Williamson, 1989: 52.

34 Strange, 1986: 193. See too Frank, 1984: 590.

35 Bank interests were divergent between small and large ones; between heavily exposed and less exposed ones; and, resulting from different legal systems, between US, European and Japanese ones, etc. See Lipson, 1981; Lipson, 1985b; Wellons, 1985; Cohen, 1989: 158 ss.

36 IMF, 1989: 54; World Bank, 1990a: 18.

37 Cohen, 1982: 459 & 475; Lipson, 1985a.

38 Waltz, 1979: 73–4. Bankers do not make profit because they love to

(although most of them probably do) but because they have to: if they did not, they would cease to be bankers. Schematically, this is what is meant with the term 'guiding principle.' The term comes from Waltz, but not the concept; in political economy it derives from structural Marxism. See Poulantzas, 1977 and Milliband, 1977.

39 Lipson, 1985a: 239.
40 Cohen with Rosati, 1982.
41 Rieffel, 1985.
42 World Bank, 1988a and 1991a. Figures of the OECD, 1988: 51, are 3 in 1978, 4 in 1979; 3 in 1980 and 7 in 1981.
43 Shatalov, 1989; 192; Humphreys & Underwood, 1989: 51 write that only about one third of Soviet claims is being regulalrly reimbursed.
44 Conway, 1987; Bogdanowicz-Bindert, 1985 and 1986; see also, for the banks' view: Morgan Guarantee Trust *World Financial Markets*, February 1986.
45 Sachs, 1989; Cohen, 1989; Williamson, 1989. All authors agree that no political solution to the debt crisis could be found without the involvement of the US: Strange, 1986. Yet, the intellectual origins of the Plan are to be found in Japan, France and the BWI: BIS, 1989: 154; *The Economist*, March 25, 1989.
46 See *Financial Times*, June 6, 1989; *The Economist*, April 29, 1989; BIS, 1989: 155. The banks vehemently criticized this increased power of the IMF: Le Monde, 20 sept. 1989.
47 Sachs, 1989: 88.
48 For example Mexico: Van Wijnbergen, 1991; World Bank, 1990: Table 11.
49 World Bank, 1988a: XXXVII. Note that the Bank is only talking about public concessional debt – not about public non-concessional debt, such as export credits and guarantees, or about private debts.
50 *Financial Times*, May 26, 1989; *The Economist*, July 12, 1989.
51 World Bank, 1990: Table 9.
52 IMF, 1988: 47.
53 World Bank, 1988a: XXXVIII; BIS, 1989: 152–3. The three options are: partial debt write-off, longer repayment periods, or lower interest rates. The Toronto facilities are conditional on agreement with the IMF.
54 Singer, 1988: 45.
55 On the definition and measurement of capital flight, see Deppler & Williamson, 1987; Lessard and Williamson, 1987; Cuddington, 1986; Dooley, 1988.
56 Koht Norbye, 1988. The Brady Plan included the return of flight capital as one of the elements of the solution of the debt crisis. This is either a case of gross naivity or, more probably, an example of convenient rhetoric.
57 World Bank, 1991a: 44; *The Economist*, June 8: 93–4; also Van Wijnbergen, 1991: 37.
58 BIS, 1989: 156. At present, now that their financial situation has started to improve, flight capital is indeed returning to Mexico, Chile and Venezuela: *The Economist*, Oct. 19, 1991: 21–4.

59 For interesting discussions of the definition and the historical pre-cedents of default, see Dommen, 1989; Lever and Hune, 1987: chapter 7 and Eichengreen & Portes, 1989: *passim* plus the comments by Skiles following it. Branford and Kucinski, 1988, and Hayter and Watson, 1985: 33, among others, argue in favor of default.

60 Mendelsohn, 1984: 54. For a radical view, see Dietz, 1989.

61 Mendelsohn, 1984: 2.

62 Polak, 1988: 120; IMF, 1989: 56.

63 See L'Hériteau, 1982 and 1986 for an excellent description.

64 *South*, July 1989: 10.

65 And nor, as 'conspiracy theorists,' such as Cypher, 1989, have it, to serve the interests of the rich countries, or the US. Some of the measures they impose on debtor LICs are not to the interests of the rich countries: for example, the limitation of food imports: Byerlee, 1987: 323. See too Cohen, 1982; L'Hériteau, 1986; Durufl, 1988: 197.

66 Gardner, 1956, chapter 7. See too Forster, 1990.

67 Singer, 1988: 12.

68 For example, as the World Bank's Husain and Diwan, 19889: 2, point out, in the 1930s debt crisis, creditor country governments pressured debtors and creditors alike to solve the crisis.

69 Haggard, 1985: 182 mentions the cases of Gabon, Kenya, Egypt, Mexico, and possibly India and Pakistan. See too Krueger & Ruttan, 1983: 2–6. For the case of the US and El Salvador, Honduras and Costa Rica, see Dabene, 1989: 136; for Haiti and the US, see Riddell, 1987: 255.

70 Killick, 1984: 219 and Hayter and Watson, 1985: 57–48, hold that the degree of harshness of IMF conditions depends on the importance attached to the survival of its government by the major powers, and especially the US. They mention the cases of Pakistan, Turkey, Lib-eria, Egypt, South Africa and El Salvador.

71 For a similar argument, see Ascher, 1983.

72 In the words of the World Bank, 1988(a): XXVII: 'the IMF and the World Bank ... have exerted moral suasion to increase concerted lending.'

73 See *The Economist*, 13/5/89. According to Mistry, 1989, this was a huge policy mistake, adding to the payment problems of these countries.

74 Faaland, 1981: 10.

75 Lipson, 1985a.

76 From the Marxist notion of the 'relative autonomy' of the state: see Milliband, 1969.

77 As Singer 1988: 61, states it: 'it ressembles more a brand of religious fundamentalism than a school of thought.' This is now also admitted by Bank economists: f.ex. Nicholas, 1988: 36.

78 In 1983, for example, the Bank published *Focus on Poverty*, where one can read that 'macro-economic growth is no guarantee for improvement in the situation of the poor.' See too Lipton's *The Poor*

and the Poorest, published by the Bank in 1988, whose conclusions were opposed to current Bank policy.

79 See too Zaki Laidi, 1989.
80 See the World Bank's regular evaluations of its own activities, such as 1988b and the evaluation of 20 years of IDA activity: World Bank, 1982; see too OCDE, 1988: 26–7.
81 Hans Singer; personal communication
82 Especially the famous radical liberal troika of top World Bank consultants: Anne O. Krueger, at the time World Bank vice-president of Research and Economics, Bela Balassa and Deepak Lal.
83 Loxley, 1987: 51.
84 Stiles, 1990: 971.
85 Haggard and Kaufman, 1989; Waterbury, 1989; Bienen and Gersowitz, 1985.
86 See Braverman & Kanbur, 1987: 1181; Mosley, 1987: 235; Streeten, 1988: 109.
87 'The government's commitment to and ownership of the program and some degree of popular support for its implementation are crucial:' World Bank, 1988c: 6.
88 For a typical defense along these lines, see World Bank, 1991b: 9.
89 It has been documented that, especially in the early years, the BWI did attempt to impose unduly harsh conditions on debtor countries: Cassen, 1986b.
90 Cassen, 1986a: 69 ff.; McNeill, 1981: chapter 3.
91 See too Krueger and Ruttan, 1983: 2–3; Cassen, 1986a: 70. Effective conditionality is thus an operational version of the ubiquitous phenomenon of power. Note that effectiveness as defined by us does not express itself on the economic impact of the policy reform finaly adopted.
92 Killick, 1984: 194 and 250–254.
93 Faaland, 1981.
94 World Bank, 1988c.
95 Mosley, 1987: 40–1.
96 Mosley, 1987: 42.
97 Also observed by Kenen, 1987: 1445.
98 Mosley et. al., 1991.
99 Stiles, 1990; Mosley, 1987b: 9.
100 Haggard, 1985: 157–8.
101 According to some authors, it is not in the interest of the BWI to be hard on problem countries: their 'self-interest [is] to renegotiate on conditionality ex post and ad hoc:' Nunnekamp, 1989: 102; Mosley e.a., 1991: *passim*.
102 Streeten, 1988: 109. See too Paul Mosley, 1987: 235: 'by artful juggling, the recipient can often confine his policy changes to the ones he would have undertaken anyway.'
103 Mosley, 1987: 240.
104 Colclough & Green, 1988; Streeten, 1988: 109–10; Krueger & Ruttan, 1983: 2–5.
105 Remark by White, in ODA, 1983: 91.

106 One of the central inovative themes of Mosley e.a., 1991.

107 Ravenhill, 1988: 210; 205; Krueger & Ruttan, 1983: 2–8.

108 1988: 183: own translation.

109 World Bank, 1988c. See too O'Brien, 1991: 36–7.

110 Mosley, 1987: 44.

111 The latter sentence we added to differentiate ourselves from those authors who reason that if system-level factors fail to explain outcomes, one should have recourse to actor-level ones; if the latter fail also, personality factors should be added. We believe this to be wrong: there is no explanatory hierarchy between these different (levels of) explanations, nor are they independent. One should be able to use them all, if not at the same moment, then at least while specifying more than *ad-hoc* the relations between them.

112 The data look precise and serious in the thick books published by the various UN bodies, but those who have seen the functioning of the system that collects them know better. See Chander, 1990: *passim.*

113 Everyone who has looked up Latin American unemployment statistics – betwen 4% and 10% for major countries all through the 1980s – must have considered this possibility.

114 For example Heller e.a., 1988: 10 & 34.

115 Jacquemot, 1988: 202; Ravenhill, 1988: 184–5.

116 Hugon, 1989: 60 – 62; Hugon, 1986: 10; also Goldstein & Montiel, 1986.

117 Theoretically, in order to assess the effects of SA, it is necessary to 1) precisely identify the changes in the economy; 2) separate those which result from SA policies from those which do not, and 3) compare the former with what would have happened if SA had not taken place. Kafka, 1988: 122. As this is quite impossible, authors can attack each other's conclusion by reproaching to have omitted one of these steps.

118 World Bank/UNDP, 1989(a); ECA, 1989(a). Some months later, in july 1989, the ECA published an even more critical report: ECA, 1989(b).

119 O'Brien, 1991: 31.

120 IMF, 1989: 45; World Bank, 1988(a): XI and XIX; BIS, 1989: 153; Huizinga, 1989: *passim* presents a good overview..

121 Sachs, 1989: 90.

122 World Bank, 1988a; *The Economist*, March 25, 1989: 95; BIS, 1989: 151: due to differences in legislation, this is not easy to do for US and Japanese banks.

123 World Bank, 1988a: XI. See too BIS, 1989 and UNICEF, 1989: 20.

124 Papic, 1989: 81.

125 World Bank, 1991a: 124 & 152.

126 George 1989: 29.

127 IMF, 1989: 46. For a good overview, see Corden & Dooley, 1989: *passim*

128 World Bank, 1988a: 15; BIS, 1989: 150.

129 Hugon, 1989: 67. For some, such as George, 1988: chapter 14, this

is no accident, but a deliberate construction of rich country governments to keep the Third World under control.

130 According to a 1986 World Bank study, in 14 out of 16 countries which had received SA loans, a main objective was to increase exports: Avramovic, 1989: 10.

131 For Africa: Glickman, 1988: 26 and Rau, 1991: 106.

132 WB, 1981: 121 for Africa; Husain, 1989, for Latin America.

133 Ravenhill, 1988: 179–80.

134 For the IMF, see Johnson, O.E.G., 1989: *passim*; for the World Bank, see its own documents: 1981, 1984b, 1986b.

135 Christensen, 1983: 75 a.f. As already said in chapter 3, this vision is also dominant in the academic literature: for example Asante, 1986: *passim*.

136 As suggested for example by the Bank's insistence on the fact that, if Africa had just managed to keep the export shares of primary commodities (most of which are agricultural) it had in the beginning of the 1970s, the increased income would have been equal to the full amount of debt of the continent, or twice as big as all aid it receives yearly. World Bank/UNDP, 1989a.

137 Central to the SA philosophy – WB, 1988c: 7; Heller e.a., 1988: 32 – but hard to realize under the conditions of the debt crisis.

138 About the distributional effects of devaluations under SA, an interesting literature exists: Jacquemot, 1988: 167 a.f.; Bienen & Gersovitz, 1985: 742 a.f.; Williams, 1987: 379–9.

139 World Bank, 1986a. This is a striking incorporation-neutralization of academic critique in mainstream policy-making. The 'inventor' of the urban bias critique, Michael Lipton, also worked since the end of the 1970s for the World Bank. He afterwards went to another of these institutions-that-count: the International Food Policy Research Institute in Washington.

140 Allison & Green, 1983: 5; Hirsch, 1990: 22–3. The reasoning is that if a country has a comparative advantage in food production, it should concentrate on producing food: it will be(come) self-sufficient and export food with the proceeds of which it can buy other products. If a country has no comparative advantage in food production, it should not try to achieve food self-sufficiency. Rather, it should concentrate on producing and exporting other products and buy food with the proceeds.

141 Amin, 1982: 24; see too Shaw, 1983: 335. For an excellent critique of the radical approach, see Sender & Smith, 1986: *passim*.

142 Allison and Green, 1983: 6 talk about a 'bland abstraction from distributional issues.' See too Rau, 1991: 99–106.

143 See for example, Heller, 1988: 3 and 5, writing for the IMF: 'because they encourage growth and the efficient allocation of resources, structural adjustment programs globally play a positive role, protecting the long term interests of the poor.' (my translation)

144 Hugon, 1989: 62.

145 See the case of subsidized rural credit we discussed in chapter 2. In the liberal vision underlying SA, as a result of the restoration of

the free market, all farmers should now have equal access to credit. The criterion for the allocation of credit would be the productive capacity of their proposed investment – and not their political clout, as in the previous, state-controlled system. That should benefit small farmers. Heller e.a., 1988: 15 & 33.

146 Johnson, O.E.G., 1988: 38.
147 For example: 'increasing agricultural producer prices will directly benefit between 40 and 50% of the poor in Côte d'Ivoire.' World Bank, 1988d: 29.
148 Hugon, 1989: 67.
149 The most influential version was undoubtedly Cernia, Jolly & Stewart, 1986, published for UNICEF.
150 This distinction in three phases was taken over from Farmer, 1990: 5–7.
151 World Bank, 1988b: 1–2; Nicholas, 1988: 36; Heller, 1988; Heller e.a., 1988; IMF, 1988: 34.
152 Nicholas, 1988: 37; Berg, 1987: *passim*; World Bank, 1986b: *passim*.
153 World Bank, 1988e: 1; see too World Bank, 1990(c): *passim*.
154 World Bank, 1986b: 50.
155 Mosley, 1987: 40. According to Commander, 1989: 229, price policy was part of 80% of all SALs in SSA; institutional reforms were part opf all of them.
156 World Bank, 1989d: 49.
157 Green, 1989: *passim*, especially pages 50 ff. provides an overview of all the policies included in 1982–6 IMF standby agreements with a direct impact on agriculture.
158 Johnson, O.E.G., 1988: 38.
159 WB, 1989a: 8.
160 World Bank, 1988c: 11; World Bank, 1989(a).
161 Loxley, 1988: 5.
162 Although the IMF still explicitely states that 'distributional matters do not belong to its authority.'
163 Zuckerman, 1988.
164 Its budget is assured for 5 years by the UNDP and by Canada, the EEC, Switzerland and some other bilateral donors.
165 Carera, 1989; World Bank, 1988c: 11 – 1; Frisch, 1988: 71.
166 UNICEF, 1989: 18; Scobie, 1989: 74.
167 Some good introductions of the different ways in which adjsutment affects the poor, see Scobie, 1989: *passim* and Streeten, 1989: 11.
168 Cassen e.a., 1986.
169 See also the World Bank's 1990 *World Development Report*, which makes a very different and much more nuanced reasoning concerning poverty than the hardline liberal one of the 1980s. It was the first time in four years that this important yearly document even mentions the concept of 'poverty': Korten, 1991: 64–5.
170 Coussy, 1990: 48, talks about a decline in real purchasing power of 25–50% for all urban wage earners in 16 out of 20 African countries undergoing SA in the 1980s.
171 Hugon, 1989: 77; Commander, 1989: 239..

172 World Bank, 1986d: 19. The examples mentioned are Zambia, Tanzania, Mautitania, Zaire and Guinea. Also Addison & Demery, 1987; Frisch, 1988: 68; Jammal & Weeks, 1988; Hugon, 1989: 77.

173 See for example the tables in World Bank, 1986a.

174 According to World Bank, 1991 data, the agricultural growth rate was 2.5% from 1965 to 1980 and the same from 1980 to 1989 for the least-income countries; for the lower group of middle income countries, it was respectively 3.4% and 2.1%. Food production per capita had stagnated throughout the 1980s for both categories of countries.

175 This is indeed the dominant position at present. See among others, Chhibber, 1989: *passim*.

176 The 'getting-the-prices-right-is-not-enough' argument. See Sender & Smith, 1986: 123–4; Green, 1983: 32; Hugon, 1988: 14; Jacquemot, 1988: 151; Ravenhill, 1988: 190–1; Commander, 1989: 236; Green, 1989: 39 ff.; Chhibber, 1989: 66. See too World Bank, 1988d: 50. Not only did government investment budgets dramatically decline in many countries, but also did the share of agricultural spending in these budget often decline too: WFC/1990/3: 3; Streeten, 1989: 10; Green, 1989: 42; Paarlberg & Grindle, 1991: 392.

177 See Gregoire, 1990: *passim*, based on a case study of Niger and Nigeria.

178 According to Heller e.a., 1988: 33, this has happened in three of the seven countries studied (Kenya, Sri Lanka and the Philippines). The same hapened in Zambia. This can be because, the farmers plant and harvest more agricultural produce, prices can fall dramatically in the absence of transport and storage facilities to move their new surpluses out of their region; moreover, given the weakness of monetary demand, this risks leaving them worse off than before. It is also possible that, in the absence of really competitive markets, trade liberalization (of agricultural inputs and outputs) restores local monopolies, often based on traditional powers, rather than to create a free market.

179 Bilateral donors, urged by the FAO, do give some financial and logistical aid to help these countries sell their cereal surpluses on the international market; part of it takes the form of food aid to neighbouring countries – so-called 'triangular aid.' See *Food Outlook*, August 1990: 23.

180 Predicted early on in the 1980s by i.a Loxley, 1984: 69; Godfrey, 1983: 39; Duruflé, 1988: 195.

181 According to Pourdanay & Mancini, 1984, and George, 1988 this is the main effect of the debt crisis: the end of an emerging New International Division of Labor.

182 Huang & Nicholson, 1987; WFC/1990/3: 4.

183 Green, 1989: 52.

184 This helps to explain the comparative record of different countries. See for example the comparison made between Zambia and Ghana, two early reformers, by Loxley, 1988. See too the editorial to the *IDS Bulletin* volume on SA edited by Colclough & Green, 1988.

185 Heller, 1988: 3; according to World Bank, 1987b, this applies to 30–40% of the population.
186 World Bank, 1988c: 12.
187 Heller e.a., 1988: 5.
188 Sahn & Sarris, 1991: 28.
189 Hewitt de Alcantara, 1992: *passim*.
190 All articles in Bird & Horton, 1989; Heller e.a., 1988: 4; World Bank, 1988c; Colclough & Green, 1988: 3.
191 Hopkins, 1989. The World Bank, 1988c: 18, offers interesting figures for rural Morocco. In Sri Lanka and Egypt food subsidies account for 50% of the public budget.
192 As the same World Bank figures show.
193 Heller e.a., 1988: 25; Pinstrup-Anderson, 1986 and all his other works.
194 Bates, 1983: 128. See too Christensen, 1983: 83 a.f.
195 Bates, 1981, 1984: For an excellent article concerning SA, see Herbst, 1990.
196 See too Bates, 1989: *passim*.
197 The same holds for pressures and conditionality in favor of democratization: Uvin, 1993: *passim*.
198 Scobie, 1989: 12.
199 Christensen, 1983: 96; Bienen, 1990: 714 & 727, for Kenya. Concerning the oft-discussed IMF riots, Bienen & Gersovitz, 1985: 753, argue that 'neither the collapse of a regime nor large-scale and persistent instability has commonly been caused by the acceptance and implementation of IMF policies.'
200 Or they dogmatically belive that the instauration of the free market will change all this. While Heller *e.a.*, 1988: 32, explain that 'the better-off are generally in a better position than those in poverty to protect themselves against the explicit and implicit taxes associated with unsustainable policies,' nothing seems to suggest they are aware that the rich' capacity to protect themselves will also exist during, and after, SA policy change.
201 Excellently discussed by Frisch, 1988: 69, Director-General of the EEC's Directorate of Development.
202 In the latter case, there have been attempts to convince Egypt of the necessity of policy reform along the SA orthodoxy during 1989 – suasion which seems to have been effective, for Egypt, at the end of 1989, is close to signing a stand-by agreement with the IMF.
203 See Dabene, 1989.
204 Christensen, 1983: 88.
205 Social spending always tends to be cut most easily during recessions, even in rich countries. Concerning SA, see Scobie, 1989: 44.
206 UNICEF, 1989: 18. This translates to – 10% for military spending; – 11% for education and – 14% for health. Yet, Streeten, 1989: 10 holds that social spending does not automatically suffer most: some countries, such as Brazil, Indonesia and the Phillippines, even increased their social spending during the period of adjustment.

207 Demery & Allison, 1987: 1495.
208 As Glickman, 1988: 41, writes: 'if government is the problem, if the state needs to restrict its role in the economy, the conventional funnelling of assistance, whatever the level, to present governments is doomed. That the instrument required for policy reconstruction and future development is itself suspect is a paradox thus far not fully explored.'
209 Sender & Smith, 1986: 123. What they are looking for is a Thatcherian kind of state: strong, and willing to cut itself. But such state does not exist in the Third World; not is it sure the Thatcherian state has really cut its size or control over civil society very much.
210 See for example the presentation by Johnson, O.E,G., 1989: *passim* of the model used by the IMF for designing its SA package in agriculture.

Conclusion

INTERDEPENDENCE, REGIMES AND HEGEMONY

We will now close the circle, going back to the aims we outlined at the outset of this study and recapitulating what we have done in the light of these. Our first aim was to apply and test some of the hypotheses enunciated in one of the major works of the contemporary study of international relations, Keohane and Nye's 1977 *Power and Interdependence*. In order to do so, it was necessary for the issue areas studied here to be characterized by the conditions of complex interdependence. We believe this to be the case. In the issue areas of food aid and trade, population assistance and Third World finance, there exist indeed a very large variety of private, governmental, bureacuratic and inter-governmental channels connecting societies; military force has not been used to solve conflicts in these issue areas over the last 40 years (that would be difficult to conceive of in the case of food aid anyhow, but would be possible for finance, food trade and population); and, finally, the hierarchy among these issues (and between them and other ones, including security) is unclear and changing, as was most evident in the cases of food trade and finance.

It is not difficult to consider issue areas as being in the condition of complex interdependence: after all, its characteristics are sufficiently vague and general to apply to most modern world politics. What is more difficult, and interesting, is to analyze if the consequences of complex interdependence, and a *fortiori* the 'international organization model' used to explain international politics under these conditions, also apply. For if this is the case, the usual Realist approach has to be at least amended. Our answer is positive, but nuanced.

Let us start with the first political consequence of complex interdependence according to Keohane and Nye: linkages between issues become less effective, and, as a result, the outcomes of political bargaining increasingly vary between issue areas. This effect has often not been verified. Important intellectual, ideological and practical linkages exist between the international regimes applying to the issue areas we studied (and between them and other issue areas),[1] rendering norms and principles remarkably integrated and homogenous between issue areas. Moreover, the processes in each of the issue areas we studied were strongly biased towards the preferences of only a handful of powerful states, foremost among them the United States. Hence, fundamentally, the 'outcomes of political bargaining' varied little among issue areas: they were in favor of the preferences of the same rich and strong states, and against the preferences of the same weak and poor ones. Even if the preferences of powerful states were not only of a self-interested nature, it was still clear that it was always their preferences which dominated the others, and not those of poor states. Given the fact that their preferences are linked between issue areas, the end result remains the existence of a strong linkage between issue areas, on the level of regimes as well as on the level of processes, biased in favor of the powerful.

Exceptions to this did occur, mainly when preferences *within* powerful states were conflicting, as was for example the case in the food trade issue area between the political and security preferences of the US and the EEC and their agricultural and economic ones, or in the structural adjustment issue area concerning the conflict between the preferences of the foreign policy establishment, in favor of Third World political stability, and the commercial banks, in favor of debtor financial discipline. In such cases, the process in these issue areas was often diversified and contradictory, more or less rapidly followed by redefinitions of preferences and changes in outcomes. But this proves less that linkages are absent and power differently distributed within issue areas, yielding different outcomes, than that states are no unitary actors and that different governmental units within states can have very different and changing preferences, often for exclusively domestic reasons – as Keohane and Nye also predicted.

Indeed, it has been very clear in this thesis that 'national interests [preferences in my parlance] are defined differently on different issues, at different times, and by different governmental units' and that in this process of definition, 'domestic problems created by economic growth and increased sensitivity interdependence' are of utmost importance.[2] This held very strongly for food production and food trade policies, at the side of both rich and poor countries: the preferences governments defined in these issue areas were strongly influenced by the problems and opportunities created by an interdependent world. US food trade policies were conditioned by the (negative) effect of EEC farm policies on its export earnings, while Third World food production policies were at least facilitated by the increased availability of concessional food on the international market which results from OECD agricultural protectionism. Similarly, the policies of rich countries in the structural adjustment issue area were more influenced by the feared repercussions of Third World default on their own domestic economies than by considerations of foreign policy, at least originally. As we have seen in both the international food trade and the debt crisis issue area, this situation of high sensitivity interdependence did not lead to international cooperation – on the contrary.

Finally, we were able to observe the central role played by non-state actors. Intergovernmental organizations were much more important than being merely the reflection of powerful states' interests. They were not only crucial in the creation, reinforcement and change of international regimes, but they also often were central actors in the concrete process.[3] This held most strongly for the structural adjustment and for the population issue areas, where international organizations – the Bretton Woods institutions in the case of the former; the whole United Nations system, the UNFPA and the World Bank for the latter – were perhaps the single most important actors in creating contemporary outcomes in their respective issue areas.

Non-governmental organizations – for profit and not for profit – were also important: they lobbied governments and international organizations for increased population assistance; bought, sold and/or transported almost all international commercial and concessional food flows; lavishly financed Third World deficits all through the 1970s and helped strangling the same economies in the 1980s; organized family planning and rural development projects all over the world, including in politically 'sensitive' countries such as Afghanistan, Vietnam, Nicaragua, Ethiopia and Sudan; and pushed for alternative conditionality among occidental publics. In all these issue areas, they have often been highly succesful in realizing their preferences; in some of them – population and finance for example – they had an important operational role in managing international outcomes. In-depth attention to them is thus warranted. Yet, they did not have the same (explanatory) power as states did: food trading companies, lobby groups in favor of family planning or alternative conditionality and development NGOs handling food aid all played their role only indirectly, passing through states, by influencing governments or their constituencies; if they played a direct role, it was only because states allowed them to do so, as in the case of the merchants of grain.[4]

Only commercial banks seem to have the capacity to play a role close to that of states on the international scene. They could allow Third World governments to follow expansionary policies against the will of the IMF in the 1970s; make them end these policies, this time in cooperation with the IMF, from 1982 onwards; and sabotage HIC government preferences in favor of increased lending to the same countries, as in the latter part of the 1980s. Their capacity to play an autonomous role (i.e. their power) originates in the failure of the public management of the world financial system. 'Private international credit expanded for lack of any agreement on how the official intergovernmental structures in the system could be reformed. (. . .) In the absence of agreement on management by official institutions, dollar hegemony shifted to the financial sector, that is to say, to the very largely unmanaged dollar itself.'[5] From the beginning of the 1970s onwards, states gave commercial banks a free hand to manipulate and create money flows all over the world. They used this freedom so effectively that they eventually ended up becoming fully uncontrollable by states. This important phenomenon, which can be described as the 'hegemony of capital', is new and has received only minor attention, except from some theorists daring to leave mainstream international relations theory, such as Stephen Gill, Robert Cox and Susan Strange.[6]

Hence, to recapitulate, among the effects expected of complex interdependence, some occurred but others did not. Basic patterns of outcomes did not differ very much between issue areas, while power remained the central, and very concentrated, element in explaining international outcomes; international cooperation did not necessarily increase. On the other hand, the increased importance of domestic politics was verified, and with it the notion that states cannnot be treated as unitary actors. Moreover, a variety of non-state actors, such as NGOs, private actors and international organizations, are clearly important in explaining international outcomes. Finally, states did not always act according to their narrowly defined interests. Take together, all this reinforces the challenges to the usual Realist approach that have been voiced since the 1970s; yet, it does not legitimize a liberal model. What it does plead for, is a cognitive/institutionalist approach that has started its development more recently.

In such an approach, the two innovations we suggested in the first chapter are easily integrated. These innovations centered around two points: first, the distinction between interests and preferences, giving rise to the possibility that outcomes are not always to the interests of powerful actors; and second, the sociological definition of regimes and their explanatory value as independent variables. How have they fared throughout this analysis?

All through this book, we have encountered numerous instances where states' preferences were not to their interest, even in the theoretically important case of powerful states. This was either due to misperception, as with the long-standing and unsatisfied self-interested preferences underlying US food aid or the same country's behavior in the food trade issue area; or to the fact that the preferences of powerful states were of a non-self-interested nature, as was predominantly the case in the food aid and population issue areas. This shows the usefulness of a clear distinction between interest and preference as well as the necessity to link domestic to international politics in order to interpret regime and process dynamics better.

The case of the agricultural/food trade issue area is a good example of the kind of dynamics we discussed in chapter one. After World War II, the US was hegemonically powerful, both generally and in the food trade issue area, and the international food trade regime and process consequently strongly reflected its preferences of the time. As we have seen, these were highly illiberal in nature, contrary to its preferences in other trade issues, and this for reasons of domestic politics. Thus the international food trade regime was illiberal, which left other states free, or even encouraged them, to adopt similar policies. As good as all rich states, and quite some other ones, subsequently adopted protectionist policies, which were often sanctioned by the GATT regime, as in the famous case of the EEC's variable levies. By the end of the 1960s, it became clear to US policy-makers that this outcome was against its interest, and their preferences consequently slowly began changing. But in the meantime the distribution of power in the agricultural/food trade issue area had also changed, to the disadvantage of the US and in favor of the EEC and other protectionist countries. This change in the distribution of power within the issue area was to a large extent the result of the regime and the process which had existed from 1945 onwards: if the EEC, Japan and the other European countries had not been as free as they were to adopt highly protectionist policies, they would never have acquired the power they eventually did in the issue area – the EEC even having become the world's second food exporter! Thus the US has become incapable of changing the nature of the international food trade outcome, notwithstanding the strength of its preference in favor of such a change.

All of this also points to the importance of unintended effects in international politics – as in all human behavior. The outcomes of the food production and food trade issue ares, for instance, resulted to a large extent from the unintended effects of behavior motivated by different, if not inverse, preferences. With Scott, we castigate the 'intentional fallacy,' which treats every outcome as the result of the intention of powerful states.[7] Much of international politics, especially under conditions of complex interdependence, is non-intended, mal-calculated, badly foreseen and rigidly executed: it is about 'muddling-through'[8] and not about grand design.

All the preceding is strongly related to the second important element of our pre-theory: the definition of and importance attached to international regimes. In the issue areas we studied, regimes, as defined by us, mattered, even if imperfectly. This was most clearly the case for food aid and population/ family planning, but also held for structural adjustment and food trade. Regimes mattered because they conditioned the perception of self-interest (and reputation) by states – as in the case of food trade and food aid – or because they led to the existence of non-self-interested preferences, such as we observed in the food aid and population issue areas. Regimes were regularly violated, to be sure, but that is only to be expected in international politics and hardly constitutes a proof of their non-existence or their non-importance.

All of this gives credit to what have been variously labelled as idealist, neo-institutionalist, reflectivist, sociological, neo-liberal or cognitivist approaches,[9] but it does not imply that Realism is passé. Indeed, we also observed that the fact that regimes exist. and influence behavior does not mean power, conflict or anarchy have lost their importance: all remained central in the issue areas we studied. Most preferences of states were self-interested in nature and conflicted with those of other states, while outcomes reflected the distribution of power; no central regulatory or enforcement authority existed. Thus the existence of regimes need not go against Realist assumptions. But there is more. We have seen that regimes are closely linked to the preferences of the powerful. On the basis of this observation, regimes can be inserted in a Realist framework, reinforcing the latter rather than weakening it. This most important point is what we now turn to.

The theoretical instrumentarium of classical Realism tells us much about the relation between international structure and the likely processes, about the dominant rational in international politics, self-interest, and its relation with power, about systemic constraints, etc. But there are some important gaps. One of these is that it does not supply us with concrete information on *what* the self-interest of a state in a given issue area is – especially if we are not dealing with security issues, but with issue areas of low politics – nor *how* it is defined. That is where the sociological perspective becomes interesting to the scholar of international relations: it allows us to understand concretely the way international actors think and (re)act – the day-to-day fashion of defining preferences and interests. This is all the more important for the development issues we studied in this thesis. As Megan Vaughan states it in her excellent book on African famine:

> perceptions of the longer-term viability of food production systems in semi-arid Africa, of the role of climatic change and population growth, of the functioning of the market and the effects and side-effects of food aid, all ultimately determine the institutional response of politicians and donors to the immediate spectacle of the starving.[10]

Ideas, norms and principles are thus important to the student of international relations: a sociogical/cognitivist perspective to the field of international politics is warranted. The latter can supply us with tools for understanding the behavior of the human beings acting within constraints, making policies in the concrete everyday environment of international politics.

Such preoccupation is not new: the discipline of international relations has dealt with such questions in a variety of ways, from the path-breaking work of Haas, discussing consensual knowledge and the importance of learning; Jervis, analyzing misconceptions and misperceptions; Rosenau discussing habit-driven actors; and Allison contrasting rational actors with bureacratic ones; to the literature on regimes, exemplified by Keohane or Krasner, posing questions about norms and principles and the way they matter; and the recent issue of *International Organization* about epistemological communities. Yet, many studies using these concepts suffered from one or more of the following defaults: one, they were overly theoretical, adding empirical analysis only as an afterthought, an illustration; two, they were static, failing to develop a dynamic approach of norm change; and three, they tended to be descriptive, failing to address the question of the impact and explanatory value of norms, principles, perceptions and knowledge in a more than ad hoc way. As we discussed in chapter one, the causes of these deficiencies are undoubtedly linked to the limited role sociological and interpretative factors can play in a classical Realist framework, as well as the dominant positivism of the discipline. Hence, notwithstanding the existence of an interesting theoretical literature on these factors in international relations, the greatest part of the empirical research goes on without much incorporation of its concepts or concerns. As a result, theory cannot draw on a large variety of case studies, which reinforces its tendency to move in an abstract vacuum.

Moreover, the descriptive and *ad hoc* incorporation in the Realist toolbox of some sociological or cognitive concepts is not sufficient. Norms, principles, knowledge, perceptions and other such factors can and should to good effect become corner-stones of a Realist approach, maybe sacrificing some of the parsimony and positivism so dear to its adherents, but gaining much in scope and explanatory power. This is what we set out to do. In order to achieve our objective, we introduced two innovations. One was the clear separation between the concepts of interest and preference, and the clarification of the relations between them. The second was the reassertion of the link between norms and behavior. We discussed both above. But there is a third innovation that has imposed itself throughout this analysis, and it concerns the link between norms and power; it constitutes the most important theoretical conclusion of this book.

Indeed, except in very rare cases, norms, principles, ideas and knowledge are neither neutral nor consensual. They are defended by some and questioned by others; they are of benefit to (the perceived interests of) some and to the disadvantage of (the preferences of) others. Take the above quote about famine: the dominant vision of population growth as a cause of famine and the free market as its solution are not accepted by all (not by this author, for example). Those who are starving, if they were asked, would probably disagree with both principles, and with the actions that follow from them. Yet, these principles are fully acceptable and evident for others, who have more power than the starving and who will organize relief, if relief there is, on the basis of these principles. This acceptability is largely caused by the fact that these principles are at least not considered inimical to the preferences of the powerful.

Norms and principles are fundamentally linked to the preferences of powerful actors within the issue area to which they apply, and these preferences, as Realism expects, are usually self-interested in nature. This does not mean that international regimes have been deliberately developed by powerful groups so as to serve their interests. One should avoid any kind of conspiracy theory. Powerful groups are often quite unaware of their interests, nor are these always homogenous among themselves or between issue areas. The construction of the principles and norms that make up international regimes is usually not done by powerful groups themselves, but by scientists. It is the latter that are the 'artisans' of principles and norms. Take the case of structural adjustment. The ideas underlying this regime existed for a long time: the works of economists such as Jackson Pollack, Peter Bauer, Bela Balassa, Anne Krueger, Harry Johnson, and many more, appeared from the 1960s onwards. Their sudden dominance in the 1980s cannnot be explained by their inherent scientific quality alone:[11] it is not these authors who master the process by which their ideas become dominant or (remain) marginal.

290

The dominance of certain ideas – and the marginality of others – is intimately linked to the extent to which they are at least neutral if not favorable to the perceived interests of the powerful, and, hence, to the distribution of power. All of this is subject to constant change: the preferences of the powerful change as the nature of issue areas or their perceptions of it change; in the longer run, also the groups who are powerful can change. As a result, international regimes will change: other, often already long existing but marginal norms and principles, gradually acquire dominance, while previously dominant ones lose their significance, as is the case of structural adjustment for example. The economic crisis of the end of the 1970s, and the debt crisis *sensu strictu* of the beginning of the 1980s created very strong preferences by powerful actors in favor of LIC adjustment, and against continued financing. Long existing ideas which justified such policies suddenly acquired global intellectual dominance. International organizations – in this case, the Bretton Woods institutions – can and do often play a very important role in that process of the creation, spread, reinforcement and destruction of dominant principles and norms.

This notion of the link between dominant ideas and the (perceived) interests of the powerful has been captured most clearly by Marxists: by Marx himself, in the 19th century, stating in the *Communist Manifesto* that 'the values of society are the interests of the bourgeoisie,' through Gramsci, in the first half of the 20th century, working on the concept of hegemony, to later authors who, following him, developed the notion of 'ideological state apparatus.' Also Realist scholars of international relations are aware if this: from Carr's insights we referred to in chapter one,'[12] over Hedley Bull writing that, 'any historical system of rules will be found to serve the interests of ruling or dominant elements of the society more adequately than it serves the interests of the others,'[13] to Robert Cox, attempting for most of the last decade to incorporate the Gramscian notion of hegemony 'as a fit between power, ideas and institutions' in international relations.[14]

Hence, the concept of regimes, and the important role given to it in our pre-theory, should not be seen as indicating that power or interest – those central factors of Realism – have suddenly become unimportant (or that Liberalism, rather than Realism, provides the better theoretical framework). We have seen that many regimes strongly promote the perceived self-interested preferences of the powerful elements within the issue areas to which they apply. But, even in the case of regimes not motivated by the self-interested preferences of their powerful elements, we have seen that the norms and preferences of powerful states, and of powerful groups within states, were dominant in the creation and spread of the regime – at times against the quite active resistance of the less powerful. These norms and principles, even if they do not seek to increase the power and wealth of the powerful, are always created and sustained by the powerful rather than by the powerless. As such, they tend to be at the very least neutral to their perceived interests. This suggests that the dominance of powerful actors at the international level does not only take place through military force and economic power, as classical Realism has it, but also through their capacity to create dominant principles and norms – a notion which, although perfectly compatible with Realism, has rarely been explored by Realists, partly because of their incapacity to deal with any kind of norms and partly becasuse of their consensual definition of norms. This notion of hegemony is a subject to be researched in more detail. It is a pity that Realists, with their positivist and liberal bias (especially at present, with the dominance of micro-economic approaches) seem unable, if not unwilling, to do so.

Notes

1 Take the example of the agricultural trade issue area. At present, it is linked to all other trade issues in the GATT talks; to export credit negotiations in the OECD; to the political/military issue area, as well with the USSR as with the EEC and the ASEAN; to food security discussions in the FAO and WFC; to food aid considerations of the WFP; and the like.

2 Keohane & Nye, 1977: 32.

3 See too Cox, 1983: 172.

4 Gilpin, 1971: 404, 418.

5 Cox, 1987: 302–3; Mendelsohn, 1984: 22; Arnaud, 1988: *passim*.

6 Gill, 1987 & 1988: *passim*; Cox, 1986: 237; Cox, 1987: 302–4; Strange, 1986.

7 Scott, 1982: 12 ff.: 37 ff.

8 Gordenker & Saunders, 1978.

9 Among many, see Keohane, 1988: 381 ff.; Nye, 1988; and Ashley's, 1986: 273 ff., treatment of a sociological position. See also Kratoch-

wil & Ruggie, 1986; E.B. Haas, 1982; P. M. Haas, 1992 and and Haggard & Simmons, 1986 on cognitivist approaches.

10 Vaughan, 1987: 4; see too the quote of Franke & Chasin in chapter 3, footnote 77.

11 Just as their non-dominance beforehand does not prove their scientific lack of quality. See Lindblöm, 1977: 209. Lindblöm's chapter on what he calls 'circularity' is probably the most brilliant treatment of the phenomenon under discussion by a non-marxist.

12 See footnote 27.

13 Bull, 1977.

14 Cox, 1987: 224; see too Cox, 1977: 387; Cox, 1983: 171–3.

BIBLIOGRAPHY

ABERCROMBIE, K. & McCORMACK, A. 'Population Growth and Food Supplies in Different Time Perspectives,' *Population and Development Review*, 2, 3/4 (Sept.- Dec. 1976): 479–98.

ABERCROMBIE, K.C., 'Population and food,' in TABAH, L. (ed.) *Population growth and economic development in the Third World*. Liège, International Union for the Scientific Study of Population, 1975, Vol. I: 352–4.

ACKER, D., *Developing the Third World Countries: Does it Help or Harm U.S. Agriculture?* presentation to the 121st Annual Convention of the National Grange, Syracuse, New York, Nov. 10, 1987.

ACKER, D., 'Does Foreign Aid Compete with U.S. Farm Exports?' in Avery (ed.), 1991: 209–12.

ADAMS, D.W., GRAHAM, D.H. & VON PISCHKE, J.D., *Undermining rural development with cheap rural credit*, Boulder, Co., Westview Press, 1984

ADAMS, R.H., Jr., 'The Role of Research in Policy Development: The Creation of the IMF Cereal Import Facility,' *World Development*, 11, 1 (1983): 549–63.

ADDISON, T. & DEMERY, L. 'The Alleviation of Poverty under Structural Adjustment,' *Finance and Development*, 24, 4 (Dec. 1987): 41–3.

ADDO, H. *Imperialism: the Permanent Stage of Capitalism*. Tokyo, United Nations University, 1986.

AGGARWAL, V.K. *Liberal Protectionism: the International Politics of Organized Textile Trade*, Berkeley, Univ. of California Press, 1985.

AIKEN, W. & LA FOLLETTE, H. (eds.) *World Hunger and Moral Obligation*. Englewood Cliffs, Prentice Hall, 1977.

ALAUX, J.-P. & NOREL, P. e.a. *Faim au Sud, Crise au Nord*. Paris, L'Harmattan, 1985.

ALLISON, C. & GREEN, R., 'Stagnation and Decay in sub-Saharan Africa:Dialogues, Dialectics and Doubts,' *IDS Bulletin*, vol. 14, no. 1 (1983): 1–10.

AMIN, S., 'A critique of the World Bank report entitled 'Accelerated development in sub-saharan Africa,' *Africa Development*, VII, 1/2 (1982): 23–9.

ANDERSON, K. 'Economic Growth, Structural Change and the Political economy of Protection,' in: Anderson & Hayami, 1986: 7–16.

ANDERSON, K., 'China's Recent and Prospective Economic Growth: Implications for Agriculture at Home and Abroad,' *Journal of Economic and International Relations*, 2, 1 (Spring 1988): 48–69.

ANDERSON, K. & HAYAMI, Y. *The political Economy of Agricultural Protection*. London, Allen & Unwin, 1986

ANDERSON, K. & HAYAMI, Y. 'Introduction,' in: Anderson & Hayami, 1986: 1–6.

ANDERSON, K., HAYAMI, Y & HONMA, M., 'The growth of agricultural protection,' in: Anderson & Hayami (eds.), 1986: 17–30.

AREFIEVA, E.B., 'Soviet Aid Policy and Food Aid: Yesterday and Tomorrow,' *Food Policy*, 16, 4 (August 1991): 306–10.

ARNAUD, P., *La dette du tiers monde*. Paris, Editions la Découverte, 1988.

ASANTE, S.K.B., 'Food as a Focus of National and Regional Policies in Contemporary Africa,' in: Hansen, A. & McMillan, D.E. (eds.) *Food in Sub-Saharan Africa*. Boulder, Lynne Rienner, 1986: 11–24.

ASHLEY, R.K., 'The Poverty of Neorealism,' in Keohane (ed.), 1986(a): 255–99.

AUSTRALIAN BUREAU OF AGRICULTURAL ECONOMICS *Agricultural Policies in the European Community*, Canberra, Australian Government Printing Service, 1985.

AUSTRALIAN BUREAU OF AGRICULTURAL AND RESOURCE ECONOMICS *Japanese Agricultural Policies. A time of Change*. Canberra, Australian Government Printing Service, Policy Monograph no. 3, 1988.

AVERY, D.T. *Global Food Progress 1991*. A Report from Hudson Institute's Center for Global Food Issues. Indianapolis, Hudson Institute, 1991.

AVRAMOVIC, D. *Conditionality: Facts, Theory and Policy*. Helsinki, WIDER, July 1989.

AXELROD, R. & KEOHANE, R.O., 'Achieving Cooperation under Anarchy: Strategies and Institutions,' *World Politics*, 38, 1 (October 1985): 226–54.

BACHMAN, K.L. & PAULINO, L.A. *Rapid Food Production Growth in Selected Developing Countries: A Comparative Analysis of Underlying Trends 1961–1976*. Washington D.C., IFPRI Research Report no. 11, 1979.

BAEHR, 'Review of "After Hegemony",' *Acta Politica*, 4, 1985.

BALL, N. *World Hunger: A Guide to the Economic and Political Dimensions*. Santa Barbara, Oxford, ABC-Clio, 1981.

BANK OF INTERNATIONAL SETTLEMENTS (BIS). *59th Annual Report*. Basel, BIS, June 1989.

BARKER, J. (ed.) *The Politics of Agriculture in Tropical Africa*. Beverly Hills, London, New Delhi, Sage Publ. (Sage series on African modernization and development no. 9), 1984.

BARKER, J., 'Politics and Production,' in: Barker (ed.) 1984: 11–33.

BARNEY, G.O. *The Global 2000 Report to the President*. Entering the 21st Century. Washington D.C., GPO, 1982.

BATES, R. H. *Markets and States in Tropical Africa*. Berkeley, University of California Press, 1981.

BATES, R.H., 'Pressure Groups, Public Policy and Agricultural Development: a Study of Divergent Outcomes,' in Bates & Lofchie, 1980: 170–217.

BATES, R.H., *Essays on the political economy of rural Africa*, Cambridge, Cambridge University Press, 1983a.

BATES, R.H., 'Governments and Agricultural Markets in Africa', in: Johnson & Shuh, 1983b: 153–83.

BATES, R., 'The Reality of Structural Adjustment: A Sceptical Appraisal,' in Commander (ed.), 1989: 221–7.

BATES, R.H. & LOFCHIE, M.F. (eds.) *Agricultural Development in Africa: Issues of Public Policy*. New York, Praeger, 1980.

BENDER, W.H. 'Food Aid and Hunger' in: Chen, R.S. (ed.) *The Hunger Report 1990*. Providence, Brown University, World Hunger Program, 1990.

BERARDI, G. (ed.) *World Food, Population and Development*. Ottowa, Rowman & Allenheld, 1985.

BERELSON, B., 'The World Population Plan of Action: Where Now,' *Population and Development Review*, 1, 1 (1974): 115–46.

BERG, A. *Malnutrition: What Can Be Done? Lessons from World Bank Experience*. Baltimore, Johns Hopkins University Press, 1987.

BERNSTEIN, H. e.a. (eds.) *The Food Question. Profits versus People*. London, Earthscan Publ. Ltd., 1990.

BERRY, R.A., 'Agricultural and Rural Policies for the Poor,' in Bird & Horton (eds.), 1989: 173–213.

BESSIS, S. *L'arme alimentaire*. Paris, Ed. La Découverte, 1985 (new edition).

BHAGWATI, J.N. & RUGGIE, J.G. *Power, Passions and Purpose*: Prospects for North-South Negotiations. Cambridge, MIT Press, 1984.

BHAGWATI, J.N. 'Food Aid, Agricultural Production and Welfare,' in *Dependence and Interdependence. Essays in Development Economics*, vol. 2. Oxford, Basil Blackwell, 1985: 285–97.

BHATTACHARYYA, A.K., 'Income equality and fertility: a comparative view', *Population Studies*, 29 (1975):

BIENEN, H.S. & GERSOVITZ, M., 'Economic Stabilization, Conditionality and Political Stability,' *International Organization*, 39, 4 (Autumn 1985): 729–53.

BIENEN, H. 'The Politics of Trade Liberalization in Africa,' *Economic Development and Cultural Change*, 38. 4 (July 1990): 713–32.

BIRD, R.M. & HORTON, S. (eds.) *Government Policy and the Poor in Developing Countries*. Toronto, University of Toronto Press, 1989.

BIRDSALL, N. (ed.) *The Effect of Family Planning Programs on Fertility in the Developing World*. Wash. D.C., World Bank Staff Working Paper no. 677, 1985.

BIRDSALL, N., FEI, J., KUZNETS, S., RANIS, G. & SCHULTZ, P., 'Demography and Development in the 1980s', in: Hauser (ed.), 1979: 211–95.

BLARDONE, G. *Le Fonds Monétaire International, l'ajustement et les coûts de l'homme*. Paris, Les Editions de l'Epargne, 1990.

BLOTT, F. 'The Multiple Objectives of PL 480', in: Wilhelm, J. & Feinstein, G. (eds.) *U.S. Foreign Assistance: Investment or Folly?* New York, Praeger, 1984: 157–186.

BOIRAL, P., LANTERI, J.-F. & OLIVIER DE SARDAN, J.-P. (eds.) *Paysans, experts et chercheurs en Afrique noire.* Paris, CIFACE-Karthala, 1985.

BORTON, J., UK Food Aid and the African Emergency, 1983–86, *Food Policy,* 14, 3 (August 1989): 232–240.

BOSERUP, E., *The Conditions of Agricultural Growth.* Chicago, Aldine, 1965.

BOSERUP, E., *Population and Technological Change: A Study of Long Term Trends.* Chicago, University of Chicago Press, 1981.

BOURGEOIS-PICHAT, J., 'The Role of the United Nations in the Field of Population,' *Population and Development Review,* 16, 2 (June 1990): 355–62.

BOURRINET, J. & FLORY, M. (eds.) *L'ordre alimentaire mondial.* Paris, Economica, 1982.

BOURRINET, J., 'Le spectre de la faim,' in: Bourrinet & Flory (eds.), 1982: 19–34.

BRADLEY, P.N. & CARTER, S.E. 'Food Production and Distribution – and Hunger,' in Jonhnston & Taylor (eds.), 1989: 101–24.

BRANDT, W. (chairman) *North-South: a Programme for Survival.* Cambr., Mass., MIT Press, for the Independent Commission on International Development Issues, 1980.

BRATTON, M., 'The Comrades and the Countryside: the Politics of Agricultural Policy in Zimbabwe', *World Politics,* XXXIX, 2 (Jan. 1987): 174–202.

BRAUMAN, R. (dir.) *Le Tiers Monde en question.* Paris, Olivier Orban, 1985.

BRAVERMAN, A. & KANBUR, R. , 'Urban Bias and the Political Economy of Agricultural Reform,' *World Development,* 15, 9 (Sept. 1987): 1179–87.

BRETT, E.A., 'States, Markets and Private Power in the Developing World: Problems and Possibilities,' *IDS Bulletin,* 18, 3 (July 1987): 31–7.

BROWN, R.E. *Starving Children. The Tyranny of Hunger.* New York, Springer Publ. Co., 1977.

BROWNE, W.P. & HADWIGER, D.F. (eds.) *World Food Policies. Toward Agricultural Interdependence.* Boulder, Lynne Riener, 1986.

BULL, H., 'Society and Anarchy in International Relations' in: BUTTERFIELD, H. & WIGHT, M. (eds.) *Diplomatic Investigations.* London, Allen & Unwin, 1966: 35–50.

BULL, H., 'The Grotian Conception of International Society,'in: BUTTERFIELD, H. & WIGHT, M. (eds.) *Diplomatic Investigations.* London, Allen & Unwin, 1966: 51–73.

BULL, H. *The Anarchical Society. A Study of Order in World Politics.* London, Macmillan, 1977.

BURING, P., VAN HEEMST, H.D. & STARING, G.J. *Computation of the*

Absolute Maximum Food Production of the World. Wageningen, Agricultural University, 1975.

BURNS, W.J. *Economic Aid and American Policy toward Egypt: 1955–1981.* Albany, SUNY Press, 1985.

BUTLER, N. *The international Grain Trade.* London, Croom Helm, 1986

BYERLEE; D., 'The political Economy of Third World Food Imports: The Case of Wheat,' *Economic Development and Cultural Change,* 35, 2 (Jan. 1987): 307–27.

CALEGAR, G.M. & SHUH, G.E. *The Brazilian Wheat Policy: Its Costs, Benefits and Effects on Food Consumption.* Washington D.C, IFPRI Research Report 66, 1988.

CARERA, M. *Rapport de voyage. Washington, 10–28 juillet 1989.* Lausanne, Communauté de travail Swissaid, Action de Carême, Pain pour le prochain, Helvetas, septembre 1989.

CARR, E.H. *The Twenty Years' Crisis, 1919–1939.* London, Macmillan, 1939.

CASSEN, R.H., 'Population and Development: A Survey,' in: Streeten & Jolly (eds.), 1982.

CASSEN, R. (dir.) *Does Aid Work? Report to an Intergovernmental Taskforce.* New York, Clarendon Press, 1986.

CATHIE, J. *The Political Economy of Food Aid.* Aldershot, Gower, 1982.

CATHIE, J. *Food Aid and Industrialization. The Development of the South Korean Economy.* Aldershot, Avebury, 1989.

CATHIE, J., Some Contrasts between European and US Food Aid Policies, *Food Policy,* 15, 6 (Nov. 1990): 458–60.

CATHIE, J., Modelling the Role of Food Importsm, Food Aid and Food Security in Africa: The Case of Botswana, in Clay & Stokke (eds.), 1991: 91–116.

CHALMIN, P. *Négociants et chargeurs.* Paris, Economica, 1984.

CHALMIN, Ph., 'Les marchés internationaux des matières premières au printemps 1986. Stagnation durable', *Chronique d'actualité de la SEDEIS,* XXXIV, 6 (juin 1986): 220–33.

CHALMIN, Ph., 'Les marchés mondiaux des matières premières à la fin de 1986. Le grand vent de la déprime!', *Chronique d'actualité de la SEDEIS,* XXXV, 1 (jan.1987): 18–28.

CHALMIN, Ph., 'L'Afrique dans le jeu alimentaire mondial: fragile et perdante,' *Politique Africaine,* 37 (Mars 1990): 8–16.

CHAMBERS, R. *Rural Development. Putting the Last First.* Essex, Longman, Harlow, 1983.

CHANDER, R. *Information Systems and Basic Statistics in Sub-Saharan Africa. A Review and Strategy for Improvement.* Washington D.C., World Bank Discussion Paper No 73, 1990.

CHARVET, J.-P. *Le désordre alimentaire mondial. Surplus et pénuries: le scandale.* Paris, Hatier, 1987.

CHASLE, R. 'Annotations,' in Cahiers Nord-Sud, *La faim dans le monde.* Ligue de l'enseignement et de l'éducation permanente, I, 2, mai 1983: 1–10.

CHEN, R.S. (ed), *The Hunger Report: 1990,* Providence, Brown University World Hunger Program, HR–90–1, June 1990(a).

CHEN, R.S. 'Refugees and Hunger' in Chen (ed.) *The Hunger Report: 1990*, Providence, Brown University World Hunger Program, HR–90–1, 1990(b): 49–70.

CHEN, R.S. & PITT, M.M. *Estimating the Prevalence of World Hunger: A Review of Methods and Data.* Providence, Brown University World Hunger Program, HR–91–5, 1991.

CHERNIKOVSKY, D. & MEESOK, O.A. *Patterns of Food Consumption and Nutrition in Indonesia. An Analysis of the National Socioeconomic Survey*, 1978. Washington D.C., World Bank Staff Working Paper No. 670, 1984.

CHHIBBER, A. & WILTON, J., 'Macro-economic Policies and Agricultural Performance,' Finance and Development, 23, 3 (Sept. 1986): 6–9.

CHHIBBER, A., 'The Aggregate Supply Response: A Survey,' in Commander (ed.), 1989: 55–68.

CHONCHOL, J. *Le défi alimentaire. La faim dans le monde.* Paris, Larousse, 1987.

CHRISTENSEN, C., DOMMEN, A. & RILEY, P., 'Assessing Africa's food policies,' *Africa Report*, July-August 1984: 57–61.

CHRISTENSEN, C., 'Food Security in Sub-Saharan Africa,' in Ladd Hollist & Lamond Tullis (eds.), 1987: 67–97.

CILSS/OECD *Espaces céréaliers régionaux en Afrique de l'Ouest. Recueil d'études sur les agricultures sahéliennes, le commerce régional et les marchés mondiaux.* Paris, CILSS (Sahel D(89)332), April 1989.

CLARK, C. *Starvation or Plenty?* London, Secker & Warburg, 1970.

CLARK, C. 'Review of the World Development Report, 1984,' *Population and Development Review*, 11, 1 (March 1985): 120–6.

CLAY, E.J., 'The changing world food aid system: some implications of the proliferation of donors and recipients', *IDS Bulletin*, 14, 2 (April 1983): 3–9.

CLAY, E.J. *Review of food aid policy changes since 1978.* Rome, WFP Occasional Paper no. 1, 1985.

CLAY, E.J., 'Food Aid, Development and Food Security,' in Timmer (ed.), 1991: 202–36.

CLAY, E.J. & BENSON, C. (1991) 'Triangular Transactions, Local Purchases and Exchange Arrangements in Food Aid: A Povisional Review with Special Reference to Sub-Saharan Africa' in: CLAY & STOKKE (eds.): 143-79.

CLAY, E.J. & EVERITT, E. (1983) 'The Record so Far: a Review of the Literature.' *IDS Bulletin*, 14, 2: 58–64.

CLAY, E. & SINGER, H. (1983) 'Food as Aid: Food for Thought.' *IDS Bulletin*, 14, 2.

CLAY, E.J. & SINGER, H.W. (1985) *Food Aid and Development: Issues and Evidence. A Survey of the Literature since 1977 on the Role and Impact of Food Aid in Developing Countries.* Rome, WFP Occasional Papers no. 3.

CLAY, E.J. & STOKKE, O. (eds.) (1991) *Food Aid Reconsidered: Assessing the Impact on Third World Countries.* London, Frank Cass.

CLAY, E.J. & STOKKE, O. (1991) 'Assessing the Performance and Economic Impact of Food Aid: the State of the Art' in CLAY & STOKKE (eds.): 1–36.

CLEAVER, K.M. *The Impact of Price and Exchange Rate Policies on Agriculture in Sub-Saharan Africa.* Washington D.C., World Bank Staff Working Paper no. 728, 1985.

COALE, A.J. & HOOVER, E.M. *Population Growth and Economic Development in Low Income Countries.* Princeton, Princeton University Press, 1958.

COHEN, B. *Banks and the Balance of Payments: Private Lending in the International Adjustment Process.* Montclair, Allenheld, 1981.

COHEN, B., 'Balance-of-Payments Financing: Evolution of a Regime,' *International Organization,* 36, 2 (Spring 1982): 457–78.

COLANDER, D. (ed.) *Neo-classical Political Economy.* Cambridge, Ballinger, 1985.

COLCLOUGH, C. 'Are African governments as unproductive as the Accelerated Development Report implies?' *IDS Bulletin,* 14, 1 (1984): 24–9.

COLCLOUGH, C. & GREEN, R.H., 'Editorial: Do Stabilisation Policies Stabilise?' *IDS Bulletin,* vol. 19 no. 1, 1988: 1–6.

COLE, H.S.D. (ed.) *Models of Doom.* New York, Universe, 1973.

COLLIARD, C.-A. *Institutions des relations internationales.* Paris, Dalloz, 1988 (8th ed.).

COMMANDER, S. *The State and Agricultural Development in Egypt since 1973.* London, Ithaca Press, for Overseas Development Institute, 1987.

COMMANDER, S. (ed.) *Structural Adjustment and Agriculture. Theory and Practice in Africa and Latin America.* London, Overseas Development Institute in collaboration with James Currey and Heinemann, 1989.

COMMANDER, S., 'Prices, Markets and Rigidities: African Agriculture 1980–1988,' in Commander (ed.), 1989: 228–243.

CORDEN, M.W. & DOOLEY, M.P., 'Issues in Debt Strategy: An Overview,' in: Frenkel, J.A., Dooley & Wickham (eds.), 1989: 10–37.

CORNIA, G.A., JOLLY, R. & STEWART, J. *Adjustment with a Human Face.* Oxford, Clarendon Press, for UNICEF, 1986.

COSER, L.A., 'Sociological Theory from the Chicago Dominance to 1965,' *Annual Review of Sociology,* 57, (June 1976): 182–207.

Cour des Comptes: Critiques à l'encontre des dépenses pour l'aide alimentaire en 1986,' *Telex Afrique,* 317, August 1988: 3–5.

COUSSY, J., 'Les importations alimentaires urbaines et l'ajustement structurel,' *Politique Africaine,* 37 (Mars 1990): 45–56.

COX, R.W., 'Labor and hegemony', *International Organization,* 31, 3 (summer 1977): 385–424.

COX, R., 'Gramsci, hegemony and international relations: an essay in method', *Millenium,* 12, 2 (summer 1983): 162–75.

COX, R.W., 'Social Forces, States and World Orders: Beyond International Relations Theory,' in Keohane (ed.), 1986: 204–54.

COX, R.W. *Production, Power and World Order. Social Forces in the Making of History.* New York, Columbia University Press, 1987.

CRANE , B.B. & FINKLE, J.L., 'The United States, China and the United Nations Population Fund: Dynamics of US Policymaking,' *Population and Development Review,* 15, 1 (March 1989): 23–59.

CROW, B., 'Moving the Lever: A New Food Aid Imperialism?' in Bernstein e.a. (eds.). 1990: 32–42.

CUDDINGTON, J.T., The Extent and Causes of the Debt Crisis of the 1980s,' in Husain & Diwan (eds.), 1989: 15–41.

DABENE, O., 'L'assistance Américaine à l'Amérique Centrale (1979–1981): pourquoi et pour qui?,' Problèmes d'Amérique Latine, 91 (1er trimestre 1989): 115–37.

DAHRENDORF, R. Class and Class Conflict in Industrial Society. Stanford, Stanford University Press, 1959.

DAHRENDORF, R., 'In Praise of Thrasymachus,' in: Essays in the Theory of Society. Stanford, Stanford University Press, 1968a.

DAHRENDORF, R., 'Out of Utopia,' in: Essays in the Theory of Society. Stanford, Stanford University Press, 1968b.

DANDEKAR, V.M. The Demand for Food and the Conditions governing Food Aid during Development. Rome, WFP Studies No. 1, 1965.

DANIEL, P. 'Accelerated Development in Sub-Saharan Africa: an Agenda for Structural Adjustment Lending?' IDS Bulletin, 14, 1 (1983): 11–17.

DAVIRON, B., 'Produits alimentaires. Qui vend et qui achète?' La Lettre du Solagral, 93–94, (Juin-Juillet 1990): 10–13.

DAVIS, K. Human Society. New York, Macmillan, 1949.

DAVIS, K., 'Population policy: will current programmes succeed?' Science, 158 (10 Nov. 1967): 730–739.

DAWSON, A., 'Défense de l'aide alimentaire et réponse à certains critiques,' Revue Internationale du Travail, 124, 1 (1985): 17–33.

DE HOOGH, J. e.a., 'Food for a growing world population', in: Food needs of developing countries: projections of production and consumption to 1990., Washington D.C., I.F.P.R.I. (Research Report no.3), 1977.

DE JANVRY, A. The Agrarian Question and Reformism in Latin America. Baltimore, Johns Hopkins University Press, 1981.

DE JANVRY, A., 'Why do governments do what they do? The case of food price policy.' in: Johnson & Shuh (eds.), 1983: 185–214.

DELL, S., 'On Being Grandmotherly: the Evolution of IMF Conditionality,' CEPAL Review, April 1982: 177–86.

DELMAS, R. La stabilisation des prix des matières premières. Un dialogue manqué. Paris, Economica, 1983.

DEMERY, L. & ADDISON, T., 'Stabilization Policy and Income Distribution in Developing Countries,' World Development, 15, 12 (Dec. 1987): 1483–98.

DEMYANENKO, V., 'Structure of the Soviet and US Food Systems: a Comparative Analysis,' Food Policy, 16, 4 (August 1991): 284–90.

DEPPLER, M. & WILLIAMSON, M. Capital Flight: Concepts, Measurements and Issues. Washington, Staff Studies for the World Economic Outlook, by the Research Department of the IMF, August 1987.

DESTLER, I.M., 'United States Food Policy 1972–1976: Reconciling Domestic and International Objectives.' in: Hopkins & Puchala (eds.), 1978: 41–77.

DINHAM, B. & HINES, C. Agribusiness in Africa. London, Earth Resources Research Ltd., 1983.

DONALDSON, P.J. & ONG TSUI, A. 'The International Family Planning Movement', *Population Bulletin*, 454, 3 (Nov. 1990) 1–45.

DONNELLY, J., 'International Human Rights: a Regime Analysis', *International Organization*, 40, 3 (Summer 1986): 599–624.

DONALDON, G. 'Government-Sponsored Rural Development: the Experience of the Wolrd Bank' in Timmer (ed.), 1991: 156–90.

DOYLE, J., U.S. Foreign Agricultural Policy and the Less Developed Countries, in Yesilada *e.a.* (eds.), 1987: 305–35.

DREZE, J. & SEN, A. *Hunger and Public Action*. Oxford, Pergamon Press, 1989.

DUMONT, R. & MOTTIN, M.-F. *Le mal-développement en Amérique latine*. Paris, Editions du Seuil, 1981.

DUMONT, R. *La croissance . . . de la famine! Une agriculture repensée*. Paris, Seuil, 1973.

DUPUY, G., 'Les associations villageoises au Sénégal: fonctions économiques et modalités de financement,' *Revue Tiers Monde*, XXXI, 122 (Avril-Juin 1990): 351–75.

DURUFLE, G. *L'ajustement structurel en Afrique (Sénégal, Côte d'Ivoire, Madagascar)*. Paris, Karthala, 1988.

EASTBY, J., *Functionalism and Interdependence*. Lanham, University Press of America, 1985.

ECONOMIC COMMISSION FOR AFRICA (ECA) *Adjustment for Transformation: An African Blueprint for Sustainable Development*. Nairobi, United Nations, 1989.

EICHENGREEN, B. & PORTES, R., 'Dealing with Debt: The 1930s and the 1980s,' in Husain & Diwan (eds.), 1989: 69–85.

EISENSTADT, S.N., 'The Concept of Social Institutions,' in SILLS, D.L. (ed.) *International Encyclopedia of the Social Sciences*. New York, London, The MacMillan Company and the Free Press, 1968, vol. 14.

EUROPEAN ECONOMIC COMMUNITY (EEC), COMMISSION *Cereals Food Aid Programme*. Brussels, Commission of the EC, COM (76) 546, 1977.

E.E.C., COMMISSION, *Food Strategies. A new form of cooperation between Europe and the countries of the Third World*. Brussels, Europe Information, Development, DE 40, Dec. 1982(a).

E.E.C., COMMISSION *Food aid from the Community. A new Approach*. Brussels, Europe Information, Development, DE 42, Dec. 1982(b).

E.E.C., COMMISSION, *The situation of agriculture in the Community*. Brussels, 1983.

E.E.C., COMMISSION, *Comparaison entre les agricultures des Etats-Unis et de la Communauté Européenne*, Bruxelles, Europe Verte, no. 200, 4/1984

E.E.C., COMMISSION, *EEC-US Relations. Relations between the EC and the USA in the field of agriculture: the Commission's view*. by: Andriesen, M. Brussels, Newsflash-Green Europe no. 31, 1985(a).

E.E.C., COMMISSION *Community Imports of Food and other Agricultural Products*. Brussels, Commission of the EC , Green Europe. 213, 1985(b):

E.E.C., COMMISSION, *The European Community's Food Aid*. Brussels, Green Europe, 216, March 1986(a).

E.E.C., COMMISSION *Mise en Oeuvre des stratégies alimentaires et perspectives d'avenir*. Bruxelles, COM(86)198 final, 1986(b).

E.E.C., COMMISSION, *The Agricultural Situation in the Community*. Rapport 1985. Bruxelles, Luxembourg, 1986(c).

E.E.C., COMMISSION *General Report on the Activities of the European Community*. Brussels, various years (1987–1991).

E.E.C., COMMISSION *L'aide alimentaire de la CEE. Instrument d'une politique de développement ou moyen d'utiliser les excédents*. Brussels, Europe Information, Development, DE 56, 1988.

E.E.C., COMMISSION, *Rapport de la Commission au Conseil et au Parlement Européen sur la politique et la gestion de l'aide alimentaire de la Communauté en 1985*. Bruxelles, COM(89)183 final, April 1989(a).

E.E.C., COMMISSION, *The Agricultural Situation in the Community*. Rapport 1988. Brussels, EEC, 1989(b).

E.E.C., COMMISSION, *The Agricultural Situation in the Community*. Rapport 1989. Brussels, EEC, 1990.

E.E.C., COUNCIL, *Food Aid for Development*. Brussels, Council of the EEC, COM(83) 141, April 1983.

EGG, J., GABAS, J.-J. & LEMELLE, J.-P., 'De l'espace régional aux espaces régionaux,' in: CILSS/OECD, 1989: 133–46.

ELIAS, V.J. *Government Expenditures on Agriculture and Agricultural Growth in Latin America*. Washington D.C., IFPRI Research Report No. 50, Oct. 1985.

ELLIOTT, C. *Patterns of Poverty in the Third World. A Study of Social and Economic Stratification*. New York, Praeger, 1975.

ELLIOTT, C. (chairman) *Real Aid: a Strategy for Britain*. Oxford, The Parchment press, for The Independent Group on British Aid, 1982.

L'ETAT du monde, 1988–89. Paris, La Découverte, 1988.

ETEMAD, B., 'Le bilan céréalier du Tiers Monde 1800–1982,' *Revue Tiers Monde*, 98, (1984): 387–408.

ETIENNE, G. 'Comment réduire la pauvreté: l'exemple de l'Asie rurale,' in Brauman (ed.), 1985: 124–30.

FAALAND, J.(ed.) *Aid and influence. The case of Bangladesh*. London, Basingtoke, Macmillan (Chr.Michelsen Institute, Bergen), 1981.

FABER, M. *Beware of Debtspeak*. Brigton, IDS Discussion Papers no. 251, Sept. 1988.

FEINBERG, R.E., 'The changing relations between the World Bank and the International Monetary Fund,' *International Organization*, 42, 3 (1988): 545–60.

FINKLE, J.L. & CRANE, B.B., 'The politics of Bucharest: Population, Development and the New Internatinal Economic Order,' *Population and Development Review*, 1, 1 (1974): 87–114.

FINKLE, J.L. & CRANE, B.B., 'Ideology and Politics at Mexico City: The United States at the 1984 International Conference on Population,' *Population and Development Review*, 11, 1 (March 1985): 1–28.

FITCHETT, D., 'Agriculture,' in: FINGER, J.M. & OLECHOWSKI, A. (eds.) *The Uruguay Round. A Handbook on the Multilateral Trade Negotiations*. Washington D.C., World Bank, 1987: 162–170.

FLETCHER, J., 'Give if it helps but not if it hurts' in: Aiken & La Follette (eds.), 1977: 103–14.

FOOD AND AGRICULTURE ORGANIZATION (FAO), *Trade Yearbook*. Rome, various years.

F.A.O. *Production Yearbook*. Rome, various years.

F.A.O. *Agricultural Protection and Stabilization Policies: A Framework of Measurement in the Context of Agricultural Adjustment*, Rome, FAO, C78/LIM/2, 1975

F.A.O. *Agriculture: Toward 2000*, Rome, FAO, 1981.

F.A.O. *Food Outlook Statistical Supplement*, 1981. Rome, FAO, Jan. 1982.

F.A.O., *Food Outlook Statistical Supplement*. Rome, FAO, various years.

F.A.O. *Capacité potentielle de charge démographique des terres du monde en développement*. Rome, FAO, 1984(a).

F.A.O, *Land, Food and People*. Rome, FAO (Economic and Social Development Series, 30), 1984b(b).

F.A.O. *Food Outlook Statistical Supplement*, 1984. Rome, FAO, Jan. 1985(a).

F.A.O. *Food aid and food security: past performance and future potential*. Rome, FAO Economic and Social Development Paper no. 55, 1985(b).

F.A.O. *The State of Food and Agriculture 1984*. Rome, FAO, 1985(c).

F.A.O. *World Food Security: selected themes and issues*, Rome, FAO Economic and Social Development paper no. 53, 1985(d)

FAO *La situation mondiale de l'alimentation et de l'agriculture 1986*. Rome, FAO, 1987.

F.A.O. *Fifth World Food Survey*. Rome, 1987(b).

F.A.O. *Food Outlook. Statistical Supplement. 1988*. Rome, FAO, Feb. 1988(c).

F.A.O. *World Agriculture Toward 2000*. An FAO Study. (directed by N.ALEXANDRATOS). New York, New York University Press, 1988(b). (translation in French: L'agriculture mondiale: Horizon 2000. Paris, Economica, 1989.)

F.A.O. *The State of Food and Agriculture 1987–88*. Rome, FAO, 1988(c).

F.A.O., *Food Outlook Statistical Supplement 1990*. Rome, 1991(a).

F.A.O., *Food Outlook*, October 1991. Rome, 1991(b).

F.A.O. *The State of Food and Agriculture 1991*. Rome, FAO, 1992.

F.A.O/Committee on World Food Security (C.F.S). *Assessment of the Current World Food Security Situation and Recent Policy Developments* Rome, CFS 1986/2.

F.A.O./C.F.S. *Prepositioning Food Stocks to Expedite Delivery of Emergency Food Aid*. Rome, FAO/CFS, 1986/5.

F.A.O./C.F.S. *Impact on World Food Security of Agricultural Policies in Industrialized Countries*. Rome, FAO/CFS/1987/3.

F.A.O./W.H.O./U.N.U. *Energy and Protein Requirements*. Geneva, Technical Report Series no. 742, 1985.

FORSTER, J., 'Preface,' to Blardonne, 1990.

FOTTORINO, E. *Le festin de la terre. L'histoire secrète des matières premières*. Paris, Lieu Commun, 1988.

FOTTORINO, E. 'Est: à la recherche du paysan perdu,' *Le Monde*, mardi 10 octobre 1989: 41.

FRANCE, Ministry of Cooperation. *Food Aid: International Code of Good Conduct*. Working Document, Draft, September 1988.

FRANK, A.G., 'Quand les solutions apparentes deviennent des réelles problèmes,' *Revue Tiers Monde*, XXV, 99 (Juillet-Sept. 1984): 585–602.

FRANKE, R.W. & CHASIN, B.H. *Seeds of Famine. Ecological Destruction and the Development Dilemma in the West African Sahel.* Totowa, Rowman & Allanheld (LandMark Series), 1980.

FRANKEL, J. *International Relations in a Changing World.* Oxford, Oxford University Press, 1979 (orig. 1964).

FRENKEL, J.A., DOOLEY, M.P. & WICKHAM, P. (eds.) *Analytical Issues in Debt.* Washington, IMF, 1989.

FREUD, C. *Quelle coopération? Un bilan de l'aide au développement.* Paris, Karthala, 1988.

FRISCH, D., 'Ajustement, développement et équité,' in *Le Courrier*, 111 (Sept. -Oct. 1988): 67–72.

FRYER, J. *Food for Thought: the Use and Abuse of Food Aid in the Fight against World Hunger.* Report prepared for the World Council of Churches, 1981. (translated in french: L'aide alimentaire: un marché des dupés. Genève, Centre Europe-Tiers Monde, s.d.)

FURLONG, W.L., Hunger, Poverty and Political Instability, in Wennergren e.a., 1989: 129–151.

GAI, D. & SMITH, L. *Food Policy and Equity in Sub-Saharan Africa.* Geneva, World Employment Research Programme, ILO, August 1983.

GARDNER, R.N. *Sterling-Dollar Diplomacy.* Oxford, Clarendon Press, 1956.

GARDNER, R.N., 'Towards a World Population Programme,' in GARDNER, R.N. & MILLIKAN, M.F. (eds.) Global Partnership: *International Agencies and Economic Development.* New York, Praeger, 1968.

GARST, R. & BARRY, T. *Feeding the Crisis. U.S. Food Aid and Farm Policy in Central America.* Lincoln, University of Nebraska Press, 1990.

GATT *Focus*, 41, October 1986: 2–5.

GEORGE, A. & SAXON, E., 'The politics of Agricultural Protection In Japan,' in Anderson & Hayami (eds.), 1986: 91–110.

GEORGE, S. *How the other half dies.* Harmondsworth, Pelican Books, 1976.

GEORGE, S. *Les stratèges de la faim.* Genève, Grounauer, Institut Universitaire d'Etudes de Développement, 1981.

GEORGE, S. *Ill Fares the Land. Essays on Food, Hunger and Power.* London, Readers and Writers Cooperative, 1984.

GEORGE, S., 'Some Effects of Bilateral and Multilateral Aid Organizations on Food and Nutrition,' in Lapham, e.a. (eds.), 1988: 96–131.

GEORGE, S. *A Fate Worse than Debt.* New York, Grove Press, 1988.

GEORGE, S., 'La dette du Tiers Monde, un état de guerre,' in *L'état du Tiers Monde*, Paris, Ed. La Découverte, 1989: 28–33.

GILL, S., 'Global Hegemony and the Structural Power of Capital,' paper presented at the 83d Annual Convention of the American Political Science Association, Chicago, 3–6 Sept. 1987.

GILL, S., *American Hegemony and the International Economic Order.* Presentation to the Graduate School of International Studies, Geneva, 7 March 1988.

GILPIN, R. 'The Politics of Transnational Economic Relations,' *International Organization*, XXV, 3 (Summer 1971): 398–419.

GILPIN, R. *War and Change in World Politics*. New York, Cambridge University Press, 1981.

GILPIN, R., 'The Richness of the Tradition of Political Realism,' in Keohane (ed.), 1986: 301–21.

GILPIN, R. *The Political Economy of International Relations*. Princeton, Princeton University Press, 1987.

GIRI, J., 'Les pénuries dans les Pays les Moins Avancés: ni injustice ni fatalité,' in: Brauman (dir.), 1985: 103–12.

GLICKMAN, H. (ed.) *The Crisis and Challenge of African Development*. New York, Greenwood Press, 1988.

GLICKMAN, H., 'The Present and Future of the African State in an Age of Adversity,' in Glickman (ed.), 1988: 24–43.

GLUCKSMAN, A. & WOLTON, T. *Silence, on tue!*. Paris, Grasset, 1986.

GODFREY, M., 'Export Orientation and Structural Adjustment in sub-Saharan Africa,' *IDS Bulletin*, 14, 1 (1983): 39–44.

GOLDSTEIN, M. & MONTIEL, P., 'Evaluation of Trend Stabilization Programs with Multicountry Data: Some Methodological Pitfalls,' *IMF Staff Papers*, vol. 33, June 1986: 304–34.

GONZALEZ-VEGA, C.,'Cheap agricultural credit: redistribution in reverse,' in Adams e.a., (eds.), 1984: 120–32.

GORDENKER, L. & SAUNDERS, P.R., 'Organisation Theory and International Organisation,' in TAYLOR, P. & GROOM, A.J.R. (eds.) *International Organisation. A Conceptual Approach*. London, Pinter, 1978.

GOUROU, P. & ETIENNE, G. (dirs.) *Des Labours de Cluny à la Révolution Verte*. Paris, PUF, 1985.

GREEN, E., 'U.S. Population Policies, Development and the Rural Poor of Africa,' *The Journal of Modern African Studies*, 20, 1 (1982): 45–67.

GREEN, R. 'Incentives, Policies, Participation and Response: Reflections on World Bank Policies and Priorities in Agriculture,' *IDS Bulletin*, 14, 1 (1983): 30–38.

GREEN, R.H., 'Articulating Stabilisation Programmes and Structural Adjustment: Sub-Saharan Africa,' in Commander (ed.), 1989: 35–54.

GREEN, S.J. *International Disaster Relief: Toward a Responsive System*. New York, MacGraw Hill, 1977.

GREENE, J., 'External Debt Problem of Sub-Saharan Africa,' in Frenkel, J.A., Dooley, M.P. & Wickham, P. (eds.), 1989: 38–74.

GREGOIRE, E., 'L'Etat doit-il abandonner le commerce des vivres aux marchands?' *Politique Africaine*, 37 (Mars 1990): 63–70.

GRIECO, J.M., 'Anarchy and the Limits of Cooperation: a Realist Critique of the Newest Liberal Institutionalism,' *International Organization*, 42, 3, (Summer 1988): 485–507.

GRIFFIN, K. *The Political Economy of Agrarian Change. An Essay on the Green Revolution*. London & Basingtoke, Macmillan, 1974.

GRIFFIN, K., 'World Hunger and the World Economy,' in: Ladd Hollist & LaMond Tullis, 1986.

GRILLI, E.R. & YANG, M.C., 'Primary Commodity Prices, Manufactured Goods Proces, and the Terms of Trade of Developing Countries: What the Long Run Shows,' *The World Bank Economic Review*, 2, 1 (1988): 1–47

GUEYDAN, C., 'Les limites des institutions actuelles,' in: Bourrinet & Flory (eds.), 1983: 119–49.

HAAS E.B. (1982) 'Words can hurt you; or, who said what to whom about regimes' *International Organization*, 36, 2 (Spring 1982): 23–59.

HAAS, P. M. (1992) 'Introduction: epistemic communities and international policy coordination' *International Organization*, 46, 1 (Winter 1992): 1–35.

HADWIGER, D . & TALBOT, R., 'The United States: A Unique Development Model,'in HOPKINS, R., PUCHALA, D. & TALBOT, R. *Food, Politics and Agricultural Development: Case Studies in the Politics of Rural Modernization.* Boulder, Westview Press, 1979.

HAEN, DE, H., JOHNSON, G.L., TANGERMAN, S., *Agriculture and International Relations.* London, MacMillan, 1985.

HAGGARD, S., 'The politics of adjustment: lessons from the IMF's Extended Fund Facility,' in: Kahler (ed.), 1985: 157–86.

HAGGARD, S. & SIMMONS, B., 'Theories of International Regimes,' *International Organization*, 41,1 (Summer 1986): 491–517.

HAGMAN, G (ed.) *From Disaster Relief to Development.* Geneva, Henri Dunant Institute Studies on Development No. 1, 1988.

HAMMER, J.S., 'Population Growth and Savings in LDCs. A Survey Article,' *World Development*, 14, 5 (May 1986): 579–91.

HARDIN, G., 'Lifeboat ethics: the case against helping the poor'. in: *Psychology Today*, 8, 1974, p. 38–43 & 123–6.

HARVEY, C. (ed.) *Agricultural Pricing Policy in Africa. Four Country Case Studies.* London, Macmillan, 1988.

HARVEY, C., 'Introduction' and 'Summary and Conclusions' in Harvey, 1988: 1–9 and 220–50.

HATHAWAY, D.E. 'Food Issues in North-South Relations' *World Economy*, 3, 4 (Jan. 1981): 447–59.

HATHAWAY, D. *Agriculture and the GATT: Rewriting the Rules.* Washington D.C., Institute for International Economics (Policy Analyses in International Economics: 20), December 1987.

HAUB, C. 'Understanding Population Projections,' *Population Bulletin*, 42, 2 (Dec. 1987).

HAUSER, Ph. M. (ed.), *World Population and Development. Challenges and Prospects.* Syracuse, Syracuse University Press (by the United Nations Fund for Population Activities), 1979.

HAVNEVIK, K.J. (ed.) *The IMF and the World Bank in Africa. Conditionality, Impact, Alternatives.* Uppsala, Scandinavian Institute of African Studies, Seminar Proceedings No 18, 1987.

HAYTER, T. & WATSON, C. *Aid Rhetoric and Reality.* London, Pluto Press, 1985.

HAZELL, P. 'Changing Patterns of Variability in Cereal Prices and Production,' in: Mellor & Ahmed (eds.), 1988: 27–53.

HEAD, I.L., 'South-North Dangers,' *Foreign Affairs*, 68, 2 (Summer 1989): 71–86.

HEIDHUES, T. *World Food Interdependence and Farm and Trade Policies.*

London, Trade Policy Research Centre, International Issues, no. 3, 1977.

HELLEINER, G.K., 'Stabilization, Adjustment and the Poor,' in: Bird & Horton (eds.), 1989: 23–48.

HELLER, P., 'Les programmes d'ajustement appuyés par le Fonds et les pauvres,' *Finances et Développement*, Déc. 1988: 2–5.

HELLER, P.S., BOVENBERG, A.L., CATSAMBAS, T., CH, K.-Y., SHOME, P. *The Implications of Fund-Supported Adjustment Programs for Poverty. Experiences in Selected Countries.* Washington D.C., IMF Occasional Paper no. 58, May 1988.

HERBST, J., 'The Structural Adjustment of Politics in Africa,' *World Development*, 18, 7 (July 1990).

HERZ, B.K., *Official Development Assistance for Population Activities. A Review.* Washington D.C., World Bank, Staff Working Paper no 688 (Population and Development Series no 13), 1984.

HEWITT DE ALCANTARA, C. *Economic Restructuring and Rural Subsistence in Mexico: Maize and the Crisis of the 1980s.* Geneva, UNRISD Discussion Paper 31, 1991.

HIRSCH, R., 'Ajustement structurel et politique alimentaire en Afrique Subsaharienne,' *Politique Africaine*, 37 (Mars 1990): 17–31.

HIRSCHMAN, A.O. *A Bias for Hope. Essays on Development and Latin America.* New Haven, Yale University, 1971

HOFFMEYER, B. *The EEC's CAP and the ACP States.* Copenhagen, Centre for Development Research Research Report no 2, 1982.

HOLSTI, K.J. *The Dividing Discipline: Hegemony and Diversity in International Relations.* Boston, Allen & Unwin, 1985.

HONMA, M. & HAYAMI, Y., 'Structure of Agricultural Protection in Industrial Countries,' *Journal of International Economics*, 20 (1986): 115–29.

HOPKINS, R.F., 'Food Aid and Development: Evolution of Regime Principles and Practices' in: W.F.P./ Government of the Netherlands, 1983: 73–92.

HOPKINS, R.F., 'Overburdened Government and Underfed Populace: The Role of Food Subsidies in Africa's Economic Crisis,' in: Glickman (ed.), 1988: 129–45.

HOPKINS, R.F., *Reform in International Institutions: Consensual Knowledge and the International Food Aid Regime.* Paper prepared for the Meetings of the International Studies Association, London, April 1, 1989.

HOPKINS, R.F. Reform in the International Food Aid Regime: the Role of Consensual Knowledge' *International Organization*, 46, 1 (Winter 1992): 225–63.

HOPKINS, R.F. & PUCHALA, D.J., *The Global Political Economy of Food*, Madison, Wisconsin Univ. Press, 1979a.

HOPKINS, R.F. & PUCHALA, D.J., 'Perspectives on the international relations of food', in: Hopkins & Puchala, (eds.), 1979b: 3–38.

HOPKINS, R.F. & PUCHALA, D.J. *Global Food Interdependence.* New York, Columbia Univ. Press, 1980.

HOSSAIN, M. *Nature and Impact of the Green Revolution in Bangladesh.* Washington D.C:, IFPRI Research Report No. 67, July 1988.

HUANG, Y. & NICHOLAS, P., 'The Social Cost of Structural Adjustment,' *Finance and Development*, 24, 3 (June 1987): 22–4.

HUGON, P., 'L'Afrique subsaharienne face au Fonds Monétaire International,' *Revue Tiers Monde*, XXVIII, 109 (Janv.-Mars 1987): 95–122.

HUGON, Ph., 'Incidences sociales de l'ajustement,' *Revue Tiers Monde*, XXX, 117 (Jan.-Mars 1989): 59–84.

HUIZINGA, H., 'The Commercial Bank Claims on Developing Countries: How Have Banks Been Affected?' in Husain & Diwan (eds.), 1989: 129–42.

HUMPHREYS, C. & UNDERWOOD, J., 'The External Debt Difficulties of Low-Income Africa,' in Husain & Diwan (eds.), 1989: 45–65.

HUSAIN, S.S., 'Relance de la croissance en Amérique Latine,' *Finances et Développement*, Juin 1989: 2–5.

HUSAIN, I. & DIWAN, I. (eds.) *Dealing with the Debt Crisis*. Washington D.C., World Bank, 1989.

HUSAIN, I. & DIWAN, I. 'Introduction' in Husain & Diwan (eds.), 1989: 1–12.

ILO *L'ajustement: un défi pour l'Afrique*. Genève, ILO, 1989.

IMF. *Annual Report 1988*. Washington D.C., IMF, 1988.

IMF. *World Economic Outlook April 1989*. Washington D.C., IMF, 1989.

INDEPENDENT COMMISSION ON INTERNATIONAL HUMANITARIAN ISSUES *Famine. A Man-Made Disaster?* London, Pan Books, 1985.

INSEL, B., 'A World Awash in Grain', *Foreign Affairs*, 63, 4 (Spring 1985): 892–911.

INTERFUTURES, *Facing the Future*. Paris, OECD, 1979.

ISENMAN, P.J. & SINGER, H.W:, 'Food aid: disincentive effects and their policy implications,' *Economic Development and Cultural Change*, 25, 2 (Jan. 1977)

JACKSON, T. & EADE, D. *Against the Grain*. Oxford, Oxfam, 1982.

JACQUEMOT, P., 'Le F.M.I. et l'Afrique Subsaharienne,' *Le Mois en Afrique*, 211–212, (Aug-Sept. 1983): 107–120.

JACQUEMOT, P. & ASSIDON, E. *Politiques de change et ajustement en Afrique. L'expérience de 16 pays d'Afrique subsaharienne et de l'océan indien*. Paris, Ministère de la coopération et du développement, Etudes et Documents, 1988.

JACQUET, F., 'La Méditerranée: un marché privilégié pour les Etats-Unis,' in: Lerin (ed.), 1986: 303–10.

JAMMAL, V. & WEEKS, L., 'Le reserrement de l'écart entre villes et campagnes en Afrique sub-Saharienne,' *Revue Internationale du Travail*, 127, 3 (1988).

JEPMA, C.J. *North-South Cooperation in Retrospect and Prospect*. London, Routledge, 1988.

JERVIS, R. *Perceptions and Misperceptions in International Politics*. Princeton, Princeton Univ. Press, 1976.

JOHNSON, D.G., 'Famine,' *Encyclopedia Britannica* (1970 ed.): 58–9.

JOHNSON, D.G. *World Food Problems and Prospects*. Wash. D.C., American Enterprise Institute for Public Policy Research, Foreign Affairs Study, 1975.

JOHNSON, D.G., 'The world food situation: recent and prospective developments', in Johnson & Shuh (eds.), 1983: 1–33.

JOHNSON, D.G., HEMMI, K. & LARDINOIS, P. *Agricultural Policy and Trade*. New York, New York University Press (A Report to the Trilateral Commission, 29), 1985.

JOHNSON, D.G. & LEE, R.D. *Population Growth and Economic Development: Issues and Evidence*. Madison, University of Wisconsin Press, 1987.

JOHNSON, D.G. & McCONNELL BROOKS, K. *Prospects for Soviet Agriculture in the 1980s*. Bloomington, Indiana Press (in association with the Centre for Strategic International Studies, Georgetown University), 1983.

JOHNSON, D.G. & SHUH, G.E. *The Role of Markets in the World Food Economy*. Boulder, Westview press, (Westview Special Studies in Agricultural Science and Policy), 1983.

JOHNSON, O.E.G., 'Agriculture and Fund-Supported Adjustment Programmes,' *Finances and Development*, June 1988: 38–40.

JOHNSON, O.E.G. 'The Agricultural Sector in IMF Stand-By Agreements,' in Commander (ed.), 1989: 19–34.

JOHNSON, S.P. *World Population and the United Nations: Challenges and Responses*. Cambridge, Cambridge University Press, 1987.

JOHNSTON, R.J. & TAYLOR, P.J. (eds.) *A World in Crisis? Geographical Perspectives*. Cambridge, Basil Blackwell, 1989 (2nd ed.)

JONES, S. *The Impact of Food Aid on Food Markets in Sub-Saharan Africa. A Review of the Literature*. Oxford, Queen Elizabeth House, International Development Center, Food Studies Group, Paper No. 1, Jan. 1989.

JONSSON, U., 'A Conceptual Approach to the Understanding and Explanation of Hunger and Malnutrition in Society,' in LATHAM e.a. (eds.), 1988: 20–43.

JOST, S. *L'aide alimentaire au Sahel*. OECD, Etude préparée pour le Colloque CILLS/Club du Sahel sur les politiques céréalières des Etats sahéliens, 1986.

JOST, S., An Introduction to the Sources of Data for Food Aid Analysis with Special Reference to Sub-Saharan Africa, in Clay & Stokke (eds.), 1991: 191–201.

KAFKA, A., 'Comment,' in Jepma (ed.), 1988: 122–4.

KAHLER, M. (ed.) *The Politics of International Debt*. Ithaca, Cornell University Press, 1985.

KEELEY, J.F., 'Toward a Foucauldian Analysis of International Regimes,' *International Organization*, 44, 1 (Winter 1990): 83–105.

KEGLEY, C.W. & HOOK, S.W., 'U.S. Foreign Aid and U.N. Voting: Did Reagan's Linkage Strategy Buy Deference or Defiance?' *International Studies Quarterly*, 35, 1991: 295–321.

KELLEY, A.C., 'Review of 'Population Growth and Economic Development' by the NRC,' in *Population and Development Review*, 12, 3 (Sept. 1986): 563–8.

KEMAN, H. & BRAUN, D., 'Economic Interdependence, International Regimes and Domestic Strategies of Industrial Adjustment,' *European Journal of Political Research*, 15, 1987.

KENEN, P.B., 'What Role for IMF Surveillance?,' *World Development*, 15, 12 (Dec. 1987): 1445–56.

KEOHANE, R.O., 'The Demand for International Regimes,' *International Organization*, 36, 2, (Spring 1982): 325–56.

KEOHANE, R.O., *After Hegemony.* Cambridge, Harvard University Press, 1984.

KEOHANE, R.O. (ed.), *Neorealism and its Critics.* New York, Columbia University Press, 1986(a).

KEOHANE, R.O., 'Realism, Neorealism and the Study of World Politics,' in Keohane (ed.), 1986(b): 1–26.

KEOHANE, R.O., 'Theory of World Politics: Structural Realism and Beyond,' in Keohane (ed.), 1986(c): 158–203.

KEOHANE, R.O., 'International Institutions: Two Approaches,' *International Studies Quarterly,* 32 (1988): 379–96.

KEOHANE, R.O. & NYE, J.S., *Power and Interdependence.* Boston, Little & Brown, 1977.

KEOHANE, R.O. & NYE, J.S., 'Power and Interdependence Revisited', *International Organization*, 42, 2 (Fall 1987).

KERN, C.R., 'Looking a Gift Horse in the Mouth,' *Political Science Quarterly,* 83, 1 (March 1968): 59–75.

KEYFITZ, N., 'How do We Know the Facts of Demography?' *Population and Development Review,* 1, 2(Dec. 1975): 267–88.

KILLICK, T. e.a. *The quest for economic stabilisation: the IMF and the Third World.* Vol.1, London, Heinemann Books, 1984.

KLATZMANN, B. *Nourrir dix milliards d'hommes?* Paris, PUF (Le géographe; 16), 2nd edition 1983 (orig. 1975).

KLATZMANN, B. *Aide alimentaire et développement rural.* Paris, PUF (Politique d'aujourd'hui), 1988.

KOESTER, U. *Policy Options for the Grain Economy of the European Community: Implications for Developing Countries.* Wash.D.C., IFPRI, Research Report 35, 1982.

KOHT NORBYE, O.D. 'The World Economy: Trade, Debt and Development – an Assessment from a Developing Country Perspective,' in KOHT NORBYE, O.D. *Development and the International Community. A Collection of Lectures and Other Papers 1987–88.* Bergen, Chr. Michelsen Institute, DERAP Working Papers (A 376), 1988.

KONINKLIJK INSTITUUT VOOR DE TROPEN. *Les stratégies alimentaires dans quatre pays d'Afrique. Une étude sur la politique alimentaire, formulation et mise en oeuvre au Kenya, Mali, Rwanda et en Zambie.* Amsterdam, Institut Royal des régions tropicales; Etude préparée pour la Commission des CE, 1984.

KORTEN, D.C. *Getting to the 21st Century. Voluntary Action and the Global Agenda.* West Hartford, Kummarian Press, 1990.

KRASNER, S.D., 'Structural Causes and Regime Consequences: Regimes as Intervening Variables,' *International Organization*, 36, 2, Spring 1982(a): 185–206.

KRASNER, S.D., 'Regimes and the Limits of Realism: Regimes as Autonomous Variables,' *International Organization*, 36, 2, Spring 1982(b): 497–510.

KRASNER, S.D. (ed.), *International Regimes*. Ithaca, Cornell University Press, 1984.

KRASNER, S.D., *Structural Conflict. The Third World against Global Liberalism*. Berkeley, University of Berkeley Press, 1985.

KRATOCHWIL, F. & RUGGIE, J.G., 'International Organization: A State of the Art on the Art of the State,' *International Organization*, 40, 4 (Autumn 1986): 753–76.

KRAUSS, M., 'The (Negative) Role of Food Aid and Technical Assistance' in HORWICH, G. & LYNCH, G.J. (eds.) *Food, Policy and Politics. A Perspective on Agriculture and Development*. Boulder, Westview Special Studies in Agriculture Science and Policy, 1989: 120–9.

KRUEGER, A.O. & RUTTAN, V.W. *The Development Impact of Economic Assistance to LDCs*. Vol. I. University of Minnesota, for AID and the Department of State, March 1983.

KRUEGER, A.O., SCHIFF, M. & VALDES, A. 'Agricultural Incentives in Developing Countries: Measuring the Effect of Sectoral and Economy-wide Policies,' *The World Bank Economic Review*, 1, 3 (1988): 255–71.

KRUGMAN, P.R., 'Debt Relief is Cheap,' Foreign Policy, 80 (Fall 1990): 141–52.

L'HERITEAU, M.-F., 'Endettement et ajustement structurel: la nouvelle canonnière,' *Revue Tiers Monde*, XXIII, 91 (Juillet-Sept. 1982): 517–48.

L'HERITEAU, M.-F., *Le Fonds Monétaire International et les pays du Tiers Monde*, Paris, IEDES/PUF, 1986.

LACHEEN, C., 'Population Control and the Pharmaceutical Industry,' in MCDONNELL, K. (ed.) *Adverse Effects. Women and the Pharmaceutical Industry*. Penang, Malaysia, International Organisation of Consumers Unions, Regional Office for Asia and the Pacific, 1986: 89–136.

LADD HOLLIST, W., 'The politics of hunger in Brazil', in: Ladd Hollist & LaMond Tullis (eds.), 1986: 230–45.

LADD HOLLIST, W. Poverty and Hunger amidst Growing Plenty: A Comparative Analysis of Brazil, Mexico, South Korea, Taiwan and Yugoslavia. Paper prepared for delivery at the annual meeting of the International Studies Association and the British International Studies Association, London, 29/3–1/4 1989.

LADD HOLLIST, W. & LAMOND TULLIS, F. (Eds.) *Pursuing Food Security. Strategies and Obstacles in Africa, Asia, Latin America and the Middle East*. Boulder, London, Lynne Riener, 1987.

LAMPERT, D.E., FALKOWSKI, L.S. & MANSBACH, R.W., 'Is there an international system?', *International Studies Quarterly*, 22, 1 (Sept. 1972): 321–49.

LATHAM, M.C., BONDESTAM, L., CHORLTON, R. & JONSSON, U. *Hunger and Society*. Vol. 1. An Understanding of the Causes. Ithaca, Cornell University Program in International Nutrition, Monograph Series no. 17, 1988.

LAWRENCE, P. (ed.) *World Recession and the Food Crisis in Africa*. London, James Currey, 1986.

LE COURRIER, *Dossier Aide Alimentaire*. no 118 (Novembre-Décembre 1989): 48–78.

LEE, R.D., ARTHUR, W.B., KELLEY, A.C., RODGERS, G. & SRINIVA-

SAN, T.N. (eds) *Population, Food and Rural Development*. Oxford, Clarendon Press, 1988.

LEMARCHAND, R., 'The Political Economy of Food Issues,' in Hansen, A. & McMillan, D.E. *Food in Sub-Saharan Africa*. Boulder, Lynne Rienner, 1986: 25–42.

LERIN, F. (ed.) *Céréales et produits céréaliers en Méditerranée*. Actes du Colloque de Rabat, Maroc, 6–8 mars 1985. Montpellier, CIHEAM/IAM, 1986.

LERIN, F. & TUBIANA, L., 'Marché mondial et marché méditerranéen des céréales.' in: Lerin (ed.), 1985: 265–74.

LERIN, F., 'Le champ de bataille méditteranéen,' *Le Monde Diplomatique*, Nov. 1986.

LESSARD, D.R. & WILLIAMSON, J. *Capital Flight and Third World Debt*. Washington D.C., Institute for International Economics, 1987.

LEWIS, R.G., 'Agriculture américaine: les ricochets de la crise,' *CERES*, 19, 2, no. 110, (mars-avril 1986): 41–45.

LEYS, C., 'The State and the Crisis of Simple Commodity Production in Africa,' *IDS Bulletin*, 18, 3 (July 1987): 45–48.

LINDBLOM, C.E., *Politics and Markets. The World's Political-Economic Systems*. New York, Basic Books, 1977.

LINDERT, P. H., 'Historical Patterns of Agricultural Policy,' in Timmer (ed.), 1991: 29–83.

LIPSON, C., 'The International Organization of Third World Debt,' *International Organization*, 35, 4 (Autumn 1981): 603- 631.

LIPSON, C., 'International Debt and International Institutions,' in: Kahler, M. (ed.), 1985: 219–243.

LIPTON, M. *Why Poor People Stay Poor: the Urban Bias in Development*. London, Maurice Temple Smith, 1977.

LIPTON, M., 'African Agricultural Development: the EEC New Role,' *IDS Bulletin*, 14, 3 (1983a): 21–32.

LIPTON, M. *Demography and Poverty*. Wash. D.C., World Bank Staff Working Paper no. 623, 1983(b).

LIPTON, M. *The Poor and the Poorest. Some interim findings*. Washington D.C, World Bank Discussion Papers 25, 1988.

LIPTON, M., 'Agriculture, Rural People, the State and the Surplus in Some Asian Countries: Thoughts on Some Implications of Three Recent Approaches in Social science,' *World Development*, 117, 10 (1989): 1553–1571.

LIU, C.Y., 'Chinese Agricultural Development Strategy since 1979,' in Purcell & Morrison (eds.), 1987: 97–114.

LOFCHIE, M.F., 'The External Determinants of Africa's Agrarian Crisis,' in Ladd Hollist & Lamond Tullis (eds.), 1987: 98–120.

LOXLEY, J. 'The World Bank and the Model of Accumulation,' in: Barker, (ed.), 1984.

LOXLEY, J., 'IMF and World Bank Conditionality and Sub-Saharan Africa,' in: Lawrence, (ed.), 1986: 96–103.

LOXLEY, J., 'The IMF, the World Bank and Sub-Saharan Africa: Policies and Politics,' in: Havnevik (ed.), 1987: 47–64.

LOXLEY, J. & YOUNG, R., 'Stabilization and Structural Adjustment:

Some Lessons from the Experiences of Ghana and Zambia,' in: North-South Institute, 1988: 7–14.

LUCAS, G.R. Jr. & OGLETREE, T.W. *Lifeboat Ethics. The Moral Dilemmas of World Hunger*. New York, San Fransisco, London, Harper & Row, 1976.

MACDONALD, A.S. *Nowhere to Go but Down? Peasant Farming and the International Development Game*. London, Unwin Hyman, 1989.

MADAULE, S. *Commerce et développement. Le cas des céréales*. Paris, L'Harmattan, 1990.

MALISH, A.F., 'Soviet Agricultural Policies in the 1980s,' in Browne & Hadwiger (eds.), 1986: 77–90.

MALTHUS, T.R. *An Essay on the Principle of Population*. London, Macmillan, 1960.

MAMDANI, M. *The Myth of Population Control*. New York, Monthly Review Press, 1972.

MAREI, S.A. *The World Food Crisis*. London, L:ongeman, 1978.

MATIN, E.M. *Conference Diplomacy: A Case Study of the World Food Conference*. Washington D.C., Georgetown University, Center for the Study of Diplomacy, School of Foreign service, s.d.

MATZKE, O. *Der Hunger Wartet Nicht*. Bonn, Deutsche Welthungerhilfe, 1974.

MAULDIN, W.P. & LAPHAM, R.J., 'Measuring family planning program effort in LDCs: 1972 and 1982,' in Birdsall (ed.), 1985: 1–40.

MAUNDER, A. & VALDES, A. *Agriculture and Governments in an Interdependenent World*. Proceedings of the 20th International Conference of Agricultural Economists. Oxford, Oxford University Press, 1990.

MAURER, J.-L., 'Commentaire,' in Brauman (ed.), 1985: 130–6.

MAXWELL, S.J. & SINGER, H.W., 'Food Aid to Developing Countries: A survey', *World Development*, 7, (1979): 225–47.

MAXWELL, S.J., The Disincentive Effect of Food Aid: A Pragmatic Approach, in Clay & Stokke (eds.), 1991: 66–90.

MAYNARD, G. & BIRD, G., 'International monetary issues and the developing countries: a survey,' in Streeten & Jolly (eds.), 1982: 343–66.

McCALLA, A.F. & SCMITZ, A., 'State Trading in Grain,' in: Kostecki, M.M. *State Trading in International Markets*. London, Macmillan, 1982: 55–77.

McLIN, J., 'Surrogate Internatiopnal Organization and the Case of World Food Security 1949–1969,' *International Organization*, 33, 1 (Winter 1979): 35–55.

McMILLAN, J., WHALLEY, J. & ZHU, L., 'The Impact of China's Economic Reforms on Agricultural Productivity Growth,' *Journal of Political Economy*, 97,4 (Aug. 1989): 781–807.

McNAMARA, R. *Address to the Board of Governors*, 30 September 1968. Washington D.C., World Bank, 1968.

McNAMARA, R. *The Population Problem: Time Bomb or Myth?* Washington D.C., s.l., 1984 (also in *Foreign Affairs*, Summer 1984).

McNEILL, P. *The Contradictions of Foreign Aid*. London, Camberra, Croom Helm, 1981.

MEADOWS, D.H. e.a. *The Limits to Growth*. A Report for the Club of

Rome's Project on the Predicament of Mankind. London, Earth Island, 1972.

MELLOR, J.W. *The New Economics of Growth*. Ithaca, Cornell University Press, 1976.

MELLOR, J.W., 'Food Aid and Nutrition,' *American Journal of Agricultural Economics*, 62, 5 (December 1980).

MELLOR, J.W., 'Food, Employment and Growth Interactions,' *American Journal of Agricultural Economics*, 64, 2 (June 1982): 304–11.

MELLOR, J.W., 'Opportunities in the International Economy for Meeting the Food Requirements of the Developing Countries, in Ladd Hollist & Lamond Tullis (eds.), 1987: 47–63.

MELLOR, J.W., 'Global Food Balances and Food Security,' *World Development*, 16, 9 (Sept. 1988a): 997–1011.

MELLOR, J.W., Food policy, food aid an structural adjustment programmes: the context of agricultural development, *Food Policy*, 13, 1 (Feb. 1988b): 10–17.

MELLOR, J.W. & AHMED, R. (eds.) *Agricultural Price Policy for Developing Countries*. Baltimore, London, Johns Hopkins University Press (for IFPRI), 1988.

MELLOR, J.W. & AHMED, R., 'Agricultural Price Policy for Accelerating Growth,' in Mellor & Ahmed (eds.), 1988: 265–92.

MENDELSOHN, N.S. *The Debt of Nations*. New York, Priority Press Publications (A Twentieth Century Fund Paper), 1984.

MERRILL, A.K. *PL480 and Economic Development in Recipient Countries*. Washington D.C., National Security and International Affairs Division, Congressional Budget Office, mimeo, 1977.

MERTON, R.K. *Social Theory and Social Structure*. New York, London, The Free Press, Collier MacMillan, 1986 enlarged edition (orig. 1949).

MESAROVIC, M. & PESTEL, E. *Mankind at a Turning Point*. The Second Report to the Club of Rome. New York, Dutton/Reader's Digest Press, 1974.

MESSER, E. *The 'Small but Healthy' Hypothesis: Historical, Political and Ecological Influences on Nutritional Standards*. Providence, World Hunger Program RP–87–4, March 1987. (reprint from Human Ecology, 14, 1 (March 1986).

MESSER, E. *Food Wars: Hunger as a Weapon of War in the 1990s*. Providence, World Hunger Program, RR–91–3, August 1991.

MESSERLIN, P.A., *Bureaucracies and the political economy of protection. Reflections of a Continental European*, Wash. D.C., World Bank Staff Working Papers no. 568, 1983

METTETAL, G., 'Inventaire des mesures de matrise des échanges céréaliers dans les pays de l'Afrique de l'Ouest, du Cameroun et du Tchad,' in: CILSS/OECD, 1989: 125–32.

MILLIBAND, R. *The State in Capitalist Society*. London, Weidenfeld & Nicolson, 1969.

MILLIBAND, R., 'The Problem of the Capitalist State: a Reply to Poulantzas,' in BLACKBURN, R. (ed.) *Ideology in Social Science*. Glasgow, Collins/Fontana, 1977, 5th impression.

MILLMAN, S. R., ARONSON, S.M., FRUZZETTI, L.M., HOLLOS, M.,

315

OKELLO, R. & WHITING, V., Jr. 'Organization, Information and Entitlement in the Emerging Global Food System,' in Newman (ed.), 1990: 307–30.

MILLMAN, S.R. *The Hunger Report: Update 1991*. Providence, Brown University World Hunger Program, HR–91–1, April 1991.

MILLMAN, S.R. & CHEN, R.S. *Measurement of Hunger: Defining Thresholds*. Providence, Brown University World Hunger Program, HR–91–6, 1991.

MINEAR, L., 'Development through food: some nongovernmental reflections', in: WFC/Government of the Netherlands, 1983, pp. 55–66.

MINEAR, L. *Humanitarianism under Siege. A Critical Review of Operation Lifeline Sudan*. Trenton, Red Sea Press, Bread for the World and Institute on Hunger and Development, 1991.

MIRANDA, A., 'The Demographic Perspective,' in: Parkinson, J.R. (ed.) *Poverty and Aid*. London, Basil Blackwell, 1983: 40–51.

MIROW, K.R. *La dictature des cartels. Un siècle de colonisation industrielle*. Grenoble, Presses Universitaires de Grenoble, 1982.

MISTRY, P. *The Problem of 'Official' Debt owed by Developing Countries*. s.l., commissioned by the European Secretariat of the Forum on Debt and Development (FONDAD), August 1989.

MOBIUS, U., 'L'aide alimentaire de la CEE,' *Problèmes Economiques*, no. 2038, 2 sept. 1987: 24–29.

MÖNCKEBERG, F., 'Food and World Population: Future Perspectives', in: Hauser (ed.), 1979: 124–44.

MOORE-LAPPE, F. & COLLINS, J. *Food First*. New York, Ballantine Books, 1977.

MOORE-LAPPE, F., COLLINS, J. & KINLEY, D. *Aid as an Obstacle*. San Fransisco, Institute for Food and Development Policy, 1980.

MORGAN, D. *Merchants of Grain*. Harmondsworth, Penguin Books, 1980 (orig.:1979).

MORGENTHAU, H.J. *Politics Among Nations*. New York, A.A. Knopf, 2nd enlarged edition, 1949 (orig. 1945).

MORRIS, M.L. & NEWMAN, M.D., 'Official and Parallel Cereals Markets in Senegal: Empirical Evidence,' *World Development*, 17, 2 (Dec. 1989): 1895–906.

MORROW, D 'The International Wheat Agreement,' in Valdes (ed.), 1981: 213–39.

MOSLEY, P. *Overseas Aid: Its Defence and Reform*. Brighton, Wheatsheaf Books, 1987.

MRAK, M. (ed.) *External Debt Problem: Current Issues and Perspectives*. Ljubljana, Center for International Cooperation and Development, 1989.

MURDOCH, W.W. *The Poverty of Nations*. Baltimore, John Hopkins University Press, 1980.

NAFZIGER, E.W. *Inequality in Africa. Political Elites, Proletariat, Peasants and the Poor*. Cambridge, Cambridge University Press, 1988.

NAU, H.R., 'The diplomacy of world food: goals, capabilities, issues and arenas', in Hopkins & Puchala (eds.), 1979: 201–36.

NDULU, B.J., 'Governance and Economic Management,' in: Berg, R.J. &

Whitaker, J.S. (eds.) *Strategies for African Development*. Berkeley, Berkeley University Press, 1986.

NELSON, G., 'Food Aid and Agricultural Production in Bangladesh,' *IDS Bulletin*, 14, 2 (April 1983): 40–52.

NELSON, J. and contributors *Fragile Coalitions*. The Politics of Economic Adjustment. New Brunswick, Transaction Books, 1989.

NEWMAN, L.F. (ed.) *Hunger in History: Food Shortage, Poverty and Deprivation*. Oxford, Basil Blackwell, 1990.

NICHOLAS, P. *The World Bank's Lending for Adjustment. An interim Report*. Washington D.C., World Bank Discussion Papers no. 34, 1988.

NICHOLSON, N.K., 'Landholding, Agicultural Modernization, and Local Institutions in India,' *Economic Development and Cultural Change*, 32, 1984: 569–592.

NICHOLSON, N.K. & ESSEKS, J.D., 'The Politics of Food Scarcities in Developing Countries,' in Hopkins & Puchala (eds.), 1978: 103–45.

NOGUES, J.J., 'Agriculture and developing countries in the GATT,' *The World Economy*, 8, 2, (June 1985): 119–34.

NORTH-SOUTH INSTITUTE, *Structural Adjustment in Africa. External financing for development*. Ottawa, North-South Institute and CIDA, 1988.

NORTMAN, D.L. *Family Planning Program Funds: Sources, Levels and Trends*. New York, The Population Council, Center for Policy Studies Working Paper no. 113, August 1985.

NUNNENKAMP, P. *The international Debt Crisis of the Third World. Causes and Consequences for the World Economy*. Brighton, Wheatsheaf Books, 1986.

NUNNENKAMP, P., 'Capital Drain, Debt relief, and Creditworthiness of Developing Countries,' in: Mrak (ed.), 1989: 95–120.

NYE, J., 'Neorealism and Neoliberalism,' *World Politics*, XL,' (1988): 235–51.

O'BRIEN, S., 'Structural Adjustment and Structural Transformation in sub-Saharan Africaa,' in Gladwin, C.H. (ed.) *Structural Adjustment and African Women Farmers*. Gainesville, University of Florida Press, 1991.

O'MANIQUE J. & LERNER, M. *World Leadership and International Development*. Dublin, Tycooly International Publishing Ltd., published for the UNITAR, 1984.

O'MEARA, R.L., 'Regimes and their Implications for International Theory,' *Millenium*, 13, 3 (Fall 1984): 245–64.

O'NEILL, 'Lifeboat Earth,' in Aiken & La Follette (eds.), 1977: 148–64.

OECHSLI, F.W. & KIRK, D., 'Modernization and the Demographic Transition in Latin America and the Carribean', *Economic Development and Cultural Change*, 23, 3 (April 1975): 391–420.

OLSON, M. *The Rise and Decline of Nations*. New Haven, Yale University Press, 1982.

ORGANISATION FOR ECONOMIC COOPERATION AND DEVELOPMENT (OECD) *L'agriculture dans les pays de l'O.E.C.D.: problèmes et défis dans les années 1980*. Paris, OECD, 1984(a)

O.E.C.D. *Agricultural trade with developing countries*, Paris, OECD, 1984(b)

O.E.C.D. *Revised Methodology for the Implementation of Part I of the Ministerial Trade Mandate*, Paris, 1984 (c).

O.E.C.D. *National Policies and Agricultural Trade – EEC*. Paris, OECD, 1987(a).

O.E.C.D. *National Policies and Agricultural Trade – Japan*. Paris, OECD, 1987(b).

O.E.C.D. *National Policies and Agricultural Trade – US*. Paris, OECD, 1987(c).

O.E.C.D. *National Policies and Agricultural Trade – A Synthesis Report*. Paris, OECD, 1987(d).

O.E.C.D. *L'évaluation dans les PVD. Une étape du dialogue*. Paris, OCDE, 1988(a).

O.E.C.D. *Monitoring and Outlook of Agricultural Policies, Markets and Trade*. Paris, OECD, May 1988(b).

O.E.C.D. *Financement et dette extérieure des pays en voie de développement*. Etude 1987. Paris, OCDE, 1988(c).

O.E.C.D. *Agricultural Policies, Markets and Trade*. Paris, OECD, 1989.

O.E.C.D. *Development cooperation: efforts and policies of the members of the Development Assistance Committee*. 1989 Report. Paris, OECD, 1990(a).

O.E.C.D. *Modelling the Effects of Agricultural Policies*, Paris, OECD Economic Studies no 13, 1990(b).

O.E.C.D. *Politiques, marchés et échanges agricoles. Suivi et perspectives 1990*. Paris, OECD, 1990(c).

OSGOOD, R.E. *Ideals and Self-Interest in America's Foreign Relations*. London, University of Chicago Press, 1964, 4th impression (orig.: 1953).

OVERSEAS DEVELOPMENT ADMINISTRATION, (ODA) *The Evaluation of Aid Projects and Programmes*. London, ODA, 1984.

OXFAM *Already Too Many. An Oxfam Special Report on Population, Family Planning and Development* by B. Llewellyn. Oxford, Oxfam, s.d.

PAARLBERG, R.L., 'Shifting and sharing adjustment burdens: the role of the food importing nations,' in: Hopkins & Puchala, (eds.), 1978: 79–101.

PAARLBERG, R., 'Discussion,' in Johnson & Shuh (eds.), 1983: 213 – 218

PAARLBERG, R.L. *Food Trade and Foreign Policy*. Ithaca, Cornell University Press, 1985.

PAARLBERG, R.L. *Fixing Farm Trade*. Cambridge, Mass., Ballenger Publ. Co. (Council on Foreign Relations), 1988

PAARLBERG, R.L. & GRINDLE, M.S., 'Policy reform and reform myopia: agriculture in developing countries' *Food Policy*, 16, 5 (Oct. 1991): 383–94.

PAARLBERG, R.L. & WEBB, A.J., 'Public Policy and the Reemergence of International Economic Influences on U.S. Agriculture,' *Agricultural Economic Research*, 38, 1 (Winter 1986).

PADDOCK, W. & PADDOCK, P. *Famine 1975! America's Decision: Who Will Survive?* Boston, Toronto, Little, Brown & Co., 1967.

PALMER; I. *Food and the New Agricultural Technology*. Geneva, UNRISD, 1972.

PAPIC, A., 'The Interconnection between International Trade, Finance and Debt – The Implications for North-South Relations,' in Mrak (ed.), 1989: 62–93.

PARKINSON, J., 'Food Aid,' in: FAALAND, J.(ed.) *Aid and influence. The case of Bangladesh.* London, Basingtoke, MacMillan (Chr.Michelsen Institute, Bergen), 1981: 82–101.

PAROTTE, J.H., 'The Food Aid Convention: its history and scope', *IDS Bulletin*, 14, 2 (1983): 10–15.

PATNAIK, U., 'Some Economic and Political Consequences of the Green Revolution in India,' in Bernstein e.a. (ed.), 1990: 80–90.

PAULINO, L.A. *Food in the Third World: past trends and projections to 2000.* Wash.D.C., IFPRI Research Report no. 52, June 1986.

PAULINO, L.A., 'Trends in Cereal Supply, Demand, Trade and Stocks,' in Mellor & Ahmed, 1988: 13–26.

PEARSE, A. *Seeds of Plenty, Seeds of Want.* Oxford, UNRISD & Clarendon Press, 1980.

PERELMAN, M., 'Marx, Malthus, and the Concept of Natural Resource Scarcity,' in: Berardi (ed.), 1985:

PETHE, V.P., 'Beyond Demography. Toards Interdisplinary Exploration,' *Economic and Political Weekly*, January 6, 1990: 57–60.

PHILIPPE, B., 'Intervention des Etats dans l'économie. Externalités et développement: l'example des politiques agricoles,' *Mondes en développement*, 1984.

PHILIPPE, B. *Politique Agricole Européenne et marchés mondiaux. Enjeux et conflits de 1958 à 1984.* Paris, Economica, 1986.

PHYSICIANS' TASK FORCE ON HUNGER IN AMERICA. *Hunger in America: the Growing Epidemic.* Boston, Harvard University School of Public Health, 1985.

PINSTRUP-ANDERSEN, 'Nutrition Intervention,' in Cornia, Jolly & Stewart (eds.), 1986: 241–256.

PIOTROW, P.T., *World Population Crisis. The US Response.* NY, Wash., London, Praeger (Special Series on International Economics and Development), 1974, 2nd printing (first ed.: 1973).

POLAK, J.J., 'Comment,' in Jepma (ed.), 1988: 120–1.

POLEMAN, T.N., 'Quantifying the Nutrition Situation in Developing Countries', *Food Research Institute Studies*, 18, 1 (1981).

POLEMAN, T.N., 'World Hunger: Extent, Causes and Cures', in: Johnson & Shuh (eds.), 1983: 41–76.

POULANTZAS, N., 'The Problem of the Capitalist State,' in BLACKBURN, R. (ed.) *Ideology in Social Science.* Glasgow, Collins/Fontana, 1977, 5th impression.

POURDANAY, N. & MANCINI, J., 'Endettement et insertion dans la division internationale du travail: pays endettés,' *Revue Tiers Monde*, XXV, 99 (Juillet-Sept. 1984): 539–550.

PRASADA RAO, D.S., SHEPHERD, W.F. & SHARMA, K.C., 'A Comparative Study of National Price Levels, Agricultural Prices and Exchange Rates,' *World Development*, 18, 2 (Febr. 1990): 215–29.

PUCHALA D.J. & HOPKINS, R.F., 'International Regimes: Lessons from

Inductive Analysis,' *International Organization*, 36, 2, (Spring 1982): 245–76.

PULT, G. 'La fuite des capitaux en Suisse: un commentaire,' in: *Annuaire Suisse-Tiers Monde 1990*. Genève, Institut Universitaire d'Etudes de Développement, 1990: 193–8.

PURCELL, R.B. & MORRISON, E. U.S. *Agriculture and Third World Development. The Critical Linkage*. Boulder, Lynne Riener, for the Curry Foundation, 1987.

PYM, F. *Speech to the Royal Commonwealth Society on Britain's Contribution to Development*. London, 7 December 1982.

RAIKES, P., 'Flowing with milk and honey: food production in Africa and the policies of the EEC,' in: Lawrence (ed.), 1986: 160–76.

RAIKES, P. *Modernising Hunger. Famine, Food Surplus and Farm Policy in the EEC and Africa*. London, CIIR and James Currey, 1988.

RAMSES. *Rapport mondial 1986/87*. Paris, Institut Français de Rélations Internationales, 1986.

RAO, H., 'Urban vs Rural or Rich vs Poor,' *Economic and Political Weekly*, 13 (7 Oct. 1978): 1285–92

RAU, B. *From Feast to Famine. Official Cures and Grassroots Remedies to Africa's Food Crisis*. London, Zed Books, 1991.

RAVENHILL, J., 'Adjustment with Growth; A Fragile Consensus,' *The Journal of Modern African Studies*, 26, 2 (1988): 179–210.

RAY, A., 'Trade and Pricing policies in World Agriculture,' *Finance and Development*, September 1986: 2–5.

REISEN, H., 'Public Debt, North and South,' in Husain & Diwan (eds.), 1989: 116–26.

REPETTO, R. *Economic equality and fertility in developing countries*. Baltimore, Johns Hopkins University Press, 1979.

REUTLINGER, S. *Food Insecurity: Magnitude and Remedies*. Washington D.C., World Bank Staff Working Paper no. 267, July 1977.

REUTLINGER, S. & KNAPP, K. *Food Security in Food Deficit Countries*. Washington D.C., World Bank Staff Working Paper no. 393, June 1980.

REUTLINGER, S. & SELOWSKY, M., *Malnutrition and Poverty: Magnitude and Policy Options*, Wash. D.C., World Bank Staff Working Paper no. 23, 1976.

REVEL, A. & RIBOUD, C. *Les Etats-Unis et la stratégie alimentaire mondiale. Paris, Callman-Lévy*, 1981. (Translation: American Green Power. Baltimore, London, Johns Hopkins University Press, 1986.)

REVELLE, R., 'International cooperation in food and population', *International Organization*, 22, 1968: 362–91.

REVIEW SYMPOSIUM. *World Development Report*, 1984. Population and Development Review, 11, 1 (March 1985): 113–38.

RICHARDS, A., 'Food Problems and State Policies in the Middle East and North Africa,' in: Ladd Hollist & LaMond Tullis (eds.), 1987: 287–311.

RIDDELL, R.C., *Foreign Aid Reconsidered*. London, Baltimore, The Johns Hopkins University Press, London, James Currey, in association with ODA, 1987.

ROCHE, F., 'The demographic transition in Sri Lanka: Is development really a prerequisite?', *Cornell Agricultural Economics Staff Paper* no. 776, 1976.

ROSENAU, J.N., 'Pre-Theories and Theories of Foreign Policy,' in Rosenau, J.N. *The Scientific Study of Foreign Policy.* New York, Free Press, London, Collier-Macmillan, 1970.

ROSENAU, J.N., 'Before Cooperation; Hegemons, Regimes, and Habit-Driven Actors in World Politics,' *International Organization*, 40, 4 (Autumn 1986): 849–94.

ROSENBLATT, J., MAYER, T., BARTHOLDY, K. e.a. *The Common Agricultural Policy of the European Community, Principles and Consequences.* Washington D.C., IMF Occasional Paper no. 62, November 1988.

RUGGIE, J.D., 'International Regimes, Transactions and Change: Embedded Liberalism in the Post-War Economic Order', *International Organization*, 36, 2 (Spring 1982): 379–416.

RUSSETT, B.M., 'Elite Perception and Theories of World Politics,' in: Goodwin, G.L. & Linklater, A. *New Dimensions of World Politics*, New York, Toronto, John Wiley and Sons, 1975

RUSSETT, B.M. & STARR, D. *World Politics. The Menu for Choice.* San Fransisco, Freeman & Co., 1981.

SACHS, J., 'Making the Brady Plan Work,' *Foreign Affairs*, 68, 3 (Summer 1989): 87–104.

SAHN, D.E. & SARRIS, A. *Structural Adjustment and Rural Smallholder Welfare: A Comparative Analysis from Sub-Saharan Africa.* Ithaca, Cornell Food and Nutrition Policy Program, Working Paper 3, January 1991.

SALAS, R.M. *Reflections on Population.* New York, Oxford, Pergamon Press, 1985.

SALEH, A., 'Disincentives to Agricultural Production in Developing Countries: A Policy Survey,' *Foreign Agriculture*, 13 (Supplement 1975): 1–10.

SANDERSON, F.H., *The Great Food Fumble*, Wash.D.C., The Brookings Institute, General Reprint Report 303, July 1975.

SANDERSON, F.H. *US Farm Policy in Perspective*, Wash. D.C., The Brookings Institute, General Reprint Series 393, July 1983.

SARAN, R. & KONANDREOS, P., 'An Additional Resource? A Global Perspective on Food Aid Flows in Relation to Development Assistance,' in Clay & Stokke (eds.), 1991: 37–65.

SCANDIZZO, P. & KNUDSEN, O. *Nutrition and Food Needs of Developing Countries.* Washington D.C., World Bank Staff Working Paper No. 328, 1979.

SCHATZ, S.P., 'Africa's Food Imports and Food Production: An Erroneous Interpretation,' *Journal of Modern African Studies*, 24, 1 (1986): 177–8.

SCHIFF, M. *An Econometric Analysis of the World Wheat Market and Simulation of Alternative Policies, 1960–1980.* Washington D.C., USDA, International Economics Division (ERS Staff Report, AGE850827), 1985.

SCHUBERT, J.N., 'The Impact of Food Aid on World Malnutrition,' *International Organization*, 32 (1981): 3292–354.

SCHUBERT, J.N., 'The Social, Developmental and Political Impacts of Food Aid,' in Browne & Hadwiger(eds.), 1986: 185–201.

SCHULTZ, T.W., 'Value of U.S. Farm Surpluses to Underdeveloped Countries,' *Journal of Farm Economics*, 42, 5 (December 1960): 1019–30.

SCHWARZENBERGER, G. *Power Politics. A Study of World Society.* London, Scribner & Sons, 3rd edition, 1964 (orig. 1941).

SCOBIE, G.M. *Macroeconomic Adjustment and the Poor: Toward a Research Policy.* Ithaca, Cornell Food and Nutrition Policy Program Monograph No. 1, April 1989.

SCOTT, A.M., *The Dynamics of Interdependence.* Chapel Hill, University of North Carolina Press, 1982.

SEERS, D., 'What types of governments should be refused what types of aid?' *IDS Bulletin*, 4, 2/3 (June 1973).

SEEVERS, G.L., 'Food Markets and Their Regulation,' in: Hopkins & Puchala (eds.), 1979: 147–69.

SEN, A. *Levels of Poverty: Policy and Change.* Washington D.C., World Bank Staff Working Paper No. 401, 1980.

SEN, A. *Poverty and Famines. An Essay on Entitlement and Deprivation.* Oxford, Clarendon Press (for ILO), 1981(a).

SEN, A., 'Family and food: sex bias in poverty,' in Bardhan, P. & Srinivasan, T.N. (eds.) *Rural Poverty in South Asia.* New York, Columbia University Press, 1981(b).

SEN, A., 'The Food Problem: Theory and Policy,' *Third World Quarterly*, 4, 3 (July 1982): 447–59.

SEN, A., 'Food Entitlement and Food Aid programmes,' in: W.F.P./Government of the Netherlands, 1983: 111–22.

SEN, A. *Property and Hunger.* Wilhamstown, Mass., Center for Development Economics (Research Memorandum Series, RM–102), 1985.

SEN, A. *Hunger and Entitlements: Research for Action.* Helsinki, World Institute for Development Economics Research (WIDER), United Nations University, 1987.

SENDER, J. & SMITH, S., 'What's right with the Berg Report and what's left of its criticisms?' in: LAWRENCE, P. (ed.), 1986: 114–28.

SHAPOURI, S. & MISSIAEN, M. *Food Aid: Motivation and Allocation Criteria.* Washington D.C., USDA, ERS FAER no. 204, Feb. 1990.

SHATALOV, S., 'African Debt: Options for Cooperative Approach,' in: Mrak (ed), 1989: 189–202.

SHAW, T.M., 'Debates about Africa's Future: the Brandt, World Bank and Lagos Plan Blueprints,' *Third World Quarterly*, 5, 2 (April 1983): 330–44.

SHAWCROSS, W. *Le poids de la pitié.* s.l., Balland, 1985. (original: *The Quality of Mercy. Cambodia, Holocaust and Modern Conscience*, New York, Simon & Shuster, 1984.)

SHUH, G.E., 'The Role of Markets and Governments in the World Food economy, ' in Johnson & Shuh (eds.), 1983: 277–301

SIMANTOV, A., 'L'option d'une intégration économique internationale,' in: Bourrinet & Flory (eds.), 1982: 253–68.

SIMON, J.L. *The Ultimate Resource.* Princeton, New Jersey, Princeton University Press, 1981.

SIMON, J.L., 'On Aggregate Empirical Studies Relating Economic Development to Population Growth,' *Population and Development Review*, 15, 2 (June 1989): 323–32.

SINGER, H.W., *Terms of trade controversy and the evolution of soft financing; early years in the U.N.: 1947–51*, Sussex, IDS Discussion Papers no. 181, 1982.

SINGER, H.W., 'Development through food: 20 years' experience' in: W.F.P./Government of the Netherlands, 1983: 31–46.

SINGER, H.W., 'Food Aid: Development Tool or Obstacle to Development?' *Development Policy Review*, 5 (1987): 323–39.

SINGER, H.W. *Lessons of Post-War Development Experience 1945–1988*. paper presented at the Conference on four decades of development, Erasmus University Rotterdam, June 1988.

SINGER, H. W., The African Food Crisis and the Role of Food Aid, *Food Policy*, 14, 3 (August 1989): 196–206.

SINGER, H., Food Aid and Structural Adjustment in Sub-Saharan Africa, in Clay & Stokke (eds.), 1991: 180–90.

SINGER, H., WOOD, J. & JENNINGS, T. *Food Aid. The Challenge and the Opportunity*. Oxford, Clarendon Press, 1987.

SINGH, S. *Sub-Saharan Agriculture. Synthesis and Trade Prospects*. Washington D.C., World Bank Staff Working Paper no. 608, 1983.

SIVARD, R.L. *World Military and Social Expenditures 1991*. Washington D.C., World Priorities, 1991.

SIZOV, A.E., 'Soviet Food Imports: the Growing Necessity for Change,' *Food Policy*, 16, 4 (August 1991): 291–298.

SOBHAN, R. *The Crisis of External Dependence. The Political Economy of Foreign Aid to Bangladesh*. Dhaka & London, The University Press & Zed Press, 1982.

SOLAGRAL, 'Le bluff de la pénurie,' *La lettre du Solagral*, 81 (Mai 1989): 1.

SOWELS, N. *World Food. A Crisis of Overproduction*. London, A Hudson Letter Special Report, s.d.

SPERO, J. E., *The Politics of International Economic Relations*. London, Allen & Unwin, 1977.

SPITZ, P., 'Violence silencieus, famine et inégalités,' in UNESCO, *La violence et ses causes*. Paris, UNESCO, 1980.

SRINIVASAN, T.N., 'Hunger: Defining, Estimating, Alleviating it,' in: Johnson & Shuh (eds.), 1983a: 77–108.

SRINIVASAN, T.N., 'La mesure de la malnutrition,' CERES, 16, 2 (mars-avril 1983b): 23–27.

SRINIVASAN, T., 'Population Growth and Food. An Assessment of Issues, Models and Projections,' in: Lee, R.D., Arthur, W.B., Kelley, A.C., Rodgers, G. & Srinivasan, T.N. (eds) *Population, Food and Rural Development*. Oxford, Clarendon Press, 1988: 11–39.

STANILAND, M. *What is Political Economy? A Study of Social Theory and Underdevelopment*. New Haven, Yale University Press, 1985.

STAVENHAGEN, R. *Social Classes in Agrarian Societies*. New York, Anchor Books, 1975.

STERLING, R.W., *Macropolitics. International Relations in a Global Society*. New York, A.A. Knopf, 1974.

STEVENS, C. *Food Aid. An Assessment*. Antwerp, Center for Development Studies, UFSIA, Paper 85/87, January 1985.

STEWART, F., 'Should Conditionality Change?' in Havnevik (ed.), 1987: 29–46.

STEWART, F., 'Adjustment with a Human Face: the Role of Food Aid,' *Food Policy*, 13, 1 (1988): 18–26.

STILES, K.W., 'IMF Conditionality: Coercion or Compromise?' *World Development*, 18, 7 (July 1990): 959–74.

STOCKHOLM INTERNATIONAL PEACE RESEARCH INSTITUTE (SIPRI), *Yearbook*. Stockholm, SIPRI, 1986

STRANGE, S. 'IMF: Monetary managers,' in Jacobson, H.K. & Cox, R. (eds.) *The Anatomy of Influence. Decision-Making in International Organization*. New Haven, Yale University Press, 1974: 263–97.

STRANGE, S., 'Cave! Hic Dragones: a critique of regime analysis,' *International Organization*, 36, 2 (1982): 497–510.

STRANGE, S. *Casino Capitalism*. Oxford, Basil Blackwell, 1986.

STRANGE, S., 'The Persistent Myth of Lost Hegemony,' *International Organization*, 41, 4 (Autumn 1987): 551–574.

STREETEN, P. & JOLLY, R. (eds.) *Recent Issues in World Development*. Oxford, Pergamon Press, 1982.

STREETEN, P., 'Conditionality: a double paradox,' in JEPMA, C.J. *North-South Cooperation in Retrospect and Prospect*. London, Routledge, 1988.

STREETEN, P., 'A Survey of the Issues and Options,' in Commander (ed.), 1989: 3–18.

SUKHATME, P.V., 'Assessment of Adequacy of Diets at Different Income Levels,' *Economic and Political Weekly*, XIII, 13, March 27, 1978.

SUKHATME, P.V., 'Measurement of Undernutrition,' *Economic and Political Weekly*, XVII, 50, Dec. 11, 1982: 2000–16.

SUKIN, H.E., US food aid for countries implementing structural adjustment, *Food Policy*, 13, 1 (Febr. 1988): 98–103.

SVEDBERG, P. *Undernutrition in Africa: a Critical Assessment of the Evidence*. Helsinki, World Institute for Development Economics Research (WIDER), June 1987.

SWANK, C.W., 'International Food Reserves,' in Brown, P.G. & Shue, H. (eds.) *Food Policy. The Responsibility of the United States in the Life and Death Choices*. New York, The Free Press, 1979 (paperback ed.).

SYMONDS, R. & CARDER, M. *The United Nations and the Population Question. 1945–1970*. New York, McGraw-Hill Book Co., (A Population Council Book), 1973.

TALBOT, R.B., 'The Role of World Food Organizations,' in Browne & Hadwiger (eds,), 1986: 171–84.

TALBOT, R.B. & MOYER, A.W., 'Who Governs the Rome Food Agencies?,' in Yesilada e..a. (eds.), 1987: 281–304.

TALBOT, R.B. *The Four World Food Agencies*. Ames, Iowa State University, 1990.

THOMPSON, S.B., International Organizations and the Improbability of A Global Food Regime, in BALAAM, D.N. & CAREY, M.J. (eds.) *Food Policies. The Regional Conflict*. Totowa, Allanheld, Osan & Co, 1981: 191–206.

TIMMER, C.P. (ed.) *Agriculture and the State. Growth, Employment and Poverty in Developing Countries*. Ithaca, London, Cornell University Press, 1991.

TIMMER, C.P., 'Agricultural Employment and Poverty Alleviation in Asia,' in Timmer, 1991: 123–55.

TIMS, W., 'EC Agricultural policies and the Developing Countries,' in Mennes, L.B.M. & Kol, J. (eds.) *European Trade Policies and the Developing Countries*, London, Croom Helm, 1988: 145–96.

TISSIER, P., ' "Modèle Chinois" de lutte contre la faim,' in: TRICONTINENTAL, *Famines et pénuries. Le faim dans le monde et les idées reçus*, Paris, Tricontinental no.3, 1982: 149–55.

TODARO, M.P. *Economic development in the Third World*. New York, London, Longman, 1981, 2nd ed. (orig.: 1977).

TOLLEY, G.S., THOMAS, V. & WONG, C.M. *Agricultural Price Policies and the Developing Countries*. Baltimore & London, John Hopkins University Press (for the World Bank), 1982.

TOMCZAK, F., 'Food and Agriculture Policy in Poland: from Peasant Agriculture to Market Economy,' *Food Policy*, 16, 3 (June 1991): 206–12.

TUDGE, C. *The Famine Business*. Harmondsworth, Pelican Books, 1979.

ULYUKAYEV, A., 'Agrarian Crisis and Economic Reforms in the USSR,' *Food Policy*, 16, 4 (August 1991): 277–83.

UNITED NATIONS (U.N.) *The Determinants and Consquences of Population Trends. Vol. I. New Summary of Findings on Interaction of Demographic, Economic and Social Factors*. New York, 1973 (E.71.XIII.5)

U.N. *Report of the World Food Conference*, Rome, 5–16 November 1974. New York, 1975.

U.N. *World Food Conference, Assessment of the World Food Situation: Present and Future*. New York, 1975.

U.N. *Report of the International Conference on Population*. Mexico City, 6–14 August 1984. New York, 1984 (E.84.XIII.8)

U.N. *Socio-economic diffrentials in child mortality in LDCs*. New York, Department of Inernational Economic and Social Affairs, 1985. (ST/ESA/SER.A/9)

U.N. *World Population Prospects. Estimates and Projections as assessed in 1984*. New York, UN, 1986(a) (ST-ESA-SER.A–98)

U.N. *Demographic Yearbook*. New York, 1986(b).

U.N. *Review and Appraisal of the World Population Plan of Action*. New York, Department of International Economic and Social Affairs, Population Studies no. 99, 1986(c).

U.N. *Fertility Behaviour in the Context of Development. Evidence from the World Fertility Survey*. New York, Department of International Economic and Social Affairs, Population Studies no. 100, 1987a.

U.N. *World Population Trends and Policies. 1987 Monitoring Report*. New York, Department of International Economic and Social Affairs, Population Studies No. 103, 1988.

U.N. *Long-Range World Population Projections. Two Centuries of Population Growth 1950–2150*. New York, UN Department of International Econmic and Social Affairs, (ST/ESA/SER.A/125), 1992.

U.N. ADMINISTRATIVE COMMITTEE ON COORDINATION-SUB-

COMMITTEE ON NUTRITION (ACC/SCN) *First Report on the World Nutrition Situation.* Rome, UN, November 1987.

UNITED NATIONS CONFERENCE ON TRADE AND DEVELOPMENT (U.N.C.T.A.D.) *Protectionism and Structural Adjustment in the World Economy.* Geneva, E.82.II.D.14., 1982.

U.N.C.T.A.D. *Reviving Multilateral Cooperation for Growth and Development.* Report by the Secretary-General of UNCTAD to UNCTAD VII. Geneva, 1987 (TD/329)

U.N.C.T.A.D. *UNCTAD Handbook.* Geneva, UNCTAD, various years.

UNITED NATIONS EXPERT GROUP ON POPULATION AND HUMAN RIGHTS. *Population Trends and Policies in the 1980s.* Geneva, IESA/P/AC.28/2, 28 March 1989.

UNITED NATIONS FUND FOR POPULATION ACTIVITIES (U.N.F.P.A.) *Guide to Sources of International Population Assistance 1985.* New York, UNFPA, 1985

U.N.F.P.A. *State of the World Population, 1988.* New York, 1988.

U.N.F.P.A. *State of the World Population, 1990.* New York, 1990.

U.N.F.P.A. *Global Population Assistance Report, 1982–1989.* New York, UNFPA 90/31006 1000, Feb. 1991(a).

U.N.F.P.A. *Etat de la population Mondiale 1991.* New York, UNFPA, 1991(b)

UNITED NATIONS INTERNATIONAL CHILDREN EMERGENCY FUND (U.N.I.C.E.F.) *State of the World's Children 1982- 1991.* New York, UNICEF, various years.

U.N.I.C.E.F. *State of the World's Children 1989.* New York, UNICEF, 1990.

UNITED STATES AGENCY FOR INTERNATIONAL DEVELOPMENT (U.S.A.I.D.) *PL480 Title I: A Discussion of Impact Evaluation Results and Recommendations.* Washington D.C., AID Program Evaluation Report No 13, February 1985.

U.S.A.I.D. *The U.S. Response to the African Famine, 1984–86. Vol. I. An Evaluation of the Emergency Food Assistance Program: Synthesis Report.* Washington D.C., AID Program Evaluation Report No 16, November 1986(a).

U.S.A.I.D. *The U.S. Response to the African Famine, 1984–86. Vol. II. An Analysis of Policy Formation and Program Management.* Washington D.C., AID Program Evaluation Report No 17, November 1986 (b)

UNITED STATES CONGRESS. *American Foreign Food Assistance PL480 and Related Materials.* Washington, Committee on Agriculture and Forestry, US Senate, 1976.

U.S. DEPARTMENT OF AGRICULTURE (U.S.D.A.) *Global Food Assessment, 1980.* Washington D.C., prepared by the Economics, Statistics and Cooperatives Service of the USDA, GPO, 1980.

U.S.D.A. *Government Intervention in Agriculture. Measurement, Evaluation and Implications for Trade Negotiations.* Washington, Economic Research Service, Staff Report No. AGES 861216, 1987.

U.S.D.A. *Global Food Assessment. Situation and Outlook Report, 1990.* Washiongton D.C:, Economic Research Service (GFA 1), November 1990.

U.S.D.A. *The World Food Situtation and Prospects to 1985.* Washington

D.C., Economic Research Service, Foreign Agricultural Economic Report no 98, December 1975.

U.S. DEPARTMENT OF STATE. *World Food Situation*. Washington D.C., Bureau of Public Affairs Special Report No. 3, July 1974.

U.S. DEPARTMENT OF STATE. *U.S. Position at the 29th United Nations General Assembly*. Washington D.C., Bureau of Public Affairs Special Report No. 13, Febr. 1975(a).

U.S. DEPARTMENT OF STATE. *Crisis in Food*. Washington D.C., Bureau of Public Affairs Special Report No. 14, June 1975(b).

U.S. DEPARTMENT OF STATE. *Silent Explosion*, US Dept. of State Bulletin, Washington, 78, Fall 1978.

UNITED STATES DEPARTMENT OF STATE 'Fourty Years of PL480', by President Ronald Reagan, No. 2089, August 1984: 47.

UNITED STATES GENERAL ACCOUNTING OFFICE (GAO) *Nutrition Monitoring. Mismanagement of Nutrition Survey Has Resulted in Questionable Data*, Washington D.C., GAO/RCED–91–117, July 1991.

U.S. G.A.O. *Famine in Africa. Improving US Response Time for Emergency Relief*. Washington D.C., GAO/NSIAD–86–56, April 1986.

U.S. G.A.O. *Foreign Aid. Information on U.S. International Food Assistance Programs*. Washington D.C., GAO/NSIAD–87–94BR, March 1987.

U.S. HOUSE OF REPRESENTATIVES, *Enhancing the Developmental Impact of Food Aid*. Hearing before the International Task Force of the Select Committee on Hunger, Washington D.C., GPO Serial No. 100–9, 1987.

U.S. HOUSE OF REPRESENTATIVES, *Renewed Challenge in Ethiopia*, Hearing before the International Task Force of the Select Committee on Hunger, Washington D.C., GPO, Serial 100–18, 1988.

UVIN, P., 'Le débat sur le crédit rural: un Etat de la question,' in Uvin, P. & Piquet, F. (eds.) *Le rôle des systèmes d'épargne-crédit dans la matrise du processus de développement*. Genève, Institut Universitaire d'Etudes de Développement, Itinéraires, 1988: 1–16.

UVIN, P., 'Interests, Surpluses and Regimes: the International Political Economy of Food Aid,' *International Studies Quarterly*, 36, 3, Sept. 1992: 293–312.

UVIN, P., 'The Limits of Political Conditionality,' *European Journal of Development Studies*, July 1993.

VALDES, A. (ed.) *Food Security for Developing Countries*. Boulder, Westview, 1981.

VALDES, A., 'Agricultural Development and Trade in Latin America: Prospects for Reform,' in Purcell & Morrison (eds.), 1987: 73–96.

VALDES, A., 'The Role of Agricultural Exports in Development,' in Timmer (ed.), 1991: 84–115.

VALDES, A. & KONANDREAS, P. 'Assessing food security based on national aggregates in developing countries,' in Valdes (ed.), 1981: 25–43.

VALDES, A. & DEL CASTILLO, A. *The Role of Food Trade in the Food Security of Developing Countries*. Geneva, U.N.C.T.A.D., TD C.1/256, 1984.

VAUGHAN, M. *The Story of an African Famine*. Cambridge, Cambridge University Press, 1987.

VENGROFF, R., 'Food Aid and Dependency: PL480 Aid to Black Africa,' *The Journal of Modern African Studies*, 20, 1 (1982): 27–43.

VIATTE, 'Comment' in Haen, De, e.a. (eds.), 1985: 266–70.

VON BRAUN, J. & HUDDLSTON, B., 'Implications of Food Aid for Price Policy in Recipient Countries,' in: Mellor & Ahmed, (eds.) 1988: 253–63.

WADEKIN, K.-E., 'Agrarian Reforms in Eastern Europe,' *Food Policy*, 16, 3 (June 1991): 182–6.

WALLERSTEIN, M.B. *Food for War-Food for Peace. US Food Aid in a Global Context*. Cambridge, London, MIT Press, 1980.

WALTON, D.J., 'Hunger and Food,' in: *The World Ten Years After the Brandt Report*. A Conference Report. Vienna, Vienna Institute for Development and Cooperation, Report Series 2/88, 1989: 14–23.

WALTZ, K. *Man, State and War*. New York, Columbia University Press, 1959.

WALTZ, K.N. *Theory of International Politics*. Reading, Addison-Wesley, 1979.

WARNOCK, J.W. *The Politics of Hunger: the Global Food System*. New York, London, Methuen, 1987.

WEAVING, R., 'Mesurer la dette des pays en développement: présentation des principales sources d'information,' *Finances et Développement*, Mars 1987.

WEINBAUM, M.G., 'Politics and Development in Foreign Aid: US Economic Assistance to Egypt, 1975–82.' *The Middle East Journal*, 37, 4 (Autumn 1983): 636–55.

WEINER, T., 'The World Bank,' in ODA, 1984: 94–101.

WEISS, T.G. & JORDAN, R.S. *The World Food Conference and Global Problem Solving*. New York, Praeger, in cooperation with UNITAR, 1976.

WENNERGREN, E.B., 'The History and Nature of US Foreign Assistance,' in Wennergren e.a., 1989: 33- 78.

WENNERGREN, E.B., PLUCKNETT, D.L., SMITH, J.H., FURLONG, W.L. & JOSHI, J.H. *The United States and World Poverty. A Survey of the History, Current Operationns and Issues of the U.S. Foreign Assistance Program*. Washington D.C., Seven Locks Press, 1989.

WHITE, J. 'Discussion' in ODA, 1984: 24.

WHITE, J. *The Politics of Foreign Aid*. London, The Bodley Head, 1974.

WILBER, C.K. *The Role of Population in Western Economic Development Theory*. Hastings-on-Hudson, Institute of Society, Ethics and the Life Sciences, 1977.

WILHELM, J. & FEINSTEIN, G. (eds.) *U.S. Foreign Assistance: Investment or Folly?* New York, Praeger, 1984.

WILLIAMS, G., 'The World Bank and the Peasant problem' in: Heyer, J., Roberts, P. & Williams, G. *Rural Development in Tropical Africa*. New York, St.Martin's Press, 1981.

WILLIAMS, G., 'Les Contradictions de la Banque Mondiale et la crise de l'Etat en Afrique,' in Terray, E. (dir.) *L'Etat contemporain en Afrique.* Paris, Harmattan, 1987: 359–385.

WILLIAMS, R.M., 'The Concept of Norms,' in: SILLS, D.L. (ed.) *International Encyclopedia of the Social Sciences.* New York, London, The Macmillan Company and the Free Press, 1968, vol. 11.

WILLIAMSON, J., 'The Brady Initiative: Alternatives and Evaluation,' in: Mrak (ed.), 1989: 49–61.

WOLF, M. 'Fiddling While the GATT Burns,' *The World Economy,* 9, 1, March 1986: 1–18.

WOLFSON, M. *Profiles in Population Assistance. A Comparative Review of the Principal Donor Agencies.* Paris, OECD (Development Centre Studies), 1983.

WOOD, B. 'Canada and Third World Development: Testing Mutual Interest,' in: Cassen, R., Jolly, R., Sewel, J. & Wood, R. *Rich Country Interest and Third World Development.* London, Canberra, Croom Helm, 1982.

WOOD, R.E. *From Marshall Plan to Debt Crisis. Foreign Aid and Development Choices in the World Economy.* Berkeley, University of California Press, 1986

WOODS, R. 'Malthus, Marx and the Population Crisis,' in Johnston & Taylor, 1989: 151–174.

WORLD BANK *Accelerated Development in Sub-Saharan Africa.* An Agenda for Action, Washington D.C., IBRD, 1981

WORLD BANK. *Progress Report on Development Prospects and Programs.* Washington D.C., World Bank, 1983(a).

WORLD BANK *Focus on Poverty.* Washington D.C, World Bank, 1983(b).

WORLD BANK *World Development Report 1984.* Wash. D.C., 1984(a).

WORLD BANK. *Toward Sustained Development in Sub-Saharan Africa: A Joint Program of Action,* Washington D.C., World Bank, 1984(b).

WORLD BANK. *World Development Report 1985.* Washington D.C., World Bank, 1985.

WORLD BANK *World Development Report 1986,* Wash.D.C., 1986(a).

WORLD BANK. *Financing Adjustment with Growth in Sub-Saharan Africa 1986–1990.* Washington D.C., IBRD, 1986(b).

WORLD BANK. *Poverty and Hunger: Issues and Options for Food Security in Developing Countries.* Washington D.C., World Bank, 1986(c).

WORLD BANK. *World Development Report 1987.* Washington D.C., World Bank, 1987(a).

WORLD BANK. *Programme for Adjustment and Growth.* Washington D.C., World Bank, 1987(b).

WORLD BANK. *Annual Report 1987.* Washington D.C., World Bank, 1987(c).

WORLD BANK. *World Debt Tables. 1988–89 Edition. Volume I.* Analysis and Summary Tables. Washington D.C., World Bank, 1988(a).

WORLD BANK. *Annual Report 1988.* Washington D.C., World Bank, 1988(b).

WORLD BANK. *Targeted Programs for the Poor during Structural Adjustment.* A Summary of a Symposium on Poverty and Adjustment April 1988. Washington D.C., World Bank, 1988(c).

WORLD BANK. *Adjustment Lending. An Evaluation of Ten Years of Experience.* Washington D.C., World Bank, Country Economics Department (Policy and Research Series no. 1), 1988(d).

WORLD BANK. *The Challenge of Hunger in Africa. A Call to Action.* Washington D.C., World Bank (2nd edition), Dec. 1988(e).

WORLD BANK *Project Performance Results 1986.* Washington D.C., World Bank Operations Evaluation Unit, 1988(f).

WORLD BANK. *World Development Report 1989.* Washington D.C., World Bank, 1989(a).

WORLD BANK. *Sub-Saharan Africa: from Crisis to Sustainable Growth. A Long-Term Perspective Study.* Washington D.C., World Bank, 1989(b).

WORLD BANK. *Social Indicators of Development 1989.* Baltimore, London, Johns Hopkins Press for the World Bank, 1989(c).

WORLD BANK. *World Debt Tables. 1990–91 Edition. Volume I.* Analysis and Summary Tables. Washington D.C., World Bank, 1990.

WORLD BANK. *World Debt Tables. 1991–92 Edition. Volume I. Analysis and Summary Tables.* Washington D.C., World Bank, 1991.

WORLD BANK & U.N.D.P. *Africa's Adjustment and Growth in the 1980s.* Washington D.C., World Bank/UNDP, 1989.

WORLD FOOD COUNCIL (W.F.C.) *Progrès accomplis en vue de l'élimination de la faim. Dix années d'activités multilatérales dans le domaine de l'alimentation. 1974–1984.* Rapport du Directeur Exécutif. Rome, WFC/1984/2.

W.F.C. *Current World Food Situation.* Report by the Executive Director. Rome, WFC/1984/7.

W.F.C. *La sécurité alimentaire mondiale et la stabilité du marché: pour une réserve appartenant en propre à chaque pays en développement. Rapport du Directeur Exécutif.* Rome, WFC/1985/2.

W.F.C. *Facteurs économiques extérieurs faisant obstacle à la réalisation des objectifs alimentaires-nécessité d'élargir le commerce international. Rapport du Directeur Exécutif,* Rome, 1985 (WFC/1985/5)

W.F.C. *Problèmes relatifs à la stabilité et à la securité du commerce international des produits alimentaires.* Note d'information du Directeur Exécutif, Rome, 1986 (WFC/1986/7).

W.F.C. *Rapport de la onzième session du comité de sécurité alimentaire mondiale.* Rome, 1986 (WFC/1986/10).

W.F.C. *Situation de la faim et de la malnutrition dans le monde et incidence des mesures de reajustement économique sur les problèmes alimentaires et de la faim.* Rome, 1987 (WFC/1987/2).

W.F.C. *Situation de la faim et de la malnutrition dans le monde.* Rapport de 1988. Rome, 1988 (WFC/1988/4).

W.F.C. *Vers une sécurité alimentaire durable. Questions cruciales.* Rome, WFC/1988/5.

W.F.C. *Additional and More Effective Measures by Governments to Alleviate Hunger and Poverty.* Rome, 1990 (WFC/1990/3).

WORLD FOOD PROGRAMME (W.F.P.) *Evaluation of the WFP Emergency Response. Lessons Learned from the African Food Crisis.* WFP/CFA, 21/12, May 1986a.

W.F.P. *Recent Development in Regard to the Main Aspects Covered by the*

Evaluation on WFP's Response to the African Food Crisis. WFP/CFA 21/ 12 add. 2, May 1986b.

W.F.P. *Food Aid and Relief/ Development Strategies.* by R.W. Hay. Rome, W.F.P./African Development Bank Seminar on Food Aid for Development in Sub-Saharan Africa, 1986c

W.F.P. *Food Aid Policies and Programmes.* Rome, May 1988(a).

W.F.P. *Annual Report,* 1988. Rome, May 1988(b).

W.F.P./C.F.A. *Guidelines and Criteria for Food Aid,* Rome, WFP/CFA 7/ 21, Annex 4, 1979.

WORLD FOOD PROGRAMME / GOVERNMENT OF THE NETHER-LANDS, *Seminar on Food Aid.* The Hague, 1983.

YESILADA, B.A., BROCKET, C.D. & DRURY, B. (eds.). *Agrarian Reform in Reverse. The Food Crisis in the Third World.* Boulder, Lynne Riener, 1987.

YOUNG, O., 'Regime dynamics: the Rise and Fall of International Regimes,' *International Organization,* 36, 2 (Spring 1982): 93–113.

YOUNG, O., 'International Regimes: Toward a New Theory of Institutions', *World Politics,* XXXIX, 1 (Oct. 1986): 104–22.

ZUCKERMAN, E., *Poverty and Adjustment: Issues and Practice.* Background Paper for the Symposium on Poverty and Adjustment, Country Economics Department, World Bank, March 1988.

and also various articles in

– *Le Monde,* Paris

– *Financial Times,* London

– *International Herald Tribune,* Paris

– *The Economist,* London

– *South,* London.

INDEX

Africa's food crisis, 44, 65, 71, 146, 192, 234
Agricultural policy: Communist and socialist countries, 35–7; OECD countries, 27–34; Third-World countries, 38–46, 256–60, 262–3

Banks, 235–8, 253, 285

Canada, 50, 131–3
China, 54, 97, 99, 122
Complex interdependence, 3, 7–8, 18, 120–1, 155, 282–6
Conditionality, 141, 210, 231, 232, 246–52
Consensus, 9–12, 27, 63, 148, 174, 217, 290–2
Consumption subsidies, 36, 39, 49, 167–8, 256, 258, 265

Debt crisis, 234–43, 253–5
Domestic politics, importance of, 25, 111–12, 115–16, 119, 139, 202–3, 205, 238–40, 283, 286

Eastern Europe, 35–7, 97
Economic growth and agriculture, 34, 36, 48, 256–7, 261–4
Emergency food aid, 129, 134, 138, 141–2, 146–7, 152, 155, 158–60
Entitlements, 59–60, 84–6, 173–4
European Economic Community, 26–9, 31–4, 98, 104, 113–16, 130–3, 141, 232

Family planning, 59, 198–201, 210–13, 284
Food aid: data, 130–3, 144–6, 167, 170–1; regime, 139–42, 162; outcome, 143–9; effects, 155–74
Food and Agriculture Organization (FAO), 63–4, 74, 139, 144, 191, 196–7
Food production: data, 31, 35–6, 42–5; policies, 27–31, 35, 38–41, 45–6; effects, 31–4, 35–7, 46–8, 111–12, 113–16
Food prices, 63–4, 74, 139, 144, 191, 196–7, 265
Food security, 31, 50, 86, 110–11, 119, 124, 140, 141, 157
Food trade: data, 93–102; regime, 102–6; outcome, 108–12, 284, 286–7; effects, 112–19

General Agreement on Trade and Tariffs, 102–6, 112, 119
Governments: autonomy of, 5, 40, 158, 166, 245–6, 248–52, 266; as unitary actors, 54, 116, 283

Hegemony, 106, 123, 285, 286, 288–92
Hirschman, 24, 30
Hopkins & Puchala, 13, 22, 107
Hunger: data, 63–73, 95; regime, 73–9, 258–9; and politics, 80–4

332

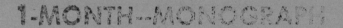